The Lyle
official
ARTS
review

Copyright © Lyle Publications 1977

Glenmayne, Galashiels, Selkirkshire, Scotland.

Printed by Apollo Press, Unit 5, Dominion Way, Worthing, Sussex.

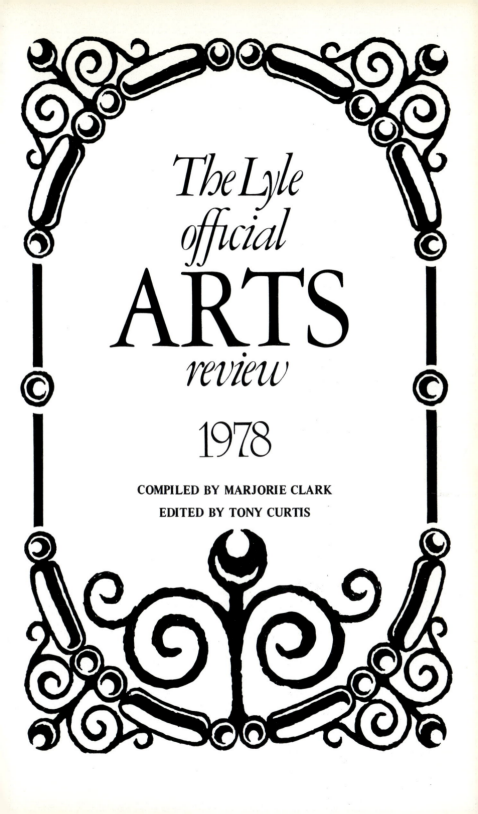

The Lyle
official

ARTS
review

1978

COMPILED BY MARJORIE CLARK
EDITED BY TONY CURTIS

Auction
Acknowledgements

Auktionshaus am Neumarkt, *Neumarkt 13, Zurich 8001, Switzerland.*
Bearnes & Watcotts, *3 Warren Road, Torquay, Devon.*
Bonham's, *Montpelier Galleries, Montpelier Street, London.*
Boulton & Cooper Ltd., *St. Michael's House, Malton, N. Yorkshire.*
Brackett's, *27-29 High Street, Tunbridge Wells, Kent.*
Bucknell & Ballard, *1A Parsons Street, Banbury, Oxfordshire.*
Butler & Hatch Waterman, *Tenterden, Kent.*
H.C. Chapman & Son, *North Street, Scarborough, Yorkshire.*
Christie's, *8 King Street, St. James', London.*
Christie's, *South Kensington, 85 Old Brompton Road, London.*
Christie's, *5025 Park Avenue, New York, N.Y. 10022.*
Chrystal Brothers & Stott, *Athol Street, Douglas, Isle of Man.*
Dacre, Son & Hartley, *1/5 The Grove, Ilkley, W. Yorkshire.*
Dee & Atkinson, *The Exchange, Driffield, E. Yorkshire.*
Edmiston's, *The Mart, 164 Bath Street, Glasgow.*
Elliott & Green, *40 High Street, Lymington, Hants.*
J. Entwistle & Co., *The Galleries, Kingsway, Lytham St. Annes, Lancs.*
Foll & Parker, *9 High Street, Woburn Sands, Bucks.*
J. Francis, T. Jones & Sons, *King Street, Carmarthen, Wales.*
Galerie Moderne, *Rue des Petits Carmes 41, Bruxelles, Belgium.*
Geering & Colyer, *Highgate, Hawkhurst, Kent.*
Graves, Son & Pilcher, *71 Church Road, Hove, Sussex.*
Hall, Wateridge & Owen, *Welsh Bridge Salerooms, Shrewsbury, Salop.*
Hollingsworths, *Westcombe House, 56/58 Whitcomb Street, London.*
Jackson-Stops & Staff, *14 Curzon Street, London.*

G.A. Key, *Market Place, Aylsham, Norwich, Norfolk.*
King & Chasemore, *Pulborough, Sussex.*
Lalonde Martin, *71 Oakfield Road, Bristol.*
Thomas Love & Sons Ltd., *St. John's Place, Perth, Perthshire.*
Morphet & Morphet, *The Mart, 4 & 6 Albert Street, Harrogate.*
Neale & Son, *30 Bridlesmith Gate, Nottingham.*
D.M. Nesbit & Co., *7 Clarendon Road, Southsea, Hants.*
Pearsons, *99 & 293 Fleet Road, Fleet, Hants.*
Charles R. Phillips, *96 High Street, Solihull, West Midlands.*
Phillips, *Blenstock House, 7 Blenheim Street, New Bond St., London.*
Phillips, *The Old House, Station Road, Solihull, West Midlands.*
Phillips in Scotland, *65 George Street, Edinburgh.*
John H. Raby & Son, *21 St. Mary's Road, Bradford, Yorkshire.*
Andrew Sharpe & Partners, *2 The Grove, Ilkley, West Yorkshire.*
Smith-Woolley & Perry, *43 Castle Hill Avenue, Folkestone.*
Sotheby's, *34/35 New Bond Street, London.*
Sotheby's, Belgravia, *19 Motcomb Street, London.*
Southam & Sons, *Corn Exchange, Thrapston, Nr. Kettering.*
Henry Spencer & Son, *20 The Square, Retford, Yorkshire.*
D.L. Staniland & Co., *3 Kingsway House, Doncaster, Yorkshire.*
Stewart & Gore, *95 High Street, Broadstairs, Kent.*
Wallis & Wallis, *Regency House, 1 Albion Street, Lewes, Sussex.*
Warner, Sheppard & Wade, *16/18 Halford Street, Leicester.*
Woolley & Wallis, *The Castle Auction Mart, Salisbury, Wilts.*
Worsfolds, *40 Station Road West, Canterbury, Kent.*

ACKNOWLEDGEMENTS

The publishers wish to thank the following for their assistance
in the production of this volume.

**Mary Mutch Alison Morrison Lynn Hall Josephine McLaren
Nicky Park Janice Moncrieff Margo Rutherford Stuart Barton**

Introduction

Here is the fourth edition of the Lyle Official Arts Review. Beside details of many thousands of oil paintings, watercolours, drawings and prints, this, the fourth edition of the Lyle Official Arts Review contains over 2,000 illustrations of selected pictures ranging in value from £1 to £1,000,000. These values are computed from auction results gathered over the past year and include, in addition to sales conducted in Britain, a broadly representative selection from some of the major European salerooms.

Every entry is listed alphabetically under the Artist's name for easy reference and includes a description of the picture, its size, medium, auctioneer and the price fetched.

As regards authenticity of the works listed, this is often a delicate matter and throughout this book the conventional system has been observed:

The full Christian name(s) and surname of the artist denote that, in the opinion of the auctioneer listed, the work is by that artist.

The initials of the Christian name(s) and the surname denote that, in the opinion of the auctioneer listed, the work is of the period of the artist and may be wholly or partly his work.

The surname only of the artist denotes that, in the opinion of the auctioneer listed, the work is of the school or by one of the followers of the artist or painted in his style.

The word 'after' associated with the surname of the artist denotes that, in the opinion of the auctioneer listed, the picture is a copy of the work of the artist. The word 'signed' associated with the name of the artist denotes that, in the opinion of the auctioneer listed, the work bears a signature which is the signature of the artist.

The word 'bears signature' or 'traces of signature' denote that, in the opinion of the auctioneer listed, the work bears a signature or traces of a signature that may be that of the artist.

The word 'dated' denotes that the work is dated and, in the opinion of the auctioneer listed, was executed at that date.

ARTS
REVIEW

The 1976/77 Auction Season has confounded all the prophets of doom. When in the past anxiety has been expressed about the commercial viability of luxury items in a receding economy, insufficient attention has been paid to the fact that people's faith in objects is in inverse proportion to their faith in money. So, despite works of art being the obvious trappings of a healthy economy, investment in works of art is a strong indication of a lack of confidence in shares and other non-aesthetic investments

With the very notable exception of Mentmore, the punitive taxation in Britain has not yet forced any of the great collections to be dispersed. However, the necessity to turn heirlooms into cash has begun an erosion of our artistic heritage, the effects of which will not be fully understood until it is too late for our myopic politicians to halt the landslide

The most galling aspect of our economic malaise lies in our inability to retain either individually or corporately art treasures that have been housed in Britain for centuries when they appear in the sale rooms. Our Continental and Colonial counterparts are so much better equipped than we to indulge their acquisitiveness that we are powerless to prevent a drain of all that once was associated with our greatness. The last year has not seen any startling new developments in taste but the patterns indicated over two years ago have be-

Fig. 1
Duccio Da Buoninsegna *(Christie's)*

come more clearly defined. Pictures of great historical importance that combine the power to stimulate the intellect as well as the senses have continued to command the most significant prices, whilst the demand for decorative objects of any period has shown a steady increase. On the other hand, the victims of the forced price growth engendered by Merchant banks injecting large sums of money into various West End dealers enabling them to create a false boom, are proving slow to recover from the bursting of the property 'Bubble' which had provided the market with so many impetuous buyers. In particular English Sporting pictures and Dutch Romantic paintings, which were eagerly adopted in the halcyon days of 1972/1973, in the case of the

first because of their connection with Society and of the second for their obvious virtuosity and the presumed financial prestige in owning them, are still wavering nervously to-day between a quarter and half of their value of five years ago.

Two years have now elapsed since the introduction of a 'Buyer's Premium' by all but Phillips of the London Auction Rooms and we are in a better position to assess the effect of this on prices. Originally it was presumed that bidders would pay 10% less than they felt an item was worth at auction. This is not the case. Partly the impracticability of reducing an arbitrary figure by 10% and partly the desire to bid until successful have nullified what was thought to be the most disadvantageous feature of the Premium to vendors.

The last year has also confirmed the position of the Germans, Belgians and Scandinavians in Britain's salerooms. Not only are they keen to take home pictures by compatriots but also are showing a marked interest in decorative British pictures, especially nineteenth century landscapes by artists whose names hardly quicken the pulse here and can mean nothing abroad. The Americans are very much in evidence in London but the old idea of them having more money than sense is a misconception illustrated by the generally high quality of their purchases and their enlightened system of taxation which encourages collecting and patronage.

The Arabs, too, engage in massive institutional buying but their dalliances with Old Masters and impressionists are sporadic and only their own works of Art, for instance Persian Qajars, which are not to be classed with European portraiture of the same period, can be said to be of unequivocal interest to them.

The Japanese, however, who were buying impressionist pictures on a large scale in the early seventies, when London auction firms were first exploring the possibilities of holding sales in Tokyo, have shown a shift of emphasis in their acquisition of European pictures. Pre-Raphaelite paintings have captured the Japanese imagination. This is not surprising when one considers the similarities between Pre-Raphaelite art which is very pure in line and conception and Japanese prints and wash drawings. Tokyo now has a gallery which specialises in works by 'The Brotherhood' and their followers and its opening catalogue illustrated pictures of a universally high standard.

While last year's Arts Review was going to press the Duke of Sutherland was offering for sale some magnificent Old Master pictures, which, together, with Duccio's ravishing panel of The Crucifixion (Fig: 1) formed the high point of the last season. The Duccio was the most expensive picture to be sold at auction since Titian's 'Diana and Actaeon' in 1971 and at £1,000,000 is the third most expensive work of art to come under the hammer. This year has not been without its masterpieces. Joos van Cleve's triptych of the Crucifixion (Fig: 2) sold last November made £85,000 a sum which explains the high prices paid for similar but less commanding works by his contemporaries Joachim Patenier and Herri Met De Bles, a picture in whose style made £4,200 last year. The mysterious landscapes of these two make on average between £20,000 and £40,000 as opposed to £8,000 to £25,000 which they made six years ago.

Among pictures of an academic nature, Italian baroque sketches and Northern mannerist works, neither of

Fig. 2
Joos Van Cleve *(Christie's)*

Fig. 3
Valerio Castello *(Phillips)*

which were favoured by collectors in the first half of this century are going from strength to strength. A modello by Valerio Castello (Fig: 3) made £10,000, an Annibale Carracci sketch of a boy and a girl playing with a cat made £14,000 and more sombre pictures by Solimena, Giordano, Vaccaro and others made consistent prices of £1,500 and £10,000 depending on their size and the importance of the frescoes for which they were studies. Of the Northern mannerist pictures to come on the market 'St. John the Baptist Preaching in the Wilderness' by Cornelis van Haarlem (Fig: 4) which made £32,000 (a world record price for the artist) was the most eminent whilst a Karel van Mander The Elder made £4,200.

However, a beautiful canvas of Ruth and Naomi (Fig: 5) by Pieter Lastman (one of Rembrandt's tutors), the surface of which was flaking, made only £2,000, a price which in no way reflects its historic and aesthetic impor-

tance. As Mr. Andrew Bowyer pointed out so eloquently in last year's review, pictures which appear to be in poor condition alarm the amateur collector, who does not have easy access to the advice of a competent restorer, to the point where although they may be works of considerable virtue they are left to the whims of the more practical Dealers.

The Dutch 'Kleinemeisters' of the seventeenth century and their Flemish counterparts have always won a place in the hearts of Northern European connoisseurs and laymen alike. The jewel-like quality of their painting and the simplicity of their subjects are irresistibly alluring. As a school they have maintained the highest level of price increase. Last year's prices were as much as a third up on those of 1975 and this year's are up as much again.

Within Netherlandish painting of the seventeenth century one genre in particular has surged ahead. Still life and flower pictures have never before

Fig. 4
Cornelis Van Haarlem *(Phillips)*

reached the heights of this year. Small panels or canvases by Simon Verelst, Jacob Marellus, Seghers, Daniels and a host of others which five or six years ago could be found for £2,000 or £3,000 would have to be of small dimensions and in poor repair to fall beneath £8,000 to-day. The pinnacle of prices for floral art was created in a sale in Holland · this June in which a minutely wrought flower piece by Jan Brueghel The Elder fetched £188,000. In the same sale a picture of flowers by Ambrosins Bosschaert realised £89,000. With these prices in mind and considering the present price range for the best works of Joris van Son, Isaac Soreau and Balthasar van der Ast to be between £40,000 and £100,000 the market in flower pictures must be thought of as the fastest growing amongst Old Master pictures.

However, the success of flower pictures has not been at the expense of some other area of the market and Venetian views, in particular, have shown how strong a demand there still is for sophisticated decoration on a large scale. A pair of Guardis of Venetian subjects sold last summer for £125,000, whilst two Canalettos (Fig: 6) sold this spring made £110,000 each.

The market in English pictures is notoriously unpredictable. They do not have the universal appeal of Old Masters and thus cannot be used as a form of international currency with exchange available through world-wide outlets. Broadly speaking only the English and Americans buy English pictures and this area of the market reflects the state of the cash flow here and in America. With the shadow of financial uncertainty hanging over Britain, Collectors here, when they are investing in art, tend to buy objects which can be realised in as many foreign countries as possible. This may seem alarmist and too severe an indictment of our political stability but it would be foolish to deny that many of those in Britain with the ability to collect pictures have not laid such contingency plans.

It is surprising, therefore, that English pictures have not been put to one side as bad debts. This is far from being the case. To say that there are too many vested interests at stake, amongst those who trade in English art, to let the market collapse, would be to imply stockpiling and incestuous dealing on a scale which does not exist. Adversity, simply, has forced our collectors to become more discriminating. Those pictures which fetch the most startling prices normally have stirred the interest of some institution or other, whilst the scarcity of masterpieces ensures that such as do appear on the market command prices well in excess of mere respectability. Turner's 'Bridgwater Sea Piece', was one such, and is now the most expensive English picture ever to have been offered at auction. It sold last summer for £340,000.

English landscape painting of the eighteenth century now offers the Collector with modest means a diversity of attractive possibilities. Prices, this year, have been much the same as those of the 1975/76 season. Views by Wilson's numerous followers (Fig: 7) as well as by artists who did not seek inspiration in Italy such as the Smiths of Chichester, John Taylor and the Barkers of Bath, Ibbetson, Rathbone and Irish painters like Bassett and Ashford can all be bought for under £500, although, their best canvases and works of topographical interest will fetch well over four figures.

Of the marine painters Monamy, Luny and Buttersworth show a wide divergence in price between their best and more hack works. The good examples have been making between £2,000 and £4,000 while the less good have sold for between £600 and £1,500.

Fig. 5
Pieter Lastman *(Phillips)*

Fig. 6
Antonio Canaletto *(Christie's)*

Fig. 7
Robert Freebairn *(Phillips)*

Whitcombe, Dodd, Chambers and Holman who are among the superior marine draughtsmen have changed little in price over the last five years and regularly make between £4,000 and £8,000 for typical works.

English portraits in oil, like their parallels in watercolour and Old Master portraits, seem rather neglected. If one, ignored portraits of great importance and rarities, such as the exciting collection of oriental portraits by Chinnery which appeared on the market last summer and made on average between £10,000 and £20,000, there is still a chance to collect interesting canvases for small sums.

Unfortunately, it need hardly be said, a high degree of expertise is required in order to take full advantage of the opportunities. Authentic works by Greenhill, Aikman, Jervas and other early English portrait painters slip through the rooms, because of the diffi-

Fig. 9
Sir Thomas Lawrence *(Phillips)*

culty of ascribing works to them with confidence, for as little as £200 or £300. Reynolds, Gainsborough, Hudson and Lawrence are painters whose names are associated with vast prices and yet they, too, need not beggar the potential buyer. A fine three-quarter length portrait of Anthony Chamier M.P. by Reynolds (Fig: 8), which had a most interesting provenance was sold last autumn for £1,900. In the same sale a sensitive bust length portrait of an American sitter by Lawrence (Fig: 9) made £1,400.

Much the same can be said of nineteenth century English portraits when one sees charming portraits like that by Frederick Goodall of his fellow painter Dighton (Fig: 10) being sold for £220, or a portrait of a lady by John Linnell, painted during his most exciting period the 1820's for under £700 or the sketch of a family group by Sir David Wilkie (Fig: 11) which was sold last summer for £1,300.

Nineteenth century landscapes

Fig. 8
Sir Joshua Reynolds *(Phillips)*

Fig. 10
Frederick Goodall *(Phillips)*

not to say that the saleability of his more interesting pictures has been affected.

Prices for English sporting pictures have been erratic. Despite a great influx of important works over the last two years the market seems buoyant, but it must be admitted that in real terms prices are no higher now than they were six years ago. Farmyard scenes by the Herrings make between £1,200 and £4,000 even if they are quite small. At the same time unattributable imitations have made as much as £1,000 last year. On the other hand a fine study of a bay hunter by Henry Barraud (Fig: 12) failed to reach £300. This was just one of a number of early or mid-nineteenth century sporting pictures by artists of the second rank which either failed to sell or made less than £500.

started the season uncertainly but have gained momentum this summer. The brightly coloured views by Pyne, Creswick, Lee and Niemann have sold for sums between £1,000 and £2,000 and even canvases or boards of slight dimensions have secured prices between £500 and £1,000. The Williams Family, who have suffered from over exposure in the last seven years, are still eagerly sought after when represented by the sort of pictures they would have exhibited. A very fine river landscape by Edward Charles Williams made £4,200 last year and a small winter scene by George Augustus Williams realised £1,100. Sidney Richard Percy is the one member of the family who appears to have suffered most. A number of large but empty highland landscapes failed to sell last year. Although that is

Fig. 11
Sir David Wilkie *(Phillips)*

Of the nineteenth century Continental pictures to come under the hammer, last season, pictures of animals were amongst the most successful. Alfred de Dreux and Wouter Verschuur are two obvious examples of Continental painters favoured by bidders in the last twelve months and the tiny panel by Verschuur (Fig: 13) which made £2,700 implies the desirability of such works to foreign collectors, who usually manage to acquire the best Continental pictures to be offered in England.

There have been no important Italian genre paintings on the market this season. No works by the Machaioli and no early nineteenth century Italian neo-classical works have appeared. However, a view on a Venetian canal by Rubens Santoro made £7,000 which bodes well for the future of the Italian market.

Dutch, Belgian and German genre scenes have replaced Northern European landscapes as the most sought after of non-impressionist nineteenth century pictures since the latter tumbled in 1973. There have been some particularly fine examples of interior scenes sold this year and without fail they have made substantial prices. Forgetting, Lesrel, Croegart and other abusers of virtuosity whose garish scenes of cavaliers and cardinals sipping madeira still make between £1,500 and £5,000, there are painters of very detailed canvases like Ferdinand De Braekeleer and Baron Hendrik Leys whose works are justifiably expensive. Two views of figures in town squares by Braekeleer

Fig. 12
Henry Barraud *(Phillips)*

Fig. 13
Wouter Verschuur *(Phillips)*

made £8,000 and £15,000, whilst a charming Leys of an artist's studio (Fig: 14) sold this spring for £7,800 The small church interiors of Johannes Bosboom are moving rapidly in price, if one takes £4,800 for a panel smaller than the one which made £1,800 last year, to be indicative of heightened interest rather than a flash in the pan.

Two superb and rare panels by Ferdinand Georg Waldmuller have shown the strength of the German market and the appeal of flower pictures in particular. A portrait of the young Count Esterhazy in a landscape (Fig: 15) made £15,500 and a study of roses (Fig: 16) fetched £32,000.

The first of the June sales indicated that Continental landscapes and sea pieces have taken a turn for the bet-ter. Two shore scenes by Hermanus Koekkoek Senior one of which made £8,000 and the other which sold for £13,000 suggest that the coming season will see a return from depression to exaltation for the works of this huge Dutch family and the other Dutch Romantics such as Kruseman, the Spohlers and Lekkert, whose recent prices had left a bad taste in the mouths of those who had collected them at the beginning of this decade.

A recent sale of Modern pictures in New York emphasised that discrimination has become the keynote in collecting pictures from any period. With 40% of the sale unsold the fact that a large proportion of the pictures had been on the market very recently was sharply underlined. However, the outstanding examples of Impressionist art have made very high prices. (Fig:17). Renoir's 'La Promenade' which sold last autumn for a record £620,000 and Monet's 'La Barque Bleue', which made £330,000 prove that those who are holding their breath in anticipation of a crash in Impressionism are liable to collapse before the market does. The best Expressionist, Cubist and Futurist pictures have also risen in price and only the mediocre and derivative have been ignored by last season's collectors.

There have been no important Modern British pictures on the market since the group of Camden Town paintings which were sold in 1975. The indifferent Sickerts (Fig: 18) and small drawings by Augustus and Gwen John (Fig: 19) are insufficient in themselves to create a rule of thumb by which to assess the saleability of more significant works. Even the Vorticists, who can claim to be Britain's only important abstract painters at work at the beginning of the twentieth century command no foreign interest. This is not so of Henry Moore, Graham Sutherland and Ben Nicholson. Yet these artists, too, have not been represented at auction by important works in the last two years and the very depressed prices that have been realised this season only reflect the paucity of important works rather than a lack of potential buyers.

However, Scottish artists, in particular the members of the Glasgow School, in common with earlier painters such as the Nasmyths have sustained the high prices of the last two years and

Fig. 14
Baron Hendrik Leys *(Phillips)*

Sotheby's sales at Gleneagles have proved immensely successful. Whether the price range of several thousand for works by Hornel, Cadell and Mactaggart or the £500 to £1,500 bracket for D.Y. Cameron, McCulloch and Macwhirter is attributable to an increased awareness amongst Scots of their political and cultural identity or to new found wealth from industry and North Sea oil is debatable. I suspect it is a combination of both these factors. At any rate, Scottish pictures are to be considered in much the same light as Colonial pictures in that they have an historical validity, which when combined with technical accomplishment sets them apart from their English equivalents and ensures that they will continue to captivate Northern Collectors.

Fig. 15
Ferdinand Georg Waldmuller *(Phillips)*

English watercolours and drawings form the one area of the market which is directly related to the British economy. Only Constable, Turner and Bonington have international reputations and thus works by the legion of other practitioners are susceptible to the frequent reverses of fortune of our balance of payments. There appears to be a direct link between the Financial Times share index and the price of English watercolours at auction! In the light of this there seems to be enormous scope for collecting without jeopardising the health of one's bank manager. The finest examples will always find buyers at high prices.

A very luminous watercolour by Bonington (Fig: 20) of a cutter and other shipping made £16,000, a record price since broken, and two landscapes by Turner, one sold last year and one this, made £21,000 each. Members of the Old Watercolour Society such as Robert Hills, John Varley, Joshua

Fig. 16
Ferdinand Georg Waldmuller
(Sotheby's)

Fig. 17
Figures in an Interior
Pierre Auguste Renoir **£180,000** *(Christie's)*

Fig. 18
Walter Sickert *(Christie's)*

great charm and distinction. £200 to £300 is sufficient to acquire even the most polished example in this vein. Pencil drawings, too, which give a fascinating insight into the way in which an artist works and which frequently appear in large albums, can be bought for as little as £5 or £10. In particular, the preparatory Drawings for topo-

Fig. 19
Augustus John *(Christie's)*

Cristall, Francis Nicholson and George Barret Junior together with Cox and De Wint, manage, because of their corporate involvement in the furthering of Watercolour as a branch of art distinct from oil painting, to attract the eye of the academic and aesthetic alike. Their most finished works realise prices between £800 and £3,000.

On the other hand, a number of eighteenth century artists such as Moses Griffiths, Joseph Farington, Jacob More, Robert Freebairn, Francis Grose and Thomas Sunderland, who at their best surpass mere topography can be obtained at auction for prices as humble as £80.

Portrait drawings, for instance those of Henry Edridge, Richard Cosway and George Richmond because of their lack of size and concomitant intimacy are a field in which a small outlay will be rewarded with a work of

Fig. 20
Richard Parkes Bonington *(Christie's)*

graphical lithographs by James Duffield Harding, Samuel Prout, David Roberts and Robert Kent Thomas (Fig: 21), despite their originality, make little more than the mass produced prints which followed. The one exception to this is Thomas Shotter Boys, whose preparatory Drawings for prints are usually in pencil and coloured washes and usually make several thousand pounds. (Fig: 22).

The present interest in all things Islamic has brought about a vast expansion in the prices of artists who worked in Arabia producing topographical views and genre scenes. Thomas Allom's Eastern views make three times as much as the average £100 to £150 paid for his scenes closer to home. David Roberts' views in the Holy Land have made as much as £8,000 and although this is

exceptional £2,000 to £3,000 is becoming commonplace and a view in Cairo made £1,400 last year, greatly in excess of what one would expect to pay for his far rarer English watercolours. Of all the English artists working in the East John Frederick Lewis is the most highly prized. £25,000 is the current auction record for a watercolour by him and two prices for his work last year, £5,000 for 'A Cavalcade in the Desert' and £22,000 for a 'Seated Carpet Seller' have kept him in the public eye.

Old Master drawings have always been considered the exclusive province of the academic and cognoscente. Until the eighteenth century, when collectors kept drawings in portfolios, the majority of sketches were retained in the workshops of painters, as they were not considered as artistic entities, but as a source of inspiration on which painters could draw when producing commissions for patrons. The drawings which were kept, tended therefore to be unfinished working studies and it is easy for the untrained eye to mistake vigour of drawing for clumsiness. Added to which, this freedom of handling can obscure the finished style of the artist and great expertise is required in order to attribute drawings. Even amongst scholars there is a greater degree of dissention about the authenticity of many artists' drawings than about their canvases.

However, the last few years have seen a growth in the number of people who wish to own Old Master drawings and as a result they have become en masse one of the 'blue chips' of the Art Market. They fulfil the needs of the investor, who seeks to protect his capital from the ravages of inflation. They are collected throughout the world and are small enough to be easily transportable. They have been collected for over two hundred years and thus are not subject to the reverses of fashion. Their record at auction is unimpeachably steady.

A number of important collections have come on the market this season, notably The Gathorne-Hardy Collection sold last year and that of the late C. R. Rudolf part of which has already been sold and part of which is to be offered this summer. The market is now quite large enough to absorb many

Fig. 21
Robert Kent Thomas *(Phillips)*

Fig. 22
Thomas Shotter Boys *(Christie's)*

masterpieces at one time and prices have continued to improve. The highest price of the year was for a preparatory drawing for a fresco by Sebastiano Del Piombo which made £104,000 arguably a greater price than one would expect for a picture by him! (Fig: 23). This is not the case with most drawings and although the market is growing steadily there is still room to buy good drawings for under £500. A vast number of pretty Dutch seventeenth century landscapes and Italian figure studies are sold for between £200 and £400. Of all the branches of the art market, Old Master drawings offer the investor the greatest certainty of capital appreciation and of enjoyment for a small outlay. Even important Netherlandish landscapes by Adriaen van de Velde, Berchem, De Vadder, Waterloo, Van Bloemen, Suycker and Saftleven can be bought for between £800 and £1,500, whilst Ciro Feri, Guercino (Fig: 24) Maratta, Cavedone, Volterrano Cambiaso and any number of other Italian Baroque painters can be acquired

for the same outlay. I am confident that drawings will assume a greater and justly deserved share of the market.

Prints are a microcosm of the whole market. They embrace in their own medium the entire range of types and nationalities expressed in oil and pencil and to some extent reflect the position of the market in the works to which they are related.

Old Master prints enjoy much the same 'blue chip' status as Old Master drawings. Lucas van Leyden, Durer and the Hoffers because of their technical accomplishment and their importance as pioneers of printing are among the more expensive print makers.

Good impressions make upwards of £1,500. However, artists like Adriaen van Ostade, among seventeenth century print makers, who produced a number of charming etchings can be bought for between £10 and £100 depending on the size and condition of the print. A lack of adequate documentation is partly responsible for the low prices of these works.

Fig. 23
Sebastiano Del Piombo *(Christie's)*

Fig. 24
Giovanni Francesco Barbieri, Il Guercino *(Christie's)*

On the other hand, academic research has begun to inflate the etchings of the Norwich School and prints by Crome and Daniell can now fetch more than the Dutch masters they emulated.

Prints of topographical interest such as the set of fifty views on the Rhine (Fig: 25) which made £22,000 are becoming very expensive. In a more humble way there is little room left for speculation in the group of Romantic print makers which comprises Griggs, Drury and Sutherland who were active in the 1920's. Last year has seen prices for the first two ranging between £60 and £120 and for the last between £80 and £250. However, their contemporaries such as Mempes who can be bought for £4 to £8 and Wyllie for between £15 and £40 must soon

Fig. 25
After Janscha Ziegler *(Christie's)*

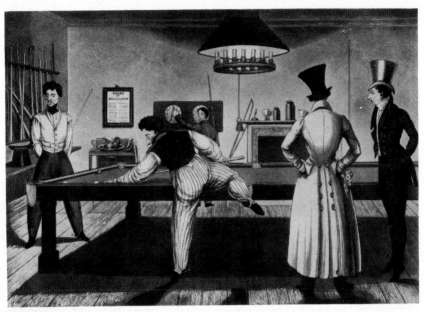

Fig. 26
W. H. Pyne *(Christie's)*

enjoy a re-assessment of their merits.

Of the Great Modern print-makers Goya, Picasso, Matisse, Leger, Chagall and Dali are fast exceeding the range of the average collector with important sets of prints, for instance Goya's 'La Tauromaquia' (a first edition of the set of 33 plates) making £34,000 last April. For those interested in nineteenth century sporting art but who cannot afford to pay £2,000 to £3,000 for a Pollard, or an Alken or a Harry Hall, prints of the same subjects offer a cheap alternative. A pair of prints of billiard players (Fig: 26) sold this season for £190, a modest price for such amusing decoration.

There is no logical way of justifying in terms of scarcity or aesthetics the prices paid for reproductions of Russell Flint's anatomically perfected ladies. This is not to say that the demand for them will not grow, perhaps it will. It is impossible to analyse the present state of this market or predict it's future, when in common with much contemporary art, the tastes of the painter or dealer are imposed on the public.

The picture market is as strong as it ever was. The dearth of important works has caused the attention of buyers to be drawn to what is available but in general sanity has governed bidding. Nevertheless, at the lower end of the market yesterday's unconsidered trifles have become today's prizes and I am sure that the tares of today will become tomorrow's wheat.

DAVID DALLAS

P. ABATTUCCI - View Of A Canal -
cartoon - signed - 70 x 86cm.
(Galerie Moderne) **£50**

PIERRE ABATTUCCI - Corner Of A
Pond - cartoon - signed - 22 x 27cm.
(Galerie Moderne) **£10**

R. VAN DEN ABBEELE - Erondegem -
oil on canvas - signed - 60 x 50cm.
(Galerie Moderne) **£470**

LOUISE ABBEMA - Portrait Of Sarah -
oil and pastel - signed and dated 1921
and inscribed - on panel - 6 x 8¼in.
(Sotheby's) **£270**

L. F. ABBOTT - Portrait Of George
Roden, half length, In Blue Coat With
White Stock - 28½ x 23in.
(Christie's) **£170**

A. ABELOOS - Portrait of a Woman - oil
on canvas - signed and dated 1929 -
1m.35 x 91cm.
(Galerie Moderne) **£50**

JOHN ABSOLON - Writing Despatches -
heightened with bodycolour - signed -
16 x 11in.
(Sotheby's Belgravia) **£60**

JOHN ABSOLON - Married - heightened
with bodycolour - signed and inscribed
on the reverse - 19 x 15¼in.
(Sotheby's Belgravia) **£65**

JOHN ABSOLON - Portrait Of A
Highlander Leaning Against A Rock -
signed - 20 x 12½in.
(Sotheby's) **£260**

JOHN ABSOLON - Mending The Nets -
12 x 9½in.
(Sotheby's Belgravia) **£40**

JOHN ABSOLON - Fisherfolk On A
Beach - 7½ x 5¾in.
(Sotheby's Belgravia) **£12**

J. ABSOLON - An Old Seafarer Holding A
Clay Pipe - 19th century watercolour -
5½ x 4½in.
(Boulton & Cooper) **£18**

LOUIS ABSOLON - Portrait Of A Girl,
head and shoulders - arched top - 12¼ x
8¾in.
(Sotheby's Belgravia) **£4**

LOUIS ABSOLON - By The Sea -
heightened with bodycolour - signed -
12½ x 9½in.
(Sotheby's Belgravia) **£55**

OSWALD ACHEBACH - An Alpine
Village - a sketch - signed - canvas -
on panel - 5 x 11½in.
(Sotheby's) **£1,050**

ANDREAS ACHIENBACH - A Beach With
Fisherfolk By A Breakwater In Stormy
Weather - signed and dated '80 - 25½ x 35in.
(Christie's) **£6,500**

JOSEPH DENOVAN ADAM - Brisbane,
1st in the Cow in Calf at Ayr, 1893 - signed
and inscribed and dated June 1893 on the
reverse - 26 x 35½in.
(Sotheby's) **£90**

JOSEPH DENOVAN ADAM - Highland
Cattle In A Mountain Landscape - oil -
signed and dated 1882 - 127.5 x 75cm.
(Phillips in Scotland) **£55**

JOSEPH DENOVAN ADAM - Bright Lady
Of Knockdon And Derby Pooly, 1st and 4th
in the Ayr Derby, 1893 - signed - inscribed
and dated June 1893 on the reverse -
26 x 35½in.
(Sotheby's) **£160**

ROBERT ADAM - Figures And Animals
On The Edge Of A Wood - signed and
dated 1784 on the mount - pencil and
watercolour - 10 x 10¾in.
(Christie's) **£550**

W. ADAM - An Eastern Desert Town -
signed and dated 1876 - 13½ x 23½in.
(Sotheby's Belgravia) **£90**

H. ADAMS - 'View Up The Thames' and
'View Of The Lea' - signed and inscribed
on the back - oil - 20 x 16in - pair.
(Warner, Sheppard & Wade) **£36**

HARRY W. ADAMS - Snow In The Hills
- signed - 29½ x 45in.
(Sotheby's Belgravia) **£190**

JOHN CLAYTON ADAMS - 'Spring Flowers' - signed and dated 1895 - oil on canvas - 23¼ x 35½in.
(Bearnes & Waycotts) **£300**

JOHN CLAYTON ADAMS - The Windings Of A Rocky River - signed and dated 1895 - 31½ x 47½in.
(Christie's) **£600**

JOHN ADAMSON - 'Halloween Ducking For Apples' - signed and dated 1895 - oil on canvas - 47 x 30in.
(Southam & Sons) **£450**

CHARLES WILLIAM ADDERTON - The Danes Watch-Tower, Near Scarborough - signed and dated '96 - watercolour - 26½ x 20in.
(Neale & Son) **£20**

JANKEL ADLER - Two Figures - oil - on canvas - signed - 7¾ x 9½in.
(Sotheby's) **£540**

LUCIEN ADRION - Nus - brush and ink and watercolour - signed and inscribed 'Paris' - 11¾ x 11¾in.
(Sotheby's) **£34**

S. D. ADSHEAD - Interior Of City, Law Courts - watercolour - 16 x 26in.
(G. A. Key) **£18**

VAN AELST - A Still Life Of Dead Game, And A Hunting Bag - canvas - on board - 29¾ x 24¾in.
(Sotheby's) **£300**

P. COECKE VAN AELST - The Rest On The Flight Into Egypt - on panel - 36½ x 28in.
(Christie's) **£2,000**

WILLIAM AFFLECK - Three Young Girls Picking Wild Flowers On The Edge Of A Cornfield - signed - watercolour - 22 x 31in.
(Geering & Colyer) **£310**

AGOSTINO AGLIO, JNR - Crossing A River; On The Coast; Country Scenes - one signed - each approx. 9 x 12in.
(Sotheby's Belgravia) **£20 Four**

AGOSTINO AGLIO, JNR - A Distant View Of London - 8¾ x 13in.
(Sotheby's Belgravia) **£12**

AGOSTINO AGLIO, JNR - A Cornfield - 12 x 18½in.
(Sotheby's Belgravia) **£10**

AGOSTINO AGLIO - Scarborough Castle; And On The Shore At Scarborough - inscribed and dated 1832 - pencil and watercolour - 6¼ x 9¼in.
(Christie's) **£75 Pair**

AGOSTINO AGLIO, JNR - Time; Evening; Glow; A Warm Argument - one heightened with bodycolour - three inscribed - each approx. 6¾ x 9½in.
(Sotheby's Belgravia) **£60 Four**

AGUAYO - Bouquet De Fleurs - oil - on canvas - signed and dated '61 - 25¼ x 31½in.
(Sotheby's) **£100**

AIKMAN

G. AIKMAN - Bay With Fishermens' Cottages, Mother And Children - 1870 - 50 x 75cm.
(Edmiston's) £200

JAMES E. AITKEN - The Line Fishermen Returning Home - watercolour - 36 x 44.5cm.
(Edmiston's) £180

J. VAN AKEN - Portrait Of A Young Lady, small three-quarter length, Seated, Holding A Basket Of Flowers, Before A Niche - on panel - 10¼ x 8½in.
(Christie's) £1,100

JOSEPH VAN AKEN - On The Terrace Of A Country House A Gentleman And Two Ladies, Seated At A Table On Which Are Cards And A Partridge, A Sportsman In A Red Coat Beside Them, A Village And A Church In The Left Distance - 26¼ x 44¼in.
(Sotheby's) £2,400

ALBANI - Venus And Putti In Landscapes: Love Triumphant; And Love Vanquished - both on panel - 11 x 14in.
(Christie's) £1,300 Pair

FRANCESCO ALBANI - Mars, Venus And Putti, in a river landscape - 50½ x 70in.
(Christie's) £7,500

L. D'ALBEEK - The Farthing - oil on canvas - signed - 32 x 27cm.
(Galerie Moderne) £16

FREDERICK JAMES ALDRIDGE - A Paddle Steamer And Sailing Ship Entering Harbour - signed - watercolour - 14½ x 21in.
(Woolley & Wallis) £100

FREDERICK JAMES ALDRIDGE - Shipping At Anchor - signed and dated '90 - watercolour - 20 x 29½in.
(Woolley & Wallis) £200

FREDERICK JAMES ALDRIDGE - Summer Weather On The Thames - signed and inscribed - 13½ x 20½in.
(Sotheby's Belgravia) £180

FREDERICK JAMES ALDRIDGE - 'Fishing Boats Entering Shoreham Harbour' - signed and dated '88 - watercolour - 10½ x 18½in.
(King & Chasemore) £70

FREDERICK JAMES ALDRIDGE - A Squall - heightened with bodycolour - signed and inscribed - 9½ x 14¼in.
(Sotheby's Belgravia) £45

HENRY ALKEN, JNR - Foxhunting
Scenes - pencil and watercolour -
10 x 14in. and 8¾ x 12¼in.
(Bearnes & Waycotts)   **£260 Four**

HENRY ALKEN, SNR - The Master Of The
Quorn In A Wooded Landscape; and Up
Over The Bank, The Quorn In Pursuit - one
signed - 11½ x 15½in
(Christie's)   **£2,000 Pair**

FRANCESCO ALEGIANI - A Trompe
L'Oeil Of La Tribuna Illustrada with a
portrait of Verdi - signed, inscribed Roma
and dated 11 March 1900 and stamped
twice by the artist - 30 x 21in.
(Christie's)   **£700**

M. McTURK ALEXANDER - The Garden
Hat, A Portrait Study - oil - on board -
signed with initials - 71.5 x 49.5cm.
(Phillips in Scotland)   **£11**

S. ALIJ - Italian and Tyrolean Child
and Peasant Subjects - oil on panel -
7 x 9 ins.
(Graves Son & Pilcher)   **£620 Three**

ALKEN - A Coach And Horses -
heightened with white - 13½ x 18in.
(Sotheby's)   **£60**

HENRY ALKEN - Partridge Shooting -
pencil and watercolour - 10½ x 14¼in.
(Christie's)   **£800**

HENRY ALKEN - Saracen Warrior
Charging - 7¼ x 10¾in.
(Buckell & Ballard)   **£34**

HENRY ALKEN, JNR - Khadidjah On
The Gallops; Corabantes, Switcher And
Hagley At The Start; Joe Miller And
Stilton; And Bourton And Allonzo -
all signed and some inscribed - on panel -
5½ x 8½in.
(Christie's)   **£3,800 Four**

ALLAN - A Riverside Inn - signed and
dated '84 - 13½ x 20½in.
(Sotheby's Belgravia)   **£95**

ROBERT WEIR ALLAN - Summer By The
Sea - signed - 23½ x 35½in.
(Sotheby's)   **£720**

ROBERT WEIR ALLAN - St. Monance -
signed - 19½ x 29½in.
(Sotheby's Belgravia)   **£70**

H. R. ALLEN - Cliftonville Arms; A
Village Church, Stormy Weather - both
signed - 9½ x 13¾in.
(Sotheby's Belgravia)   **£40 Pair**

JOSEPH ALLEN - A Group Portrait Of
The Younger Children Of John And
Anne Johnson Of Arley, all full length,
With 'Brown George' The School Pony -
signed and inscribed - 77 x 59in.
(Christie's) **£1,800**

HELEN ALLINGHAM - Study Of A
Young Girl - signed - 4 x 4in.
(Sotheby's Belgravia) **£140**

A. ALLORI - Madonna and Child with
St John the Baptist - on panel - 44 x
34 ins.
(Christie's, S. Kensington) **£1,600**

A. ALLORI - Portrait Of A Young Lady,
Standing, three-quarter length, Wearing
A White And Gold Dress, Holding A
Pair Of Gloves - on panel - 37 x 29in.
(Christie's) **£1,600**

SIR LAWRENCE ALMA-TADEMA -
Anacreon Reading His Poems At Lesbia's
House - signed and dated 1870 - on panel
- 15½ x 19in.
(Christie's) **£9,000**

NICOLAS ALPERIZ - Flirtation In
The Mill - signed - 23 x 33¼in.
(Sotheby's) **£900**

EDMOND-FRANCOIS AMAN-JEAN -
La Brouette - charcoal - 9¼ x 12in.
(Sotheby's) **£110**

GEO AMAT - Champ d'Oliviers En Provence - oil - on canvas - signed - 23¼ x 31in.
(Sotheby's) **£350**

AMIGONI - Saint Francis In Ecstasy - oval - on metal - 5¼ x 4¼in.
(Sotheby's) **£120**

CARL CHRISTIAN ANDERSEN - A Street Scene In Tunis - signed, inscribed Tunis, and dated Nov. 83 - 38¼ x 29in.
(Christie's) **£600**

J. AMIGONI - Hercules And The Dragon Of The Hesperides - 29 x 24in.
(Christie's) **£800**

J. AMIGONI - Apollo And The Muses; And Lovers In An Arcadian Landscape - 19 x 33in.
(Christie's) **£1,000 Pair**

WILLIAM ANDERSON - River Scene With Shipping - oil on panel - 5¾ x 8½in.
(Bearnes & Waycotts) **£360**

SOPHIE ANDERSON - 'Honeysuckle' - signed - on canvas - 21 x 17in.
(King & Chasemore) **£700**

ALEX DE ANDREIS - The Serenade - signed - 17¾ x 21¼in.
(Christie's) **£1,200**

ANDREOTTI - A Cavalier Enjoying A Good Drink - signed - on panel - 6 x 8¼in.
(Sotheby's) **£650**

ANDREWS

J. ANDREWS - Portrait Of Miss Alice Lister - signed and dated 1864 - 36 x 27½in.
(Sotheby's Belgravia) **£220**

CLEMENT-AUGUSTE ANDRIEUX - L'Officier A Cheval - pencil and watercolour - signed - 14¾ x 11¾in.
(Sotheby's) **£220**

ANGELIS - A Fish Seller Seated Beside Her Stand, An Elegant Couple To The Right - on metal - 13 x 11in.
(Sotheby's) **£130**

PIETRO SANTA ANGELO - Portrait Of A Girl In A Blue And White Dress Seated Reading - signed with monogram - oil on canvas - 48 x 34in.
(Bonham's) **£2,800**

THE REV. CHARLES ANNESLEY - A Village In A Wooded Landscape - dated July 20 - pen and brown ink and watercolour - 6¾ x 10¼in.
(Christie's) **£22**

RICHARD ANSDELL - Ptarmigan Shooting - signed with initials and dated 1866 - 19¾ x 26½in.
(Christie's) **£480**

RICHARD ANSDELL - The Goatsherd - signed and dated 187? - 47 x 75in.
(Christie's) **£800**

RICHARD ANSDELL - A Highland Shepherd - signed with initials and dated 1866 - 29½ x 53¼in.
(Sotheby's) **£600**

RICHARD ANSDELL - Addax'es In An Extensive Landscape - signed and dated 1842 - 30½ x 49½in.
(Christie's) **£3,000**

MARK ANSON - Fishing Boat Entering Harbour - signed and indistinctly dated - 29 x 49in.
(Sotheby's Belgravia) **£420**

ANTHONISSEN - Frigates Firing Salutes In Breezy Weather - 29 x 45½in.
(Christie's) **£1,200**

ARNOLDUS VAN ANTHONISSEN - A Dutch Man-O'-War And Other Shipping In A Choppy Sea - on panel - 16 x 25½in.
(Christie's) **£4,000**

APPIANI - Portrait Of A Young Man, half length Wearing A Blue Coat And White Cravat - 10¾ x 9in.
(Sotheby's) **£150**

ROSA APPLETON - Still Lives Of Wild Flowers And A Bird's Nest - both signed and dated '78 and 1880 - one 7 x 10in and the other 10½ x 7in.
(Sotheby's Belgravia) **£40 Two**

THOMAS VAN APSHOVEN - Peasants On A Path By A House - on panel - 9 x 12in.
(Christie's) **£1,500**

ARAGONESE SCHOOL, circa 1470 - The Annunciation - on panel - 25¼ x 20½in.
(Christie's) **£2,400**

ARELLANO - Still Lives Of Flowers, Including Tulips, Roses, And Double Ranunculuses In Vases On Ledges - 18 x 14½in.
(Sotheby's) **£600 Pair**

J. DE ARELLANO - Tulips, Carnations, Iris And Other Flowers In A Basket On A Table - 19¼ x 25¾in.
(Christie's) **£3,000**

ARMFIELD - Waiting To Go Out; After The Shoot - both on board - 8¾ x 12in.
(Sotheby's Belgravia) **£300 Pair**

ARMFIELD - A Sportsman With His Dogs In An Interior - 18¼ x 24½in.
(Sotheby's Belgravia) **£95**

A. ARMFIELD - A Horse And Two Dogs Outside A Stable - signed - oil - 20 x 30in.
(Warner, Sheppard & Wade) **£125**

GEORGE ARMFIELD - The Hot Paunch - signed - 39½ x 50½in.
(Sotheby's Belgravia) **£280**

39

ARMFIELD

G. ARMFIELD - Studies Of Spaniels
And Terriers Hunting - oil on millboard -
6½ x 8¾in.
(Bearnes & Waycotts)   **£250 Pair**

G. ARMFIELD - Studies Of Terriers Ratting
- on canvas - 16 x 12in - pair.
(Morphet & Morphet)   **£110**

GEORGE ARMFIELD - After The
Shoot - signed and dated 1867 - 23½ x
35¼in.
(Sotheby's Belgravia)   **£280**

GEORGE ARMFIELD - A View In
Thorny Island, Isle Of Wight - signed and
dated 1840 - 9½ x 11½in.
(Sotheby's Belgravia)   **£340**

GEORGE ARMFIELD - A Spaniel With
A Partridge; Terriers Beating - one signed
and dated 1875 - the other bears a signature and date - 15¾ x 21¾in.
(Sotheby's Belgravia)   **£160 Pair**

GEORGE ARMFIELD - After The
Shoot - 24½ x 43½in.
(Sotheby's Belgravia)   **£380**

ARMOUR - Waves Breaking On A Rocky
Coast - oil - 15.5 x 20cm.
(Phillips in Scotland)   **£36**

MARY ARMOUR - Auriculas - 38 x
28.5cm.
(Edmiston's)   **£140**

MARY ARMOUR - Dish Of Fruit At A
Window - signed and dated '68 -
23½ x 27¼in.
(Sotheby's)   **£540**

MARY ARMOUR - The Avenue -
55 x 68cm.
(Edmiston's)   **£150**

GEORGE ARMFIELD - Spaniels And A
Terrier In An Interior - signed - 11¼ x
15¼in.
(Sotheby's Belgravia)   **£360**

JOHN ARMSTRONG - Clowns
Fighting On A Bridge - signed and
dated - 9¾ x 14¼in.
(Phillips)   **£190**

F. ARNOLD - Glen Gaitiff, Killarney -
both signed - one inscribed on the
reverse - each 19½ x 29½in.
(Sotheby's Belgravia)   **£90 Pair**

REGINALD ERNEST ARNOLD -
Coffee, Sir? - signed - 26½ x 16½in.
(Sotheby's Belgravia)   **£480**

ALBERT ARNZ - In The Roman
Campagna At Sunset - signed and
inscribed 'Ddf' - indistinctly dated -
36 x 55in.
(Sotheby's)   **£600**

JACQUES D'ARTHOIS - A Wooded
River Landscape With Figures On A Path
- signed - on panel - 24½ x 34in.
(Christie's)   **£5,500**

GEORGE ARTHUR - Highland Loch
Scene - watercolour - 3 x 5in.
(G. A. Key)   **£11**

F. ARTIGES - Old Thatched Cottage -
oil on canvas - signed - 26 x 36cm.
(Galerie Moderne)   **£5**

A. VAN ARTVELT - A British Man-O'-
War In A Choppy Sea; And A Galley
And A Frigate In A Choppy Sea - on
panel - 20 x 24in.
(Christie's)   **£2,200 Pair**

CONSTANT ARTZ - River Landscapes
With Ducks - both signed - 19½ x 27¼in.
(Sotheby's)   **£2,500 Pair**

DAVID ADOLF CONSTANT ARTZ -
Ducks And Ducklings On A River Bank -
signed - watercolour - 14 x 20½in. and
companion.
(Bonham's)   **£950 Pair**

I. ARTZ - Man, Women And Child On
Sand Dunes - oil - on panel - 4 x 6in.
(G. A. Key)   **£76**

VAN ASCH - An Elegant Hunting
Party, In A Landscape, A Castle In
The Distance - bears Alsloot signature -
on panel - 19 x 28in.
(Christie's)   **£800**

ASCH

PIETER JANSZ. VAN ASCH - A Wooded Landscape With A Hawking Party - signed - 19 x 23½in.
(Christie's) £2,800

PIETER JANSZ. VAN ASCH - A Wooded Italianate Landscape, With Peasants And Horsemen On A Path - signed with monogram - 20 x 29in.
(Christie's) £6,500

WILLIAM ASHFORD - An Extensive River Landscape, With A Ruined Castle, Cattle in the foreground And The Wicklow Mountains in the distance - 37½ x 53in.
(Christie's) £2,800

ANDERS MONSEN ASKEVOLD - A Fjord with a sailing boat, figures in a rowing boat with a landing stage nearby - signed and dated 1890 - 20½ x 32½in.
(Christie's) £1,300

THE MASTER OF THE ASHMOLEAN PREDELLA - The Madonna And Child Enthroned, with four angels above and two music-making angels below - on gold ground, on panel - arched top - 28¾ x 16¼in.
(Christie's) £11,000

JAN ASSELIJN - An Italianate Landscape, with a horse and goats by a stable, and a muleteer near a tower - signed with monogram - on panel 20½ x 17in.
(Christie's) £6,000

MAURICE ASSELIN - La Pointe De Cobellan - watercolour - signed - titled - dated 1933 - 7¼ x 10¼in.
(Sotheby's) £35

ROBERT ASSMUS - A Snow Covered Landscape, Figures And A Coach in the foreground, A Village Beyond - 12¼ x 19½in.
(Sotheby's) £450

BALTHASAR VAN DER AST - A Basket of Grapes And Other Fruit, with flowers in a bottle - signed - on panel - 29½ x 41½in.
(Christie's) £65,000

P. J. ATKINS - A Winter Huntsman - signed - watercolour - 9¾ x 13½in.
(Warner, Sheppard & Wade) £28

SAMUEL ATKINS - A Brig Leaving Harbour In A Rough Sea - signed - watercolour - 11 x 15½in.
(Christie's) £800

SAMUEL ATKINS - Merchantmen And A Brig Off The South Coast; And A Dutch Fishing Boat And A Merchantman In Harbour - pen and grey ink and watercolour - both signed - oval - 7¼ x 9½in.
(Christie's) £300 Pair

SAMUEL ATKINS - A Pilot Cutter Approaching An Anchored Indiaman - signed - watercolour - 6 x 8¾in.
(Christie's) £350

W. E. ATKINS - A Paddle Steamer And Other Boats Off A Martello Tower; And Shipping In An Estuary - pen and ink and watercolour heightened with white - both signed - 11¾ x 17¼in.
(Christie's) £100 Pair

W. E. ATKINS - Fishing Boats In Calm - watercolour - signed - 5½ x 7¼in. - and three others by same artist.
(King & Chasemore) £100 Four

J. ATKINSON - A Castle By A River; A River Landscape - both signed - 16 x 26in.
(Sotheby's Belgravia) £180 Pair

NATALE ATTANASIO - 'The Reception' - signed and inscribed 'Roma' - 61 x 100cm.
(Phillips) £1,400

G. De L'AUBINIERE - Boats Off Shore At Sunset - signed - 14½ x 20in.
(Christie's) £150

AUMONIER

JAMES AUMONIER - A Gloucester-shire Village - signed and dated 1883 - 18½ x 29½in.
(Sotheby's Belgravia) **£70**

JAMES AUMONIER - Haymaking - signed - 20 x 30in.
(Sotheby's Belgravia) **£360**

JAMES AUMONIER - On The Sussex Downs - watercolour - signed - 19 x 28in.
(Christie's) **£85**

FRED AUSTIN - The Cock Inn, Lakenham - watercolour - 10 x 16in.
(G. A. Key) **£26**

W. F. AUSTIN - The Wensum At Drayton - watercolour - 12 x 18in.
(G. A. Key) **£28**

W. F. AUSTIN - Windsor Castle From The River - watercolour - 14 x 10in.
(G. A. Key) **£16**

W. F. AUSTIN - Drayton Bridge - watercolour - 12 x 18in.
(G. A. Key) **£26**

W. FRED AUSTIN - Cow Tower, Norwich - watercolour - 12 x 17in.
(G. A. Key) **£24**

AUSTRIAN SCHOOL, 18th Century - Saint Barbara, head and shoulders, Wearing A Crown And Holding A Golden Chalice And A Sword - oval - on metal - 3¾ x 3in.
(Sotheby's) **£100**

E. A. AUTHIAT - Interior With A Courting Couple - signed and dated 1873 - oil on canvas - 10¼ x 7¼in.
(Bearnes & Waycotts) **£150**

AVIGNON SCHOOL - The Virgin And The Child Surrounded By Saints - oil on wood - 72 x 56cm.
(Galerie Moderne) **£1,415**

P. VAN AVONT - A Wooded Landscape With The Rest On The Flight, in the foreground, The Holy Family And Two Angels - 46 x 66in.
(Sotheby's) **£4,000**

PEETER VAN AVONT - The Holy Family With The Infant Saint John The Baptist And Attendant Angels In An Extensive Landscape - on copper - 19 x 24¾in.
(Christie's) **£4,200**

B

DIRCK VAN BABUREN - Granida -
canvas - on board - 46½ x 29½in.
(Christie's) **£1,200**

ATTILIO BACCANI - Shakespearian
Scenes - one indistinctly signed and
dated - oil on canvas - 42½ x 70½in.
(Bearnes & Waycotts) **£600 Pair**

JACOB ADRIAENSZ. BACKER - Self
Portrait As A Shepherd, bust length - signed
with monogram - on panel - 20 x 15½in.
(Christie's) **£7,000**

BACON - Portrait Of A Gentleman.
Said To Be Sir William Pope, bust
length, In A White Ruff - on panel -
in a painted oval - 20¾ x 16in.
(Christie's) **£700**

LUDOLF BACKHUIZEN - A Dutch Man-O'-
War And Other Shipping On the River Y
Near Amsterdam - signed L. Back and dated
1674 - 47½ x 62in.
(Christie's) **£4,500**

W. BACON - Portrait Of A Young Girl
Resting - oil - 12 x 10in.
(G. A. Key) **£20**

SISTO BADALOCCHIO - The Holy
Family With The Infant Saint John The
Baptist - on panel - 7 x 7in.
(Christie's) **£1,500**

JAN JURRIAESZ. VAN BADEN - The
Interior Of A Gothic Church Seen From
The West End Of The Aisle, Ladies And
Gentleman, A Priest And Beggars in the
foreground - signed and indistinctly
dated - on panel - 34¼ x 51¼in.
(Sotheby's) **£2,400**

BAES

FIRMIN BAES - The Model - crayon - signed - 60 x 50cm.
(Galerie Moderne)   **£157**

GIOVANNI BAGLIONE - Judith With A Jewelled Girdle, Holding The Head Of Holofernes - 50¾ x 38in.
(Sotheby's)   **£12,000**

J. E. BAILEY - Silver Birches By A Broad On A Summers Evening - oil - 18 x 12in.
(G. A. Key)   **£24**

WILFRED BAILEY - The Day Of The Stage - signed - 19½ x 29¾in.
(Sotheby's Belgravia)   **£160**

WILFRED BAILEY - The Weekly Stage - signed - 19½ x 29¾in.
(Sotheby's Belgravia)   **£170**

WILFRED BAILEY - On The Scent - signed - 19½ x 29¾in.
(Sotheby's Belgravia)   **£160**

WILFRED BAILEY - The Elopement - signed - 19½ x 29¾in.
(Sotheby's Belgravia)   **£130**

N. BAILLY - Landscape - oil on canvas - signed - 46 x 56cm.
(Galerie Moderne)   **£11**

BAINES - Italian Scenes - watercolours - 7 x 10¼in.
(Hollingsworths)   **£50 Pair**

BLANCHE BAKER - Ham Green Pond, Near Bristol - heightened with body-colour - 18 x 14½in.
(Sotheby's Belgravia)   **£40**

E. W. BAKER - Ducks And Waterfowl On Broads - watercolour - 4 x 7in.
(G. A. Key)   **£8**

OLIVER BAKER - Farmyard At Orleton, Herefordshire - signed - 17½ x 24¾in.
(Sotheby's Belgravia)   **£80**

OLIVER BAKER - "Farmyard At Orleton" - watercolour - 13½ x 19½in.
(Thomas Love & Sons Ltd)   **£22**

OLIVER BAKER - "Church With Graveyard" - watercolour - 17 x 21½in.
(Thomas Love & Sons Ltd)   **£24**

BAKER OF LEAMINGTON - An Extensive Wooded Landscape, Children Playing On The Grass And A Hay-Cart in the foreground, A Village Beyond - 11¾ x 15¾in.
(Sotheby's) £260

THOMAS BAKER OF LEAMINGTON - Cattle In A Rocky River Landscape With Hills In The Distance - signed and dated 1858 - 51 x 77cm.
(Phillips) £720

WILLIAM BAKER - Still Life With Game Birds - signed - oil on panel - 7 x 9¼in.
(Bearnes & Waycotts) £280

HENDRIK VAN DE SANDE BAKHUYZEN - A Winter Landscape With Figures On A Frozen Waterway By A Windmill - signed and dated 1826 - on panel - 12½ x 16in.
(Christie's) £3,400

BALDI - Adoration Of The Magi - on panel - 43½ by 34½in.
(Sotheby's) £200

A. BALDUINO - 'Returning Home' - signed and dated 1878 - on panel - 25.5 x 40cm.
(Phillips) £300

C. T. BALE - Studies Of Grapes, Blossom And a Bird's Nest - canvas on panel - 9½ x 11½in.
(Bearnes & Waycotts) £115 Pair

J. BALE - Fishing Boats In Calm Waters - signed - 14½ x 22¾in.
(Sotheby's Belgravia) £95

THOMAS C. BALE - Still Life Of Fruit And An Earthenware Jug On A Table - signed and dated 1881 - 20½ x 16¼in.
(Sotheby's Belgravia) £340

THOMAS C. BALE - Still Life Of Game And Fruit On A Table - signed - 19½ x 29¼in.
(Sotheby's Belgravia) £300

THOMAS C. BALE - Still Lives Of Fruit By Mossy Banks - both signed with monogram and dated 1871 - 11½ x 15½in.
(Sotheby's Belgravia) £160 Pair

HENDRICK VAN BALEN AND JAN VAN KESSEL - The Virgin And Child With Angels In A Landscape - on copper - 19 x 14¾in.
(Sotheby's) **£5,000**

ANTONIO BALESTRA - Neptune And Aurora - 84 x 56in.
(Christie's) **£2,800**

H. VAN BALEN - The Marriage Feast Of Peleus And Thetis - on panel - 18 x 25½in.
(Christie's) **£1,100**

H. VAN BALEN - A Southern Landscape, A Herdsman, A Woman And A Child in the foreground, Mountains in the distance - 20 x 29in.
(Sotheby's) **£1,400**

WILFRED BALL - 'Chartres - With River and Arched Bridge in the middle distance and the Cathedral in the far distance' - signed and dated 1901 - watercolour - 9¾ x 8in.
(Lalonde Martin) **£30**

G. BALLESIO - A Clever Mover - heightened with bodycolour - signed and inscribed Roma - 14½ x 21in.
(Sotheby's) **£200**

J. BALLESIO - 'A Good Match' - signed - watercolour - 14¼ x 21¼in.
(Bearnes & Waycotts) **£170**

J. J. BANNATYNE - Firth Scenes - 24 x 35cm.
(Edmiston's) **£130**

B. DE BAR - A Fete Champetre - 21¼ x 19in.
(Christie's) **£1,300**

GIOVANNI BARBARO - An Arab Market - heightened with white - signed - 12¼ x 19½in.
(Sotheby's) **£30**

CHARLES BURTON BARBER - Study Of A Tabby Cat After A Tom Tit - signed and dated 1880 - oil on canvas - 9½ x 17½in.
(Bearnes & Waycotts) **£210**

CHARLES BURTON BARBER - 'Wait For It' - signed and dated 1891 - oil on canvas - 28 x 36in.
(Bonham's) **£1,600**

GEORGES BARBIER - Etudes De Robes - pen and brush and indian ink - signed and dated 1923 - 12 x 7¾in.
(Sotheby's) **£85**

J. BARCLAY - Mountain Landscape - both signed - each 9½ x 15½in.
(Sotheby's Belgravia) **£300 Pair**

J. R. BARCLAY - The Young Butterfly Catcher - 24¼ x 29¼in.
(Sotheby's Belgravia) **£90**

S. BARCLAY - The Last Stand - 20 x 27½in.
(Sotheby's Belgravia) **£120**

THOMAS BARDWELL - Portrait Of A Lady, three-quarter length, Wearing A White Dress And Blue Stole - oval - 29 x 24in.
(Christie's) **£680**

J. BARENGER - Sportsmen And Pointers In A Wooded Landscape - on panel - 13½ x 19½in.
(Christie's) **£700**

JAMES BARENGER - The Kill - 38 x 53in.
(Christie's) **£1,600**

BARKER - A Mountainous Landscape With Peasants And Donkeys On A Path - on panel - 5¼ x 7in.
(Christie's) **£170**

BARKER OF BATH - 'Morning' and 'Noon', Wooded Landscapes With Figures - inscribed on reverse - oak panels - 6½ x 5in.
(Woolley & Wallis) **£330 Pair**

BENJAMIN BARKER OF BATH - An Extensive Wooded River Landscape, With Figures, And Cattle Watering - signed and dated 1810 - 68 x 105in.
(Christie's) **£2,800**

J. BARKER - 'A Chat By The Roadside' - signed - oil on canvas - 23¼ x 35¼in.
(Bearnes & Waycotts) **£280**

JOHN BARKER - On Guard - signed 29¼ x 24in.
(Sotheby's Belgravia) **£50**

THOMAS BARKER OF BATH - A Goatherd With His Flock - oil on paper - inscribed on the reverse - 8 x 5¾in.
(Sotheby's) **£50**

THOMAS BARKER OF BATH - A Hedger With His Dog - 17¼ x 13½in.
(Sotheby's) **£120**

BARKER

THOMAS JONES BARKER - The Heroic Bugler: An Incident At The Battle Of Bassaro - signed - on panel - 11½ x 16in.
(Christie's) **£260**

WRIGHT BARKER - Highland Scene, Cattle Crossing A Stream - signed - oil on canvas - 43½ x 33½in.
(John H. Raby & Son) **£230**

WRIGHT BARKER - Scenes From Greek Mythology - signed and dated 1904/12 - oil on canvas - 46 x 29in.
(Bearnes & Waycotts) **£600**

J. NOBLE BARLOW - 'At Shere, Surrey - Country Landscape With Figures in foreground at Rivers Edge' - signed - early 20th century - oil on canvas - 11 x 13in.
(Lalonde Martin) **£60**

BARNA - The Madonna And Child - on gold ground panel - 15½ x 11in.
(Christie's) **£3,200**

E. C. BARNES - The Young Spanish Girl - signed and dated 1872 - 17½ x 13½in.
(Christie's) **£220**

BAROCCI, After - "Noli Me Tangere" - 25¼ x 19¼in.
(Sotheby's) **£300**

DESIDERIUS BARRA - The Battle Of The Downs, 1639 - on panel - 5¾ x 20½in.
(Christie's) **£600**

THOMAS BARRATT OF STOCKBRIDGE - A Chestnut Racehorse With Groom On A Racecourse - signed with initial - 22 x 29in.
(Christie's) **£1,500**

THOMAS BARRATT OF STOCKBRIDGE - 'Virago', A Chestnut Filly With Wells Up, John Day, The Trainer And W. S. Cooper, The Stable Lad - 34 x 44in.
(Christie's) **£2,400**

FRANCIS BARRAUD - In Debt - signed - 15 x 21½in.
(Sotheby's Belgravia) **£700**

FRANCIS BARRAUD - The Parsons
Brew - signed - 15 x 21½in.
(Sotheby's Belgravia) £700

FRANCIS BARRAUD - A Mare And
Foal In A Wooded Landscape - 56 x
76cm.
(Phillips) £350

HENRY BARRAUD - A Grey And A Bay
Hunter, In A Wooded Landscape - signed
and dated 1818 - 27¾ x 35in.
(Christie's) £550

WILLIAM BARRAUD - A Grey Hunter
In A Landscape - signed and dated 1830 -
24½ x 29½in.
(Christie's) £1,000

G. BARRET - Slane Castle, Co. Meath,
Ireland - watercolour - 14 x 20in.
(Christie's) £260

GEORGE BARRET, JUN - In The
Austrian Tyrol - signed and dated 1842 -
pencil and watercolour - 19¾ x 29¾in.
(Christie's) £280

GEORGE BARRET, JUN - Figures On
A Road Above A Lake - watercolour
heightened with white - inscribed on
the reverse - 25 x 30¼in.
(Christie's) £130

GEORGE BARRET, JUN - Evening:
A Classical Landscape - signed and
dated 1827 - pencil and watercolour -
6¾ x 9½in.
(Christie's) £200

G. T. BARRIE - Fruit And Leaves -
22 x 29cm.
(Edmiston's) £65

JOSEPH CHARLES BARROW -
Peterborough: The Cathedral From The
North West - signed and dated 1797 -
watercolour - 16¼ x 22½in.
(Christie's) £600

**BACCIO della PORTA, called fra
BARTOLOMMEO** - The Lying In State And
Ascension Of Saint Anthoninus - on panel -
20 x 21½in.
(Christie's) £7,500

BASSANO, After - Christ In The House
Of Martha And Mary - on panel - 8¼ x
11¾in.
(Sotheby's) £160

BASSANO - Herdsmen And Women
With Animals - 11¼ x 20¾in.
(Sotheby's) £120

BASSANO - The Supper At Emmaus -
38 x 22¾in.
(Sotheby's) £200

F. BASSANO - Women Beside A Fire,
Beneath Trees - 26½ x 23¼in.
(Sotheby's) £220

FRANCESCO BASSANO, After - A Boy
Playing a Pipe - on panel - 6¾ x 5 ins.
(Christie's)   **£2,400**

J. BASSANO - Madonna And Child -
oil on canvas - 15½ x 13½in.
(Bearnes & Waycotts)   **£150**

LEANDRO BASSANO, After - Portrait
of a White Augustinian Canon - small
half length - on panel - 6½ x 4¾ ins.
(Christie's)   **£1,900**

LEANDRO BASSANO - The Flight Into
Egypt - signed - 60 x 52in.
(Christie's)   **£3,800**

**JACOPA AND FRANCESCO DA
PONTE, Called BASSANO** - Abraham
Leading The Israelites To The Promised
Land - inscribed - 46 x 64½in.
(Sotheby's)   **£5,500**

BARTHOLOMAEUS VAN BASSEN - The
Courtyard Of A Palace, with the Return of
the Prodigal Son - on panel - 32 x 44¾in.
(Christie's)   **£900**

M. A. BASSETTI - Saint Paul, Bust Length, With A Sword And Crucifix Which He Holds Before Him - 23 x 21in. *(Sotheby's)* **£900**

ALFRED BASTIEN - The Jetty At Nieuport - on wood - signed - 24 x 45cm. *(Galerie Moderne)* **£90**

CHARLES ALBERT HECTOR BASTOGY - La Crue De La Seine - pencil and watercolour heightened with white - signed - inscribed and dated '27 - 10¾ x 12in. *(Christie's)* **£65**

BATCHELDER - Broads Scene - watercolour - 3 x 2in. *(G. A. Key)* **£11**

S. J. BATCHELDER - At Reedham On The River Yare - watercolour - 4 x 6in. *(G. A. Key)* **£105**

STEPHEN J. BATCHELDER - River Scene With Boats And Figures At Thorpe Green, Norwich - watercolour - 11 x 17in. *(G. A. Key)* **£380**

HERBERT J. BATEMAN - A Cottage Garden - signed - 12 x 18in. *(Sotheby's Belgravia)* **£40**

DAVID BATES - 'In The Wood At Capel Curig' - signed and dated 1895 - and signed, dated 1895 and inscribed on reverse - 51 x 76cm. *(Phillips)* **£900**

DAVID BATES - Wooded Landscape - signed and dated 1885 - on canvas - 9½ x 7in. *(Morphet & Morphet)* **£100**

DAVID BATES - Bridge On The River Kennet - signed and dated 1908 - 15½ x 23½in. *(Phillips)* **£750**

DAVID BATES - A Country Scene Near Bromsgrove - oil - on board - signed - 9 x 5in. *(Stewart & Gore)* **£110**

DAVID BATES - Near Windermere - heightened with bodycolour - signed, inscribed on the reverse - 13½ x 20¼in. *(Sotheby's Belgravia)* **£170**

DAVID BATES - A Moorland Stream Near Dolwyddelan - signed and dated 1878 - 23 x 35in. *(Christie's)* **£400**

DAVID BATES - A Rural Scene With Girl Picking Flowers in the foreground - oil - on board - signed - 9 x 5in. *(Stewart & Gore)* **£120**

DAVID BATES - River Landscape With Figures Pushing Off In Rowing Boat And Children Walking Along Wooded Bank; and companion - signed and dated 1878 - 23 x 35½in *(Phillips)* **£1,500 Pair**

DAVID BATES - Return from Pasture; At Wittington, near Worcester - both signed - 9¾ x 13½ ins. *(Sotheby's Belgravia)* **£220 Pair**

S. BATES - By Lake Grasmere - signed - inscribed on the stretcher - 17½ x 23½in. *(Sotheby's Belgravia)* **£60**

STEPHEN JAMES BATHELDER - Entrance To Ranworth Broad - watercolour - 11 x 19in. *(G. A. Key)* **£105**

POMPEO BATONI - Portrait Of Sir Gregory Page-Turner (1748-1805), three-quarter length in red, gold-trimmed coat - signed and dated Roma 1768 - 53 x 39in.
(Christie's) **£55,000**

F. BATTAGLIOLI - Capriccios Of Classical Architecture With Figures - 17½ x 23in.
(Christie's) **£5,000 Three**

P. BATTONI, 18th century - Hercules With Attendants - oil - 38 x 29in.
(Charles R. Phillips) **£275**

CHARLES BAXTER - A Mother And Child In A Wooded Landscape - on panel - 14 x 10½in.
(Christie's) **£170**

JAMES BAYNES - Norham Castle Overlooking The Tweed - pencil and watercolour - 13½ x 20in.
(Christie's) **£220**

T. BEACH - Portrait Of An Officer, half length, In The Austrian Hussars - 35½ x 27in.
(Christie's) **£160**

THOMAS BEACH - Portrait Of Lord Craven, three-quarter length, In A Grey Coat And Blue Waistcoat With His Dog Beside Him - signed - 49½ x 40in.
(Christie's) **£320**

THOMAS BEACH - Portrait Of William Tatersall - oil - 14 x 18in.
(G. A. Key) **£175**

BEALE - Portrait Of Mary Kemeys (Nee Long), half length, Wearing A Yellow And White Dress - in a painted oval - 29½ x 24½in.
(Sotheby's) **£180**

BEALE - Portrait Of A Gentleman, half length, Wearing A Brown Cloak And A White Ruff - in a painted oval - 29¾ x 25in.
(Sotheby's) **£60**

G. BEARE - Portraits of a Gentleman Wearing A Brown Coat; the Lady In A Blue Dress - 29½ x 25½in
(Woolley & Wallis) **£130 Pair**

WILLIAM BEATTIE-BROWN - A Wooded Highland Landscape At Sunset With Sheep - signed and dated 1881 - 16½ x 27½in.
(Christie's) **£320**

BEATTY - Norfolk River Scene With Wherrys - oils - 13 x 21in.
(G. A. Key) **£28**

BEAUMONT - A Wooded River Landscape With Animals in the foreground And A Ruined Castle Beyond - 23½ x 31½in.
(Christie's) **£140**

RICHARD BEAVIS - A View Of Okehampton Castle From The River With Cattle in the foreground - 19½ x 14½in.
(Christie's) **£70**

RICHARD BEAVIS - 'Cuirassier du Roi, Trompette 1745' - watercolour sketch - signed and dated '79 - 13½ x 19½ ins.
(King & Chasemore) **£80**

T. D. BECQUER - Spanish Travellers Outside An Inn, distant landscape - signed and dated 1844 - 21½ x 16½in.
(Woolley & Wallis) **£390**

F. BEECH - Seated Figure - signed - oil - 7½ x 9½in.
(John H. Raby & Sons) **£85**

CAPT. RICHARD BEECHEY - A Merchantman And A Smack In A Stiff Breeze Off The Coast Of Ireland - signed and dated 1874 - 92 x 140cm.
(Phillips) **£1,400**

JAN VAN BEERS - Portrait Of Clara - oil on canvas - 45 x 40cm.
(Galerie Moderne) **£116**

JAN ABRAHAMSZ. BEERSTRAATEN - A Winter Landscape, with numerous figures skating near a moated house - signed - 33½ x 57in.
(Christie's) **£19,000**

SYBRAND VAN BEEST - Vertumnus And Pomona - on panel - 17½ x 25½in.
(Christie's) **£2,600**

C. P. BEGA - Peasants In An Interior, A Man About To Break A Glass To The Right, Two Seated Figures Beside Him - 14½ x 12¼in.
(Sotheby's) **£320**

BEGEYN - Wooded Landscape With Drovers, Cattle, Sheep And Goats - 49 x 66cm.
(Edmiston's) **£900**

BELGIAN SCHOOL, 19th century - Portrait Of A Man - oil on canvas - 73 x 59cm.
(Galerie Moderne) **£37**

BELL

A. D. BELL - Continental Harbour Scene With Yachts At Anchor - watercolour - 9 x 14in.
(G. A. Key) £64

JOHN BELL - Extensive Italian Lake Scene - signed and dated '70 - 23¼ x 35½in.
(Christie's, S. Kensington) £440

ROBERT ANNING BELL - Harvest - a coloured plaster relief - signed and inscribed - 21½ x 12¼in.
(Sotheby's Belgravia) £180

R. BELLANGE - The Grumbler - on wood - signed - 23 x 19cm.
(Galerie Moderne) £130

BELLINI - The Adoration Of The Magi - on panel - 26½ x 37in.
(Christie's) £700

B. BELLOTTO - A View On The Grand Canal, Venice, With The Church Of Santa Maria Della Carita - 19 x 28¾in.
(Christie's) £99,000

BERNARDO BELLOTTO - A View Across The Tiber, Rome, With The Castel Sant' Angelo And The Church Of San Giovanni Dei Fiorentini - 33½ x 57½in.
(Christie's) £15,000

ANTONIO BELLUCCI - The Resurrection - a sketch for a ceiling - 29¼ x 24¼in.
(Christie's) £1,000

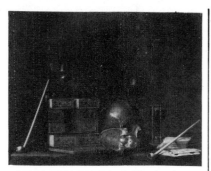

ANDREA BENEDETTI - A Pipe leaning against a small wooden chest, the fronts of whose drawers are painted with rows of houses, on top of it a roemer, grapes and a candlestick and beside it a nautilus shell, a skull, a pipe and a pack of cards - inscribed with the artist's name - 20 x 25½ ins.
(Sotheby's) **£4,200**

FRANK MOSS BENNETT - The Royal Sovereign - signed and dated 1947 - on board - 14½ x 19¾in.
(Sotheby's Belgravia) **£1,100**

FRANK MOSS BENNETT - The Early Rise - signed and dated 1934 - 14½ x 19½in.
(Christie's) **£1,600**

FRANK MOSS BENNETT - Waiting - signed and dated 1910 - on panel - 10½ x 7½in.
(Sotheby's Belgravia) **£550**

FRANK MOSS BENNETT - A Jacobean Interior - signed and dated '10 - on board - 13½ x 9½in.
(Sotheby's Belgravia) **£65**

FRANK MOSS BENNETT - Her Ladyship - signed and dated 1908 - on panel - 10½ x 7½in.
(Sotheby's Belgravia) **£600**

BENNETT

FRANK MOSS BENNETT - Temple Bar - signed and dated 1950 - 14½ x 22in.
(Christie's) £2,200

GODWIN BENNETT - A Tudor Garden - signed - oil - 10½ x 14½in.
(Neale & Son) £20

ALEXANDRE BENOIS - Maison De Campagne Au Crepuscule - pencil, pen and ink and watercolour - heightened with white gouache - signed and dated 1900 - 3½ x 5¾in.
(Sotheby's) £100

J. VAN DER BENT - An Italianate Landscape With Peasants, A Horse-Drawn Cart, Sheep And Cattle, And A Chapel By A Ruined Arch Nearby - bears signature - 38¼ x 32in.
(Christie's) £2,400

JAN VAN DER BENT - An Italianate Coastal Landscape with a lady and gentleman on horseback and fisherfolk resting - signed - 36½ x 29½in.
(Christie's) £3,200

C. BENTLEY - French Fishing Smacks At Sea - signed - 8 x 10¾in.
(Buckell & Ballard) £47.50

E. BENVENUTI - Venetian Canal Scenes - both signed - 11 x 5¼in.
(Sotheby's) £30 Pair

BERCHEM - Southern Landscape, A Herdsman With Animals By A River, A Woman Milking A Cow To The Left - 26 x 24½in.
(Sotheby's) £320

BERCHEM, After - The Annunciation To The Shepherds - 27 x 22½in.
(Sotheby's) £220

N. BERCHEM - A Southern River Landscape, A Herdsman With Animals in the foreground, Ruins On A Hill To The Right - 20 x 26½in.
(Sotheby's) £850

NICOLAES BERCHEM - Peasants With Cattle And Sheep In A Ruin - signed and dated 1652 - 40 x 50¼in.
(Sotheby's) £7,500

NICOLAES BERCHEM - An Ambush, with robbers attacking waggons in a rocky wooded landscape - signed and dated 1668 - 39 x 53in.
(Christie's) £9,500

NICOLAES BERCHEM - A Rocky Wooded Landscape with peasants gathering firewood by a stream - signed - 55½ x 68½in.
(Christie's) **£12,000**

BERCKHEYDE - Figures In A Town Square, With Monks Entering A Monastery - 17½ x 24⅛in.
(Christie's) **£750**

M. DURAND BERGER - View Of A Port - on wood - signed - 35 x 56cm.
(Galerie Moderne) **£250**

STANLEY BERKELEY - Gordons And Greys To The Front, An Incident At Waterloo - signed - 61½ x 97in.
(Sotheby's Belgravia) **£1,900**

EUGENE BERMAN - Decor Baroque Mexicain - pen and indian ink on paper - signed with initials and dated Oct 28 '40 - 12 x 9in.
(Sotheby's) **£90**

J. BERNARD - Two Beauties In A Garden - both signed - on panel - 20½ x 10½in.
(Sotheby's) **£850 Pair**

TONY DE BERGUE - 'The Connoisseurs' - signed - on panel - 73 x 59cm.
(Phillips) **£1,700**

J. BERKELINK - The Seamstress; The Violin Player - both signed and dated 1867 - each 9½ x 7½in.
(Sotheby's) **£600 Two**

BERNHARD KEIL, called MONSU BERNARDO - A Sleeping Youth Teased By An Old Man And A Boy - 29 x 38in.
(Christie's) **£2,800**

GEO. BERNIER - Cows At Grass - oil on canvas - signed - 55 x 79cm.
(Galerie Moderne) **£535**

GEO. BERNIER - Cows At Pasture - oil on wood - signed - 25 x 36cm.
(Galerie Moderne) **£141**

J-V. BERTIN - A Monastery In The Mountains, A Girl Seated By A Rock in the foreground - 38¼ x 58in.
(Sotheby's) **£400**

BALTHASAR BESCHEY - David And Abigail, Surrounded By Attendants In A Wooded Landscape; Solomon And The Queen Of Sheba, In An Architectural Setting - 18 x 22½in.
(Sotheby's) **£3,800 Pair**

BALTHASAR BESCHEY - Putti With Spinning Tops In A Wooded Landscape - on panel - 13 x 10½in.
(Christie's) **£1,300**

BETTES - Portrait Of A Gentleman, Said To Be A Member Of The Vernon Family - inscribed and dated '69 and inscribed with coat-of-arms - on panel - 19½ x 17½in.
(Christie's) **£240**

JEAN BAPTISTE BEUCHOT - The Reprimand; The New Maid, Elegant Interior Scenes - both signed - 21½ x 19½in.
(Sotheby's) **£3,900 Pair**

FR. DE BEUL - Cows At Pasture - oil on canvas - signed - 24 x 36cm.
(Galerie Moderne) **£110**

H. DE BEUL - The Church - oil on canvas - signed - 25 x 35cm.
(Galerie Moderne) **£60**

H. De BEUL - Farmyard Scene With Girl Feeding Sheep And Domestic Fowl - oil - 20 x 15in.
(G. A. Key) **£420**

H. de BEUL - Game Dogs And Wild Ducks By A Pool - dated 1874 on panel - 80 x 59cm.
(Edmiston's) **£460**

T. BEVERLEY - Three Master Sailing Home - oil - 11 x 19in.
(G. A. Key) **£13**

W. R. BEVERLEY - A Landscape With A Castle - pencil and watercolour - 5¼ x 9in.
(Christie's) **£18**

WILLIAM ROXBY BEVERLEY - A Castle In The Tyrol - watercolour on two sheets of paper - signed and dated 1870 - 53¾ x 42in.
(Christie's) **£150**

IRWIN BEVIN - The Battle Of Trafalgar - watercolour - signed and dated '05 - 10¼ x 18¼in.
(Christie's) **£75**

JOHANN BEYER - A View Of Walhalla Near Donaustauf, The Danube To The Left And Figures On A Track in the foreground - signed - 30 x 41½in.
(Sotheby's) **£380**

HENRY JOHN BIDDINGTON - A Welsh Landscape With Faggot Gatherers - dated 1853 - oil on canvas - 24 x 18in.
(Bonham's) **£550**

GEO. BIERAND - Vase Trimmed With Roses - oil on canvas - signed and dated 1927 - 81 x 66cm.
(Galerie Moderne) **£566**

BIGG - Children In The Country With A Donkey; Children Tending Sheep - both on panel - each 9¼ x 11¾in.
(Sotheby's) **£210 Pair**

W. R. BIGG - 'Rent Day In A West Country Village' - 27 x 36in.
(Warner, Sheppard & Wade) **£1,900**

JAN VAN BIJLERT - Pilate Washing His Hands, With Christ Led Away By Two Soldiers In The Background - on panel - 42½ x 32½in.
(Christie's) **£2,600**

JACOB BILTIUS - A Dead Partridge Hanging From A Nail - on panel - 21½ x 16¼in.
(Christie's) **£5,500**

FRANZ BINJE - View Of The Village - oil on wood - signed - 25 x 38cm.
(Galerie Moderne) **£86**

MARIO BIONDA - Il Pesce - oil - on canvas - signed and dated '72 - signed twice and inscribed - 23 x 19in.
(Sotheby's) **£28**

S. J. LAMORNA BIRCH - Wooded Landscape And Stream - dated 1949 - watercolour - 12 x 19.5cm.
(Edmiston's) **£44**

SAMUEL JOHN LAMORNA BIRCH - White Sand Bay, Land's End, - signed - 19 x 23in.
(Sotheby's Belgravia) **£65**

SAMUEL JOHN LAMORNA BIRCH - A Manchester Playing-Ground - signed - watercolour - 17 x 22in
(Henry Spencer & Sons) **£160**

A. BIRD - Stream With Water Wheel - oil - signed - 13½ x 9½in.
(John H. Raby & Sons) **£25**

EDWARD BIRD - Wayfarer's Rest - signed with monogram - on board - 11¾ x 9¾in.
(Christie's) **£320**

BIRKMEYER

M. BIRKMEYER - Watering The
Flowers - signed - 29 x 21¼in.
(Sotheby's Belgravia) **£240**

CARLO FELICE BISCARRA - A View Of
An Italian Lakeside Town with numerous
figures - signed and dated Torino 1881 -
41 x 57in.
(Christie's) **£1,900**

WALTER FOLLEN BISHOP - An
Autumn Afternoon - signed - 27½ x 39¼in.
(Sotheby's Belgravia) **£160**

CHARLES BISSCHOPS - Springtime -
cartoon - signed - 46 x 39cm.
(Galerie Moderne) **£19**

EUGENE DE BLAAS - On The Balcony -
signed and dated 1879 - 44 x 66in.
(Christie's) **£10,000**

L. E. BLACKALLER - Fishing Boats Off
A Pier - signed and dated 1892 - 30 x
50in.
(Sotheby's Belgravia) **£120**

A. M. S. BLACKBURN - Tintern Abbey -
pencil and wash heightened with white -
8 x 12in.
(Neale & Son) **£9**

A. BLACKLER - Portrait Of Two
Children - signed and dated 1875 -
pastel - oval - watercolour -
25 x 20in.
(Woolley & Wallis) **£120**

BLACKLOCK - Wooded Landscape - on
panel - 16 x 23cm.
(Edmiston's) **£28**

W. KAY BLACKLOCK - Evening
Scene, Young Lady In Edwardian
Dress Picking Flowers - signed - oil
on panel - 9½ x 13in.
(John H. Raby & Son) **£245**

B. BLAKE - A Larder Still Life -
9½ x 10in.
(Sotheby's) **£20**

BENJAMIN BLAKE - A Still Life Of A
Game Larder - 16¾ x 21in.
(Sotheby's) **£120**

WILLIAM BLAKE - Study Of
Theotormon - pencil - 8 x 6½in.
(Christie's) **£320**

RALPH BLAKESTON - A Fishing Town - heightened with bodycolour - signed - 16¼ x 27½in.
(Sotheby's Belgravia) £28

JACQUES BLANCHARD - The Education Of The Virgin - shaped top - 63 x 44½in.
(Christie's) £1,100

JAN THEUNISZ BLANKERHOFF - Fishing Smacks And Other Shipping In A Stiff Breeze Off A Wooded Coastline With A Church In The Distance And A Storm Approaching - 40 x 58cm.
(Phillips) £1,000

JAN THEUNISZ. BLANKERHOFF - Shipping Off A Rocky Coast With Figures On The Beach And A Fort Beyond - signed with initials - 36 x 50in.
(Christie's) £2,400

EUGEN VON BLASS - Portrait Of A Young Lady, bust length, wearing a white dress - signed - on panel - 15½ x 11½in.
(Christie's) £4,000

DIRK BLEKER - A Milkmaid With A Cow, Sheep And Goats At The Foot Of A Road Leading Up A Wooded Bank, Men At Work In A Field In The Left Background - on panel - 16¾ x 25¾in.
(Sotheby's) £2,000

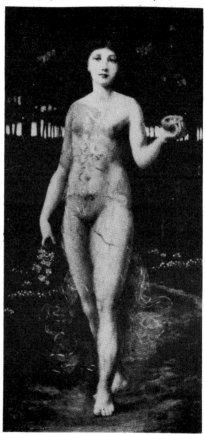

RUDOLF BLIND - Primavera - signed - on panel - 22 x 11in.
(Sotheby's Belgravia) £100

BLINKS

T. BLINKS - Pointers By A Highland Burn - bears another signature and dated - 14½ x 21¼in.
(Sotheby's) **£220**

THOMAS BLINKS - A Mishap At The Hedge - signed and dated '88 - 9½ x 13½in.
(Sotheby's Belgravia) **£650**

THOMAS BLINKS - Hounds - signed with monogram and dated 1885 - on board - 8½ x 6in.
(Sotheby's Belgravia) **£250**

THOMAS BLINKS - Studies Of Heads Of Horses - signed - on board - 18 x 11in.
(Sotheby's Belgravia) **£320**

THOMAS BLINKS - Russian Trotters - signed - on board - 11½ x 17in.
(Sotheby's Belgravia) **£600**

ADRIAEN BLOEMAERT - A Wooded Hillside With Travellers In The Distance And A Town Beyond - signed with initials and dated 1654 - on panel - 11 x 9¼in.
(Christie's) **£1,800**

ABRAHAM BLOEMAERT - The Annunciation To The Shepherds - signed - 36½ x 49½in.
(Christie's) **£3,200**

P. VAN BLOEMEN - Huntsmen At A Fountain, Others Following Hounds, An Extensive Landscape Beyond - 10¼ x 16¼in.
(Sotheby's) **£900**

PIETER VAN BLOEMEN - Horses And Soldiers In Encampment - both signed with initials - 14½ x 17½in.
(Christie's) **£2,500**

MAURICE BLUM - The Salesman, Elegant Company Outside An Inn - signed - 17¾ x 21½in.
(Sotheby's) **£950**

ANNA E. BLUNDEN - An Episode From Uncle Tom's Cabin - signed twice and dated 1853 - 24¼ x 20¼in.
(Sotheby's Belgravia) **£120**

ADRIANUS VAN BLYK - Coastal Scene With Fishing and Rowing Boats in foreground - signed - panel - 10 x 13½in.
(Morphet & Morphet) **£105**

FRANZ JACOB VAN DEN BLYK - An Estuary Scene With Shipping - signed and inscribed - oil on canvas - 42 x 66in.
(Bonham's) **£2,000**

FAUSTINO BOCCHI - A Number Of Dwarfs Playing A Stringed Instrument Constructed From A Bucket With A Tree-Branch For A Bow, One Of Them Falling On To An Upturned Chamberpot - 21 x 30½in.
(Sotheby's) **£4,200**

FAUSTINO BOCCHI - A Giant Grasshopper, Attached To A Thread Held By A Fallen Dwarf, Flying At Two Dwarfs On The Bank Of A Stream, One Of Whom Has A Lizard On A Leash - 20 x 26¼in.
(Sotheby's) **£4,000**

ANNA BOCH - Glass Trimmed With Roses - cartoon - signed - 40 x 33cm.
(Galerie Moderne) **£63**

M. BODAERT - La Garde - oil on wood - signed - 14 x 10cm.
(Galerie Moderne) **£63**

E. H. BODDINGTON - Victorian Landscape With Lake - oil on canvas - signed - 22 x 12in.
(J. Francis, T. Jones & Sons) **£85**

EDWIN H. BODDINGTON - Fishing On The Thames - bears another signature - 17½ x 21½in.
(Sotheby's Belgravia) **£240**

EDWIN HENRY BODDINGTON - Country Lanes - both signed and dated 1868 - 11¾ x 24in.
(Sotheby's Belgravia) **£480 Pair**

EDWIN H. BODDINGTON - Morning At St. Neots - watercolour - 8 x 16in.
(G. A. Key) **£90**

EDWIN H. BODDINGTON - Cader Idris; Evening - both signed and dated 1869 - one inscribed on the stretcher - one on board - each 12 x 22in.
(Sotheby's Belgravia) **£480 Pair**

EDWIN HENRY BODDINGTON - Fishing On The Bend Of A River - signed - 29½ x 49½in.
(Sotheby's Belgravia) **£280**

HENRY JOHN BODDINGTON - Near Albury, Surrey - signed and dated 1862 - 23½ x 35½in.
(Christie's) **£2,400**

HENRY JOHN BODDINGTON - Stags
Watering, Evening - signed - 35¼ x 53in.
(Sotheby's) **£700**

WILLEM BODEMAN - Rustics On A
Woodland Path Under Snow - signed and
dated 1856 - 31 x 25¾in.
(Sotheby's) **£1,900**

JAN VAN BOECKHORST - The Mystic
Marriage Of Saint Catherine - 76 x 56in.
(Christie's) **£2,600**

PIERRE LE BOEUFF - A Street Scene In
Quimper - signed - watercolour -
11 x 15in.
(Neale & Son) **£34**

J. BOFILL - Mixed Flowers In A Basket -
36 x 44cm.
(Edmiston's) **£46**

J. BOGDANI - Peaches And Grapes On
A Table; And Grapes And Plums On
A Table - 13½ x 19½in.
(Christie's) **£1,100 Pair**

BOGDANI - A Macaw, A Turkey And
Three Doves, in the foreground Of A
Wooded Landscape - on panel - 9¾ x
6¾in.
(Sotheby's) **£230**

JAKOB BOGDANI - Tulips, Lilac and other
flowers in an urn with a cockatoo and fruit
on a stone ledge - 26 x 47½in.
(Christie's) **£4,500**

**ALEXEI PETROWITSCH
BOGOLJUBOFF** - A View Of Yalta
With Fishing Boats in the foreground -
signed and inscribed - on panel -
13½ x 22in.
(Sotheby's) **£1,200**

ALEXANDER BOGOMAZOV - Study
For A Cubo-Futurist Portrait - pencil -
5 x 4in.
(Sotheby's) **£220**

ADOLF BOHM - A Monk Watching
Pigeons Feed Outside An Abbey -
signed - on panel - 14¼ x 9in.
(Sotheby's) **£500**

BOHRDT

HANS BOHRDT - A Clipper At Sea -
signed and dated 1919 - on panel -
31¼ x 46½in.
(Sotheby's) £500

BOILLY, School Of - The House Of Cards
- on wood - 05 x 07cm.
(Galerie Moderne) £232

CORNELIS BOL - A Dutch Fleet Offshore -
signed - 51½ x 76in.
(Christie's) £4,500

FERDINAND BOL - An Allegory Of
Education: three children at the feet of
Minerva - 72¼ x 55in.
(Christie's) £9,500

GIOVANNI BOLDINI - En Soiree -
23½ x 28¾in.
(Sotheby's) £9,000

BOLOGNESE SCHOOL, 17th Century -
Return From The Flight Into Egypt -
21 x 16½in.
(Sotheby's) £160

WILLIAM JOSEPH J. C. BOND - A
Castle By A Lake - signed - 27 x 35¼in.
(Sotheby's Belgravia) £260

SIR MUIRHEAD BONE - Cathedral,
Santiago - drawing - 37 x 22cm.
(Edmiston's) £10

BONHEUR - Portrait Of A Gentleman,
Seated On A Rock, Wearing A Black
Suit And A Black Hat - inscribed - 9½
x 7in.
(Sotheby's) £100

BONINGTON - A Lady Playing A Lute
In An Interior - on panel - 11 x 9in.
(Christie's) £140

BONINGTON - A Fishing Boat Leaving
A Harbour - bears signature - on board -
9 x 12½in.
(Christie's) £340

RICHARD PARKES BONINGTON -
Studies Of Figures In Medieval Costume
- inscribed with colour notes - pencil
and watercolour - 4½ x 3½in.
(Christie's) £130

RICHARD PARKES BONINGTON - Barges In An Estuary Near Dunkirk - watercolour - 6½ x 7½in.
(Christie's) £2,500

THOMAS BONNAR - Portrait Of James Ballantine, The Poet, three-quarter length, Seated - 44 x 34¼in.
(Christie's) £65

PIERRE BONNARD - La Cueillette Des Pommes - signed - on board - 21¼ x 17¼in.
(Sotheby's) £22,000

PIERRE BONNARD - Le Cavalier Cabre - stamped with signature - on panel - 16½ x 13¾in.
(Sotheby's) £16,000

PIERRE BONNARD - Paysage Du Dauphine, Environs Du Grand-Lemps - signed - 20½ x 13in.
(Sotheby's) £22,000

JULES de BONNEMAISON - A Huntsman and Hounds; A Postilion With Two Carriage Horses and a Terrier - both signed - 13 x 17½in
(Woolley & Wallis) £300 Pair

P. BOONE - Seascape - oil on canvas - signed - 14 x 19cm.
(Galerie Moderne) £16

PARIS BORDON - The Holy Family in an extensive landscape with the Infant Christ held by Saint John the Baptist and offered fruit by Saint Joseph - 39½ x 60in.
(Christie's) £65,000

WILLIAM HENRY BORROW - Riverside Towns - both heightened with bodycolour - signed - each 9¼ x 13¼in.
(Sotheby's Belgravia) £35 Pair

GIUSEPPE BORTIGNONI - An Interior Scene With A Cavalier And A Monk Playing Cards Watched By A Girl - signed - 35.5 x 48.5cm.
(Phillips) £1,200

JOHANNES BOSBOOM - A Church Interior - pen and brown ink and brown washes - signed - inscribed and dated 1849 - 19½ x 15¼in.
(Sotheby's) £400

BOSCH

PIETER VAN DEN BOSCH - A Still Life Of A Bunch Of Grapes On A Silver Tazza, A Pear, An Orange And A Peach On A Stone Ledge - signed and dated 1652 - 24 x 19½in.
(Christie's) **£4,200**

JAN BAPTISTE BOSSCHAERT - Still Lifes Of Flowers In Decorative Urns: Roses, Tulips etc. In Sculpted Stone Urns In Landscapes - both signed - 46 x 32in.
(Sotheby's) **£5,200 Pair**

FRANCOIS ANTOINE BOSSUET - A Spanish Town With A Ruined Tower By A River And Washerwoman Nearby - signed - 20½ x 28⅓in.
(Christie's) **£3,000**

J. BOTH - An Italianate Woody Landscape With Peasants On A Path By A Mountain Stream - 61½ x 48in.
(Christie's) **£3,000**

J. BOTH - A Southern Landscape, A Huntsman On A Path Near Trees in the foreground, A Town At The Foot Of A Mountain Beyond - on panel - 23 x 31in.
(Sotheby's) **£280**

EDWIN BOTTOMLEY - Fishing On The Bend Of A River - signed and dated '98 - 9¾ x 13¼in.
(Sotheby's Belgravia) **£40**

BOUCHER, Studio Of - A Seated Shepherdess Singing In A Wooded Landscape - monochrome - 27¾ x 34in.
(Christie's) **£1,700**

BOUCHER - A Young Boy And Girl On A Seesaw, In A Wooded Landscape - 23 x 19in.
(Sotheby's) **£85**

FRANCOIS BOUCHER - Le Moulin De Quiquengrogne A Charenton; And Les Environs De Beauvais - one signed - 37½ x 50½in.
(Sotheby's) **£50,000 Pair**

FRANCOIS BOUCHER - An Italianate
River Landscape With A Ferry, Country
Folk On A Jetty, Washerwomen Nearby
And A Bridge Beyond - grisaille - 21½ x
24in.
(Christie's) **£11,000**

BOUCHET - A Group Of Children Playing
Cards - signed and dated 1865 - on canvas -
15 x 18in.
(Morphet & Morphet) **£360**

AUGUSTE BOUCHET - Young Card
Players On A River Bank - signed and
dated 1865 - 14½ x 17⅓in.
(Sotheby's) **£500**

A. F. BOUDEWIJNS - An Italianate
Wooded River Landscape With Travellers
On A Path And A Ruin Beyond - canvas
laid down on panel - 15½ x 22in.
(Christie's) **£1,600**

EUGENE BOUDIN - Retour Du Terre-
neuvier A Portrieux - signed and dated
Portrieux '71 - board on panel - titled
on the reverse - 8¾ x 11¾in.
(Sotheby's) **£7,200**

EUGENE BOUDIN - Le Havre -
l'Avant-Port - signed and dated Le
Havre '85 - 16¼ x 31¾in.
(Sotheby's) **£23,000**

EUGENE BOUDIN - Trouville -
l'Entree Du Port - signed - on panel -
9¼ x 12¾in.
(Sotheby's) **£7,100**

SAMUEL BOUGH - Rough Shooting By A
Highland Loch - signed and dated 1864 -
25½ by 35in.
(Sotheby's) **£1,100**

SAM BOUGH - The Stormy Winds Do
Blow, St. Andrews Harbour With Fisher-
man in foreground And Numerous Other
Figures - signed and dated 1861-62 -
113 x 154cm.
(Edmiston's) **£3,700**

SAM BOUGH - A Castle In An Evening
Landscape - heightened with white -
signed and dated 1850 - 8½ x 13½in.
(Sotheby's) **£120**

SAMUEL BOUGH - Figures On A Path Outside A Town - signed and indistinctly dated - 18¾ x 29in.
(Sotheby's) £800

SAMUEL BOUGH - At The Head Of A Loch - signed and dated 1863 - 32½ x 55in.
(Sotheby's) £2,100

SAM BOUGH - View Of Edinburgh With The Castle And Canal With Barges - signed and dated 1862 - 100 x 125cm.
(Edmiston's) £6,000

SAM BOUGH - Southampton Water At Sunset - signed - signed and inscribed on the reverse - 21 x 31½in.
(Christie's) £350

MICHEL DE BOUILLON - Still Lives Of Dead Thrushes, Wagtails, A King-Fisher, A Partridge And Other Dead Birds In A Landscape And On A Ledge - one signed and dated 1652 - on panel - 21½ x 15½in.
(Christie's) £1,200

JOHN BOULTBEE - A Bay Hunter With A Terrier In A Landscape - 28 x 36in.
(Christie's) £800

JOHN BOULTBEE - Bay Hunters In A Wooded River Landscape - 27½ x 35in.
(Christie's) £950

PIETER BOUT - A Capriccio View Of Paris, with the Pont Neuf, the Ile de la Cite and Notre Dame - 18¼ x 22½in.
(Christie's) £4,800

PIETER BOUT - Figures On A Quayside Outside The Walls Of A Town - 11 x 17in.
(Christie's) £2,000

PIETER BOUT - A Harbour Scene, With Numerous Figures - 11½ x 16in.
(Christie's) £3,800

PIETER BOUT - An Extensive Wooded Landscape, with numerous figures, a horse and cart, and sheep and cattle - 18 x 27in.
(Christie's) £2,600

JOSEPH BOUVIER - The Grape Harvest; Music - both signed and dated 1850 - arched tops - 21½ x 33½in.
(Sotheby's Belgravia) £900 **Pair**

BOWKETT - Little Girl Playing With A Baby - 12¼ x 15½in.
(Sotheby's Belgravia) £160

ALBRECHT BOUTS - The Adoration Of The Kings - on panel - shaped top - 35½ x 25¾in.
(Sotheby's) £6,500

F. BOUTTATS - A Wooded Landscape With Figures Gathering, Fruit And Animals - on panel 7 x 9¾in.
(Christie's) £650

ANTOINE BOUVARD - A Shady Side Canal, Venice - signed - 25 x 19½in.
(Sotheby's) £1,000

ANTOINE BOUVARD - A Venetian Canal Scene - signed - 19¼ x 25in.
(Sotheby's) £1,350

JANE MARIA BOWKETT - Valuable Assistance - signed with monogram - inscribed on the stretcher - 17 x 13in.
(Sotheby's Belgravia) £350

JANE MARIA BOWKETT - Out Of Reach - signed - 29¼ x 19¼in.
(Sotheby's Belgravia) **£800**

JANE MARIA BOWKETT - The Farmer's Girl - signed with monogram and dated 1880 - 23½ x 13½in.
(Christie's) **£300**

GEORGE BOYLE - Corn Stooks - signed - 12 x 15½in.
(Sotheby's Belgravia) **£110**

GEORGE BOYLE - A Breezy Day - signed - 17½ x 23½in.
(Sotheby's Belgravia) **£85**

THOMAS SHOTTER BOYS - The Byloke, Ghent - signed and inscribed - pencil and watercolour heightened with white on buff paper - 10¼ x 14¼in.
(Christie's) **£600**

THOMAS SHOTTER BOYS - An Estuary With A Merchantman Moored By A Pier (recto); An Estuary With A Merchantman Moored By A Pier And Two Small Studies (verso) - signed with initials (recto) - pencil and watercolour - 5½ x 8¾in.
(Christie's) **£200**

HERCULES BRABAZON BRABAZON - At The Steps Of A Venetian Church, Gondolas On The Canal - signed with initials - 8½ x 11in.
(Sotheby's) **£280**

HERCULES BRABAZON BRABAZON - Syracuse - signed with initials - pencil and watercolour heightened with white on blue paper - 8¾ x 12¼in.
(Christie's) **£450**

HERCULES BRABAZON BRABAZON - Near Chillon, Lake Geneva - pencil and watercolour heightened with white - signed with initials and inscribed - 6½ x 9¼in.
(Christie's) **£85**

HERCULES BRABAZON BRABAZON - St. Maria Della Salute Venice - pastel - 6 x 9in.
(Bearnes & Waycotts) **£46**

PAUL BRADDON - French Town Scenes - both heightened with bodycolour - signed - each 21 x 14¼in.
(Sotheby's Belgravia) **£42 Pair**

BASIL BRADLEY - Study Of An Otter Hound - heightened with bodycolour - signed and dated 1872 - 13¼ x 19in.
(Sotheby's Belgravia) **£45**

WILLIAM BRADLEY - Shade Oak Ferry On The Thames Near Marlow - signed and dated 1879 - 20 x 35in.
(Sotheby's Belgravia) **£400**

FERDINAND DE BRAEKELEER - A View Of A Continental Town With Numerous Figures Outside A Tavern - signed and dated 1835 - 39 x 51cm.
(Phillips) **£3,300**

R. BRAKENBURGH - The Interior Of A Cottage, Many Figures Playing A Game - on panel - 12¼ x 14½in.
(Sotheby's)   **£1,550**

L BRAMER - King David Assembling Treasures To Build The Temple - 46 x 39in.
(Christie's)   **£500**

L. BRAMER - Soldiers in a witches' cavern - 64 x 55 ins.
(Christie's, S. Kensington) **£1,300**

LEONARD BRAMER - Christ In The Temple - bears initial R - on panel - 20 x 15in.
(Christie's)   **£3,000**

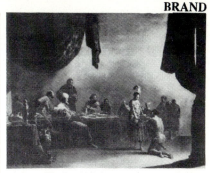

LEONARD BRAMER - Salome Presented With The Head Of Saint John The Baptist - signed - on panel - 31 x 41½in.
(Christie's)   **£3,500**

M. BRAMHALL - Figures On The Edge Of A Wood - signed - 11½ x 17½in.
(Sotheby's Belgravia)   **£80**

JOHANN CHRISTIAN BRAND - An Italianate Wooded Landscape with peasants by a torrent - 37½ x 30½in.
(Christie's)   **£1,000**

ANTONIETTA BRANDEIS - A View Of Bolgna - signed with monogram - on panel - 9¾ x 5¼in.
(Christie's) **£400**

ANTONIETTA BRANDEIS - Tomb Of The Scaligeri, Verona - signed with monogram - on panel - 9¾ x 5¼in.
(Christie's) **£500**

GIACINTO BRANDI - The Martyrdom Of Saint Sebastian - 51 x 37½in.
(Christie's) **£2,800**

A. K. BRANDYN - Portrait Of Three-Masted Sailing Ship 'Illimani' - signed - oil on canvas - 21½ x 33½in.
(Bearnes & Waycotts) **£480**

SIR FRANK BRANGWYN - Etching Of Trees - 9 x 14in.
(J. Francis, T. Jones & Sons) **£32**

CHARLES BRANSCOMBE - Mountain Landscape With Sheep in foreground - oil - on canvas - signed - 42 x 26in.
(Stewart & Gore) **£46**

CHARLES BRANWHITE - An Extensive Beach Scene, With Figures And Vegetables And A Horse-Drawn Cart Carrying A Rowing Boat Near A Windmill - signed and dated 1852 - 93 x 142.5cm.
(Phillips) **£2,000**

GEORGES BRAQUE - Nature Morte Aux Richardies d'Afrique - signed - canvas on board - 13¾ x 25½in.
(Sotheby's) **£6,000**

GEORGES BRAQUE - Bouquet Et Aquarium - signed - 24 x 19½in.
(Christie's, New York) **£35,600**

GEORGES BRAQUE - Pichet Noir Et Poissons - signed - 13 x 21¾in.
(Sotheby's) **£36,000**

GEORGES BRAQUE - Baigneuse Assise Au Bras Leve - signed and dated - oil and sand on canvas - 51½ x 29½in.
(Christie's, New York) **£103,500**

W. A. BREAKSPEARE - Bust Portrait Of A Young Woman - oil on panel - 11¾ x 9in.
(Bracketts) **£200**

ALFRED DE BREANSKI, JNR - Kew
Gardens - signed - on board - 12 x 9in.
(Sotheby's Belgravia) £75

WILLIAM A. BREAKSPEARE - A
Breton Farm Girl - signed and dated
1882 - 31 x 17in.
(Sotheby's Belgravia) **£200**

BREANSKI - Scene In Scotland With
Mill And Sluice - oil - 20 x 15in.
(G. A. Key) **£24**

ALFRED DE BREANSKI, JNR -
Hindhead, Surrey - signed - on board -
9 x 12in.
(Sotheby's Belgravia) £55

ALFRED DE BREANSKI - 'Balmoral' -
signed and dated 1897 and inscribed on
the reverse - oil on canvas - 22¼ x 38¾in.
(Bearnes & Waycotts) **£640**

ALFRED DE BREANSKI - Rob Roy's
Hut, Strowach Lacher, Loch Lomond -
signed - and signed and inscribed on
the reverse - 35½ x 23½in.
(Christie's) **£580**

ALFRED DE BREANSKI, JNR - Abingdon
On Thames - signed - 19½ x 29½in.
(Sotheby's Belgravia) £420

ALFRED DE BREANSKI, JNR - Thornton Le Dale; The Village Green - both signed - on board - each 9¼ x 12½in.
(Sotheby's Belgravia) **£50 Two**

ALFRED DE BREANSKI, SNR - 'The Dee Near Balmoral' - signed - signed and inscribed on reverse - 61 x 91cm.
(Phillips) **£1,700**

ALFRED DE BREANSKI, SNR - Loch Lomond - signed - inscribed on the reverse - 23¼ x 35¼in.
(Sotheby's) **£1,000**

ALFRED DE BREANSKI, SNR - 'Near Inversnaid, Loch Lomond' - signed and inscribed on reverse - oil on canvas - 19½ x 29½in.
(King & Chasemore) **£1,100**

ALFRED FONTVILLE DE BREANSKI - Brother's Water - signed - inscribed on the reverse - 11¾ x 19½in.
(Sotheby's Belgravia) **£130**

G. DE BREANSKI - Shipwreck Off The Goodwin Sands - 29 x 49½in.
(Sotheby's Belgravia) **£160**

JULIA DE BREANSKI - Early Morning, Richmond On The Thames - signed and dated 1871 - 11½ x 19¾in.
(Sotheby's Belgravia) **£190**

J. P. VAN BREDAEL - A River Landscape With A Hawking Party, Peasants And Cattle, And A Town in the distance - on copper - 9 x 11½in.
(Christie's) **£2,000**

P. VAN BREDAEL - A Capriccio Roman Market With A Quack Doctor, Townsfolk, And A Herdsman - 26 x 32in.
(Christie's) **£950**

VAN BREE - Game Of Draughts - signed - oil - 16½ x 15½in.
(Bonham's) **£900**

QUIRINGH GERRITSZ VAN
BREKELENKAM - The Cobbler's Shop -
signed with monogram - on panel -
23 x 32in.
(Christie's) £17,000

Q. G. VAN BREKELENKAM - A
Peasant And His Wife In An Interior With
A Jug, A Calf's Head On A Dish And A
Bread Roll On A Table - on panel - 13½ x
9½in.
(Christie's) £950

C. BREMS - The Park - on wood - signed -
50 x 60cm.
(Galerie Moderne) £6

QUIRINGH GERRITSZ VAN
BREKELENKAM - A Tailor's Shop - on
panel - 13¼ x 10¼in.
(Sotheby's) £6,200

QUIRINGH GERRITSZ VAN
BREKELENKAM - An Old Man Seated
At A Table On Which Are A Pipe, A
Roemer Of Wine And A Pewter Tobacco
Box - signed with initials - on panel -
8¾ x 6¾in.
(Sotheby's) £3,400

ALESSANDRO BONVICINO, called
MORETTO DA BRESCIA - The Madonna
And Child Enthroned With Saint
Augustine And Saint Lawrence, With An
Angel Musician - arched top - 61 x 39½in.
(Christie's) £9,500

BRETLAND

THOMAS BRETLAND - 'Gone Away' - signed and dated 1858 - 28½ x 38½in.
(Christie's) **£1,500**

JACQUELINE BRETON - Le Baliseur - grattage and white gouache - signed - titled and dated '37 - 6 x 6¼in.
(Sotheby's) **£85**

JOHN BRETT - A Coast Scene, Calm Sea - signed and dated 1877 - 11½ x 23½in.
(Sotheby's Belgravia) **£1,100**

JOHN BRETT - 'The Mouth Of The Looe, Cornwall' And 'The Cornish Coast' - one on millboard - 6½ x 13½in.
(Bearnes & Waycotts) **£210 Pair**

J. BRETT - Red Sails At Sunset - inscribed - 24 x 39in.
(Sotheby's Belgravia) **£170**

EDWARD FREDERICK BREWTNALL - A Christmas Whist Party - signed and dated 1893 - watercolour - 15 x 21 ins.
(Christie's, S. Kensington) **£95**

K. VAN BREYDEL - A Cavalry Skirmish By A Windmill In An Extensive Landscape; An Ambush In A Woody Landscape - on panel - 8½ x 11½in.
(Christie's) **£4,000 Pair**

C. BREYTLE - The Troops Halting Place - on wood - signed - 23 x 32cm.
(Galerie Moderne) **£150**

A. F. de BRIANSKI - Whitchurch Mill On Thames - watercolour - 27 x 37.5cm.
(Edmiston's) **£44**

BRIDGEMANN, French School - Mother, Babe And Monk In Landscape - signed on reverse - oil - 15 x 11in.
(G. A. Key) **£42**

SIR OSWALD WALTERS BRIERLY - Una Burrasca In The Lagoon At Venice - signed and dated 1879 - watercolour and pencil heightened with white - 22 x 39¼in.
(Christie's) **£600**

ERNEST BRIGGS - "Early Morning, Whitby" - watercolour - 13½ x 22½in.
(Thomas Love & Sons Ltd) **£35**

BRIGHT - Cattle And A Herdsman At A River By A Bridge - inscribed - 17½ x 24¼in.
(Sotheby's) **£100**

H. BRIGHT - The Prawn Catchers - bears signature - 12 x 12½in.
(Christie's) **£140**

HARRY BRIGHT - Greenfinches On A Snow Covered Branch; A Chaffinch On A Flowering Branch - both heightened with white - signed and dated 1886 - 10 x 8¼in.
(Sotheby's) **£100 Pair**

HENRY BRIGHT - By A Barn, Evening - signed - 9¼ x 14in.
(Sotheby's Belgravia) **£320**

HENRY BRIGHT - Moonlight, St. Benet's Abbey - black chalk and pastel on grey paper - 13¾ x 21½in.
(Christie's) **£900**

HENRY BRIGHT - A Cottage Scene On The Suffolk Coast - oil - 10 x 13in.
(G. A. Key) **£115**

PAUL BRIL - A Rocky Coastal Landscape With Pioneers Round A Camp Fire in the foreground And A Moored Frigate Beyond - on copper - 6 x 7½in.
(Christie's) **£9,000**

P. BRIODOU - Village Au Bord D'Une Fleuve - pencil and watercolour - signed - 11¾ x 17¼in.
(Sotheby's) **£18**

EDMUND BRISTOW - A Terrier With A Duck In A River Landscape - signed - 19 x 23½in.
(Christie's) **£200**

CHARLES EDWARD BRITTAN - Moorland Scenes - signed - oil on canvas - 29½ x 19½in.
(Bearnes & Waycotts) **£130 Pair**

CHARLES EDWARD BROCK - Earl And Joey, The Favourite Horses Of Basil R. Fleming - both signed and dated 1891 - each 10 x 13½in.
(Sotheby's Belgravia) **£310 Pair**

WILLIAM BROCKEDON - An Italian Mountain Path - heightened with bodycolour - signed - 12½ x 19in.
(Sotheby's Belgravia) **£50**

ELLEN BROCKLEHURST - A Coach And Four In Heavy Snow - signed and indistinctly dated - on board - 7¾ x 9¾in.
(Sotheby's Belgravia) **£120**

THADEUS BRODOWSKI - An Allegory Of Hunting - signed and dated 1848 on the reverse under the relining - 38 x 50¾in.
(Sotheby's) **£720**

BRONCHORST

JAN GERRITSZ VAN BRONCHORST -
A Vanitas: a young woman in front of a
mirror, with an old woman in attendance -
on panel - 30 x 39½in.
(Christie's) **£3,500**

C. BROOKING - British Men-O'-War In
Calm Seas, Offshore - 19½ x 17½in.
(Christie's) **£1,100**

JACOB BROOKS - Blowing Bubbles -
signed twice, once indistinctly -
inscribed on the reverse - 27½ x 35½in.
(Sotheby's Belgravia) **£180**

THOMAS BROOKS - Sing Birdie Sing -
inscribed on the reverse - 21 x 18¼in.
(Sotheby's Belgravia) **£220**

ADRIAEN BROUWER - Peasants Playing
Skittles In A Woody Landscape - on
panel - 10½ x 14in.
(Christie's) **£6,500**

BROUWER, After - 'Bad Medicine' -
21½ x 18in.
(Sotheby's) **£290**

BROUWER - A Boor In A Tavern
Interior - oil - on panel - 16 x 11.5cm.
(Phillips in Scotland) **£135**

A. BROUWERS - Cattle At Pasture - oil
on canvas - signed - 31 x 41cm.
(Galerie Moderne) **£66**

A. K. BROWN - Light On The Water -
113 x 75cm.
(Edmiston's) **£55**

A. K. BROWN - River Gaur - 24 x 35cm.
(Edmiston's) **£27**

FORD MADOX BROWN - The
Liberation Of St. Peter: A Cartoon For
A Stained Glass Window - signed with
monogram - inscribed and dated - grey
wash - 23 x 19¾in.
(Christie's) **£420**

GEORGE BROWN - A Gypsys' Encampment Near Maryhill - signed - inscribed
on the reverse - on board - 7 x 11¼in.
(Sotheby's Belgravia) **£30**

W. BEATTIE BROWN - Bruges - watercolour - dated Feb. 1889 - 35 x 50cm.
(Edmiston's) **£40**

WILLIAM MARSHALL BROWN -
Fisherfolk By The Sea - 9¾ x 13¾in.
(Sotheby's) **£320**

WILLIAM MARSHALL BROWN - Young
Mussell Gatherers - signed 15¾ x 20in.
(Sotheby's) **£500**

WARNE BROWNE - 'Bringing In Crab
Pots - Coastal Scene With Fishermen In
Rowing Boats' - signed - oil on panel -
10¼ x 15in.
(Lalonde Martin) **£30**

EMMA BROWNLOW - By The Gate -
signed and dated 1864 - 20 x 16in.
(Sotheby's Belgravia) **£320**

AMBROSIUS BRUEGHEL - Roses And
Other Flowers in a faience bowl on a stone
ledge - on panel - 18 x 25in.
(Christie's) **£11,000**

JAN BRUEGHEL - Peasants In A Cart
And On Foot Going Towards A Windmill,
Another Group By A Windmill Farther
Off, Other Windmills Beyond And A
Town In The Distance - on copper -
6 x 8¼in.
(Sotheby's) **£16,000**

J. BRUEGHEL THE YOUNGER - A
Village Landscape with travellers and
cattle near a stream - bears the initial B -
on copper - 5½ x 8in.
(Christie's) **£6,000**

J. BRUEGHEL, THE YOUNGER - A
Wooded Village With Peasants And
Travellers - on panel - 10½ x 11in.
(Christie's) **£12,000**

JAN BRUEGHEL, THE YOUNGER -
Two men in a boat in the foreground
by a wooded bank on which is a
Farmhouse - on copper - 3¼ x 4½ ins.
(Sotheby's) **£4,800**

BRUEGHEL

JAN BRUEGHEL THE YOUNGER -
Peasants Dancing Round A Maypole,
outside a village inn, a church and an estuary
beyond - signed with initials - on copper -
11½ x 14¼in.
(Christie's) **£22,000**

**J. BRUEGHEL, THE YOUNGER and
D. TENIERS, THE YOUNGER** - The
Temptation Of Saint Anthony, Surrounded
By Garlands Of Flowers - bears Brueghel
signature and Teniers initial - on copper -
37 x 37in.
(Christie's) **£6,000**

JAN BRUEGHEL THE ELDER - A Woody
River Landscape With Two Huntsmen
Coursing Deer - on panel - 14¾ x 21½in.
(Christie's) **£11,000**

JAN BRUEGHEL THE ELDER - A River
Landscape, with fishing boats and numerous
figures near a village - on copper -
10½ x 14½in.
(Christie's) **£28,000**

JAN BRUEGHEL THE ELDER - A Rocky
Landscape With The Flight Into Egypt, and
a bridge over a ravine by a watermill - signed
and dated 1600 - on copper - circular -
7¼in.
(Christie's) **£22,000**

J. BRUEGHEL THE ELDER - A River
Estuary Landscape with a village and
shipping - on copper - 7½ x 9½in.
(Christie's) **£15,000**

PIETER BRUEGHEL, THE YOUNGER -
A Winter Scene With A Bird-Trap - on
panel - 15 x 22in.
(Sotheby's) **£28,000**

BRUEGHEL - An Extensive Landscape,
Horse-Drawn Carriages On A Path,
Peasants Dancing to the right, A
Village In A Clearing beyond - 13¼ x
17in.
(Sotheby's) **£2,800**

LOUIS JOSEPH BRULS - 'The
Bridesmaid' - signed - dated 1859 and
inscribed 'Roma' - 74.5 x 62.5cm.
(Phillips) **£1,000**

L. BURLEIGH BRUNT - The Wye At
Bullingham, Hereford, a river scene, with
cottages and mountains in background -
signed - watercolour - 54 x 37in.
(Boulton & Cooper) **£24**

A. CAMPBELL BRUNTON - 'A Girl In
Period Costume In Landscape' - signed -
oil - on canvas - 24 x 20in.
(Butler & Hatch Waterman) **£45**

B. BRUYN - Portrait Of An Ecclesiastic,
small half length, In A Black Habit,
Holding A Book - inscribed with coat-of-
arms - on panel - 16½ x 12½in.
(Christie's) **£1,700**

H. C. BRYANT - A Cool Place - signed -
17 x 22in.
(Sotheby's Belgravia) **£500**

PETER BUCHAN - Early Spring, Near
Row - signed - 15½ x 23¼in.
(Sotheby's Belgravia) **£110**

ADAM BUCK - The Expiation Of
Orestes - signed and dated 1813,
pencil and watercolour - 9 x 9¾in.
(Christie's) **£140**

JOHN CHESSEL BUCKLER - Askham
Hall, Westmorland; And Entrance To
Askham Hall - both signed and dated
1819 - pencil and watercolour - 7¾ x
10½in.
(Christie's) **£260 Pair**

J. E. BUCKLEY - The Walled Garden -
heightened with bodycolour - signed
and dated 1864 - 17¾ x 29in.
(Sotheby's Belgravia) **£240**

85

BUCKLEY

C. F. BUCKLEY - Figures Near A Castle Beside A Highland Loch - watercolour on London Board - 8¾ x 11in.
(Christie's)   **£35**

BUCKLEY - Portrait Of A Girl Wearing A Wreath And Coronet In A Landscape, three-quarter length - 52 x 32¾in.
(Sotheby's Belgravia)   **£50**

ERNEST P. BUCKNALL - The Haywain - signed - 34 x 48½in.
(Sotheby's Belgravia)   **£420**

JOHANN RUDOLF BUHLMANN - Sunset Over The Bay - signed and dated 1846 - 14 x 21½in.
(Sotheby's)   **£400**

JOHANN RUDOLF BUHLMANN - Sunset Over The Isle Of Ischia - signed and dated 1847 - inscribed on a label on the reverse - 14 x 21½in.
(Sotheby's)   **£900**

EDGAR BUNDY - 'Flirtation' - signed - watercolour - 14¼ x 20½in.
(Bearnes & Waycotts)   **£190**

EDGAR BUNDY - An Interior Scene - watercolour - signed and dated 1892 - 19 x 26in.
(King & Chasemore)   **£420**

J. BUNTING - On The Coast - signed - 9½ x 17½in.
(Sotheby's Belgravia)   **£55**

DUCCIO DI BUONINSEGNA - The Crucifixion: Christ crucified between the two thieves surrounded by six angels in attitudes of grieg - on gold ground - on panel - 23½ x 15in.
(Christie's)   **£1,000,000**

HENDRICUS JACOBUS BURGERS - A Youthful Romance In Danger - signed and dated '66 and indistinctly inscribed - 12½ x 18in.
(Sotheby's)   **£1,000**

JOHN BAGNOLD BURGESS - A Venetian Lady At A Well - signed and dated 1869 - 24 x 20in.
(Christie's)   **£320**

WILLIAM BURGESS - Near Towen In Merionethshire - etched outline and watercolour - etched signature and date 1783 - 9½ x 12½in.
(Christie's)   **£60**

HEINRICH BURKEL - A View Outside Rome - a sketch - on paper - 8¼ x 18¼in.
(Sotheby's)   **£1,300**

HEINRICH BURKEL - A Distant View Of The Zugspitz - on paper - 8 x 17in.
(Sotheby's) £2,800

SIR EDWARD COLEY BURNE-JONES - Three Figures At A Window - pencil - 7½ x 5¼in.
(Sotheby's Belgravia) £140

SIR EDWARD COLEY BURNE-JONES - A Preparatory Drawing For An Illustration To 'The Earthly Paradise', Possibly Danae And The Infant Perseus - black chalk - 3½ x 4¾in.
(Sotheby's Belgravia) £220

SIR EDWARD COLEY BURNE-JONES - Study Of A Girl's Head - gouache - oval - 12½ x 10¼in.
(Sotheby's Belgravia) £900

JAMES BURNET - A Farmyard, With A Herdsman And Cattle - 19 x 33in.
(Christie's) £350

ROBERT BURROWS - Landscape With Sheep And Shepherd In Lane, River With Boat in background - 13 x 19in.
(G. A. Key) £175

EDMUND BUSH - Men-O'-War In The Open Sea - pen and ink and watercolour - signed and dated Anno Domini, 1715/6 in an ornamental cartouche - 20 x 28½in.
(Christie's) £350

WILLIAM BUSK - A Young Primrose Seller - signed - 24 x 16in.
(Sotheby's Belgravia) £30

SIMON BUSSY - Taormina, The Roman Theatre - pastel - signed - 6 x 4½in.
(Sotheby's) £45

THOMAS BUTTERSWORTH - The Battle Of Trafalgar, With The 'Royal Sovereign' Breaking Through The French Line - signed - 27¼ x 41½in.
(Christie's) £5,000

THOMAS BUTTERSWORTH - The Surrender Of Two English Men-O'-War - oil on panel - signed - 24 x 36in.
(King & Chasemore) £660

WILLEM BUYTEWECH - Ladies And Gentlemen Merrymaking At A Feast - on panel - 16½ x 26in.
(Christie's) £4,800

BYZANTINE SCHOOL, 12th Century - The Virgin And Child Between Two Apostles - gilded panel - 20 x 23½in.
(Buckell & Ballard) £1,150

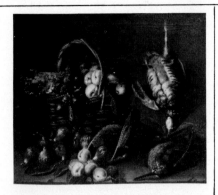

F. CABANES - Still Life With Dead Game And Fruit - signed and dated 1747 - oil on canvas - 24½ x 29in.
(Bearnes & Waycotts) **£1,150 Pair**

FRANCIS CAMPBELL BOILEAU CADELL - An Interior - signed - inscribed on the reverse - 39½ x 29½in.
(Sotheby's) **£2,000**

FRANCIS CAMPBELL BOILEAU CADELL - Iona - signed and dated '14 - on board - 14½ x 17½in.
(Sotheby's) **£300**

FRANCIS CAMPBELL BOILEAU CADELL - The Embroidered Cloak - signed - inscribed on the reverse - 29¼ x 24¼in.
(Sotheby's) **£900**

J. CADEYNE - Seascape - oil on canvas - signed - 17 x 29cm.
(Galerie Moderne) **£38**

THOMAS WATT CAFE - An Interior Of A Fisherman's Cottage In Jersey - heightened with white - 12 x 18in.
(Sotheby's) **£70**

THOMAS WATT CAFE - Arundel Park; Arundel From The River - both inscribed on the reverse - 13 x 20in. and 9½ x 20in.
(Sotheby's) **£70 Pair**

J. H. CAFEINIC - Vase Of Flowers - oil on wood - signed - 36 x 28cm.
(Galerie Moderne) **£66**

HECTOR CAFFIERI - Still Life With A Vase Of Roses - heightened with white - signed - 13½ x 10¼in.
(Sotheby's) **£80**

HECTOR CAFFIERI - The Ex Voto -
signed - 22¼ x 17½in.
(Sotheby's Belgravia) **£130**

WALTER WALLOR CAFFYN - Reed
Collectors At Harvest Time - signed
and dated 1889 - 23½ x 35½in.
(Sotheby's Belgravia) **£1,400**

CHARLES CALLCOTT - Dancing In A
Croft - indistinctly signed with monogram
and indistinctly dated - 36 x 48in.
(Sotheby's) **£270**

WILLIAM CALLON - Kilgarrin Castle -
dated 1854 - watercolour - 25 x 18in.
(Boulton & Cooper) **£40**

J. CALLOW - Shipping Off The Shore -
heightened with bodycolour - 5 x 7¾in.
(Sotheby's) **£80**

JOHN CALLOW - Figures Near A Horse
And Cart On A Roadway - watercolour -
11½ x 14½in.
(Christie's) **£170**

J. CALLOW - Fishing Boats In A
Rough Sea - 27¼ x 37in.
(Sotheby's Belgravia) **£260**

WILLIAM CALLOW - The Palazzo
Pisani-Moretta On The Grand Canal,
Venice - signed - watercolour
heightened with white - 12¼ x 18½in.
(Christie's) **£1,800**

WILLIAM CALLOW - Vico, Bay Of
Naples - signed - inscribed and dated '40 -
pencil and watercolour - 10¼ x 14½in.
(Christie's) **£300**

ARTURO CALOSCI - The Violinist - signed
and inscribed 'Firenze' - on panel - 12½ x 8in.
(Christie's) **£380**

CALVERT

E. CALVERT - Mussel Gatherers, Evening - signed - 11½ x 19½in.
(Sotheby's Belgravia) £70

E. S. CALVERT - Hayfield And Sheep - 24 x 34cm.
(Edmiston's) £62

SIR DAVID YOUNG CAMERON - Culloden - pen and sepia wash - signed and inscribed - 12½ x 17¾in.
(Sotheby's) £150

F. CALVERT - Shipping In A Storm - indistinctly inscribed - 9½ x 11½in.
(Sotheby's Belgravia) £220

FREDERICK CALVERT - Shipping In Calm Waters - signed - 9½ x 13½in.
(Sotheby's Belgravia) £420

CALVI - The Madonna And Child With Saint Mary Magdalene And Saint Lucy - oval - 10 x 13½in.
(Sotheby's) £120

LOUIS CAMBIER - The Pool - oil on canvas - signed and dated 1902 - 39 x 50cm.
(Galerie Moderne) £69

T. CAMBIER - House And Garden At Uccle - oil on canvas - signed and dated 1914 - 47 x 35cm.
(Galerie Moderne) £15

D. CAMERON - Solway Coast Scene - 29 x 44cm.
(Edmiston's) £66

SIR DAVID YOUNG CAMERON - A Pool In Badenoch - signed - on board - 9½ x 13½in.
(Sotheby's) £550

SIR DAVID YOUNG CAMERON - Old Cairo - signed - 16¾ x 7½in.
(Sotheby's) £270

HUGH CAMERON - The Sleeping Drummer - signed and dated 1884 - 26½ x 19½in.
(Christie's) £300

KATHERINE CAMERON - Loch Leven - signed - 8½ x 11¾in.
(Sotheby's) £75

KATHERINE CAMERON - Carnations And Red Admirals - signed - 20½ x 11¼in.
(Sotheby's) £80

H. CAMPBELL - River Landscape With Bridge - watercolour - 10 x 5in.
(Thomas Love & Sons Ltd) £4

JAMES CAMPBELL - 'A Whitesmith's Cellar' - signed with monogram - signed and inscribed on reverse - 35 x 47cm.
(Phillips) £600

OLIVER CAMPBELL - A Barn Owl - gouache - signed - 10 x 12½ ins.
(Sotheby's Belgravia) £45

MICHELE PACE, called MICHELANGELO DA CAMPIDOGLIO - Melons, Apples, Peaches, Grapes And Plums On A Table - 27½ x 41¼in.
(Christie's) £2,200

CAMPION - A Mountainous Landscape; A Mountainous River Landscape - both heightened with white on buff paper - 8½ x 12¼in.
(Sotheby's) £18 Pair

CAMPION

GEORGE BRYAN CAMPION - The
Highland Royal Mail Crossing The Burn -
heightened with bodycolour - signed and
inscribed - 13 x 21in.
(Sotheby's) £240

FREDERICO DEL CAMPO - The Canale
Del Sastro, Venice - signed and dated
Venezia 1893 - on panel - 7½ x 4½in.
(Christie's, S. Kensington) £1,000

SCHOOL OF CANALETTO - Venetian Canal
Scene With Boats And Figures - 30 x 35in.
(Woolley & Wallis) £340

ANTONIO CANAL, IL CANALETTO -
The Grand Canal, Venice Looking East
From The Campo San Vio, With Gondolas
And Sailing Vessels - 18 x 30½in.
(Christie's) £110,000

ANTONIO CANAL, IL CANALETTO -
The Piazza San Marco, Venice, With The
Basilica And Two Religious Processions -
18½ x 28in.
(Christie's) £40,000

ANTONIO CANAL, IL CANALETTO -
The Molo, Venice From The Bacino Di
San Marco With A Gondola, A Sandalo
And Numerous Other Vessels - 18 x
30½in.
(Christie's) £110,000

CANALETTO - The Bacino Di San
Marco, Venice - 20 x 32in.
(Christie's) £700

A. CANALETTO - The Tiber and the Ponte
Cestio, Rome, with two men fishing -
18¼ x 24¼in.
(Christie's) £7,500

CANELLA - A Street Scene With A
Church - 7¾ x 6¾in.
(Sotheby's) £140

VINCENTIUS CAPOBIANCHI -
Portrait Of A Nobleman, three-quarter
length, Wearing A Black Tunic And
White Ruff - signed and dated 1857 -
inscribed 'Romae' on the reverse -
44 x 30¾in.
(Sotheby's) £360

VINCENZO CAPRILE - The Old
Guitar Player - signed - 38 x 26in.
(Sotheby's) £2,400

JULIA CAPRON - Patterns - cartoon -
signed - 45 x 38cm.
(Galerie Moderne) £6

JACQUES CARABAIN - An Italianate
Street Scene - signed - on panel - 15½ x
11½in.
(Christie's) £1,700

CARACCI, Style of - Marriage Of Cana
In Galilee - 13½ x 18in.
(Charles R. Phillips) £100

SCRAFINA CARAFO - The Death Of
Miss Bathurst In The River Tiber,
Rome, 1824 - 8½ x 13¾in.
(Graves Son & Pilcher) £190

CARAVAGGIO, After - The Card
Players - 14 x 17in.
(Sotheby's) £300

TONY CARDELLA - South Of France -
oil - 17¾ x 23½in.
(Charles R. Phillips) £100

CLAUDE CARDON - Calves And
Domestic Fowls In Barns - oils -
6 x 10in
(G. A. Key) £500 Pair

CONSALVE CARELLI - The Bay Of
Naples - oil - on board - signed and
inscribed 'Napoli' - 10½ x 11½in.
(King & Chasemore) £1,000 Pair

CARELLI - Bay Of Naples - on panel -
9½ x 13½in.
(Sotheby's Belgravia) £38

GABRIELE CARELLI - Monaco, The
Old Town From The East - signed - 4¾ x
8in.
(Sotheby's) £100

GABRIELE CARELLI - The Royal Tombs
In The Church Of San Lorenzo, Naples -
signed and dated 1851 - 30 x 24in.
(Christie's) £450

GIUSEPPE CARELLI - A View Of The
Pozzuoli In The Bay Of Naples -
inscribed 'Pozzuoli' - on panel - 9¾ x
15in.
(Sotheby's) £800

CAREY

J. W. CAREY - The Misty Hills Of Skye - heightened with bodycolour - signed - inscribed and dated 1910 - 6½ x 14½in.
(Sotheby's Belgravia) **£22**

ONORATO CARLANDI - An Italian Woman Holding A Wool Carder - signed - 19 x 12¼in.
(Sotheby's) **£65**

C. CARLONE - The Last Supper, In An Architectural Setting - 20 x 30in.
(Sotheby's) **£1,800**

GIOVANNI BATTISTA CARLONE - The Assumption Of The Magdalene - 67 x 47¾in.
(Sotheby's) **£2,500**

GIOVANNI BATTISTA CARLONE - Joseph Interpreting Dreams - 48 x 56in.
(Christie's) **£1,300**

JOHN WILSON CARMICHAEL - Salvaging A Wreck Off The Coast - inscribed 'sketch' - on board - 12¾ x 16½in.
(Sotheby's Belgravia) **£700**

JOHN WILSON CARMICHAEL - Dutch Sailing Vessels Moored Offshore In A Calm; and Dutch Fishing Boats And A Man-O'-War Offshore In Breezy Weather - both signed with initials - on panel - 8 x 10½in.
(Christie's) **£2,700 Pair**

JOHN WILSON CARMICHAEL - Hexham Abbey - grey wash - inscribed - 5 x 4in.
(Sotheby's) **£90**

JOHN WILSON CARMICHAEL - St. Michael's Mount, Cornwall - signed and dated 1847 - on panel - 11¾ x 16in.
(Sotheby's Belgravia) **£1,000**

JOHN WILSON CARMICHAEL - Fisherfolk Bringing In The Catch - inscribed 'sketch' - on board - 12¾ x 16½in.
(Sotheby's Belgravia) **£200**

JOHN WILSON CARMICHAEL -
Soldiers And Travellers On A Road Near
Lake Geneva - watercolour - signed and
dated 1837 - signed again and inscribed
on the reverse - 16½ x 23½in.
(Christie's) **£240**

JOHN WILSON CARMICHAEL - Shipping
In An Offshore Scene - signed and dated
1845 - oil on canvas - 12 x 18½in.
(King & Chasemore) **£420**

B. DE CARO - Geese, Frogs And A
Tortoise In A Pool - 35 x 48½in.
(Christie's) **£1,400**

A. CAROLUS - Landscape - oil on
canvas - signed and dated 1927 - 45 x
26cm.
(Galerie Moderne) **£7**

JEAN CAROLUS - Interior With
Figures - signed - oil on panel - 25 x 19in.
(Bonham's) **£1,800**

JEAN CAROLUS - The Dressmaker's
Visit - signed and dated Bruxelles 1866 -
34 x 48½in.
(Christie's) **£3,200**

JOSEPH CARON - Les Diseaux - oil on
canvas - signed - 41 x 51cm.
(Galerie Moderne) **£25**

HENRY JOSEPH CARPENTERO - Two
Pipe Smokers - signed and dated '43 - on
panel - 6½ x 5½in.
(Sotheby's) **£170**

MARGARET CARPENTER - Portrait Of
A Gentleman Said To Be Of George
Davis, Grandson Of John Spicer, As A
Child, standing half length, Holding A
Dog - 23 x 19in.
(Christie's) **£350**

GUILIO CARPIONI - Kingdom Of
Hypnos - oil on canvas - 29 x 26in.
(Bonham's) **£2,600**

ANNIBALE CARRACCI, After - The
Annunciation - 10¾ x 8½in.
(Sotheby's) **£40**

CARRACCI - The Flight Into Egypt -
28 x 37in.
(Christie's) **£1,200**

CARRACCI, After - The Holy Family -
on panel - 5¼ x 6¾in.
(Sotheby's) **£200**

CIRCLE OF LODOVICO CARRACCI -
The Holy Family, In The Workshop Of
Saint Joseph, A Wooded Landscape
Beyond - on panel - 14 x 11in.
(Sotheby's) **£380**

CARRACCI

SCHOOL OF CARRACCI - 'The Nativity' - oil on canvas - 36½ x 26½in.
(Bearnes & Waycotts)   **£190**

JOHN MULCASTER CARRICK - A Barge at Richmond-on-Thames - signed and dated 1888 - 15½ x 23½in.
(Christie's, S. Kensington)   **£460**

EUGENE CARRIERE - L'Indiscret - signed and dated '74 - signed and dated on the reverse - 16 x 12½in.
(Sotheby's)   **£550**

A. CARSE - Figures Drinking In A Highland Interior - 25 x 29½in.
(Christie's)   **£190**

H. B. CARTER - Shipping Off Scarborough In Stormy Weather - heightened with bodycolour - inscribed - 12¼ x 26¼in.
(Sotheby's Belgravia)   **£40**

HENRY BARLOW CARTER - 'Mount Orgueil, Jersey' - signed - inscribed and dated 1876 - watercolour - 13¼ x 24¼in.
(Bearnes & Waycotts)   **£120**

G. CASENZA - Boating Scene With A Family Group - signed and dated Napoli 1884 - oil on panel - 11 x 6¾in.
(Bearnes & Waycotts)   **£340**

GIOVANNI FRANCESCO CASSANA - A Woman Plucking Fowl In A Kitchen - 52½ x 38in.
(Christie's)   **£2,400**

MARY CASSAT - Sketch Of A Young Woman Picking Fruit - 23½ x 28¾in.
(Sotheby's)   **£7,000**

P. CASTEELS - A Peacock, Chickens, Doves And A Squirrel In A Woody Landscape - 48 x 38½in.
(Christie's)   **£1,100**

PIETER CASTEELS - Aesop's Fable of the Stolen Feathers - signed and dated 1732 - 48½ x 47½in.
(Christie's) **£3,000**

VALERIO CASTELLO - The Charity Of Saint Louis - 24½ x 34in.
(Christie's) **£1,600**

FRANCESCO CASTIGLIONE - The Crossing Of The Red Sea - 44 x 49½in.
(Christie's) **£2,000**

MASON CHAMBERLIN - Portrait Of Mr. and Mrs Gale Of Catgill Hall, Cumberland, And Their Daughter, full lengths - signed and inscribed - dated 1761 - 65½ x 81½in.
(Christie's) **£1,300**

SEBASTIAN CASTRO - A Naval Battle Between Turks And Crusaders With Shipwrecked Sailors in the foreground - signed - 46¼ x 65½in.
(Christie's) **£2,000**

SEBASTIAN CASTRO - A Naval Engagement Between Turks And Crusaders With Galleys in the fore-ground - 46¼ x 64¼in.
(Christie's) **£1,700**

R. CATTERI - Playmates - signed and dated 1896 - inscribed 'Roma' - 16½ x 12in.
(Sotheby's) **£600**

GEORGE CATTERMOLE - The Defence Of Latham House - heightened with bodycolour - 16½ x 22in.
(Sotheby's Belgravia) **£65**

CATTERMOLE

GEORGE CATTERMOLE - Venetian
Merchants - watercolour and bodycolour
- 13 x 18¼in.
(Christie's) £70

L. F. G. CATTERMOLE - The London to
Brighton Coach At Speed In A Summer
Landscape - signed and dated 1868 -
16 x 30in.
(Warner, Sheppard & Wade) £360

HENRI CAUCHOIS - Pitcher Trimmed
With Flowers - oil on wood - signed -
30 x 40cm.
(Galerie Moderne) £12

L. DE CAULLERY - The Exiled
Marie De Medicis Landing At Antwerp -
on panel - 26½ x 38in.
(Christie's) £850

LA CAVE - Figures And Farm Animals
In Rural Landscapes - on metal - each
6¾ x 8¼in.
(Sotheby's) £200 Pair

LOUIS G. CAWKER - Still Life Of
Fruit, By A Mossy Bank - signed and
dated 1864 - 8 x 10¾in.
(Sotheby's Belgravia) £130

CAYAN - Spanish Dancers - signed - on
panel - 6½ x 12½in.
(Sotheby's) £250

JEAN CHARLES CAZIN - Farm Buildings
In A Landscape - signed - 13 x 16in.
(Sotheby's) £220

CORNEILIUS CELS - Portrait Of A Man
- oil on canvas - signed and dated 1829 -
75 x 63cm.
(Galerie Moderne) £220

MARC CHAGALL - Les Maries Et Le
Coq - signed and dated 1939-1947 -
35½ x 25½in.
(Sotheby's) £115,000

A. CHALON - Study Of A Young
Girl Holding A Canary - inscribed with
monogram - in a painted oval - 13½ x
11½in.
(Sotheby's) £130

ALFRED EDWARD CHALON -
Portrait Of A Young Lady, half length -
watercolour - signed and dated 1836 -
10½ x 9in.
(Christie's) £55

ALFRED EDWARD CHALON - Portrait
Of Mrs. Thomson And Her Daughter
Caroline, small full length, In An Interior -
inscribed - 35 x 27in.
(Christie's) £800

GEORGE CHAMBERS, JNR - Yachts Off
The Coast, Evening - inscribed - on panel
- 6¾ x 13½in.
(Sotheby's Belgravia) £200

GEORGE CHAMBERS - A British Man-O'-War And Other Sailing Vessels Off Shore - signed - 18½ x 25½in.
(Christie's) **£1,700**

F. CHAPLIN - Still Life Of Fruit By A Bank - signed and dated 1881 - 11¼ x 17¼in.
(Sotheby's Belgravia) **£100**

EDWARD FRANCIS CHAPMAN - Boats In A Cove At Colpetty, Near Colombo, Ceylon - 12 x 19¼in.
(Sotheby's) **£25**

SERGE CHARCHOUNE - Le Pianiste - oil - on board - 14 x 19¼in.
(Sotheby's) **£150**

R. CHARLOT - View Of A Park - oil on canvas - signed - 40 x 67cm.
(Galerie Moderne) **£345**

F. J. DU CHATTEL - Leafy Country Road With Worker, Horse And Cart - signed - watercolour - 24.5 x 15.25cm.
(Edmiston's) **£150**

GEORGE CHAMBERS - Study For The Bombardment Of Algiers - pencil and brown wash - dated 27 August 1816 - 8 x 12½in.
(Christie's) **£280**

G. CHAMBERS, JNR. - An action between the English and French Fleets - bears signature and a date 1836 - 24½ x 35 ins.
(Christie's) **£1,100**

PETER CHAMPION - 'Horsa Gliders on Tow, D Day' - oil - 19 x 29 ins.
(Wallis & Wallis) **£26**

PETER CHAMPION - 'Breakfast For Luke' - oil - 23 x 26in.
(Wallis & Wallis) **£28**

PETER CHAMPION - 'Fireflies At Twilight' - oil - 23 x 26in.
(Wallis & Wallis) **£20**

GEORGES CHAUDET - Nature Morte Aux Pommes - oil - on canvas - signed - 18 x 16¾in.
(Sotheby's) **£350**

VALENTIN CHAVES - The Fountain - on wood - signed 43 x 38cm.
(Galerie Moderne) **£26**

CHELMINSKI

JAN VAN CHELMINSKI - The Honeymoon Sleigh - signed 25 x 30in.
(Sotheby's)   **£1,600**

JOSEPH CHELMONSKI - Morning After The Soiree - signed and dated 1877 - 21 x 55¼in.
(Sotheby's)   **£1,700**

JULES CHERET - Bateaux Sur La Plage - oil on panel - 8 x 11¼in.
(Sotheby's)   **£100**

JULES CHERET - Pierrot - pastel on canvas - signed - 31¾ x 23¼in.
(Sotheby's)   **£420**

JULES CHERET - La Faune - charcoal - signed - 14 x 9¼in.
(Sotheby's)   **£60**

G. CHERICI - Playing With Baby - bears signature - 19 x 24¾in.
(Sotheby's)   **£550**

F. CHESHIRE - Seascape With Figures In A Boat - signed - watercolour - 7½ x 14½in.
(Butler & Hatch Waterman)   **£22.50**

G. O. CHESTER, Attributed To - Clearing Up After The Storm' - oil on canvas - 54 x 35in.
(Southam & Sons)   **£675**

J. CHESTERTON - Mixed Fruit On A Slab - oil - 20 x 15in. - oval.
(G. A. Key)   **£140**

GIUSEPPE CHIARI - Christ And The Woman Of Samaria At The Well - 53 x 38¼in.
(Sotheby's)   **£1,800**

GIUSEPPE CHIARI - Christ And The Woman Of Samaria - 19½ x 22in.
(Christie's) **£700**

A. CHICHEITER - L'Impasse - oil on canvas - signed - 53 x 43cm.
(Galerie Moderne) **£25**

CHINESE SCHOOL, Late 18th or Early 19th Century - Portrait Of A Young Woman In European Dress, three-quarter length - watercolour on ivory - 5¼ x 3½in.
(Bearnes & Waycotts) **£120**

GEORGE CHINNERY - Chinese Playing Cards By A Wall - 6½ x 5¾in.
(Christie's) **£1,500**

GEORGE CHINNERY - Portrait Of John Robert Morrison And His Father's Secretary, Mr Thomas - 19 x 17½in.
(Christie's) **£13,000**

GEORGE CHINNERY - Indian Men Washing In A River By A Mosque - 5½ x 6¾in.
(Christie's) **£4,000**

GEORGE CHINNERY - A View Of The Praya Grande At Macao From The North, With The Portugese Settlement And Junks in the foreground And Penha Hill Beyond - 10½ x 18in.
(Christie's) **£9,000**

GEORGE CHINNERY - Portrait Of A Young Eurasian Lady, small full length, Wearing A Blue Komono, White Trousers And Cloggs, Holding A Fan And Seated By A Circular Window With A View Of Mountains Beyond - 17¾ x 14¾in.
(Christie's) **£22,000**

GEORGE CHINNERY - Portrait Of A Lady - small full-length - seated on a sofa with a child - 25 x 18½in.
(Christie's) **£2,800**

GEORGE CHINNERY - Entrance To A Dutch Folly Fort With A Goat in the foreground - 6½ x 7in.
(Christie's) **£1,200**

GEORGE CHINNERY - An Indian Watchman And His Goat Outside A Hut In A Wooded Landscape - 12½ x 15½in.
(Christie's) **£2,800**

GEORGE CHINNERY - Portrait Of A Gentleman, standing by a table with a view of the Franciscan Fort At Macao beyond - 24½ x 19¼in.
(Christie's) **£9,000**

CHINNERY - Chinese Port With Ships And Figures - 20.5 x 28cm.
(Edmiston's) **£130**

MISS CHIPPINGDALE - Studies Of Children - 11 x 10in.
(Sotheby's Belgravia) **£14 Three**

A. CHOLER - Vase Trimmed With Flowers - oil on wood - signed - 31 x 38cm.
(Galerie Moderne) **£15**

N. H. CHRISTIANSEN - Autumn Woodland Scene With Sheep And Figures - oil - 20 x 30in.
(G. A. Key) **£220**

N. CHRISTIANSEN - A Winter Landscape With Cottages And Figures - oil on canvas - 29¾ x 50in.
(Bearnes & Waycotts) **£360**

JAMES ELDER CHRISTIE - A Paisley Loom - signed and dated '83 - 19½ x 29½in.
(Sotheby's) **£280**

J. E. CHRISTIE - Hide And Seek - 40 x 50cm.
(Edmiston's) **£100**

CHURCHYARD - Wooded Landscape - 6 x 8in.
(Sotheby's) **£85**

EUGENE CICERI - Au Bord De La Seine - charcoal and white chalk - signed and dated Bougival '49 - 8¾ x 11¾in.
(Sotheby's) **£25**

EUGENE CICERI - Le Sentier A l'Oree d'un Village - pencil - stamped with signature - 7¾ x 10¼in.
(Sotheby's) **£20**

EUGENE CICERI - Bateaux A Voile Au Port - pencil and white chalk - stamped with signature - 9 x 12¼in.
(Sotheby's) **£170**

CIGNANI - A Wooded Landscape, A Woman In Yellow, Covering Another Woman With Blue Drapery, A Young Boy To The Right - 14 x 12in.
(Sotheby's) **£180**

G. B. CIPRIANI - The Worship Of Venus With The Rape Of Proserpine Beyond - on panel - oval - 36 x 44in.
(Christie's) **£700**

MIGUEL CIRY - Solitude Minerale - oil - on canvas - signed and dated '64 - signed - titled - dated '64 on the reverse - 19 x 25in.
(Sotheby's) **£300**

PIETER CLAESZ - A Broken Roemer On A Pewter Plate, An Earthenware Mustard-Pot, A Ham On A Dish, An Overturned Silver Beaker, A Bread Roll On A Plate, A Roemer Of Wine And A Pewter Wine-Pot, On A Table Covered By A White Cloth - inscribed with monogram - 23¾ x 33in.
(Sotheby's) **£7,500**

F. CLAETENS - Les Dizeaux - oil on canvas - signed - 37 x 62cm.
(Galerie Moderne) **£50**

ALBERT CLAEYS - The Sea - oil on canvas - signed - 38 x 46cm.
(Galerie Moderne) **£59**

CLARE - Still Lives Of Fruit By Mossy Banks - both heightened with bodycolour - 6 x 8¾in.
(Sotheby's Belgravia) **£25 Pair**

G. CLARE - Still Life Of Grapes And Holly - oil - 7 x 10in.
(Warner, Sheppard & Wade) **£45**

CLARE

GEORGE CLARE - Still Lives Of Fruit
And Flowers - both signed - each 11½ x
9½in.
(Sotheby's Belgravia) **£1,000 Pair**

OLIVER CLARE - Still Lives Of Fruit
By Mossy Banks - both signed - on
board - 5¾ x 8½in.
(Sotheby's Belgravia) **£450 Pair**

OLIVER CLARE - Still Lives Of Plums,
Apples, Grapes, Gooseberries and
Raspberries By Mossy Banks - both
signed - on board - 6 x 9in.
(Sotheby's Belgravia) **£500 Pair**

GEORGE CLARE - Still Life Of Fruit
By A Bank - signed - 8¼ x 6¼in.
(Sotheby's Belgravia) **£170**

OLIVER CLARE - Still Life Of Fruit
On A Mossy Bank;   And Companion -
signed - on board - 13 x 19cm.
(Phillips) **£540 Pair**

OLIVER CLARE - Still Life, Fruit -
signed - oil - 17½ x 13½in.
(Charles R. Phillips) **£700**

VINCENT CLARE - Primulas in a
basket, with roses and chrysanthemums -
signed, signed and inscribed on the
reverse - 16 x 14 ins.
(Christie's, S. Kensington) **£320**

ALBERT CLARK - A Dark Bay Hunter -
signed and dated 1888 - 19½ x 23in.
(Sotheby's)   **£140**

ALBERT CLARK - A Dappled Grey
Hunter Standing By A Barn - signed and
dated 1889 - 19½ x 23½in.
(Sotheby's)   **£140**

DIXON CLARK - Cattle Watering In A
Wooded River Landscape - oil - on
canvas - signed - 19½ x 24½in.
(King & Chasemore)   **£550**

J. COSMO CLARK - Gas Victim, The
Somme - chalk - 36 x 51cm.
(Edmiston's)   **£2**

JACK CLARK - Village Scene With Figures,
Wagons And Horses, 'Approach To
Ipswich' - inscribed on stretcher - signed -
22 x 30in.
(Woolley & Wallis)   **£170**

JAMES CLARK - A Heavy Dray Horse
In Stable - oil - 16 x 24in.
(G. A. Key)   **£80**

O. T. CLARK - Landscape With
Cottages And Cattle - oil - 16 x 24in.
(G. A. Key)   **£104**

S. J. CLARK - Donkeys And Chickens,
In The Shade - signed and indistinctly
dated - 15½ x 19½in.
(Sotheby's Belgravia)   **£700**

S. J. CLARK - The Midday Rest - bears
another monogram and dated - 23 x
31in.
(Sotheby's Belgravia)   **£1,700**

W. A. CLARK - Horse And Trap -
dated 1911 - 50 x 60cm.
(Edmiston's)   **£120**

EVELYN CLARKE - A Chestnut
Hunter In A Stable - signed and dated
'02 - 21¼ x 25¼in.
(Sotheby's Belgravia)   **£75**

J. D. CLARKE - Coastal Scene - oil -
7 x 15in.
(G. A. Key)   **£16**

LIZZIE CLARKE - A Rural Bouquet -
signed - signed, inscribed and dated
'89 on the reverse - on board - 23¼ x
14½in.
(Sotheby's Belgravia)   **£120**

O. T. CLARKE - Coming Home From The Market - signed - 29½ x 49½in.
(Sotheby's Belgravia) **£250**

E. CLASSENS - Vase Trimmed With Flowers - oil on canvas - signed - 54 x 40cm.
(Galerie Moderne) **£10**

CLAUDE - A Capriccio Mediterranean Harbour At Sunset, With A Tower And Roman Buildings - 31 x 39½in.
(Christie's) **£1,100**

CLAUDE - A River Landscape, A Herdsman With Animals And Other Figures in the foreground, A Fortress On A Hill To The Right - 11¾ x 13¾in.
(Sotheby's) **£180**

PIERRE DE CLAUSADES - Coup De Soleil Sur Le Rive - signed and dated '77 - oil on canvas - 23 x 36in.
(Bonham's) **£300**

SIR GEORGE CLAUSEN - Reapers - signed and dated 1901 - 7½ x 5¾in.
(Sotheby's Belgravia) **£190**

H. CLEMENTS - By An Overshot Mill - signed - 19½ x 29½in.
(Sotheby's Belgravia) **£300**

ROBERT CLEMINSON - Two Retrievers Putting Up Pheasant - oil - signed - 29.5 x 39.5cm.
(Phillips in Scotland) **£130**

WILLIAM CLERIHEW - Allyghur - inscribed and dated 1843 on the reverse - 7¼ x 10in.
(Sotheby's) **£25**

LOUIS CLESSE - The Fishing Boats - oil on canvas - signed and dated 1935 - 80cm. x 1m.
(Galerie Moderne) **£500**

LOUIS CLESSE - The Undergrowth - oil on canvas - signed and dated 1946 - 90 x 1m.10cm.
(Galerie Moderne) **£534**

LOUIS CLESSE - Le Tombereau - oil on canvas - signed and dated 1915 - 80 x 90cm.
(Galerie Moderne) £534

LOUIS CLESSE - Vie Ille Ferme - on wood - signed and dated 1916 - 72 x 76cm.
(Galerie Moderne) £465

CORNELIS VAN CLEVE - The Adoration Of The Shepherds - on panel - 31¼ x 21½in.
(Christie's) £2,400

HENDRICK VAN CLEVE - The Burning Of Troy - on panel - 21½ x 35in.
(Christie's) £1,300

JOHN CLEVELEY - British Men-O'-War In The English Channel - 35 x 77in.
(Christie's) £3,500

ALFRED CLINT - Study Of Waves Breaking Over Rocks - watercolour heightened with white - 9¼ x 13½in.
(Christie's) £8

ALFRED CLINT - A Mountain Torrent With A Watermill - signed and dated 1857 - 24 x 36in.
(Christie's) £150

GEORGE CLINT - Miss Foote As Maria Darlington In John Madison Morton's Musical Entertainment 'A Roland For An Oliver' At Covent Garden, 1819 - 49 x 39in.
(Christie's) £4,000

R. M. CLOCK - In The Grounds Of A Country Mansion - signed and dated 1828 - 17½ x 20½in.
(Sotheby's Belgravia) £160

F. CLOETENS - Farm Yard Scene - oil on canvas - signed - 48 x 70cm.
(Galerie Moderne) £66

J. CLOSSET - Vieille Ferme - oil on canvas - signed - 40 x 50cm.
(Galerie Moderne) £19

CLOSTERMAN

JOHANN BAPTISTE CLOSTERMAN - Portrait Of A Gentleman, Said To Be Vice-Admiral John Benbow, half length, Wearing Armour And A White Stock - oval - 29 x 24½in.
(Sotheby's) £200

C. CLUICENS - Stag In A Landscape - oil on canvas - signed - 42 x 66cm.
(Galerie Moderne) £73

ANDRE CLUYSENAER - Landscape - oil on wood - signed - 29 x 40cm.
(Galerie Moderne) £94

COCCORANTE - A River Landscape, Figures Near The Ruins Of A Bridge, Mountains in the distance - on metal - 6 x 7¼in.
(Sotheby's) £260

L. COCCORANTE - Architectural Capriccios With Elegant Figures - one inscribed - 32 x 43½in.
(Christie's) £2,200 Pair

LEONARDO COCCORANTE - A Landscape With A Roman Ruin; And A Ship In A Storm - both signed in monogram - 24 x 18¾in.
(Sotheby's) £3,500 Pair

WILLIAM COCK - A Rustic Cottage - signed and dated '98 - 35 x 19in.
(Sotheby's Belgravia) £80

V. CODAZZI - Classical Buildings With Figures in the foreground - 23½ x 17½in.
(Christie's) £550

VIVIANO CODAZZI - A Capriccio Of Classical Ruins, with the Colosseum in the distance - 29½ x 35½in.
(Christie's) £2,400

P. CODDE - Cavaliers Playing Backgammon In An Interior - on panel - 12 x 15in.
(Christie's) £850

CONSTANTINUS FIDELIO COENE - Figures Drinking In A Tavern - signed and dated 1808 - on panel - 11¼ x 13in.
(Sotheby's) £950

G. COLE - Wooded Landscape and River Scenes - oil - 16 x 12in
(G. A. Key) £36 Pair

GEORGE COLE - Rick Making; Lunch Time - signed and dated 1882 - 23½ x 35½in.
(Christie's) £3,200

GEORGE VICAT COLE - At Albury, Surrey - signed - 17¾ x 23½in.
(Christie's) £2,100

GEORGE VICAT COLE - A Hilly Wooded Landscape With Cows in the foreground - signed with monogram and dated 1877 - 10 x 21½in.
(Christie's) **£500**

JAMES WILLIAM COLE - Meet Of The Limerick Hunt - A Bye-Day - Foxhounds At Croom Castle - signed and dated 1853 and inscribed with the names of the principle figures on the reverse - 38½ x 59in.
(Christie's) **£3,000**

L DE COLEREWNE - 'Woodslade' - signed and dated 1892 - oil - 31½ x 47½in.
(Charles R. Phillips) **£185**

WILLIAM STEPHEN COLEMAN - Watering Flowers - heightened with bodycolour - signed and dated 1903 - 13 x 9in.
(Sotheby's Belgravia) **£120**

T. COLIS - 'On The Avon, Warwickshire' - signed and dated 1893 - oil - 30 x 50in.
(Warner, Sheppard & Wade) **£50**

S. D. COLKETT - A Woody Landscape With Figures, Ducks And Sheep By A Cottage Pond - 24¼ x 29½in.
(Christie's) **£600**

S. R. COLKETT - Farmyard Scene With Figure - oil - 8 x 11in.
(G. A. Key) **£48**

IMOGEN COLLIER - Stable Interior - signed - oil on canvas - 36 x 46in.
(Bearnes & Waycotts) **£125**

THE HON. JOHN COLLIER - Portrait Of Christabel Hopkins, Later Mrs H. C. Harillier - signed - 62 x 39in.
(Sotheby's Belgravia) **£90**

THE HON. JOHN COLLIER - A Balcony Overlooking A Continental Lake - signed and dated 1932 - 44 x 31in.
(Sotheby's Belgravia) **£50**

THOMAS COLLIER - Moorland Landscape With Three Ponies - signed and dated 1884 - oil on canvas - 19 x 29in.
(Bearnes & Waycotts) **£140**

THOMAS COLLIER - Moorland Landscape - signed and dated 1873 - watercolour - 9½ x 13½in.
(Woolley & Wallis) **£125**

CHARLES COLLINS - On The Arun, Sussex - signed and dated 1886 - 19½ x 29½in.
(Sotheby's Belgravia) **£700**

H. COLLINS - 'A Figure Fishing In Woodland Landscape' - oil - on canvas - 10 x 14in.
(Butler & Hatch Waterman) **£27.50**

HUGH COLLINS - The Family Concert - Interior With Numerous Figures - 64 x 91cm.
(Edmiston's) **£1,500**

HUGH COLLINS - Robbing The Miser - signed - 20 x 26in.
(Sotheby's Belgravia) **£35**

ALBERT H. COLLINGS - Portrait Of A Girl, half length - signed - 23¼ x 19in.
(Sotheby's Belgravia) **£110**

WILLIAM COLLINGWOOD - Near Ingelberg - heightened with bodycolour - signed - inscribed and dated 1883 - 9½ x 30¾in.
(Sotheby's) **£60**

ALFRED COLLINS - A View In Italy, Early Morning - inscribed on the stretcher - 27¼ x 35¼in.
(Sotheby's Belgravia) **£320**

C. COLLINS - In The Druids' Grove, Norbury Park, Mickleham - on paper - 5 x 8in.
(Sotheby's Belgravia) **£35**

CHARLES COLLINS - 'A Misty Morning, Mickleham, Surrey' - signed - inscribed and dated 1876 on the reverse - oil on canvas - 17¼ x 32¼in.
(Bearnes & Waycotts) **£520**

W. COLLINS, After - Happy As A King - 28 x 36in.
(Sotheby's Belgravia) **£620**

COLLINSON - A Girl Sewing, Summer Time, oval - 11¼ x 9¼in.
(Sotheby's Belgravia) **£250**

SCHOOL OF COLOGNE - A Burgher Offering Clothes To A Pauper (one of The Seven Acts Of Mercy) - on panel - 21½ x 20in.
(Christie's) **£2,600**

JEAN FRANCOIS COLSON - Portrait Of A Young Boy, three-quarter length, Holding A Bunch Of Grapes; And Portrait Of A Young Boy, three-quarter length, Beating A Drum - ovals - 23½ x 19½in.
(Christie's) **£380 Pair**

CHARLES COMPTON - The Dance - signed and dated 1874 - 23½ x 17½in.
(Sotheby's Belgravia) **£75**

PIERRE CHARLES COMTE - Portrait Of A Renaissance Lady Seated In A High Backed Chair, full length - signed - on panel - 30 x 21½in.
(King & Chasemore) **£1,400**

CONDY - A Barge And Other Shipping Off The Dutch Coast - on panel - 7½ x 10½in.
(Sotheby's) **£240**

NICHOLAS CONDY - Figures Smoking And Drinking In A Cottage Interior - on panel - 11½ x 15½in.
(Christie's) **£700**

NICHOLAS CONDY - Fisherfolk Examining Nets, A Devonshire Scene - oil on board - signed and dated 1831 - 11¾ x 15in.
(King & Chasemore) **£850**

NICHOLAS CONDY - A Fine Cottage
Interior with figures seated at a table -
signed and dated 1830 - on panel -
18 x 21in.
(King & Chasemore) **£1,150**

NICHOLAS MATTHEW CONDY -
Cashel, Co.· Leitrim - brown and yellow
wash heightened with white on pink
prepared paper - 4½ x 5¾in.
(Christie's) **£25**

ALFRED CHARLES CONRADE - A
Shrine To Napoleon - signed - 12¾ x 9in.
(Sotheby's) **£30**

CONSTABLE - A Distant View Towards
A Castle, Probably Arundel - 9¾ x 13½in.
(Sotheby's) **£220**

JOHN CONSTABLE - A Woody Landscape With A Farmhouse And Haystacks
- 7½ x 10½in.
(Christie's) **£6,000**

J. CONSTABLE - 'The Norfolk Broads' -
oil on panel - 5½ x 10in.
(King & Chasemore) **£130**

JOHN CONSTABLE - A Sketch Of
Dedham Vale - on panel - 13½ x 11½in.
(Christie's) **£350**

JOHN CONSTABLE - A View In Suffolk -
Figures And Cattle In A Wooded Landscape
- on paper laid down in canvas - 9½ x 13in.
(Christie's) **£2,000**

TITO CONTI - The Departure - signed
and dated 1879 - 22 x 31in.
(Christie's) **£2,200**

HERBERT MOXOM COOK - On The
Coast - heightened with bodycolour
- signed and dated 1888 - 15 x 27¼in.
(Sotheby's Belgravia) **£80**

EDWARD WILLIAM COOKE - Sailing
Vessels At Anchor Near Flushing,
Holland - signed and dated 1857 - 14¾ x
25¼in.
(Christie's) **£2,600**

EDWARD WILLIAM COOKE - Sunset
Over Venice - signed and dated 1860 -
7 x 15in.
(Sotheby's Belgravia) **£550**

EDWARD WILLIAM COOKE - The Entrance To The Harbour At Marseilles With Numerous Fishing Boats And Fisherfolk Hauling In Their Nets in the foreground - signed and dated 1850 - 91 x 127cm.
(Phillips) £3,800

EDWARD WILLIAM COOKE - Dutch Pincks Coming Ashore - signed and dated 1855 - 107.5 x 171.5cm.
(Phillips) £3,200

EDWARD WILLIAM COOKE - Dutch Sailing Barges in a river estuary - oil on canvas - 8 x 16in.
(King & Chasemore) £340

EDWARD WILLIAM COOKE - Alicante; Alicante From The East - Sunset - pencil - both inscribed and dated 1860 - 6¼ x 10½in. and 3½ x 10½in.
(Sotheby's) £55 Two

HUBERT COOP - A Steamer In Rough Seas - heightened with bodycolour - signed - 13½ x 25½in.
(Sotheby's Belgravia) £35

COOPER - Sheep In The Meadow - bears signature - 17½ x 23½in.
(Sotheby's Belgravia) £220

COOPER - Cattle Resting - bears signature - 19½ x 29in.
(Sotheby's Belgravia) £370

COOPER - Cattle And Sheep In An Extensive Landscape - inscribed and dated 1848 - 11½ x 15½in.
(Sotheby's) £180

A. COOPER - The Death Of A Faithful Steed - 11½ x 14½in.
(Sotheby's) £50

A. COOPER - Study Of A Racehorse In A Stable Interior - oil - 24.5 x 29.5cm.
(Phillips in Scotland) £260

BYRON COOPER - Low Tide, A Sandy Bay Under A Cloudy Sky - signed - oil - 24 x 36in.
(Warner, Sheppard & Wade) £35

EDWIN COOPER - Horses In A Paddock - signed and dated 1829 - pencil and brown wash on Bristol Board - 12¼ x 14¾in.
(Christie's) £240

EDWIN COOPER - A Curricle And Pair - signed and dated 1815 - 24 x 33in.
(Christie's) £1,500

EDWIN COOPER - A Polled Warwick-shire Longhorn, Standing In A Landscape, An Extensive River View Beyond - signed and dated 1806 - 17¼ x 23¼in.
(Sotheby's) £220

THOMAS GEORGE COOPER - On The Bridge Between Pastures - signed and dated 1870 - 21 x 35½in.
(Sotheby's Belgravia) **£1,300**

T. S. COOPER - Cattle And Sheep In A Woodland Glade - oil - 12 x 9in.
(H. C. Chapman & Son) **£410**

T. S. COOPER - In The Meadows - signed and dated - 19½ x 23in.
(Sotheby's Belgravia) **£140**

GERALD COOPER - A Still Life Painting Of Spring Flowers In A Glass Vase - signed - on board - 23½ x 19½in.
(King & Chasemore) **£540**

THOMAS SIDNEY COOPER - A Cow, A Goat, And Sheep, In An Extensive Landscape - signed and dated 1866 - 25 x 36in.
(Christie's) **£1,400**

THOMAS SIDNEY COOPER - Mountaineers - signed and dated 1852 - on panel - 17½ x 23½in.
(Sotheby's Belgravia) **£1,000**

GERALD COOPER - Anemones, Irises, Jonquils, A Tulip And Other Flowers, In A Glass Vase On A Stone Ledge - signed - on board - 51 x 40.5cm.
(Phillips) **£850**

HENRY COOPER - A Deserted Coast - signed - 19½ x 29½in.
(Sotheby's Belgravia) **£45**

THOMAS SIDNEY COOPER - A
Pensioner - signed and dated 1886 -
stamped with initials on the stretcher -
30 x 42in.
(Sotheby's Belgravia)   **£2,800**

WILLIAM SIDNEY COOPER - Highland
Cattle On The Banks Of A Loch - signed
and dated 1900 - 19½ x 29½in.
(Sotheby's Belgravia)   **£150**

ALEXANDER COOSEMANS - A Still Life
With Grapes And Figs On A Tazza, And
With Peaches, Melons And Two Plums On A
Pedestal in a landscape - signed - 39½ x 34in.
(Christie's)   **£2,600**

JOSEPH COOSEMANS - Pond At Boits-
fort - oil on lined canvas - signed - 20 x
32cm.
(Galerie Moderne)   **£235**

CHARLES WEST COPE, JNR - The
Tiber From The Ponte Molle -
inscribed - 4¼ x 9in.
(Sotheby's)   **£1**

COPLEY - A Late 18th century
Interior Scene Depicting A Man Being
Helped On With A Red Cloak By A
Young Girl - oil on canvas - 29 x 24in.
(Geering & Colyer)   **£250**

A. V. COPLEY-FIELDING - Coastal
Scene With Figures On Beach - water-
colour - 7 x 10in.
(G. A. Key)   **£24**

OMER COPPENS - Old Bridge At
Mechlin - oil on wood - signed and dated
1917 - 33 x 24cm.
(Galerie Moderne)   **£78**

ALBERIC COPPIETERS - Ferme A
Dixmunde - oil on canvas - signed -
2 x 2m.
(Galerie Moderne)   **£250**

MARY CORBETT - Portrait of Young
Girl Seated In Red Dress - oil - 24 x 29in.
(G. A. Key)   **£12**

CORBOULD - Crusaders Fighting The
Infidels - on panel - 11½ x 16in.
(Sotheby's Belgravia)   **£38**

EDWARD HENRY CORBOULD - 'Amor
Omnia Vincit' - signed - watercolour -
23½ x 18½in.
(Bearnes & Waycotts)   **£130**

115

CORBOULD

E. H. CORBOULD - Bar The Door -
watercolour - 12 x 14.5cm.
(Edmiston's) **£12**

VICTOR CORDEN - Relieving The
Castle Guard, Windsor - signed with
initials - on panel - 4¾ x 8¼in.
(Christie's) **£220**

CORDERY - A Horse-Drawn Coach In
A Landscape - 16½ x 21 in.
(Christie's) **£220**

M. CORELLI - The Reluctant Kiss -
signed and inscribed 'Napoli' - 23½ x
30in.
(Sotheby's) **£650**

JOHN CORNISH - Portrait of William
Henry Chauncy - signed and dated
1765 on the reverse - 12 x 9½ ins.
(Christie's, S. Kensington) **£70**

WILLIAM CORNISH - A General
View Of Calcutta - 8 x 16¼in.
(Sotheby's) **£30**

CAMILLE COROT - Cavalier Sous
Un Arbre - on panel - signed - 5 x
11¼in.
(Sotheby's) **£9,000**

JEAN BAPTISTE CAMILLE COROT -
Pommiers et Chaumieres, Normandie -
signed - on panel - 9 x 16 ins.
(Christie's) **£8,500**

CORREGGIO, After - The Madonna
Adoring The Christ Child - 31½ x 26in.
(Sotheby's) **£70**

CORREGGIO, After - Young Woman
Reading - 28 x 39cm.
(Edmiston's) **£88**

**After CORREGIO, ITALIAN SCHOOL,
Mid 19th century** - The Virgin And Child
and St Joan in a Romantic Landscape -
in pastels - 40 x 40in.
(King & Chasemore) **£350**

T. CORRIE - The Cottage - oil on
canvas - signed and dated 1920 -
26 x 36cm.
(Galerie Moderne) **£75**

**HERMANN DAVID SALOMON
CORRODI** - A Fisherman's Shrine -
signed and inscribed 'Roma' - 29 x 17in.
(Sotheby's) **£600**

HENDRIK FRANS DE CORT - The Abbey Gate of Neat in Glamorganshire, South Wales - oil on copper panel - inscribed on reverse - 11½ x 15 ins.
(King & Chasemore) **£700**

G. CORTESE - Cupid Holding A Bowl Of Roses in a landscape - 35½ x 27in.
(Christie's) **£1,100**

H. CORTVRIENDT - The Hermit's Pool - oil on canvas - signed - 32 x 46cm.
(Galerie Moderne) **£2**

J. CORTVRINT - Paysage Avec Voilier - oil on canvas - signed - 35 x 55cm.
(Galerie Moderne) **£15**

C. COSTA - Cavaliers Relaxing And Recounting Their Fortunes - both signed - 23½ x 19½in.
(Sotheby's) **£600 Pair**

GIOVANNI COSTA - An Evening In The Cascine, Florence: A Lady With Two Children In A River Landscape - signed - on panel - 14½ x 25½in.
(Christie's) **£4,400**

R. COSWAY - A Woman, Possibly Charlotte Ramsden, With A Child, Standing In A Park - 28½ x 34½in.
(Christie's) **£650**

JUAN SANCHEZ COTAN - A Still Life Of Plates Of Nuts, Mulberries And Blackberries, Pastry And Plums In Bowls, Bread, Wine Glasses And A Knife On A Ledge - 28 x 32½in.
(Christie's) **£24,000**

JUAN SANCHEZ COTAN - A Still Life Of A Basket of Apricots, Asparagus And Peppers On A Ledge And Two Dead Pigeons Suspended Above - 27½ x 32½in.
(Christie's) **£13,000**

COTMAN - Cathedral Interior With Sexton - watercolour - 22 x 16in.
(G. A. Key) **£14**

FREDERICK GEORGE COTMAN - A Fishing Town Around A Harbour Mouth With Vessels At Sea - signed and dated 1893 - oil on canvas - 35¼ x 25¼in.
(Geering & Colyer) **£180**

JOHN JOSEPH COTMAN - Lame Dog Lane, Norwich - signed - pencil and watercolour - 15¾ x 26½in.
(Christie's) **£950**

JOHN SELL COTMAN - An Angler At The Foot Of A Waterfall Near Montreuil - pencil and ochre and red wash heightened with white on buff paper - 6¼ x 5½in.
(Christie's) **£200**

JOHN SELL COTMAN - Fribourg - inscribed - pencil and watercolour heightened with white on buff paper - 7 x 10½in.
(Christie's) **£900**

JOHN SELL COTMAN - An East Anglian River Landscape - oil on canvas laid on board - 6½ x 8¾in.
(King & Chasemore) **£170**

MILES EDMUND COTMAN - View Near Llangollen, Wales - watercolour - 9 x 14in.
(G. A. Key) **£46**

H. S. COTTRELL - The Bath-London Royal Mail Coach - signed - 11 x 15½in.
(Christie's) **£550**

FREDERIC COUPIL - A Soldier Helping A Woman; The Wounded Turk - both signed - one inscribed à Florence - 14½ x 10¾in.
(Sotheby's) **£70 Pair**

J. COURTOIS - A Cavalry Skirmish By A Castle - 8¼ x 12½in.
(Christie's) **£700**

H. COURTOY - View Of A Village - oil on canvas - signed and dated 1925 - 40 x 50cm.
(Galerie Moderne) **£12**

THOMAS COUTURE - A Study Of An Arab Girl - 18½ x 14½in.
(Sotheby's) **£550**

JAN VAN COUVER - 'Marken', Holland oil on canvas - signed - 18 x 24 ins. and companion
(King & Chasemore) **£700 Pair**

JAN VAN COUVER - Fishing Boats Moored In The Estuary At Zyst, Holland - signed and inscribed on the reverse - 19¼ x 21in.
(Sotheby's) **£650**

JAN VAN COUVER - 'The Sluice Gates', An Extensive Dutch Canalside Scene - signed - oil on canvas - 33 x 44in.
(King & Chasemore) **£400**

R. M. G. COVENTRY - Glasgow Exhibition Scene, Kelvingrove - watercolour - 24 x 19cm.
(Edmiston's) **£230**

ROBERT McGOWN COVENTRY - Old Net Menders - signed - 33½ x 49½in.
(Sotheby's) **£360**

JANET COWAN - A Young Flower Picker - heightened with bodycolour - signed and dated '83 - 18½ x 9½in.
(Sotheby's Belgravia) **£16**

COX - A Fisherman By A Wooded River - bears signature and dated 1845 - 7¾ x 11½in.
(Sotheby's) **£40**

COX - A Rustic Cottage In A Wooded Landscape - 14 x 18in.
(Sotheby's) **£100**

D. COX - 'Crossing The Sands' - signed - watercolour - 7½ x 11¾in.
(Bearnes & Waycotts) **£180**

D. COX - A Gypsy Encampment - oil - 10 x 18in.
(G. A. Key) **£30**

DAVID COX, SEN. and DAVID COX, JUN - Llanilltyd Village And Bridge Near Dolgelly, Wales - inscribed 'David Cox, Sen. finished by D. Cox, Jun.' - watercolour heightened with white - 29¾ x 42½in.
(Christie's) **£300**

DAVID COX - Cavalry Approaching Stirling Castle - signed and dated 1838 - watercolour heightened with white - 8½ x 12¾in.
(Christie's) **£1,400**

G. COX - The Old Thatched Cottage - crayon - signed - 60 x 1m.20cm.
(Galerie Moderne) **£173**

ANTOINE COYPEL - Lot And His Daughters - 64½ x 51 in.
(Christie's) **£2,600**

CRABTREE - Figures By The Side Of A Boating Pool - oil - 40 x 35cm.
(Phillips in Scotland) **£35**

M. CRADOCK - Ducks And Ducklings In A River Landscape; and Peacocks And Other Birds In A Woody Landscape - 11½ x 13½in.
(Christie's) **£1,300 Pair**

MARMADUKE CRADOCK - A Peacock, Turkey And Other Birds In A Wood Landscape; and A Peacock, Mallard And Other Birds By A Barn - 24½ x 29¼in
(Christie's) **£2,200 Pair**

LAURENS CRAEN - A Still Life With A Peeled Lemon, A Bunch of Grapes, Plums, Nuts And Two Glasses, On A Ledge - signed and dated '35 - on panel - 17 x 23in.
(Christie's) **£16,000**

J. VAN CRAESBEEK - A Peasant Family In An Interior, Eating And Drinking Near A Fire - on panel - 10½ x 13½in.
(Sotheby's) **£850**

J. CRANCH OF BATH - Portrait Of Henry Knight Of Bath Mounted On A Bay Hunter Near Landsdowne - 26½ x 36in.
(Christie's) **£1,400**

CRANE - Night - arched top - 15 x 27in.
(Sotheby's Belgravia)   **£220**

LEFEVRE JAMES CRANSTONE - St.
Leonards From The West - pen and
brown ink, brown and grey wash
heightened with white on grey paper -
inscribed and dated 1852 on the reverse -
5½ x 8¾in.
(Christie's)   **£50**

J. H. CRANSTOUN - A View Of Perth -
15 x 26in.
(Sotheby's)   **£140**

JAMES H. CRANSTOUN - A Scottish
Country Seat - signed - inscribed 'Edinburgh'
and dated 1866 - 28 x 36in.
(Sotheby's)   **£420**

EDMUND THORNTON CRAWFORD -
Holy Island - oil on canvas - signed and dated
1851 - 40 x 60in.
(King & Chasemore)   **£600**

EDMUND THORNTON CRAWFORD -
Fishing Boats, Loch Fyne - signed and dated
1847 - 30 x 41½in.
(Sotheby's)   **£1,050**

E. T. CRAWFORD - 'On The Esk', Wooded
River Landscape With Cattle Grazing in the
middle distance and with Castle Ruins
beyond - signed - 19th century - oil on card -
11 x 15in.
(Lalonde Martin)   **£30**

R. C. CRAWFORD - Portrait Of A Girl
Under A Tree - 23½ x 18½in.
(Sotheby's Belgravia)   **£100**

ROBERT CREE CRAWFORD - The
Cottage Door - signed and dated 1877 -
19 x 25in.
(Sotheby's)   **£300**

CRAWHALL - Cows In A Landscape -
oil - on board - 13.5 x 21.5cm.
(Phillips in Scotland)   **£55**

LORENZO DI CREDI, Circle Of - The Madonna And Child With The Infant St. John The Baptist - on panel - 58 x 46.5cm.
(Phillips) £9,500

ARTHUR CREP - A Mountainous River Landscape - indistinctly signed and dated 1850 - 7¼ x 12½in.
(Sotheby's) £35

ADOLPHE CRESPIN - The Track - cartoon - signed - 26 x 35cm.
(Galerie Moderne) £7

HORTENSE CRESSONNIER - Still Life Of Fruit - oil on canvas - signed and dated 1909 - 52 x 40cm.
(Galerie Moderne) £107

T. CRESWICK - A Forest Glade - signed and dated - 23½ x 17½in.
(Sotheby's Belgravia) £150

THOMAS CRESWICK - The Yew Tree Walk At Haddon Hall - signed with initials - on panel - 11½ x 15½in.
(Sotheby's Belgravia) £320

T. CRESWICK - 'In Derbyshire' - inscribed on the reverse - oil on panel - 11¼ x 8¾in.
(Bearnes & Waycotts) £100

CRESPI - A Shepherdess Surrounded By Flowers, A Basket Of Fruit, Hares, A Cat And A Dog, In A Wooded Landscape - 70 x 52in.
(Woolley & Wallis) £1,850

THOMAS CRESWICK - An upland river landscape with angler in foreground - oil on canvas - signed and dated 1851 - 17 x 28 ins.
(King & Chasemore) **£450**

THOMAS CRESWICK and HENRY BRITTAN WILLIS - 'The Ford' - signed by the artists - 50.5 x 76 cm.
(Phillips) **£1,050**

GEORGE CROEGAERT - The Hidden Letter - signed and inscribed 'Paris' - on panel - 10½ x 8¾in.
(Sotheby's) **£1,800**

W. E. CROFT - A Harvest Scene, Evening - canvas laid on board - 14¼ x 18½in.
(Sotheby's Belgravia) **£80**

ERNEST CROFTS - A Roundhead Military Camp - signed and dated '42 - 14½ x 18 ins.
(Christie's, S. Kensington) **£720**

CROME - A Wooded Landscape With Travellers Resting By A Path Under A Tree - on panel - 8½ x 12½in.
(Christie's) **£65**

JOHN CROME - Figures On A Track Near A Cottage In Woodland - pencil - 8¾ x 6½in.
(Christie's) **£270**

J. B. CROME - Windmill And Cottages By Moonlight - oil - 8 x 10in.
(G. A. Key) **£26**

J. B. CROME - A Wooded River Landscape With A Cottage - on panel - 8 x 5½in.
(Christie's) **£180**

W. H. CROME - 'Marlingford' - Treed Landscape With Figure Fishing And Cattle Watering - oil - 24 x 30in.
(G. A. Key) **£40**

WILLIAM HENRY CROME AND CHARLES DUKES - On The Tay At Stab Hill - signed by both artists and dated 1855 - 27½ x 35½in.
(Sotheby's) **£700**

F. CROOKE - 'The Highwayman' - oil - 23½ x 19½in.
(Charles R. Phillips) **£165**

A. J. VAN CROOS - A River Landscape, With Cottages - on panel - 12 x 15½in.
(Christie's) **£900**

ANTONIE JANSZ VAN CROOS - A Wooded River Landscape with fishermen in the foreground and a monastery beyond - signed with initials and dated 1630 - 22½ x 19in.
(Christie's) **£5,500**

WILLIAM CROSBY - Attractive Portrait Group Of Florence Moore And Her Two Brothers On A Rocky Seashore - inscribed and dated 1868 - oil on board - 11¾ x 9¾in.
(Graves Son & Pilcher) **£720**

NICHOLAS J. CROWLEY - Guy Fawkes Eve - 27½ x 36in.
(Sotheby's Belgravia) **£1,800**

H. CROWTHER - A Hunter In A Stable - signed and dated 1918 - oil - 16½ x 21in.
(Neale & Son) **£42**

A. B. CULL - The Taj Mahal - signed and dated 1923 - 10½ x 18in.
(Sotheby's) **£30**

CHARLES ERNEST CUNDALL - Edinburgh - signed - on panel -19¼ x 23¼in.
(Sotheby's) **£200**

CYRUS CINCINNATI CUNEO - View Of The Rocky Mountains - signed - oil on canvas - 29¼ x 24¼in.
(Bearnes & Waycotts) **£80**

JAMES CURNOCK - The Confidant - signed and dated 1857 - oval - 34 x 25¾in.
(Sotheby's Belgravia) **£500**

CURNOCK

JAMES JACKSON CURNOCK - Welsh Riverside In Autumn - heightened with white - signed and dated 1874 - inscribed on the reverse - 10½ x 16in.
(Sotheby's) **£120**

JOSE CUSACHS Y CUSACHS - Spanish Soldiers Crossing A Mountainous Terrain - signed and dated 1896 - 19½ x 39½in.
(Sotheby's) **£4.400**

F. CUSTERS - Vase Trimmed With Flowers - oil on canvas - signed and dated 1895 - 70 x 30cm.
(Galerie Moderne) **£15**

A. VAN CUYLENBURG - Diana And Her Nymphs In An Italiante Landscape - 9½ x 13in.
(Christie's) **£600**

ABRAHAM VAN CUYLENBORCH - Diana And Her Attendants Bathing By The Entrance To A Cave - signed and dated 1645 - on panel - 52 x 74cm.
(Phillips) **£2,200**

CUYP - A River Landscape, With Cattle, Figures And A Milkmaid By A Ruin - 40 x 53in.
(Christie's) **£500**

AELBERT CUYP - An Extensive Landscape With Herdsmen - inscribed with the artist's name and a date - on panel - 17¼ x 21½in.
(Sotheby's) **£16,000**

AELBERT CUYP - A Wooded River Landscape with a peasant woman milking a cow, cows, horses and duck nearby, and an eel-trap in the foreground - signed - 54¼ x 69½in.
(Christie's) **£20.000**

AELBERT CUYP - A Young Herdsman Piping To Cattle, an overhanging rock nearby and an extensive river landscape beyond - signed - 37 x 45in.
(Christie's) **£6,500**

BENJAMIN GERRITSZ. CUYP - A Religious Subject, A Priest, In A Purple Robe With Gold Ornamentation, Holding A Baby; A Group Of Men And Women Around Them - on panel - 15¼ x 17¼in.
(Sotheby's) **£1,300**

BENJAMIN GERRITSZ. CUYP - A Fishwife On A Quayside - on panel - 29 x 42in.
(Christie's) **£2,000**

CYNICUS - "Drink To Me Only With Thine Eyes" - oil - signed and inscribed - on panel - 21 x 16cm.
(Phillips in Scotland) **£36**

MICHAEL DAHL - Portrait Of A Lady, three-quarter length, In Blue Dress, Holding A Sprig Of Orange-Blossom - signed and dated 1724 - 48¼ x 29¼in.
(Christie's) **£110**

E. DALBONO - A Band Of Horsemen Passing Across A Wooded Landscape - signed - 6¼ x 16¼in.
(Sotheby's) **£500**

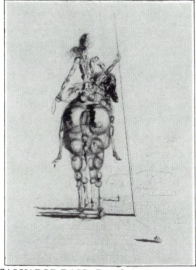

SALVADOR DALI - Don Quixote - signed in pencil and dated 1935 - Indian ink drawing - 40¼ x 28½in.
(Phillips) **£4,800**

FRANS VAN DAMME - Cattle At The Water's Edge - signed - 30 x 50in.
(Sotheby's) **£340**

SYLVIA VAN DAMME - Herd Leading The Cows - oil on canvas - 41 x 33cm.
(Galerie Moderne) **£72**

SYLVIA VAN DAMME - Cows At Pasture - oil on canvas - signed - 31 x 43cm.
(Galerie Moderne) **£157**

EMILE VAN DAMME-SYLVA - A Woman With Cattle By A Pond - signed - on panel - 8½ x 14¾in.
(Sotheby's) **£600**

JAN JACOBUS MATTHYS DAMSCHRODER - Baby's First Steps - signed - 14 x 17¾in.
(Sotheby's) **£550**

J. F. DANBY - Evening - 14¼ x 21¼in.
(Sotheby's Belgravia) **£150**

THOMAS DANBY - A Highland Landscape, With Herdsmen, Sheep And Cattle On A Road - signed and dated '51 - 29½ x 50in.
(Christie's) **£900**

P. DANDBY - An Aracadian Landscape With Figures in the foreground - 8 x 10¼in.
(Sotheby's) **£190**

DANCKERTS

DANCKERTS - An Extensive View Of London From Greenwich - 24 x 29in.
(Christie's) **£900**

SAMUEL DANIELL - Study Of A Native, Seen From Behind - pencil and grey wash - 8¾ x 5¾in.
(Christie's) **£130**

THOMAS DANIELL - The Entrance To Muscat Harbour, Arabia - inscribed and dated June 1793 beneath the mount - pencil, pen and grey ink and watercolour - 11½ x 15½in.
(Christie's) **£11,000**

THOMAS DANIELL - Tappacollum, Near Madura - pencil and grey wash - inscribed and numbered on the reverse - oval - 12 x 19in.
(Christie's) **£65**

THOMAS DANIELL - An Excavated Hindu Temple On The Island Of Salsette In The East Indies - 24 x 29in.
(Christie's) **£800**

WILLIAM DANIELL - Deer Resting In A Wooded Landscape - 23 x 30in.
(Christie's) **£2,400**

WILLIAM DANIELL - Study Of An Elephant Running - pencil - 6 x 7¾in.
(Sotheby's) **£8**

WILLIAM DANIELL - The Citadel, Plymouth - signed on the mount and inscribed - pencil and brown wash heightened with white on buff paper - 6½ x 9¼in.
(Christie's) **£200**

J. B. DANLOUX - Portrait Of A Woman, half length, Wearing A White Dress And Holding A Rose - oval - 27 x 20½in.
(Christie's) **£400**

JOHANN GEORG DATHAN - An Old Woman Reading To A Young Girl, A Basket Filled With Books Before Them - signed and dated 1732 - on panel - 13¾ x 10½in.
(Sotheby's) **£550**

CHARLES FRANCOIS DAUBIGNY - 'Blanchisseuses Au Bord D'Une Riviere' - signed - 38 x 62cm.
(Phillips) **£1.300**

HENRI DAURIAC - 'Preparing The Meal' - signed - 116 x 96cm.
(Phillips) **£1,400**

LESLIE DAVENPORT - View Of Norwich Cathedral From The Gas Works - 20 x 27in.
(G. A. Key) **£30**

A. DAVIDSON - Joan Of Arc Leading A Procession - on board - 9¾ x 9¼in.
(Sotheby's Belgravia) **£48**

JOHN DAVIDSON - A Cottage Scene Near The Pentland Hills - signed - inscribed on the reverse - 19 x 26in.
(Sotheby's Belgravia) **£220**

ARTHUR E. DAVIES - Cromer Beach - watercolour - 13 x 18in.
(G. A. Key) **£165**

ARTHUR E. DAVIES - St. Pauls Across The Thames - watercolour - 10 x 15in.
(G. A. Key) **£160**

WILLIAM DAVIES - Glen Ogwen, Carnarvonshire - signed and dated 1894 - inscribed on the reverse - 19½ x 29¼in.
(Sotheby's Belgravia) **£360**

E. DAVIS - Loch Lomond Side - 39 x 60cm.
(Edmiston's) **£28**

R. DAVIS - Lads And Farm - on panel - 23 x 15cm.
(Edmiston's) **£10**

R. B. DAVIS - Children Among Dunes - watercolours - 23 x 34cm
(Edmiston's) **£25 pair**

RICHARD BARRETT DAVIS - Ralph Lambton On A Bay Hunter, A Chestnut Hunter And Terrier Nearby, In A Wooded Landscape - signed and dated 1836 - 24 x 28½in.
(Christie's) **£2,500**

WILLIAM HENRY DAVIS - A Pair Of Carriage Horses - signed with initials and dated 1828 - 17 x 31in.
(Christie's) **£480**

W. H. DAVIS - 'Belville', Study Of A Shorthorn Bull In An Open Landscape - signed and dated 1846 - on canvas - oil - 21½ x 29in.
(Morphet & Morphet) **£250**

WILLIAM DAVIS - Wallasey Mill, Cheshire - 15 x 22½in.
(Sotheby's Belgravia) **£200**

A. H. MILTON DAWKINS - Durham Cathedral From The River - signed and dated 1896 - 23½ x 35in.
(Sotheby's Belgravia) **£170**

ALFRED DAWSON - In Windsor Park - signed and dated 1874 - 16 x 24in.
(Sotheby's Belgravia) **£800**

ALFRED DAWSON - Ancient Nottingham, a view of the Castle from the Hermitage - watercolour - signed with monogram and dated '84 - with key - 6¾ x 9¾in.
(Neale & Son) **£39**

HENRY DAWSON - Shipping At Dusk - oil on board - signed with initials and dated 1861 - 10 x 14in.
(King & Chasemore) £220

HENRY DAWSON - Shipping In A River Estuary - on canvas - 22½ x 33⅓in.
(King & Chasemore) £360

MONTAGUE DAWSON - Cowes With Prince Phillip In 'Cowslip' Passing The Anchored 'Britannia' - signed - 26¾ x 41in.
(Phillips) £3,700

EDWARD DAYES - Bolton Castle - pencil and watercolour - signed and dated 1791 - 5½ x 8½in.
(Christie's) £250

EDWARD DAYES - Lancaster - pencil and watercolour - signed and dated 1791 - 5½ x 8½in.
(Christie's) £320

FRANK DEAN - Springtime - coloured chalks - signed and inscribed - on buff paper - 14½ x 27in.
(Sotheby's Belgravia) £25

DEANE - The Pool Of London By Moonlight - on panel - 17½ x 23½in.
(Christie's) £120

EDOUARD BERNARD DEBATPONSAN - A Watermill In Summer - signed - 12½ x 15½in.
(Sotheby's) £250

ALEXANDRE DECAMPS - Landscape - oil on lined canvas - signed - 20 x 29cm.
(Galerie Moderne) £85

GABRIEL ALEXANDRE DECAMPS - The Medicants - heightened with bodycolour - signed - 7¼ x 8¾in.
(Sotheby's) £50

C. DECKER - A River Landscape, With Vessels And Figures On The Bank By A House - on panel - 15½ x 20½in.
(Christie's) £2,200

CORNELIS DECKER AND ADRIAEN VAN OSTADE - The Edge Of A Wood; A Peasant With A Boy And A Dog Talking To A Woman Seated At The Side Of A Road - 37¼ x 32½in.
(Sotheby's) £7,000

JAN DECLERCO - Landscape - oil on canvas - signed 40 x 50cm.
(Galerie Moderne) £50

HENRI DECOENE - A Pause For Refreshment: Peasants At A Table In An Interior - signed - on panel - 19 x 22in.
(Christie's) £4,800

EDGAR DEGAS - Femme A Son Lever - La Boulangere - pastel - 30¾ x 19¾in.
(Sotheby's) **£23,000**

DELEN - The Tribute Money, In A Marble Interior - on alabaster - oval - 6 x 8in.
(Sotheby's) **£130**

CHARLES DELHOMMEAU - Etudes de Lions - brown crayon - 11¼ x 18½in.
(Sotheby's) **£25**

F. DELINCE - The Anger Of The Hunchback - oil on canvas - signed - 70 x 50cm.
(Galerie Moderne) **£15**

ANDREA DELITIO - The Madonna And Child Against A Red And Brown Curtain - on panel - 27 x 20in.
(Christie's) **£4,000**

E. DELPEREE - Portrait Of A Monk Contemplating, full length - oil - on canvas - signed and dated 1873 - 30 x 42in.
(Locke & England) **£160**

A. DEMART - View Of A Beach - oil on canvas - signed - 33 x 41cm.
(Galerie Moderne) **£10**

DENNER - A Merchant Counting His Stock Of Gold - 29 x 24in.
(Sotheby's) **£580**

C. DENNONE - View Of A Busy Village - oil on canvas - signed - 70 x 60cm.
(Galerie Moderne) **£66**

E. DENONLER - The Life Of The Virgin - oil on canvas - signed - 54 x 45cm.
(Galerie Moderne) **£40**

L. DERAYMACKER - Landscape - oil on canvas - signed - 30 x 40cm.
(Galerie Moderne) **£10**

A. DERBYSHIRE - 'Drawing Room In Lyme Hall, Cheshire' - signed and dated 1859 - watercolour - 13 x 32in.
(Butler & Hatch Waterman) **£20**

R. DERRY - Manx Coast Scenes - both signed - inscribed on the reverse - each 11½ x 23¼in.
(Sotheby's Belgravia) **£40 Pair**

GUILLAUME DESIRE JOSEPH DESCAMPS - A Moroccan Soldier - 6 x 4in.
(Sotheby's) **£120**

CHARLES DESPIAU - Femme Assise Au Bras Leve - red chalk - 13¼ x 9½in.
(Sotheby's) **£35**

A. F. DESPORTES - 'Lisette', A Spaniel, Flushing A Pheasant With A View Of A Bavarian Town Beyond - inscribed - 45½ x 66in.
(Christie's) £2,600

A. F. DESPORTES - A Still Life, A French Silver Chocolate Pot With Straight Side Handle Standing On Three Feet, A Silver Beaker, Peaches And A Walnut On A Stone Ledge - 21½ x 17in.
(Sotheby's) £950

A. F. DESPORTES - A Dead Deer And Partridge, With A Dog Barking At A Parrot On A Pedestal, And Implements Of The Chase In A Woody Landscape - 76 x 50½in.
(Christie's) £1,100

ALPHONSE DESSENIS - Undergrowth - oil on canvas - 30 x 40cm.
(Galerie Moderne) £16

HERBERT CLAYTON DESVIGNES - Going To Market - signed and dated 1860 - arched top - 35½ x 27½in.
(Sotheby's Belgravia) £850

EDWARD JULIUS DETMOLD - 'Drawing His Scimitar Aimed At Him A Blow Which, Had It Found Him, Must There And Then Have Ended The Fight' (The Arabian Nights) - pen and black ink and watercolour heightened with white and gold - signed with monogram - 32 x 22¾in.
(Christie's) £820

CESARE AUGUSTE DETTI - Market Day - signed and dated Paris '82 - 32 x 41in.
(Christie's) £6,500

CESARE AUGUSTE DETTI - The Afternoon Siesta - signed - on panel - 5¾ x 9in.
(Christie's) £1,300

WILLEM ANTONIE DEVENTER - Figures Logging On The Amstel - signed and dated 1849 - on panel - 35 x 52.5cm.
(Phillips) **£1,550**

ANTHONY DEVIS - A Drover With His Herd In A Wooded Landscape - signed - pen and grey ink, black chalk and watercolour - 10 x 15in.
(Christie's) **£280**

ANTHONY DEVIS - A Castle Near A Lake In A Mountain Landscape; And Figures Near A Fortified Town - pen and grey ink and watercolour - 11½ x 16½in.
(Christie's) **£150 Pair**

ARTHUR DEVIS - Portrait Of A Gentleman In Brown Coat, Seated Under A Tree Holding A Telescope - small full length - signed and dated 1765 - 29 x 24in.
(Christie's) **£800**

GUILLAIM VAN DEYNUM - A Peeled Lemon, Grapes And Other Fruit With A Shell On A Table - signed - 19 x 25in.
(Christie's) **£2,000**

N. DIAZ - A Nude Woman Reclining With A Tambourine - bears signature and date '62 - 23 x 41¾in.
(Christie's) **£600**

THOMAS COLEMAN DIBDIN - Rouen, Part Of The Cathedral - heightened with bodycolour - signed and dated 1886 - 30½ x 21½in.
(Sotheby's Belgravia) **£95**

MARGARET K. DICKER - Horning Ferry And Ranworth Church - watercolour - 10 x 14in.
(G. A. Key) **£9**

SIR FRANK DICKSEE - The Wedding Of Canaan - grisaille - signed - arched top - 15¾ x 22½in.
(Sotheby's Belgravia) **£60**

CHARLES DICKSON - 'Sunset Limehouse Reach On The Thames' - signed and dated 1889 - oil on canvas - 19¼ x 35¼in.
(Bearnes & Waycotts) **£400**

R. VAN DIER - A Boat On A Lake - oil on canvas - signed and dated 1882 - 56 x 46cm.
(Galerie Moderne) **£72**

A. VAN DIEST - An Italianate Coastal Landscape With Figures in the foreground And A Fort Beyond - 21 x 31in.
(Christie's) **£1,000**

A. VAN DIEST - An Extensive River Landscape With A Herdsman And A Milkmaid Tending Cattle And Sheep By A Castle - 19½ x 40½in.
(Christie's) **£900**

PIERRE DIETMAN - A Sheep Drinking From A Stream In An Extensive Landscape - indistinctly signed and dated - on panel - 13 x 16¾in.
(Sotheby's) **£300**

C. W. E. DIETRICHY - Portraits Of Two Old Men - on panel - each 3 x 2¼in.
(Sotheby's) **£200 Two**

131

A. VAN DIEST - Italianate river landscape with figures and animals - 35 x
48 ins.
(Christie's, S. Kensington) **£700**

ADRIAEN VAN DIEST - A Wooded
Italianate River Landscape With A
Fisherman in the foreground; And A
Mountainous Woody Landscape With
Figures By A River - one signed - 24½ x
29½in.
(Christie's) **£3,800 Pair**

W. VAN DIEST - Shipping In A Calm Sea,
A Ferry Filled With Passengers in the
centre foreground, A Man-Of-War To The
Left - on panel - 9¼ x 16½in.
(Sotheby's) **£3,400**

IERONYMUS VAN DIEST - Dutch
Shipping In An Estuary, A Jetty in the
foreground - signed with monogram -
on panel - 17¾ x 25in.
(Christie's) **£14,000**

DIETRICH, Attributed to - Personnages -
on wood - 30 x 26cm.
(Galerie Moderne) **£265**

CHRISTIAN WILHELM ERNST DIETRICH
- A Mountainous Landscape with figures by
a stream and a castle beyond - 31½ x 39½in.
(Christie's) **£5,000**

MASTER OF DILIGHEM ABBEY - The Adoration Of The Magi, Flanked By The Adoration Of The Shepherds And The Presentation In The Temple - a triptych - on panel - in shaped frame pierced with Gothic tracery central panel - 41½ x 27½in. - laterals - 42 x 12¼in.
(Christie's)   **£17,000**

CHARLES DIXON - Above Woolwich - heightened with bodycolour - signed - inscribed and dated '04 - 10¼ x 30in.
(Sotheby's Belgravia)   **£320**

CHARLES DIXON - A Yacht Race - heightened with bodycolour - signed and dated '05 - 29¼ x 39in.
(Sotheby's Belgravia)   **£1,200**

CHARLES DIXON - A Steam Boat In Open Seas - heightened with body-colour - signed - 9½ x 25in.
(Sotheby's Belgravia)   **£30**

CHARLES DIXON - Shipping In An Estuary - watercolour - signed and dated 1921 - 7¼ x 10½in.
(King & Chasemore)   **£145**

CHARLES DIXON - 'Off Tilbury' - water-colour - signed, inscribed and dated '18 - 7½ x 10½in.
(King & Chasemore)   **£100**

ANTONIO DIZIANI - An Italianate Woody River Landscape With Peasants And Cattle Outside A Farmstead - 46 x 68in.
(Christie's)   **£2,800**

H. J. DOBSON - Cottage Interior With Old Man Seated By Fire - oil - 11½ x 15½in.
(Thomas Love & Sons Ltd)   **£50**

WILLIAM THOMAS CHARLES DOBSON - The Pet - watercolour heightened with white - signed with monogram and dated 1867 - 7 x 5¾in.
(Christie's)   **£150**

ALEXANDER BROWNLIE DOCHARTY - The Falls of Dochart, Killin, Perthshire, Autumn - signed - 27 x 35in.
(Sotheby's) £120

ALEXANDER BROWNLIE DOCHARTY - Loch Laggan, Perthshire - with snow-capped mountains - signed - 27¾ x 39½in.
(Sotheby's) £300

ROBERT DODD - Shipping Off Gravesend - 32½ x 57in.
(Christie's) £4,200

VAN DER DOES - A Landscape, Animals Resting By A Tree To The Right, Others Grazing By A River Beyond - on panel - 10 x 9in.
(Sotheby's) £150

DOLCI - The Young Christ, Holding Flowers - on metal - 11¾ x 8¾in.
(Sotheby's) £100

DOLCI - The Madonna And Child - 25¼ x 20in.
(Sotheby's) £130

CARLO DOLCI - St Jerome In A Landscape, The Saint In Purple Drapery, A Rock In His Hand, Kneeling On A Rock Before A Crucifix, An Open Book In Front Of Him - on panel - oval - 11½ x 8½in.
(Sotheby's) £1,200

CARLO DOLCI - Saint Philip Benizi renouncing the Papal Triple Crown - octagonal - 46½ x 36½in.
(Christie's) £3,200

JOHN CHARLES DOLLMAN - 'The Elopement' - oil on canvas - signed - 36 x 60in.
(King & Chasemore) £340

JOHN CHARLES DOLLMAN - Portrait Of A Girl, head and shoulders - signed with initials - inscribed on the reverse - 11½ x 9½in.
(Sotheby's Belgravia) £70

JEAN-GABRIEL DOMERGUE - Eve Au Miroir - oil - on board - signed - 19½ x 23½in.
(Sotheby's) £480

FRANCISCO DOMINGO - A Halt At The Inn - signed and dated Paris 1898 - 19½ x 23½in.
(Christie's) £8,000

CORNELIUS CHRISTIAN DOMMERSEN - The Pool Of London Bridge - signed and dated 1899 - on board - 23¼ x 17¾in.
(Christie's) £2,100

PETER CHRISTIAN DOMMERSEN - A Dutch Estuary With Shipping - signed and dated 1884 - oil on canvas - 41 x 60in.
(Bonham's) £2,400

PIETER CHRISTIAN DOMMERSEN - A Street View, Rouen, France - signed and dated 1908 - 19½ x 29½in.
(Sotheby's) £1,700

PIETER CORNELIS DOMMERSEN - 'On The Maas, Nr. Maasluis, Holland' - signed and dated 1889 - signed with initials on a seal and inscribed on reverse - on panel - 30 x 40cm.
(Phillips) £1,150

DOMMERSEN

PIETER CORNELIS DOMMERSEN -
An Estuary Scene With Fishing Boats
Moored Offshore, Figures in the
foreground - signed and dated 1869 -
28 x 41cm.
(Phillips) **£1,200**

W. DOMMERSEN - Views Of Chinsi
And Corte - signed and inscribed on the
reverse - oil on canvas - 11½ x 9½in.
(Bearnes & Waycotts) **£320 Pair**

W. R. DOMMERSEN - 19th century canal
Scene - oil on canvas - 12 x 9in.
(J. Francis, T. Jones & Sons) **£70**

WILLIAM DOMMERSEN - Canal
Views, Possibly In Delft - both
signed and dated 1872 - each 11½ x
15½in.
(Sotheby's) **£2,500 Pair**

**CORNELIS CHRISTIAN
DOMMERSHUIZEN** - A Street Scene In
Turnhout - signed and dated 1887 -
12½ x 11in.
(Christie's) **£1,500**

DONALD - Landscape And Loch -
16 x 20.5cm.
(Edmiston's) **£14**

M. DONAT - Country Scenes With
Figures - signed - oil on panel - 7½ x 5½in.
(Bearnes & Waycotts) **£150 Pair**

G. DONCK - Group Portrait Of A Lady
And Gentleman, With Two Children In
A Landscape - 56 x 68½in.
(Christie's) **£2,600**

GERARD DONCK - The Vegetable Seller -
21¾ x 25¼in.
(Christie's) **£2,200**

L DONNAY - Man In Armour - oil on
canvas - signed and dated 1912 - 80 x
60cm.
(Galerie Moderne) **£22**

L DONNAY - Portrait Of A Man - oil
on canvas - signed and dated 1913 -
74 x 56cm.
(Galerie Moderne) **£10**

DORCY - Portraits Of Girls, One Wearing
A White Shawl, The Other Wearing A
White Dress With A Garland Of Leaves In
Her Hair - both signed - oval - on panel -
each 20 x 16in.
(Sotheby's) **£260 Two**

DOU - Violinist At An Arched Window -
35.5 x 29.5cm.
(Edmiston's) **£250**

GERARD DOU - A Kitchen Maid at a well -
on panel - 9½ x 7½in.
(Christie's) **£12,000**

G. DOU - A Old Woman, bust length,
Wearing A Black Hat And Fur Coat
With White Collar - oval - on panel -
6 x 4¾in.
(Christie's) **£600**

ANDREW DOUGLAS - Cattle In Pasture -
80 x 116cm.
(Edmiston's) **£130**

**EDWARD ALGERNON STEWART
DOUGLAS** - The London To Bristol
Mail Coach; And The Cambridge To
London Coach - both signed - water-
colour heightened with white - 8¼ x
13¼in.
(Christie's) **£420 Pair**

**EDWARD ALGERNON STEWART
DOUGLAS** - Figures Driving A Trap;
And Following A Hunt - both signed -
watercolour heightened with white -
7¾ x 13¼in.
(Christie's) **£170 Pair**

W. H. DOUST - Fishing Boats - 11½ x
15½in.
(Sotheby's Belgravia) **£160**

W. H. DOUST - Pleasant Seascapes With
Ships And Barges - oils - 9 x 12in.
(G. A. Key) **£480 Pair**

MARIE DOVASTON - A Chip Off The
Old Block - signed - 19½ x 26½in.
(Christie's) **£2,600**

EBENEEZER NEWMAN DOWNARD - Locked Out - signed and dated 1875 - 33 x 21¼in.
(Sotheby's Belgravia) **£320**

PATRICK DOWNIE - A Summer Breeze, Firth of Clyde - 70 x 90cm.
(Edmiston's) **£310**

PATRICK DOWNIE - Bass Rock - watercolour - 34 x 51cm.
(Edmiston's) **£126**

DOWNMAN - Portrait Of Mr Dyne, A Vicar Choral Of St. Paul's Cathedral, bust length, Wearing A Blue Coat - dated 1779 - pencil and watercolour - oval - 6 x 4½in.
(Christie's) **£20**

JOHN DOWNMAN - Portrait Of Edith Potter, Daughter Of The Archbishop Of Canterbury, Wife Of The Dean Of Exeter - signed with initials - dated 1780 - stump and orange chalk heightened with white - oval - 7½ x 5¼in.
(Christie's) **£60**

JOHN DOWNMAN - Portrait Of A Gentleman, half length, Wearing A Grey Coat - stump and watercolour heightened with white - oval - 9½ x 8in.
(Christie's) **£75**

RICHARD DOYLE - The Guardian Angel - pencil and watercolour heightened with white - 11¾ x 18in.
(Christie's) **£190**

ALFRED DE DREUX - 'Etalon En Liberte' - signed and dated 1857 - on canvas - 32 x 39½in.
(King & Chasemore) **£4,100**

JACOB CORNELISZ DROOCHSLOOT - Prince Maurice Of Nassau Disbanding The Mercenaries On The Neude At Utrecht, 1618 - 35¼ x 53½in.
(Sotheby's) **£3,600**

JOOST CORNELISZ DROOCHSLOOT - Peasants Feasting In An Interior - signed and dated 1637 - on panel - 20 x 27½in.
(Christie's) **£6,500**

JOOST CORNELISZ. DROOCHSLOOT -
A Village Street, with numerous peasants -
signed with monogram and dated 1652 - on
panel - 23½ x 33in.
(Christie's) £5,000

CORNELIS DROOGSLOOT - Peasants
Eating And Drinking Outside An Inn -
signed - on panel - 16½ x 23in.
(Christie's) £3,500

F. DROUAIS - A Lady of Virtue - oil on
canvas - 81 x 64 cm.
(Galerie Moderne) £258

DRUMMOND - Portrait Of An Artist,
small three-quarter length, Seated,
Holding A Sketch Book And Wearing
A Green Coat, In A Woody Landscape -
13½ x 11in.
(Christie's) £150

J. DRUMMOND - A Sailor And His Family -
signed and dated 1879 - 23½ x 35½in.
(Sotheby's) £320

JAMES DRUMMOND - 'The Devil's Cave' -
A Coastal Scene With Danish Invaders -
watercolour - 13 x 20in.
(Warner, Sheppard & Wade) £17

J. T. DRYSDALE - Study Of A Lady
Sewing, in an interior - signed and
dated 1891 - on panel - 8¾ x 11¾in.
(Sotheby's Belgravia) £50

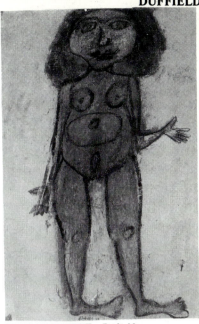

JEAN DUBUFFET - Petit Nu
Verdatre - signed and dated - paper
on board - 24½ x 16½in.
(Sotheby's) £13,200

JEAN DUBUFFET - Mute Permute -
signed with initials and dated - vinyl
and acrylic paint on Klegecell, glazed
with polyster and fiberglass - 113½ x
151½ x 1½in.
(Christie's, New York) £116,500

CHARLES DUDLEY - Surprised - signed
- 13½ x 9½in.
(Sotheby's Belgravia) £120

MARY ELIZABETH DUFFIELD -
Roses And Marigolds By A Vase; And
Roses And Peonies On A Ledge - water-
colour heightened with white - one
signed - 8¼ x 12½in.
(Christie's) £220 **Pair**

RAOUL DUFY - Atelier Au Violon -
signed - 15 x 18¼in.
(Sotheby's) **£6,000**

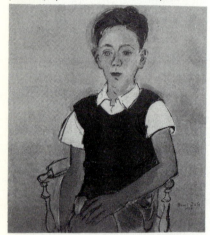

RAOUL DUFY - Portrait De Michel
Bignou - signed and incorrectly dated
1934 - 32¼ x 25½in.
(Sotheby's) **£8,000**

RAOUL DUFY - Quintet Au
Pupitre Bleu - signed - 18¼ x 21¾in.
(Sotheby's) **£13,000**

RAOUL DUFY - Femme Nue Debout -
pencil - signed with monogram - 8¼ x
5in.
(Sotheby's) **£180**

K. DUJARDIN - A Peasant On A
Donkey, And A Traveller On A Road
In A Woody Lake Landscape - 15¾ x
13½in.
(Christie's) **£600**

KAREL DU JARDIN - A Shepherd Boy
With His Sheep - oil on canvas - 14 x 18in.
(King & Chasemore) **£370**

EDMUND DULAC - 'The Mermaid' -
watercolour - signed - 12½ x 9¾in.
(King & Chasemore) **£1,550**

L. DUMINI - Old Master Self Portraits -
Rembrandt, Rubens, da Vinci, Michael
Angelo, Tiziano, Reni - 8½ x 7in - six
copies.
(Woolley & Wallis) **£200**

EDWARD DUNCAN - Fishermen
Mending The Nets By Derelict Buildings
- sepia and pen wash - 10 x 20in.
(G. A. Key) **£75**

EDWARD DUNCAN - Fishing Boats
Off Duntroon Castle, Loch Crinan In
Argyllshire - watercolour heightened
with white - signed and dated 1869 -
9 x 20in.
(Christie's) **£130**

ALBERT DUNINGTON - Loch Maree;
Loch Nieve - both signed and dated
1901 - 15 x 23in.
(Sotheby's Belgravia) **£170 Pair**

ALBERT DUNINGTON - Herding Sheep
Over The Hills - signed and dated 1892 -
29½ x 24½in.
(Sotheby's Belgravia) **£85**

JOHANNES BARTHOLOMAUS DUNTZE
A Village In Winter, With Figures Skating
On A Frozen Canal And A Horse-Drawn
Sleigh Near A Windmill - signed and
dated 1864 - 37½ x 53½in.
(Sotheby's) **£6,600**

JOHANNES BARTHOLOMAUS DUNTZE -
German River Landscape With Figures -
signed and dated 1871 - oil on canvas - 23 x
36in.
(Bonham's) **£1,600**

JOHANNES BARTHOLOMAUS DUNTZE -
A Winter Landscape With a Castle, and a
wood gatherer and other figures on a frozen
lake - signed and dated 1872 - 23 x 37½in.
(Christie's) **£3,500**

JOHANNES BARTHOLOMAUS DUNTZE -
Summer; and Winter - both signed and
dated 1893 - 12½ x 18in
(Christie's) **£3,000 Pair**

H. DUPOIS - Vue de Bruges Animee -
oil - signed - 1m. x 80cm.
(Galerie Moderne) **£345**

B. DUPOND - 'The Golden Apple',
Elegant Figures In An Interior -
signed - on panel - 12½ x 17in.
(Sotheby's) **£350**

A. DUPONT - La Lenpont, Saint-Hubert -
wood - signed - 34 x 56cm.
(Galerie Moderne) **£11**

GAINSBOROUGH DUPONT - The
Milkmaid - pastel - 26½ x 20¼in.
(Sotheby's) **£60**

GAINSBOROUGH DUPONT - Portrait
Of The Prince Of Wales, small bust
length, Wearing The Insignia Of The
Order Of The Garter - on board -
5¾ x 4in.
(Christie's) **£220**

G DUPRE - Cattle, Figure And Goats By
A Lake - bears signature - 9¾ x 13¾in.
(Sotheby's) **£170**

VICTOR DUPRE - A Wooded Landscape,
A Figure Crossing A Bridge - signed - on
panel - 9¾ x 12¾in.
(Sotheby's) **£800**

A. DURANT - The Pool - oil on canvas -
signed - 40 x 60cm.
(Galerie Moderne) **£31**

FRIEDRICH DURCK - The 'Schafhirt's
Abendgluhen' - signed - dated 1853 -
stamped on the reverse 'Henry Wimmer,
Munich' - 40 x 46½in.
(Sotheby's) **£1,500**

DURER - The Head Of John The Baptist
Upheld by Angels - oak panel - 15½ x 19in.
(Woolley & Wallis) **£610**

MICHEL DUREUIL - Voiliers Dans Un
Port - oil - on canvas - signed and dated
'60 - 19¼ x 23½in.
(Sotheby's) **£280**

DURIEUX

E. DURIEUX - The Firewood Gatherer -
oil on canvas - signed 65cm. x 1m.
(Galerie Moderne) **£215**

R. DURIEUX - The Sail Makers - oil on
wood - signed - 13 x 23cm.
(Galerie Moderne) **£19**

V. DURIEUX - Flowers And Fruit -
oil on canvas - signed - 70 x 90cm.
(Galerie Moderne) **£21**

LEOPOLDO DURNINI - Titian, bust
length; Rubens, head and shoulders -
each after his self-portrait in the
Uffizi - each signed and inscribed on
the reverse - oval - on board - 8½ x 7in.
(Sotheby's) **£100 Pair**

A. H. DUROBA, Paris - An Extensive
Evening Landscape With Animals And
Figures - signed - inscribed and dated
1797 - 25 x 35½in.
(Woolley & Wallis) **£270**

DU ROY - Cattle In A Sunlit Evening
Landscape - on panel - 9½ x 11½in.
(Sotheby's) **£180**

DUTCH SCHOOL, mid 17tn century -
Shipping in a calm - oil on panel - 9 x
12 ins.
(King & Chasemore) **£480**

DUTCH SCHOOL, Late 17th century -
A Landscape with Hawking Party in the
style of Adrien Van Der Velde, with three
gentlemen on horseback, two servants and
many dogs at their feet - 23 x 29in.
(Henry Spencer & Sons) **£4,800**

DUTCH SCHOOL, 19th century -
Packet Boat With Fishing Boats On The
Scheldt - 24 x 34in.
(Worsfolds) **£200**

DUTCH SCHOOL - Fruit And Flowers
And Wicker Basket On A Table - 56 x
43cm.
(Edmiston's) **£500**

DUTCH SCHOOL, 19th century - The
Skaters - on wood - 26 x 35cm.
(Galerie Moderne) **£230**

DUTCH SCHOOL, 19th century -
Canal Near Utrecht - oil - on board -
inscribed Jongkind - 36¼ x 29½in.
(Sotheby's) **£320**

DUTCH SCHOOL, 18th century - Rocky
Coastal Scene with Shipwreck and Survivors
in Mountainous Seas - canvas - 24 x 33in.
(Morphet & Morphet) **£280**

DUTCH SCHOOL - Comestibles, Fruit
And Still Life On A Table - 62 x 109cm.
(Edmiston's) **£4,800**

DUTCH SCHOOL - Extensive Farm Scene
With Figures And Animals - 85 x 111cm.
(Edmiston's) **£1,300**

DUTCH SCHOOL - A still life of a
vase of flowers and a bird's nest on
stone ledge - oil on canvas - 31 x 25½ ins.
(King & Chasemore) **£480**

DUTCH SCHOOL - Dutch Men-O'-War
And Hagboats Off A Coastal Town -
bears signature 'W. Van De Velde' -
dated 1770 - 60 x 90cm.
(Phillips) **£1,700**

DUTCH SCHOOL - Coast Scene With
Sailing Ships And Figures - 43 x 63cm.
(Edmiston's) **£950**

DUTCH SCHOOL - The Hunt. Extensive
Wooded Landscape With Stags, Dogs,
Figures And Horses With Carriage In
Distance - 92 x 137cm.
(Edmiston's) **£1,500**

DUTCH SCHOOL - Interior With Figures -
15½ x 11½in.
(Woolley & Wallis) **£125**

DUTCH SCHOOL - Extensive Landscape
With Buildings And An Open Market
Place With Numerous Figures - 76 x
102cm.
(Edmiston's) **£2,500**

DUTCH SCHOOL

DUTCH SCHOOL - Preparing Carrots - on panel - 34 x 28cm.
(Edmiston's) £200

DUTCH SCHOOL - Harbour Scene With Boats - 48 x 64cm.
(Edmiston's) £290

DUTCH SCHOOL - Interiors With Figures - 15 x 11in.
(Woolley & Wallis) **£125 Pair**

DUTCH SCHOOL - A Still Life with a dead Bird suspended above Table with Pestle and Mortar - 34 x 25½in.
(Phillips) £300

THEOPHILE EMMANUEL DUVERGER - Making-Up - signed - on panel - 13 x 10in.
(Christie's) **£1,600**

F. DUYK - The Harvest - oil on wood - signed - 20 x 29cm.
(Galerie Moderne) £12

VAN DYCK - Portrait Of A Man, head and shoulders - on panel - 14 x 12in.
(Sotheby's) £90

A. VAN DYCK - A Portrait Of A Lady And Her Daughter, The Latter To The Left Handing A Basket Of Roses To Her Mother - 35 x 45½in.
(Sotheby's) **£1,650**

SIR A. VAN DYCK - Portrait Of Queen Henrietta Maria, three-quarter length, Wearing A Yellow Dress With Lace Collar And Cuffs - 40½ x 30½in.
(Christie's) **£1,400**

SIR ANTHONY VAN DYCK - Portrait of a Lady, seated, three-quarter length, in a black dress and white ruff, against a red draped curtain - 40 x 27in.
(Christie's) **£13,000**

SIR ANTHONY VAN DYCK - Portrait Of The Marchese Filippo Spinola, in half-armour, with his helmet on the ground beside him - 86 x 55in.
(Christie's) **£85,000**

W. H. DYER - The Cheese Ring, Lynton, North Devon - watercolour - 13 x 18in.
(G. A. Key) **£4**

SIR ANTHONY VAN DYCK - The Virgin And Child - on panel - 57 x 42½in.
(Christie's) **£200,000**

MARCEL DYF - Flowers in a jug - signed - 20½ x 18 ins.
(Christie's, S. Kensington) **£150**

JOHN EARDLEY - Winter Sea -
122 x 189cm.
(Edmiston's) **£510**
E. EARL - Setters - signed - on board -
6½ x 8½in.
(Sotheby's Belgravia) **£65**

GEORGE EARL - Waiting For Master -
signed with initials - on board - oval -
19½ x 23½in.
(Sotheby's Belgravia) **£190**

MAUD EARL - Study Of A Terrier -
oil - 15½ x 21½in.
(Thomas Love & Sons Ltd) **£50**

PERCY EARL - Deerslayer, A Chestnut Hunter in a landscape - signed, inscribed and dated 1912 - 25 x 30in.
(Christie's, S. Kensington) **£320**

THOMAS EARL - Study Of A Terrier's
Head - on board - 10½ x 8½in.
(Sotheby's Belgravia) **£300**

J. EARP - A River In A Landscape - signed -
13½ x 8½in.
(J. Francis, T. Jones & Sons) **£16**

HENRY EARP, SNR - A View From
The Fields Of Steyning - heightened
with white - signed - 7¼ x 18in.
(Sotheby's Belgravia) **£110**

HENRY EARP, SNR - Haymaking -
signed - 10 x 20½in.
(Sotheby's Belgravia) **£150**

SIR ALFRED EAST - Hale - a sketch
for the picture in Birmingham Art
Gallery - signed - 13½ x 29¾in.
(Sotheby's Belgravia) **£320**

SIR ALFRED EAST - Gay Spring -
signed - 39½ x 59½in.
(Christie's) **£800**

H. EAST - Figures By A Wooded River -
signed - 11½ x 15½in.
(Sotheby's Belgravia) **£135**

GERARD EDEMA - A Mountainous
Italianate Landscape With A Cottage
By A Torrent - signed - 37 x 36in.
(Christie's) **£2,000**

J. C. EDGAR - Portrait Of Lady With
Flowers In Landscape - oil - 11 x 9in.
(G. A. Key) **£62**

EDRIDGE - Portrait Of A Lady, small
full length, In A Black Dress, Seated On A
Terrace, With A Landscape Beyond -
29½ x 24½in.
(Christie's) **£160**

A. SANDERSON EDWARD - Near Loch
Awe, Argyllshire - signed - 19½ x 29½in.
(Sotheby's Belgravia) **£50**

GEORGE EDWARDS - The Jay From
Carolina - watercolour - varnished -
inscribed on the reverse - 10¾ x 8¾in.
(Christie's) **£140**

J. EDWARDS - Sailing Ships Off The South
Coast - signed - 20 x 30in.
(Woolley & Wallis) **£220**

LIONEL EDWARDS - The Bronco
Buster - watercolour - signed with
initials - 20½ x 13 ins.
(King & Chasemore) **£300**

GERBRAND VAN DEN EECKHOUT -
The Spurning Of The Crown By The
Child Moses In Pharaoh's Palace -
signed and dated - 45½ x 52½in.
(Christie's) **£2,800**

VICTOR EECKHOUT - Studies Of
Arabian Horsemen - signed - oil on
panel - 9½ x 7in.
(Bearnes & Waycotts) **£540 Pair**

WILHELM VON EHRENBERG -
Figures Outside A Palace, in the fore-
ground Groups Of Ladies And Gentlemen
And A Fountain With Statuary - 25¾ x
47½in.
(Sotheby's) **£3,200**

O. EICHINGER - An Old Bavarian
Peasant - signed - on panel - 10¾ x
8¼in.
(Sotheby's) **£300**

EGG - A Rest From Embroidery -
dated '60 - on board - 11¾ x 7½in.
(Sotheby's Belgravia) **£110**

AUGUSTUS LEOPOLD EGG - Portrait
Of An Artist, small half length, Seated
Wearing A Blue Jacket - on board -
18½ x 15½in.
(Christie's) **£100**

SUZANNE EISENDIECK - L'Absinthe -
oil - on canvas - signed and inscribed -
24¼ x 15¼in.
(Sotheby's) **£1,100**

SUZANNE EISENDIECK - Jeune Femme
Au Chapeau De Paille Orne De Coque-
licots - oil - on canvas - signed - 17¾ x
21¼in.
(Sotheby's) **£1,050**

EISMAN-SEMENOWSKY

EMILE EISMAN-SEMENOWSKY - The Flower Arranger; An Eastern Beauty Refuelling A Lamp - both signed and inscribed 'Paris' - on panel - 34 x 10½in.
(Sotheby's) **£1,500 Pair**

F. C. ELLERMAN - View Of A Waterfall With Two Fishermen in the foreground - signed - oil on canvas - 17½ x 13½in.
(Bearnes & Waycotts) **£140**

EDWIN ELLIS - The Beach At Rhos Neigr, Anglesey, With A Fisherman Drying Nets Near A Beached Boat - oil - signed - 29½ x 49in.
(Henry Spencer & Sons) **£330**

CHRISTIAN ELIESON - A Steamer In A Fjord - signed and dated '97 - 17 x 27¼in.
(Sotheby's) **£300**

A. ELMORE - A Gap In The Fence - signed with initials - on panel - 12¼ x 7¼in.
(Sotheby's Belgravia) **£150**

ELSHEIMER, After - The Martyrdom Of Saint Stephen - in copper - 13½ x 11in.
(Christie's) **£2,800**

ADAM ELSHEIMER - Tobias and the Archangel Raphael returning with the Fish - 'The Small Tobit' - on copper - 4½ x 7 ins.
(Christie's) **£15,000**

P. TETAR VAN ELVEN - Algerian Interior With Figures - signed - 10¼ x 13½in.
(J. Francis, T. Jones & Sons) **£40**

P. TETAR VAN ELVEN - Algerian Street Scene - signed - 10¼ x 13½in.
(J. Francis, T. Jones & Sons) **£40**

EMMS - Portrait Of A Dog In A Landscape - 29½ x 37¼in.
(Sotheby's Belgravia) **£22**

JOHN EMMS - Run To Ground - signed - 47½ x 35½in.
(Christie's) **£1,100**

JOHN EMMS - The Young Huntsman -
signed - 19 x 23in.
(Christie's)   **£850**

JOHN EMMS - Taking A Fence - signed
and dated 1903 - on board - A Still Life -
12 x 14¾in.
(Sotheby's Belgravia)   **£200**

JOHANN ENGELA - In The Transvaal -
29 x 39cm.
(Edmiston's)   **£82**

E. E. ENGLAND - Poultry Feeding In A
Barn - oils - 9 x 13in.
(G. A. Key)   **£105 Pair**

E. S. ENGLAND - Studies Of Poultry In A
Farmyard - signed - on board - 9½ x 11½in.
(Morphet & Morphet)   **£110 Pair**

ENGLISH SCHOOL, 18th century - Portrait
Of A Boy Holding A Bow And Arrow, With
Dog in Landscape Background - three-
quarter length - 30 x 25in.
(Woolley & Wallis)   **£195**

ENGLISH SCHOOL, Early 19th century -
A Half-Length Seated Portrait Of A Lady
In A White Dress With Flowers At Her
Breast, And Wearing A Plumed Hat, - oil
on canvas - 29¼ x 24¼in.
(Geering & Colyer)   **£55**

ENGLISH SCHOOL, circa 1641 - Portrait
Of John Evelyn, The Diarist, half-length,
Wearing A Breastplate And Yellow Jerkin,
His Hands Resting On A Helmet, With A
Landscape Beyond - 29 x 24in.
(Christie's)   **£3,000**

ENGLISH SCHOOL, 18th century - Sir
Baptist Hicks - oil on canvas - 1m.26 x
1m.02cm.
(Galerie Moderne)   **£365**

ENGLISH SCHOOL, 18th century - Interior
With Five Figures Around A Spinet -
30 x 40½in.
(Woolley & Wallis)   **£360**

ENGLISH SCHOOL

ENGLISH SCHOOL, Early 19th Century - View Of A Village Shop At Tickhill, Near Doncaster, With Figures in the foreground - oil on canvas - 18 x 25in.
(Bearnes & Waycotts) **£300**

ENGLISH SCHOOL, Mid 19th century - Woolwich from Charlton Pier - on canvas - 20 x 29in.
(King & Chasemore) **£160**

ENGLISH SCHOOL, 19th century - Coastal Shipping Scenes - 20½ x 14¼in.
(D. M. Nesbit & Co.) **£370 Pair**

ENGLISH SCHOOL, mid 19th century - Haddon Hall And The Old Hall, Hardwick, Derbys. - pencil heightened with white - 11½ x 8in.
(Neale & Son) **£8 Pair**

ENGLISH SCHOOL, Early 19th century - 'A Boy Archer With King Charles Spaniel In Landscape' - oil - on canvas - 16 x 12in.
(Butler & Hatch Waterman) **£140**

ENGLISH SCHOOL, 19th century - A Study Of Master Of Foxhounds - oil on canvas - signed - 34¾ x 51in.
(King & Chasemore) **£340**

ENGLISH SCHOOL, 19th century - 'Buckland Bridge, 1839' - A Company Of Soldiers Before A Rural Inn - on canvas - 24 x 36in.
(King & Chasemore) **£550**

ENGLISH SCHOOL, 19th Century - A Gipsy Encampment - signed with monogram - oil on canvas - 18¼ x 24½in.
(Bearnes & Waycotts) **£180**

ENGLISH SCHOOL, 19th century - Landscape With Plough Team - watercolour - 7 x 10in.
(Woolley & Wallis) **£134**

ENGLISH SCHOOL, 19th century - A British Military Garrison In The Far East, With Hill-Top Fort And Parade Ground in the foreground - oil on canvas - 8¾ x 16¼in.
(Geering & Colyer) **£150**

ENGLISH SCHOOL, 19th century - Still Life And A Bird's Nest And Flowers - oil - 12 x 10in.
(Warner, Sheppard & Wade) **£38**

ENGLISH SCHOOL - An Extensive
View Of Plymouth, With A Drover And
Cattle in the foreground And Shipping
Beyond - dated 1800 - 92 x 154cm.
(Phillips) **£2,800**

ENGLISH SCHOOL, 19th century - Still
Lives Of Birds' Nests And Roses On A
Mossy Bank - oil - 7¼ x 9in.
(Warner, Sheppard & Wade) **£28 Pair**

ENGLISH SCHOOL - Portrait Of George
III - oil on canvas - 2m. 35 x 1m. 47cm.
(Galerie Moderne) **£943**

ENGLISH SCHOOL - A Young Woman
With A Greyhound By A Standing Folio -
watercolour heightened with white - 8¼ x
7in.
(Christie's) **£80**

ENGLISH SCHOOL - Portrait Of A
Naval Officer - on board - 8 x 6½in.
(Sotheby's Belgravia) **£40**

ENGLISH SCHOOL - Country Landscape
With Pony And Trap And Figure - oil -
9 x 14in.
(G. A. Key) **£38**

ENGLISH SCHOOL - Portraits Of A
Gentleman Wearing A Brown Coat; the
Lady In A Pink Dress - 29½ x 25½in.
(Woolley & Wallis) **£150 Pair**

ENGLISH SCHOOL, 19th Century - The
Palace of Westminster from across the
Thames; and London Bridge and St Paul's
Cathedral from the Thames - oil on canvas
- 60 x 90 cm
(Henry Spencer & Sons) **£400 Pair**

M. ENSOR - 'Still Life Flowers' - oil -
11½ x 17¾ ins.
(J. Entwistle & Co.) **£20**

MAX ERNST - Frau mit Fleur de Lis -
signed - collage and black chalk - 17¾ x
11½ ins.
(Christie's) **1800 gns.**

MAX ERNST - Trois Figures - signed
twice - signed on the reverse - on
panel - 7 x 4½in.
(Sotheby's) **£9,000**

RUDOLPH ERNST - 'The Favourite' -
signed - on panel - 62 x 49.5cm.
(Phillips) **£3,800**

ERTE

ERTE - Danseuse En Mauve; Danseuse En Rose - gouache - signed - each 13¼ x 9in.
(Sotheby's) **£140 Two**

ANDRIES VAN ERTVELT - French Men-O'-War Bombarding A Town On A River Estuary - 27¾ x 44¼in.
(Christie's) **£1,300**

JACOB VAN ES - A Basket of Apples, Grapes, A Melon, and other fruit on a stone ledge - signed - on panel - 25½ x 34in.
(Christie's) **£4,500**

RICHARD HAMILTON ESSEX - The Interior Of A Georgian Church - watercolour - 6¾ x 4¾in.
(Christie's) **£38**

W. ETTY - Portrait Of A Lady, three-quarter length, Seated On A Sofa, Wearing A White Dress - on panel - 13¾ x 11¾in.
(Sotheby's) **£130**

WILLIAM ETTY - Study Of A Man, small full length - on panel - 28 x 22in.
(Christie's) **£300**

BERNARD EVANS - Hexham, From Fell Side Northumberland - watercolour - signed - 19½ x 26½in.
(King & Chasemore) **£360**

J. EVERS - Vieille Ferme - oil on wood - signed and dated 1933 - 24 x 35cm.
(Galerie Moderne) **£11**

WILLEM EVERSDYCK - A Capriccio Of Classical Ruins, With Rebecca And Eleazer - signed and dated 1632 - on panel - 7¾ x 12in.
(Christie's) **£1,500**

ADRIANUS EVERSEN - A Dutch Street Scene With Figures in the foreground - signed with monogram - on panel - 19 x 15cm.
(Phillips) **£1,200**

ADRIANUS EVERSEN - Figures In The Market Square Of A Dutch Town; And Peasants In A Street With A Cathedral Beyond - both signed - 13½ x 16½in.
(Christie's) **£9,000 Pair**

ADRIANUS EVERSEN - A Winter Street Scene In Amsterdam - signed - on panel - 12½ x 10½in.
(Christie's) **£3,200**

JAN EYCKELBACH - After The Apple Harvest - oil on canvas - signed - 69 x 1m.01cm.
(Galerie Moderne) **£66**

JAN EYCKELBOSCH - Portrait Of A Woman - oil on canvas - signed and dated 1873 - 48 x 40cm.
(Galerie Moderne) **£125**

F

MASTER OF THE FABRIANO ALTARPIECE - The Madonna And Child, half length, behind a stone ledge, the Christ child holding a goldfinch - on gold ground panel - shaped top - 28 x 18½in.
(Christie's) **£5,500**

PIETRO FABRIS - Naples Seen From The West; And A View Of Vesuvius From Naples - 24½ x 51in.
(Sotheby's) **£15,000 Pair**

B. FABRITIUS - The Departure Of The Prodigal Son - 46¼ x 37¾in.
(Sotheby's) **£2,000**

BARENT FABRITIUS - Saint Mary Magdalen, half length - 27½ x 20in.
(Christie's) **£480**

FABRITIUS

B. FABRITIUS - Group Of Agitated
Figures With A Dog - oil - 29 x 24in.
(Graves Son & Pilcher) £270

CAREL FABRITIUS - Portrait of a Man
wearing a white collar and a cloak - signed
and dated 1650 - on panel - oval - 11½ x
9 ins.
(Christie's) £6,500

CARLO FACHINETTI - Tobias And The
Angel - signed - 15¼ x 18in.
(Sotheby's) £120

FAED - Jealousy - bears signature and
date - 11¼ x 9½in.
(Sotheby's Belgravia) £100

JAMES FAED, JNR - Wild Sutherlandshire -
signed - 34½ x 55½in.
(Sotheby's) £350

JOHN FAED - Kitchen Interior With A
Family Group - oil on millboard - 10 x
13in.
(Bearnes & Waycotts) £520

THOMAS FAED - 'The Artist's
Scullery' - oil on canvas - on panel -
13¼ x 9in.
(Bearnes & Waycotts) £130

S. FANGIAMORE - Attentive Admirers -
signed and dated 1897 - inscribed 'Roma'
- 22½ x 17½in.
(Sotheby's) £1,500

JOSEPH FARINGTON - The First
Bridge Over The River Forth - pen
and brown ink, brown wash - inscribed -
7½ x 12in.
(Christie's) £85

DAVID FARQUHARSON - A Glimpse Of
The Tay - signed and dated 1881 -
12¼ x 17¼in.
(Sotheby's) £150

DAVID FARQUHARSON - A Ross-
Shire River With Cattle Watering -
signed and dated 1879 - signed, inscribed
and dated on the reverse - 14½ x 23½in.
(Christie's) £680

DAVID FARQUHARSON - In The
Turnip Field - signed - 19 x 29½in.
(Christie's) £750

DAVID FARQUHARSON - A Rocky
Coastal Landscape, With Figures On
The Shore - signed and dated 1880 -
9½ x 15½in.
(Christie's) £500

JOSEPH FARQUHARSON - A Corner Of
The Rose Garden - signed - 24 x 19¼in.
(Sotheby's) £200

PERICLES FAZZINI - Testa D'Uomo -
pen and ink - signed and dated Roma
1950 - 11 x 8¾in.
(Sotheby's) £80

FRITZ FEIGL - Bei Dem See - pen and
ink and watercolour - Strassenszene -
charcoal, brush and ink - both signed -
5¾ x 7¾in. and 8½ x 11in.
(Sotheby's) £55 Two

G. FELTHAM - Off The Coast - signed -
on board - 5¼ x 11in.
(Sotheby's Belgravia) £22

R. FENSON - Country Scenes - one
signed with initials - millboard - 12 x
24in.
(Bearnes & Waycotts) £170 Pair

SERGE FERAT - Maisons Parmi Des
Arbres - pencil on paper - on board -
signed - 7 x 4½in.
(Sotheby's) £60

FRANZ DE PAULA FERG - Italianate
Landscapes, With Ruined Castles And
Figures - one signed with initial - on
copper - 8¼ x 10½in.
(Christie's) £5,000 Pair

F. DE PAULA FERG - An Extensive
Landscape With Travellers Resting Near
A Classical Ruin - on copper - 10 x 14in.
(Christie's) £750

W. G. FERGUSON - Classical Ruins
With A Monk At Prayer - 41½ x 44in.
(Christie's) £110

J. D. FERGUSSON - Study Of A
Parisian - chalk drawing - 20 x 12cm.
(Edmiston's) £17

J. D. FERGUSSON - A Lady Of Fashion -
33 x 23.5cm.
(Edmiston's) £180

JOHN DUNCAN FERGUSSON -
Parisienne - coloured chalk and wash -
8½ x 6¾in.
(Sotheby's) £170

JOHN DUNCAN FERGUSSON - Flowers
And Pink Box, 1911 - signed - inscribed
Paris and dated 1911 on the reverse -
18 x 14¾in.
(Sotheby's) £450

FERNELEY - Family Group In Landscape,
With Mother Standing Behind Baby On Pony,
With Daughter Holding The Reins -
27 x 35in.
(Phillips) £200

JOHN FERNELEY, JNR - Feeding Ponies -
signed - inscribed 'York' and dated 1819 -
24 x 30in.
(Sotheby's) £320

JOHN FERNELEY, JNR - Officers And Troopers Of The 10th Hussars Parading In An Extensive Landscape, With A Castle, signed and dated 1835 - 18½ x 26½in.
(Christie's) £2,000

JOHN E. FERNELEY, SNR - Captain Hampson's Favourite Chestnut Hunter - signed and dated Melton Mowbray, 1837 - 27 x 35½in.
(Christie's) £2,000

JOHN E. FERNELEY, SNR - The Game Larder - 30 x 24in.
(Christie's) £380

JOHN E. FERNELEY, SNR - Portrait Of H. Wormald, Of Sawley Hall, Ripon, Yorkshire, Standing, Small Full Length In Highland Dress, By A Dead Stag, In A Landscape - 24½ x 19in.
(Christie's) £400

LUIGI FERRAZZI - Decorating a Tabernacle In Lower Stiria - signed and dated 1887 - 49 x 19¼in.
(Christie's) £1,000

JAMES FERRIER - A Scottish River Valley - signed and dated 1872 - 12 x 21in.
(Sotheby's Belgravia) **£50**

WALTER FIELD - Henley Regatta - signed and dated 1884 - 55 x 95in.
(Sotheby's Belgravia) **£8,000**

DOMENICO FETTI, After - Saint Margaret victorious over Sin - on panel - 8¾ x 6¼ ins.
(Christie's) **£4,000**

D. FIASELLA - The Rest On The Flight Into Egypt - 79 x 58½in.
(Christie's) **£1,600**

A. V. COPLEY FIELDING - Shipping In A Gale - bears signature - 7 x 10in.
(Sotheby's) **£200**

ANTHONY VANDYKE COPLEY FIELDING - On The Downs - signed - watercolour - 6 x 8¾in.
(Christie's) **£550**

EUGENE FICHEL - The Toast - signed and dated 1863 - on panel - 8½ x 6¼in.
(Christie's) **£1,400**

G. FIELDING - A Sheltered Glade - signed - inscribed on the reverse - 29½ x 24½in.
(Sotheby's Belgravia) **£160**

G. FIELDING - A Woodland Path -
signed - 29½ x 24in.
(Sotheby's Belgravia)   **£180**

G. FIELDING - Billingsgate 5 a.m. -
signed - inscribed on the stretcher -
13½ x 9½in.
(Sotheby's Belgravia)   **£26**

LADY KATHERINE FIELDING -
Portraits Of Girls, head and shoulders -
one heightened with white - oval -
10 x 8¼in.
(Sotheby's Belgravia)   **£30 Four**

PEDRO FIGARI - Introduction - oil -
on board - signed - titled on the reverse -
12¾ x 18¾in.
(Sotheby's)   **£800**

FILDES - Portrait Of A Girl Seated,
three-quarter length - 35½ x 27½in.
(Sotheby's Belgravia)   **£40**

FRANCIS OLIVER FINCH - The Flight
Into Egypt - pencil and watercolour -
6¼ x 8¾in.
(Christie's)   **£28**

A. H. FINDLEY - Belgrave Hall And Church -
signed - watercolour - 7 x 10¾in.
(Warner, Sheppard & Wade)   **£30**

LEONOR FINI - Le Narcisse
Incomparable - 67 x 43¼in.
(Sotheby's)   **£13,000**

HANS FINK - The Antiquarian's
Study - signed - on panel - 11½ x 7¾in.
(Sotheby's)   **£250**

HERBERT JOHN FINN - Radcliffe Camera And All Souls, Oxford - signed and dated 1899 - 27½ x 20in.
(Sotheby's Belgravia)   **£55**

Circle of **ANDREA BONAIUTI called ANDREA DA FIRENZE** - The Madonna and Child - on gold ground panel - shaped top - 31 x 19¾in.
(Christie's)   **£3,800**

BENNO JOACHIM THEODOR FISCHER - Portrait Of A Gentleman, half length, Seated, Wearing A Black Suit And White Waistcoat - signed and dated (I)848 - 30½ x 24½in.
(Sotheby's)   **£250**

FISCHEZl - News From The Stock Exchange - signed and dated 1878 - 38½ x 28½in.
(Sotheby's)   **£200**

JONATHAN FISHER - An Extensive Landscape In Ireland, With Herdsmen And Cattle in the foreground - 21½ x 40½in.
(Christie's)   **£900**

MARK FISHER - "Returning Home" - signed - on canvas - 18½ x 23¾in.
(Charles R. Phillips)   **£175**

THOMAS FISHER - Llanbadarn Vawr, Near Aberystwyth - inscribed - water-colour - 3¼ x 4½in.
(Christie's)   **£40 Two**

WILLIAM MARK FISHER - Cattle At Pasture - 20 x 29in.
(Sotheby's Belgravia)   **£500**

WILLIAM MARK FISHER - Cattle In A Shady Wood - signed - 14 x 20¼in.
(Sotheby's Belgravia)   **£320**

JOHN ANSTER FITZGERALD - Sweet Violets - signed - inscribed on the reverse - 22½ x 17¼in.
(Sotheby's Belgravia)   **£420**

FITZWALTER-GRACE

ALFRED FITZWALTER-GRACE -
Bringing In The Cows, Evening - signed -
on board - 9¼ x 12¾in.
(Sotheby's Belgravia) £55

FRANCOIS FLAMENG - An Elegant Lady
In A White Dress with the coast beyond -
signed and inscribed - 45¾ x 19in.
(Christie's) £1,300

EUGENE NAPOLEON FLANDIN - The
Royal Mosque In Isfahan - signed and
inscribed Isfahan - 49½ x 79in.
(Christie's) £21,000

J. FLEMING - Loch scene, with steam
yacht, other vessels and country house
beyond - 44 x 62 ins.
(Christie's, S. Kensington) £800

FLEMISH SCHOOL, 1600 - An Alpine
Town with a bridge over a rocky river -
signed with initials H.S. and dated 1600 -
on panel - 10 x 14in.
(Christie's) £3,200

FLEMISH SCHOOL, 17th century -
Portrait Of Antoine Grandvelle - oil on
canvas - 69 x 54cm.
(Galerie Moderne) £230

FLEMISH SCHOOL, 18th century - The Hunting Trophy - oil on canvas - 46 x 39cm.
(Galerie Moderne) **£830**

FLEMISH SCHOOL, 18th century - A Busy Scene - on wood - 19 x 25cm.
(Galerie Moderne) **£250**

FLEMISH SCHOOL, 18th Century - A Still Life Of Flowers, Including Roses, Blue Convolvulus, And Peonies - 38 x 31in.
(Sotheby's) **£800**

FLEMISH SCHOOL, 18th Century - A River Landscape, Figures Resting Near A Village - 13½ x 11½in.
(Sotheby's) **£260**

FLEMISH SCHOOL - Venus Rising From The Waves - copper panel - oval - 5¼ x 7¼in.
(Bearnes & Waycotts) **£170**

FLEMISH SCHOOL - The Madonna And Child Adored By Angels, In A Rocky Landscape - on panel - 31.5 x 33cm.
(Phillips) **£3,500**

FLEMISH SCHOOL - Portrait Of A Prelate - oil on canvas - 92 x 71cm.
(Galerie Moderne) **£102**

FLEMISH SCHOOL, 18th century - Man With A Frilled Collar - oil on canvas - 89 x 71cm.
(Galerie Moderne) **£157**

FLEMISH SCHOOL, Circa 1600 - The Feast Of Dives, Lazarus To The Left - on panel - 19 x 25in.
(Sotheby's) **£1,250**

FLEMISH SCHOOL, circa 1600 - The Discovery Of Erichthonius By The Daughters Of Cecrops - 55 x 63in.
(Christie's) **£2,800**

EDWIN FLETCHER - St. Paul's from the Thames - signed, inscribed on the reverse 20 x 30 ins.
(Christie's, S. Kensington) **£150**

J. V. DE FLEURY - A Continental Street Scene - heightened with white - signed and dated 1869 - 12¾ x 19½in.
(Sotheby's Belgravia) **£60**

GOVAERT FLINCK - Portrait of a Lady wearing a black dress and white collar and cuffs - signed - 29 x 24 ins.
(Christie's)　　　　　**£2,200**

SIR WILLIAM RUSSELL FLINT - Summer Sprawl - coloured chalks - signed - 8 x 13½in.
(Sotheby's)　　　　　**£720**

SIR WILLIAM RUSSELL FLINT - A Sunburned Pandora - watercolours - signed, signed again and inscribed on reverse of frame - 9½ x 14¼in.
(Phillips)　　　　　**£2,850**

SIR WILLIAM RUSSELL FLINT - Lucy, Caroline And Dorothy - signed - 19 x 26in.
(Sotheby's)　　　　　**£1,000**

SIR WILLIAM RUSSELL FLINT - Two Female Nudes - brown and black crayon - signed - 8 x 11¼in.
(Woolley & Wallis)　　　　　**£290**

SIR WILLIAM RUSSELL FLINT - Cecilia Reclining - signed, signed again and inscribed on reverse of frame - watercolours - 10¾ x 15in.
(Phillips)　　　　　**£3,500**

SIR WILLIAM RUSSELL FLINT - Early Morning, Loch Earn - watercolour - 26 x 33cm.
(Edmiston's)　　　　　**£340**

SIR WILLIAM RUSSELL FLINT - On The Beach - signed - 13 x 19in.
(Sotheby's) £750

SIR WILLIAM RUSSELL FLINT - Study Of A Reclining Nude - watercolour - 9¾ x 14½in.
(Bonham's) £2,300

FLORENTINE SCHOOL, 17th Century - David Playing The Harp, A Wooded Landscape Beyond - 64 x 38in.
(Sotheby's) £360

ENRICO FOGGATI - Capriccio Views Of Venice - both signed - 14½ x 29¾in.
(Sotheby's) £450 **Pair**

H. FOLEY - On The Lagoon, Venice - signed - 5½ x 15½in.
(Sotheby's Belgravia) £75

SCHOOL OF FONTAINEBLEAU, 16th Century - Cupid Asleep Surrounded By Putti - on panel - 26¼ x 37½in.
(Sotheby's) £2,500

LEO FONTAN - Devant La Glace - pencil and watercolour - heightened with white gouache - signed - 19 x 13in.
(Sotheby's) £130

LAVINIA FONTANA - The Pieta With Numerous Mourning Angels - 68 x 133in.
(Christie's) £2,200

FRANCESCO FONTEBASSO - Judith With The Head Of Holofernes - 27 x 35in.
(Christie's) £3,800

FRANCESCO FONTEBASSO - Alexander The Great And His Physician Philip - shaped canvas - 168 x 134.5cm.
(Phillips) £4,000

FRANCESCO FONTEBASSO - Alexander The Great And His Physician Philip - shaped canvas - 66 x 53in.
(Christie's) **£3,800**

FRANCESCO FONTEBASSO - Sophonisba About To Drink The Poisoned Cup - shaped canvas - 66½ x 99½in.
(Christie's) **£7,500**

J. B. BELIN DE FONTENAY - Roses, Poppies, Carnations, An Iris, Fritillaries And Other Flowers In A Kakiemon Bowl On A Ledge - 24 x 20in.
(Christie's) **£5,000**

A. FONTVILLE - Between the Showers, Scotland - signed and signed and inscribed on the reverse - 24½ x 20 ins.
(Woolley & Wallis) **£30**

JEAN-LOUIS FORAIN - Nude drying herself - oil on linen - 73 x 61 cm.
(Auktionshaus am Neumarkt) **£6,667**

JEAN-LOUIS FORAIN - Le Lit matrimonial - pencil, pen and indian ink - 11½ x 18½ ins.
(Sotheby's) **£450**

JEAN-LOUIS FORAIN - Chez l'Atelier Du Sculpteur - pen, brush and brown ink and blue wash - signed - 10½ x 16in.
(Sotheby's) **£480**

JEAN-LOUIS FORAIN - Le Juge Chez Le Redacteur - charcoal and pen and indian ink - signed and inscribed - 10¾ x 13in.
(Sotheby's) **£80**

STANHOPE ALEXANDER FORBES - Portrait of a gentleman with his dog and a shotgun - signed and dated 1880 - oil on canvas - 35½ x 27½ ins.
(Bearnes & Waycotts) **£150**

J. D. FORD - Figure On A Path In A Summer Landscape - oil - signed - 39.5 x 49.5cm.
(Phillips in Scotland) **£20**

CHARLES FORSTER, JNR - Pet Goat -
38 x 42½in.
(Sotheby's Belgravia) £380

L FORTE - A Basket Of Grapes, A
Pot Of Flowers And Vegetables On A
Stone Ledge - 39½ x 56in.
(Christie's) £2,500

DE LA FOSSE - A Wooded Landscape,
Nymphs And Putti in the foreground,
Mountains in the distance - 21 x 26in.
(Sotheby's) £180

B. FOSTER - Children Gathering Wild
Flowers - signed - 5¾ x 8½in.
(Buckell & Ballard) £75

BIRKET FOSTER - Children Resting By A
Stile - bears monogram - watercolour -
7 x 9¾in.
(Woolley & Wallis) £150

DERYCK FOSTER - Sailing Dinghies -
all signed - on board - 11 x 15in.
(Sotheby's Belgravia) £20 Three

H. FOSTER - Down Channel, Sailing
Vessels And Steam Ship - watercolour -
7 x 14in.
(G. A. Key) £16

M. B. FOSTER - Shipping Off The Coast -
heightened with bodycolour - 6½ x 9¼in.
(Sotheby's Belgravia) £25

M. B. FOSTER - Crossing The Brook;
Taking A Rest - both heightened with
bodycolour - bears monograms - 9½ x
16½in.
(Sotheby's Belgravia) £110 Pair

MYLES BIRKET FOSTER - Washing
Day - pencil and watercolour heightened
with white - signed with monogram and
inscribed - 6 x 4¾in.
(Christie's) £140

HENRY JUSTICE FORD - "You'll Have To
Make Me Your Wife" said the Elf Maiden -
watercolour - signed and dated 1906 -
12 x 7in
(King & Chasemore) £260 Pair

165

MYLES BIRKET FOSTER - Dedham -
impressed with artist's stamp - on
panel - 9½ x 13½in.
(Sotheby's Belgravia) **£650**

MYLES BIRKET FOSTER - Going For
A Ride - heightened with bodycolour
- signed with monogram - 11½ x 16in.
(Sotheby's Belgravia) **£1,500**

MYLES BIRKET FOSTER - A Young
Shepherd By Farm Buildings - heightened
with bodycolour - signed with monogram
- 6 x 9¼in.
(Sotheby's Belgravia) **£250**

MYLES BIRKET FOSTER - The Ferry -
heightened with bodycolour - signed with
monogram - 9½ x 13½in.
(Sotheby's Belgravia) **£650**

MYLES BIRKET FOSTER - The Broken
Egg - heightened with bodycolour -
signed with monogram - 6 x 8¼in.
(Sotheby's Belgravia) **£350**

MYLES BIRKET FOSTER - Children
Playing Near A Croft - signed with
monogram - watercolour - 6 x 8in.
(Bonham's) **£340**

TSUGUHARU FOUJITA - Diane -
signed and dated 1948 - also signed in
Japanese - 20¾ x 31½in.
(Sotheby's) **£28,000**

ELIZABETH FOUNTAIN - Loch Katrine
With Boats And Figures - oil - 20 x 26in.
(G. A. Key) **£60**

THEODORE FOURMOIS - Le Depart
Du Troupeau - oil on canvas - signed -
43 x 60cm.
(Galerie Moderne) **£204**

THEODORE FOURMOIS - Landscape - on wood - signed - 29 x 29cm.
(Galerie Moderne) **£36**

WILLIAM FOWLER - The Village Ford - signed and dated 1841 - 39 x 55in.
(Sotheby's Belgravia) **£2,800**

E. M. FOX - A Chestnut Hunter By A Cottage - signed and dated 1846 - 24½ x 29½in.
(Christie's) **£230**

GEORGE FOX - 'The Winner Of The Stakes' And 'Cleaned Out' - signed - oil on panel - 7¾ x 5½in. and 8¼ x 8½in.
(Bearnes & Waycotts) **£240 Two**

HENRY CHARLES FOX - Cattle Watering; Workhorses Returning - both heightened with bodycolour - signed and dated 1917 - 14 x 20½in.
(Sotheby's Belgravia) **£130 Pair**

HENRY CHARLES FOX - Stapleford, Hertfordshire - heightened with bodycolour - signed, inscribed and dated 1888 - 14 x 20½in.
(Sotheby's Belgravia) **£55**

A. FOXCROFT - The Cavalier's Letter - signed - 24¼ x 29¼in.
(Sotheby's Belgravia) **£120**

FRACANZANO - Joseph Interpreting The Dreams Of Two Egyptian Prisoners - 21¼ x 46¼in.
(Sotheby's) **£440**

JEAN HONORE FRAGONARD - Portrait Of Honore-Leopold German Maubert, half length, in a green coat and broad-brimmed hat, holding the barrel of a gun - 25 x 20½in.
(Christie's) **£16,000**

FRANCOIS LOUIS THOMAS FRANCIA - A Cutter And Other Shipping In Heavy Seas - pencil and watercolour - 3¾ x 6½in.
(Christie's) **£500**

CONSTANTIJN FRANCKEN - William III At The Siege Of Namur, 1695, in the foreground William III On A Rearing Horse Among A Large Group Of Officers - signed - 56½ x 175¾in.
(Sotheby's) **£5,500**

F. FRANCKEN - The Feast Of Esther: In The Centre A Large Banquet Presided Over By The Queen, in the foreground an Angel - on metal - 18½ x 23¼in.
(Sotheby's) **£480**

FRANS FRANCKEN, THE YOUNGER -
The Story Of Esther - on copper - 19 x 25in.
(Christie's) **£3,200**

FRANS FRANCKEN, THE YOUNGER -
Christ In The House Of Martha And Mary - signed - on panel - 22 x 30in.
(Christie's) **£4,000**

FRANS FRANCKEN, THE YOUNGER -
David And Abigail - on copper - 19 x 25in.
(Christie's) **£4,000**

FRANS FRANCKEN, THE YOUNGER -
Death And The Miser - bears signature - on panel - 13 x 10in.
(Christie's) **£2,400**

FRANS FRANCKEN THE YOUNGER -
King Solomon Worshipping False Gods - signed - on panel - 28½ x 22in.
(Christie's) **£1,400**

L. FRANK - The Undergrowth - oil on canvas - signed - 46 x 32cm.
(Galerie Moderne) **£40**

BENJAMIN FRANKS - A Yugoslavian Scene At Interlaken - watercolour - 11 x 15in.
(G. A. Key) **£24**

D. FRANS - Cows At Pasture - cartoon - signed - 40 x 50cm.
(Galerie Moderne) **£18**

FRASER - Wallace Monument - 25 x 34cm.
(Edmiston's) **£16**

ALEXANDER FRASER - Among The Welsh Hills - signed with initials - inscribed on the reverse - 11¾ x 16¼in.
(Sotheby's Belgravia) **£50**

ALEXANDER FRASER - Neidpath
Castle On The Tweed - 62 x 85cm.
(Edmiston's) **£240**

JOHN FRASER - Shipping In Open Seas -
signed - on panel - 9½ x 13½in.
(Sotheby's Belgravia) **£160**

ROBERT W. FRASER - On The Ouse,
Bromham - heightened with bodycolour - signed and dated '82 - 18 x
30in.
(Sotheby's Belgravia) **£85**

ANDRE FRAYE - La Derniere Cartouche - oil on canvas - signed -
49 x 64cm.
(Galerie Moderne) **£33**

WILLIAM MILLER FRAZER - Collecting
the day's catch - signed - 21 x 29 ins.
(Sotheby's) **£280**

WILLIAM MILLER FRAZER - Sheep On A
Sunlit Lane - signed and dated '95 -
15½ x 23½in.
(Sotheby's) **£180**

WILLIAM MILLER FRAZER - Whitkirk -
signed - inscribed on the stretcher -
24½ x 29½in.
(Sotheby's) **£160**

WILLIAM MILLER FRAZER - Kings Lynn,
Norfolk - signed - 11½ x 17½in.
(Sotheby's) **£160**

WILLIAM MILLER FRAZER - Old woman
driving cows along a wooded road - signed
and dated 1902 - 24 x 34 ins.
(Christie's, S. Kensington) **£180**

JAMES EDWARD FREEMAN - An
Italian Girl With Her Dog - signed -
48½ x 36½in.
(Sotheby's) **£350**

W. P. B. FREEMAN - Burgh St. Peters,
Nr. Beccles - watercolour - 10 x 17in.
(G. A. Key) **£170**

FRENCH SCHOOL

FRENCH SCHOOL, 17th century -
Portrait Of A Man - oil on canvas -
74 x 59cm.
(Galerie Moderne) **£300**

FRENCH SCHOOL, 18th century - A
Peasant Family in an interior - 23½ x 29in.
(Christie's) **£1,000**

FRENCH SCHOOL - Catherine - oil -
80 x 65cm.
(Galerie Moderne) **£660**

FRENCH SCHOOL, 18th century -
Portrait Of A Lady - oil on canvas -
77 x 61cm.
(Galerie Moderne) **£141**

FRENCH SCHOOL, 18th century -
Portrait Of A Woman - oil on canvas -
73 x 59cm.
(Galerie Moderne) **£94**

FRENCH SCHOOL, 16th Century -
Mutius Curtius Scaevola Before King
Porsenna, Holding His Right Hand Over
The Fire - on panel - 38 x 49in.
(Sotheby's)   **£2,200**

FRENCH SCHOOL, 18th century -
Woman Drinking From A Goblet - oil on
canvas - 46 x 37cm.
(Galerie Moderne)   **£332**

FRENCH SCHOOL, 18th century -
Diane, The Huntress - oil on canvas -
1m.05 x 84cm.
(Galerie Moderne)   **£366**

FRENCH SCHOOL, 18th century -
Diane, Bacchus & Nymphs - oil on
canvas - 1m.24 x 95cm.
(Galerie Moderne)   **£830**

**FRENCH SCHOOL, Second Quarter Of
The 17th Century -** Portrait Of Two Royal
Children, Both Wearing The Order Of The
Saint-Esprit - 45¼ x 37¾in.
(Sotheby's)   **£4,400**

FRENCH SCHOOL - King David Playing
The Harp, With Cherubs, Landscape In
Left Distance - 86 x 74cm.
(Edmiston's)   **£300**

FRIEND

DONALD FRIEND - Three Nude Negro Boys - signed and dated '53 - watercolour - 19 x 14¼in.
(Woolley & Wallis) £190

HOLLAND FRINGHAM - A Woodland Scene - heightened with bodycolour - signed with monogram - 12¾ x 9½in.
(Sotheby's Belgravia) £30

GEORGE ARTHUR FRIPP - A Highland Waterfall - watercolour heightened with white - signed and dated 1847 - 22¾ x 39¼in.
(Christie's) £140

W. FRISTON - Cattle Watering By A Cottage - signed - 9½ x 13½in.
(Sotheby's Belgravia) £100

WILLIAM POWELL FRITH - A Scene From The Vicar Of Wakefield - signed and dated 1868 - 18½ x 14in.
(Christie's) £1,600

WILLIAM POWELL FRITH - Lovers - paper laid on board - 8¼ x 7in.
(Sotheby's Belgravia) £550

WILLIAM POWELL FRITH - Sterne's Maria - signed and dated 1868 - 34½ x 27¼in.
(Sotheby's Belgravia) £1,900

WILLIAM POWELL FRITH - Lovers At A Style - paper on board - 8 x 5½in.
(Christie's) £120

WILLIAM POWELL FRITH - The Forester's Daughter, With A Sick Fawn - signed - 22 x 17½in.
(Christie's) £420

W. E. FROST - A Fairy And A Child In A Wooded Landscape - on panel - 5 x 4in.
(Christie's) £50

J. FULLEYLOVE - North Wales Landscape With Shepherd And Sheep - signed - oils on board - 9 x 15in.
(Staniland's) £110

JOHN FULLEYLOVE - From The Ring Given To Venus In 'The Earthly Paradise' - William Morris - heightened with bodycolour - signed and dated 1871 - 24 x 36in.
(Sotheby's Belgravia) **£150**

DAVID FULTON - Tending Cattle, Evening - signed - 15½ x 17½in.
(Sotheby's) **£180**

SAM FULTON - Study Of Two Dogs - oil - 20 x 24in.
(Thomas Love & Sons Ltd) **£90**

HENRY FUSELI - Daniel - pen and brown ink, brown wash - on the reverse of a letter to the artist - 8½ x 5in.
(Christie's) **£850**

J. FYFE - Country Scenes With Roses And Figures - 23 x 29in and 25 x 30in.
(Edmiston's) **£170 Two**

TADDEO GADDI - St. Dominic Holding A Book With A Red Cover Decorated With Gold And A Branch Of Lilies - gold ground - on panel - 8½ x 6in.
(Sotheby's) **£3,500**

GASPARE GABRIELLI - The Forum, Rome - signed with initials and dated Roma 1827 - 30 x 39½in.
(Christie's) **£1,800**

ADRIAEN GAEL - Shadrach, Mesach And Abednego In The Fiery Furnace - signed - on panel - 22½ x 32½in.
(Christie's) **£550**

GAINSBOROUGH, After - Portrait Of Sir Paul Pechell, 1st Bt. Of Paglesham, Essex, 10th Baron de la Boyssonade Et St. Cranberre - inscribed - 30 x 25in.
(Sotheby's) **£70**

THOMAS GAINSBOROUGH - A Landscape With A Clump Of Trees - black chalk, grey wash heightened with white on pale green paper - 5¾ x 7½in.
(Christie's) **£220**

THOMAS GAINSBOROUGH - Portrait Of A Gentleman, Apparently Captain John Simcoe R.N., Of Wolford, Honiton, Wearing A Naval Uniform - half length - 29 x 24in.
(Christie's) **£2,500**

THOMAS GAINSBOROUGH - Portrait Of Lady Blackstone In A Blue Dress - half length - 29 x 24½in.
(Christie's) **£6,000**

THOMAS GAINSBOROUGH - Oak Trees By A Lane - black chalk - 6 x 7½in.
(Christie's) **£450**

THOMAS GAINSBOROUGH - Two Cows By A Wood And Rustic Lovers in the foreground - 25 x 30in.
(Christie's) **£11,500**

THOMAS GAINSBOROUGH - Portrait Of James, Viscount Maitland, Later Earl Of Lauderdale - oval - 28 x 23in.
(Christie's) **£6,500**

THOMAS GAINSBOROUGH - Portrait Of William Lowndes Stone - inscribed - 49½ x 39½in.
(Christie's) **£20,000**

T. GAINSBOROUGH - A woodland
scene with figures beside a pool - oil
on canvas - 10 x 12 ins.
(King & Chasemore)   **£320**

GAISSER - A Scholar Reading A Letter -
23½ x 19⅓in.
(Sotheby's)   **£300**

WILLIAM GALE - 'Nazareth Fig
Seller' - signed with monogram - 62 x
30cm.
(Phillips)   **£430**

FRANCISCO GALLEGO - The Lamen-
tation - on panel - 33 x 22in.
(Christie's)   **£9,000**

ROBERT GALLON - A Rocky Coastal
Landscape - signed - 19½ x 29½in.
(Christie's)   **£60**

ROBERT GALLON - A River Landscape - signed and dated '75 - 23½ x
39½in.
(Sotheby's Belgravia)   **£1,600**

GALVEN - Study Of An Old Man And A
Glass Of Wine - oil - signed - 42.5 x 35cm.
(Phillips in Scotland)   **£34**

GIUSEPPE GAMBARINI - A Peasant Family
In A Landscape - 25½ x 18½in.
(Christie's)   **£2,200**

GIUSEPPE GAMBARINI - A Group Of
Washerwomen - 25½ x 18½in.
(Christie's)   **£1,700**

GAMBOGI

EMILE GAMBOGI - Reading In The Garden; The Scene Of The Carnation - both signed - one on panel - 18 x 15in.
(Sotheby's) **£400 Pair**

H. GAMLEY - Dordrecht - signed with monogram and inscribed on the reverse - 13½ x 9½in.
(Sotheby's) **£35**

ANTONIO GANDINI - Sheet of Figure Studies - pen and brown ink - signed 'Gandini' (recto); and a drawing of later date of a girl dancing (verso) - 97 x 24.5 cm.
(Sotheby's) **£90**

YVES GANNE - Nature Morte Aux Fruits - oil - on canvas - signed and dated '61 - signed - titled - dated '61 on the reverse - 23½ x 28½in.
(Sotheby's) **£100**

EDWIN GANZ - The Hunter - oil on canvas - signed - 54 x 40cm.
(Galerie Moderne) **£18**

WILLIAM FRASER GARDEN - Hemingford Mill, Hampshire - heightened with bodycolour - signed and dated '01 - 7¾ x 11in.
(Sotheby's Belgravia) **£190**

WILLIAM FRASER GARDEN - Watery Shadows - signed and dated '01 - 5½ x 7¾in.
(Sotheby's Belgravia) **£240**

MASTER OF THE GARDNER ANNUNCIATION - The Madonna and Child - inscribed with coat-of-arms - on gold ground panel - 17 x 10in.
(Christie's) **£4,000**

DANIEL GARDNER - Portrait Of Charles Blomfield Of Bury-St. Edmunds, bust length - pastel and bodycolour - oval - 10 x 8in.
(Christie's) **£400**

H. GARLAND - Highland Cattle
Crossing A Bridge - signed - 13½ x 20½in.
(Buckell & Ballard) **£82.50**

HENRY GARLAND - In The Highlands -
signed and dated 1879 - 19½ x 29½in.
(Sotheby's Belgravia) **£260**

FREDERICK GARNER - Donkey
Rides - signed and dated 1900 - 23¾ x
36in.
(Sotheby's Belgravia) **£220**

DAVID GARNIER - Costume Militaire -
pencil, brush and indian ink and brown
wash - 12½ x 7in.
(Sotheby's) **£30**

L. GAROT - Undergrowth - oil on
canvas - signed - 50 x 40cm.
(Galerie Moderne) **£50**

L. GARZI - The Adoration Of The
Golden Calf, Moses Destroying The
Commandments Above To The Right -
40¼ x 54½in.
(Sotheby's) **£300**

Circle of **LUCAS GASSEL** - The Pieta with
scenes from the Passion, and a capriccio
view of Jerusalem set in a mountainous
landscape beyond - 21½ x 33½in.
(Christie's) **£9,000**

HENRY GASTINEAU - A Fortified
Town In Germany - pencil and water-
colour - 10½ x 17¾in.
(Christie's) **£55**

HENRY G. GASTINEAU - A Sketch Of
Edinburgh Castle From The Grass Market -
signed - inscribed and dated 1821 -
12½ x 17½in.
(Sotheby's) **£190**

L. GATTI - Dante with a Young Messenger -
signed and dated 1855 - on the reverse four
portraits of Raphael, Del Sarto,
Michaelangelo and Leonardo mounted in a
Florentine frame - 31½ x 24 ins.
(Sotheby's) **£340**

PAUL GAUGIN - Ferme En Bretagne -
signed and dated '86 - 29 x 42in.
(Sotheby's) **£44,000**

DAVID GAULD - "Study Of Three Calves
In A Landscape" - oil - 30 x 40in.
(Thomas Love & Sons Ltd) **£560**

DAVID GAULD - Cattle In The Marshes -
signed - 23½ x 35½in.
(Sotheby's) **£420**

DAVID GAULD - Female Musicians -
colour sketch - 51 x 41cm.
(Edmiston's) **£350**

GAVARNI

PAUL GAVARNI - Jeune Femme Au Bord De l'Eau - pen and ink and water-colour on paper - on board - signed - 9¾ x 6in.
(Sotheby's) **£300**

WALTER GAY - A Young Lady Seated In A Parkland Reading To An Elderly Gentleman - signed - inscribed and dated 1880 - oil on panel - 15½ x 12½in.
(Bonham's) **£480**

DE'GECHY - 'The James Baines' At Anchor Off Seaside Town - oil - 34 x 35in.
(G. A. Key) **£195**

W. VAN GEEST - Portrait Of An Old Woman, Seated, three-quarter length, In Black Fur-Lined Dress, White Ruff And Head Dress, Holding Spectacles In Her Right Hand And A Book In Her Left - bears inscription and date 1619 - 42½ x 23in.
(Christie's) **£420**

WILLI GEIGER - Zeit Und Augenblick - pen and brush and indian ink on paper - signed - titled - 13 x 10¼in.
(Sotheby's) **£180**

WILLY GEIGER - Landschaft Mit Kaktus - oil - on canvas - signed and dated Teneriffe '25 - 24 x 27¼in.
(Sotheby's) **£380**

AERT DE GELDER - An Old Woman Plucking A Duck Beside A Table On Which Are A Bird Of Paradise And, On A Wooden Box Partly Covered By A Cloth, A Snipe; A Partridge And Another Bird Suspended On The Wall Behind - on panel - 39 x 28¾in.
(Sotheby's) **£3,000**

G. GELDORP - Portrait Of A Gentleman, three-quarter length, In A Black Coat And White Ruff, Standing By A Table - 40 x 30½in.
(Christie's) **£950**

GENOESE SCHOOL, 17th Century - Two Pigeons - 21 x 24in.
(Sotheby's) **£340**

GENOESE SCHOOL, 17th century - Portrait Of Pope Innocent X, half length, seated, his right hand raised in benediction - 33½ x 27½in.
(Christie's) **£1,300**

W. PETTITT GEORGE - Villa Lodge, Evening, Cromach Water, Cumberland - signed - 17½ x 29½in.
(Sotheby's Belgravia) **£80**

LUCIEN GERARD - Portrait Of A Woman - oil on wood - signed - 24 x 19cm.
(Galerie Moderne) **£40**

LUCIEN GERARD - Le Repos Du Chasseur - oil on wood - signed - 27 x 35cm.
(Galerie Moderne) **£251**

GERMAN SCHOOL - River Landscape, Figures Resting On A Bank in the foreground, Mountains in the distance - dated 1720 - 11½ x 13½in.
(Sotheby's) **£1,150 Pair**

GERMAN SCHOOL, Circa 1850 - Tending Geese; The Nature Lesson - both on panel - each 7¾ x 6½in.
(Sotheby's) **£220 Pair**

GERMAN SCHOOL - The Martyred Saint Sebastion - on panel - dated 1800 - 10½ x 8in.
(Sotheby's) **£120**

GERMAN SCHOOL, 19th Century - Philipp Melanchton and other figures seated around a table with books, papers and an hour glass - signed with monogram and dated 1853 - oil on panel - 14 x 18 ins.
(Bearnes & Waycotts) **£500**

GERMAN PROVINCIAL SCHOOL, circa 1845 - Portrait Of Emile Gammelien, Born Hamburg 1840, Riding A Toy Horse - 34 x 24½in.
(Sotheby's) **£750**

MATTHIAS GERUNG - The Martyrdom Of St. Margaret - on panel - 28¾ x 20¼in.
(Sotheby's) **£4,500**

PAUL JEAN GERVAIS - A Reclining Nude - signed - 16 x 25in.
(Sotheby's) **£300**

P. L. GHEZZI - The Procession Of Pope Benedict XIII To The Lateran Council, 1725 - 47 x 66½in.
(Christie's) **£10,000**

GHIKA - Landscape - oil - on canvas - signed and dated '63 - inscribed A Flanc De Coteau and dated 1963 on the reverse - 28¼ x 19¾in.
(Sotheby's) **£850**

GHISOLFI - Southern Harbour Scenes, With Figures Unloading Boats Near Ruined Buildings in the foregfound, Ships At Anchor Beyond - 19¼ x 20¼in.
(Sotheby's) **£1,000 Pair**

GIANNI - An Old Couple And Two Young Spectators - water colours - signed - 16½ x 11¾in.
(John H. Raby & Son) **£160 Pair**

M. GIANNI - Bay Of Naples - gouache - bears signature - 12½ x 19½in.
(Sotheby's) **£10**

C. GIAQUINTO - The Adoration Of The Shepherds - 24½ x 12in.
(Christie's) **£1,500**

T. H. GIBB - On The Moor; Rest - both signed - inscribed on reverse - each 13½ x 20½in.
(Sotheby's Belgravia) **£60 Pair**

W. GIBBONS - The Last Sailing Barge Race From Plymouth Sound - signed and dated 1879 - oil on canvas - 16 x 29½in.
(Bearnes & Waycotts) **£880**

W. A. GIBSON - Katwyk Beach - on panel - 19 x 24cm.
(Edmiston's) **£165**

W. A. GIBSON - A Windy Day - bears two signatures - on panel - 7¾ x 10¼in.
(Sotheby's Belgravia) **£60**

R. GIL - Wooded Landscape And River - 72 x 92cm.
(Edmiston's) **£22**

ARTHUR GILBERT - A Hazy Morning In The Meadows Above Windsor - 25½ x 39½in.
(Christie's) **£450**

ALBERT THOMAS JARVIS GILBERT - Feeding Doves - signed - on board 13¼ x 9½in.
(Sotheby's Belgravia) **£160**

A. GILBERT - 'Chepstow Castle On The Wye' - oil - 9½ x 15¼in.
(J. Entwistle & Co.) **£160**

SIR J. GILBERT - Sir Roger De Coverley And The Spectator - 9¾ x 15½in.
(Sotheby's Belgravia) **£80**

SIR JOHN GILBERT - The Duke Of Wellington Leading His Troops Into Battle - on board - 10½ x 14¼in.
(Christie's) **£170**

JOHN GILBERT - A Royalist Charge - signed and dated 1872 - 12¾ x 22¾in.
(Buckell & Ballard) **£120**

J. F. GILBERT - A View Of A Country House From The Park - 18 x 26in.
(Christie's) **£160**

KUTE GILBERT - Views on the Thames signed and dated 1887 - on board - 6 x 9 ins.
(Christie's, S. Kensington) **£240**

G. D. GILES - A Huntsman And His Favourite
Hounds Of The Pytchley Hunt - oil on canvas
- signed and dated 1889 - 41 x 55in.
(King & Chasemore) **£460**

JAMES WILLIAM GILES - Shetland Ponies -
signed and dated 1858 - 24½ x 35½in.
(Sotheby's) **£300**

JAMES WILLIAM GILES - The Two
Dogs - 50 x 69cm.
(Edmiston's) **£85**

MAX GILLARD - Still Life Of
Partridge - signed and dated 1881 -
canvas - on board - 15¼ x 11½in.
(Sotheby's Belgravia) **£18**

M. GILLIES - A Full-Length Portrait Of A
Girl With Fan - watercolour drawing, signed
and dated 1871 - 14¾ x 11½in.
(H. C. Chapman & Son) **£140**

SIR WILLIAM GEORGE GILLIES - A
Midlothian Landscape - signed - on board -
19 x 24in.
(Sotheby's) **£240**

GILPIN - Figures By A Farmhouse In
The Lake District - pencil and water-
colour - 22½ x 29½in.
(Christie's) **£25**

SAWREY GILPIN - 'Gulliver Repriman-
ded And Silenced By His Master, When
Describing The Horrors Of War' - 107 x
154cm.
(Phillips) **£350**

WILLIAM GILPIN - Picturesque Mountain
Landscape - watercolour - 7 x 10in.
(G. A. Key) **£14**

WILLIAM SAWREY GILPIN - Farmyard
Scenes With Horses And Other Animals -
pencil and watercolour - 12 x 18in.
(Christie's) **£500 Pair**

WILLIAM SAWREY GILPIN - Dover -
watercolour - 11½ x 18½in.
(Christie's) £160

VICTOR GILSOUL - A Riverside Town
At Dusk - signed - 55 x 77in.
(Sotheby's) £500

VICTOR OLIVIER GILSOUL - Marias
In Campine, With a Figure In A Boat
And A Cottage in the foreground -
signed and inscribed on the reverse -
oil on canvas - 13 x 20¾in.
(Geering & Colyer) £190

GIMIGNANI - Lot And His Daughters,
Sodom Burning Beyond - 27¾ x 37¾in.
(Sotheby's) £260

GIORDANO - Saint Peter, head and
shoulders, Dressed In Blue And Brown -
21¼ x 19¼in.
(Sotheby's) £100

GIORDANO - The Assumption Of
The Virgin - 31½ x 32in.
(Sotheby's) £280

LUCA GIORDANO - Flora And Her
Attendants - 33½ x 72in.
(Christie's) £1,600

PALMA GIOVANE, Circle Of - The
Forge Of Vulcan - 48¼ x 72½in.
(Sotheby's) £3,500

PALMA GIOVANE, After - Saint
Peter - on panel - 8¾ x 6¾ ins.
(Christie's) £1,600

FOLLOWER OF PALMA GIOVANE -
The Presentation of the Virgin - pen and
brown ink and wash over black chalk -
17.6 x 20.6 cm.
(Sotheby's) £210

Workshop of APOLLONIO DI GIOVANNI -
A Nobleman And His Attendants And
Warriors In Combat - bears inscription on
the reverse - on panel - 17½ x 63¾in.
(Christie's) £6,500

PALMA GIOVANE, After - Salome with
the head of Saint John the Baptist - on
panel - 9 x 6¾ ins.
(Christie's) £2,800

183

GIRAUD

NEP GIROTTA - The Sandstorm -
heightened with bodycolour - signed
and inscribed Venezia - 13½ x 9in.
(Sotheby's Belgravia) **£9**

THOMAS GIRTIN - Melrose Abbey -
watercolour - 13¼ x 16½in.
(Christie's) **£6,000**

S. GLADYS - The Hunt - oil on canvas -
signed - 60 x 80cm.
(Galerie Moderne) **£31**

HAMILTON GLASS - The Islands Of
Loch Maree - watercolour - 33 x 50cm.
(Edmiston's) **£46**

HAMILTON GLASS - Castle And
River Landscape - 11.5 x 15.5cm.
(Edmiston's) **£18**

S. T. GLEED - Flying Fortress - watercolour - 14 x 18in.
(G. A. Key) **£20**

EDUARD GLEIM - Figures In An
Extensive Wooded Valley, At Sunset -
signed and dated '69 - 30 x 48in.
(Sotheby's) **£300**

ALFRED AUGUSTUS GLENDENING,
SNR - The path home, evening - signed
with initials and dated '88 - 7½ x 14½in.
(Sotheby's Belgravia) **£460**

ALFRED AUGUSTUS GLENDENING -
River Scene At Reedham - oil - 8 x 14in.
(G. A. Key) **£301**

A. GLENDINNING - A River Landscape
With Figures In Punt in foreground - oil
on canvas - signed with initials and dated
1853 - 12 x 20in.
(King & Chasemore) **£600**

PIERRE FRANCOIS EUGENE GIRAUD -
The Lovers' Tiff; and The Secret Letter -
both signed - on panel - 32 x 20¼in - pair.
(Christie's) **£3,500**

J. GLENDINNING - Rural Scenes Of Cottages, Trees And Characters Walking - watercolours - 10 x 14in
(Boulton & Cooper) **£26 Pair**

J. GLOVER - Sailing Vessels on River Thames at London Bridge - water-colour - signed and dated 1808 - 29½ x 43½ ins.
(Jackson-Stops & Staff) **£820**

JOHN GLOVER - A View Of Rome From The Villa Madama - on panel - 13 x 17in.
(Christie's) **£3,800**

W. GLOVER - Highland Landscapes - watercolour - dated 1915 - 8½ x 12½in.
(Thomas Love & Sons Ltd) **£7 Pair**

A. VERNON GODBOLD - A Young Girl On The Edge Of A Wood - signed - 30 x 18in.
(Sotheby's Belgravia) **£60**

SAMUEL BERRY GODBOLD - The Fern Gatherer - signed and dated 1864 - 40 x 29in.
(Sotheby's Belgravia) **£400**

CHARLES GODDARD - Listening To Carols - signed - 24 x 36in.
(Sotheby's Belgravia) **£170**

CHARLES GODDARD - Outside The Stable - signed - 24 x 36in.
(Sotheby's Belgravia) **£240**

J. W. GODWARD - 'Golden Hours', Portrait Of Lady With Fan - dated 1913 - oil - 38½in. diameter.
(J. Entwistle & Co.) **£4,200**

JOHN WILLIAM GODWARD - 'Dolce Far Niente' - signed and dated - 77 x 128cm.
(Phillips) **£3,200**

JOHN WILLIAM GODWARD - Dreaming - signed with monogram and dated 1901 - on panel - 6¼ x 12½in.
(Sotheby's Belgravia) **£280**

GODWARD

JOHN WILLIAM GODWARD - Faraway Thoughts - signed and dated 1892 - 18 x 18in.
(Christie's, S. Kensington) £800

JOHN WILLIAM GODWARD - Dolce Far Niente - signed and dated 1904 - 19½ x 29½in.
(Sotheby's Belgravia) £6,000

A. GOFINON - The Undergrowth - oil on canvas - signed - 40 x 50cm.
(Galerie Moderne) £72

VINCENT VAN GOGH - La Fin De La Journee (D'Apres Millet) - 28¼ x 37in.
(Christie's, New York) £517,600

WALTER H. GOLDSMITH - On The Thames - heightened with white - signed and dated '96 - 17½ x 25½in.
(Sotheby's Belgravia) £30

NATALIA GONTCHAROVA - Maisons Dans Une Forest - pencil - 10 x 13¾in.
(Sotheby's) £45

NATALIA GONTCHAROVA - Design For An Eighteenth Century Military Costume - watercolour and pencil - signed and inscribed Le Factionaire - 18½ x 12¼in.
(Sotheby's) £105

T. GOOCH - Blackcock Shooting - 24 x 19in.
(Sotheby's) £300

GOODALL - Egyptian Views - watercolour - 19½ x 20in. and 13 x 38½in.
(Bearnes & Waycotts) £44 Two

EDWARD GOODALL - A Young Woman Writing - signed - watercolour - 11½ x 9in.
(Christie's) £200

F. GOODALL - An Egyptian Pastoral Scene On The Banks Of The Nile With Pyramids in the background - monogram 1880 - oil on canvas - 22 x 33in.
(Foll & Parker) £325

FREDERICK GOODALL - A View On The Nile With Pyramids beyond - signed with monogram and dated 1873 - 10½ x 21in.
(Christie's) £200

FREDERICK GOODALL - The Happy Days Of Queen Henrietta Maria - signed and dated 1852 - 22 x 27in.
(Christie's) £1,200

ALFRED GOODFELLOW - Touche - signed - 15 x 24½in.
(Sotheby's Belgravia) £48

MAUD GOODMAN - Summer Flowers - signed and dated '94 - 23½ x 35½in.
(Sotheby's Belgravia) £2,000

ROBERT GWELO GOODMAN - Darjeeling - signed - inscribed on the reverse - 8½ x 11¾in.
(Sotheby's) **£50**

ALBERT GOODWIN - Venice - signed - inscribed and dated 1912 - 7¼ x 9¾in.
(Sotheby's Belgravia) **£260**

ALBERT GOODWIN - Bristol - signed - inscribed and dated '68 - 9¼ x 15¾in.
(Sotheby's Belgravia) **£100**

MAUD GOODMAN - Blowing Smoke Rings - signed and dated '99 - 35½ x 27¾in.
(Sotheby's Belgravia) **£1,000**

ALBERT GOODWIN - Rye, Sussex - signed - inscribed and dated 1910 - watercolour heightened with white, pen and black ink on brown paper - 10¼ x 14½in.
(Christie's) **£180**

ALBERT GOODWIN - The Gate In The Wall, Pevensey Castle - signed - inscribed and dated 1920 - watercolour and body-colour - 10¼ x 14in.
(Christie's) **£180**

ALBERT GOODWIN - Freybourg - signed - inscribed and dated 1900 - mixed media - 14¾ x 9¾in.
(Christie's) **£110**

MAUD GOODMAN - Amongst The Flowers - signed and dated '84 - 21¼ x 15in.
(Sotheby's Belgravia) **£1,000**

JAN VAN GOOL - A Farmyard Scene
With A Landscape Beyond - signed - on
panel - 20 x 29in.
(Christie's) **£3,500**

JAN VAN GOOL - Milking Time: peasants
and cattle in a farmyard - signed - on panel -
15½ x 23½in.
(Christie's) **£4,800**

SIR JOHN WATSON GORDON -
Portrait Of A Cleric, Standing, small full
length, Under An Arch - on board - 17½ x
11in.
(Christie's) **£55**

SIR JOHN WATSON GORDON -
Portrait Of Roger Aytoun And His Son
Professor William Edmondstowne Aytoun,
At The Age Of 4 - on panel - 35¼ x 27in.
(Sotheby's) **£150**

WILLIAM HENRY GORE - The New
Gramophone, little girls in an interior -
signed - 21½ x 29½ ins.
(Christie's, S. Kensington) **£300**

WILLIAM HENRY GORE - The Young
Model - signed - 30 x 24 ins.
(Christie's, S. Kensington) **£170**

ALESSANDRO GORI - Dead Game in a
Wooded Landscape - signed - 23½ x
28¾ ins.
(Christie's) **£900**

WILLIAM W. GOSLING - A Horse And
Cart - 14 x 31in.
(Sotheby's Belgravia) **£95**

H. GOSSELIN - Boats At Blankenberghe
- oil on wood - signed and dated 1875.
(Galerie Moderne) **£126**

T. C. GOTCH - The Good Book - dated
1886 - 70 x 42cm.
(Edmiston's) **£600**

M. GOTS - The Musketeers - oil on canvas - signed and dated 1906 - 28 x 46cm.
(Galerie Moderne) **£40**

ALEXANDER GOUDIE - Still Life In
Brittany - pastel - 29 x 40cm.
(Edmiston's) **£25**

ALEXANDER GOUDIE - Cornfield In
Brittany - pastel - 38 x 46cm.
(Edmiston's) **£60**

JOSEPH GOUPY - The calling of the first
two apostles - gouache - 19.4 x 24,8 cm.
(Sotheby's) **£66**

A. GOVAERT - The Pool - oil on canvas -
signed - 26 x 50cm.
(Galerie Moderne) **£66**

J. GOVAERTS - Landscape - oil on
canvas - signed - 26 x 35cm.
(Galerie Moderne) **£8**

JAN VAN GOYEN - A Wooded River Landscape with sailing barges and rowing boats near a village - on panel - 13½ x 16¾in.
(Christie's) **£13,000**

A. G. GOW, After - A War Despatch At The Hotel De Ville - 29½ x 19½in.
(Sotheby's Belgravia) **£70**

GOYEN - A River Landscape, A Fisherman In A Row Boat in the foreground, A Church On A Promontory To The Right - on panel - 7½ x 9½in.
(Sotheby's) **£180**

JAN VAN GOYEN - A Beach Scene: On The Left, Numerous Figures And Fishing Boats On The Shore, In The Centre Two Horsemen, With Two Wagons Outside An Inn On The Right - signed and dated 1634 - 21 x 32in.
(Christie's) **£40,000**

JAN VAN GOYEN - A Village By A River With A Ferry And A Man Fishing in the foreground - signed and dated 1623 - on panel - circular - 10in. diameter.
(Christie's) **£26,000**

JAN VAN GOYEN - Fishing Vessels Offshore In A Choppy Sea - signed with monogram and dated 1642 - 25 x 29½in.
(Christie's) **£10,000**

GOYEN

JAN VAN GOYEN - The Old Watch Tower On The Kil Near Dordrecht with numerous boats - signed with monogram and dated 1652 - on panel - 15 x 30in.
(Christie's) **£38,000**

JAN VAN GOYEN - A View Of Nijmegen Across The Rhine with fishermen hauling in a net, other figures in boats, and with the Valkhof and the Groote Kerk beyond - on panel - 16½ x 21in.
(Christie's) **£9,000**

JAN VAN GOYEN - A Woody River Landscape, with an angler, and peasants on a bridge by a cottage - signed with initials and dated 1632 - on panel - 13½ x 20¾in.
(Christie's) **£24,000**

J. W. GOZZARD - The Homeward Path - heightened with bodycolour - signed - 8 x 15¾in.
(Sotheby's Belgravia) **£14**

COLIN GRAEME - Still Life Of A Grouse On A Moorland - signed - 16 x 20in.
(Sotheby's Belgravia) **£12**

ANDREW GRAHAM - 'Highland Landscape With Cattle At Rivers Edge' - signed - 19th century - oil on canvas - 24 x 36in.
(Lalonde Martin) **£170**

GEORGE GRAHAM - A Street In Rotterdam - signed and dated 1914 - inscribed on the reverse - 15½ x 11¾in.
(Sotheby's Belgravia) **£48**

GRANT - Portrait Of Josiah Greethead Strachan Of Farnhill Park, Stroud - 29 x 24½in.
(Sotheby's) **£80**

DUNCAN GRANT - Venetian canal scene - signed and dated '57-
(Christie's, S. Kensington) **£160**

SIR FRANCIS GRANT - A Lady Of The Manners Family Riding Side-Saddle With Her Dog - 43½ x 55½in.
(Christie's) **£5,000**

SIR FRANCIS GRANT - Portrait Of Lord Alfred Henry Paget, C.B., small full length, Mounted On A Charger In The Uniform Of The Royal Horse Guards, In The Riding School Of Knightsbridge Barracks - 44½ x 30in.
(Christie's) **£180**

W. J. GRANT - Hunted Down - on board - 13¾ x 17in.
(Sotheby's Belgravia) **£15**

MARY GRANVILLE, Mrs Delany - Portrait Of Rosalba Carriera - pastel - 11¼ x 9¾in.
(Christie's) **£85**

JOSUA DE GRAVE - A Still Life With Peaches, Grapes And Plums In A Blue Chinese Bowl With A Pewter Dish On A Green Cloth - signed - on copper - 13½ x 18in.
(Christie's) **£2,600**

NORAH NEILSON GRAY - Children Among Flowers - watercolours - 27 x 44 cm
(Edmiston's) **£165 Pair**

DOMENIKOS THEOTOKOPOULOS, called EL GRECO - The Disrobing Of Christ (El Espolio) - on panel - 28½ x 17¼in.
(Christie's) **£50,000**

A. H. GREEN - Pont y Heda, Betwsy Coed - oil - 20 x 30in.
(G. A Key) **£75**

A. H. GREEN - The Herons Pool, Hidr Valley - oil - 20 x 30in.
(G. A. Key) **£75**

R. GREEN - Study Of A Stock Dove - watercolour - 12 x 10in.
(G. A. Key) **£16**

RICHARD CRAFTON GREEN - Portrait Of A Fisherwoman - signed and dated 1894 - oil on canvas - 17¼ x 13¼in.
(Bearnes & Waycotts) **£300**

WILLIAM GREEN - Windermere From Low Wood; Langdale Pikes From Langdale Head; And Wast Water - all signed - inscribed and dated 1820 on the reverse of the mounts - watercolour - 5½ x 7¾in.
(Christie's) **£350 Three**

COLIN GREENE - A Study Of Two Dogs' Heads - signed and dated '93 - oil - 16 x 14in.
(Warner, Sheppard & Wade) **£70**

COLIN GREENE - A Chestnut Horse And Two Pointers By A Thatched Shed - signed - oil on canvas - 23½ x 19¼in.
(Bearnes & Waycotts) **£200**

JAMES GREENLEES - View Of Dunblane Cathedral - oil - signed, inscribed and dated 1884 on the reverse - on panel - 22.5 x 36cm.
(Phillips in Scotland) **£66**

P. GREENWOOD - Shipping In Open Seas - signed and dated 1894 - 15½ x 23½in.
(Sotheby's Belgravia) **£25**

H. GREGTHAM - Highland Cattle In A Lake And Mountain Landscape - signed and dated 1921 - oil - 20 x 36in.
(Warner, Sheppard & Wade) **£15**

MAURICE WILLIAM GREIFFENHAGEN - Portrait Of A Lady, seated - signed and dated 1899 - 46½ x 35½in.
(Woolley & Wallis) **£175**

J. GREIG - A Village In Provence - 48 x 98cm.
(Edmiston's) **£18**

JOHN R. GREIG - A Dutch Harbour - signed - on panel - 9¾ x 11½in.
(Sotheby's Belgravia) **£35**

GREUZE - A Young Girl, bust length, Wearing White - 15½ x 12½in.
(Christie's) **£300**

J. B. GREUZE - Supper Time - 21 x 17½in.
(Christie's) **£1,300**

JEAN-BAPTISTE GREUZE - The Young Letter Writer: a young girl seated at a desk with paper and a quill pen - on panel - 26¼ x 20¾in.
(Christie's) **£9,000**

H. De GREVE - A Busy Farmyard - on wood - signed - 56 x 96cm.
(Galerie Moderne) **£25**

GEORGE GREY - River Landscape - signed and dated 1890 - oil on canvas - 29½ x 49½in.
(Bearnes & Waycotts) **£110**

LOUIS GRIER - 'Sunset Through The Trees' - signed - oil on canvas - 29¼ x 39½in.
(Bearnes & Waycotts) **£90**

J. GRIFFIER - An Extensive Mountainous Landscape With Peasants On A Path, A Ruined Castle Beyond - bears signature - 16¾ x 22in.
(Christie's) **£1,500**

JAN GRIFFIER - A View Of Greenwich Park, With The Queen's House And Observatory, The River Thames And London Beyond - 22 x 52½in.
(Christie's) **£2,400**

J. GRIFFIER - A Woody River Landscape, With Figures By A Fortified Village - 12½ x 15½in.
(Christie's) **£1,200**

G. F. GRIMALDI - Pan Playing The Pipes To Nymphs Dancing In A Wooded Landscape - 29½ x 46½in.
(Christie's) **£1,900**

GIOVANNI FRANCESCO GRIMALDI, IL BOLOGNESE - An Extensive Wooded River Landscape, with fortified buildings by a bridge, and figures in boats - 37½ x 52in.
(Christie's) **£2,400**

GRIMM, Style of, 18th century - The Temple Of Cybele, Rome, With Figures, Dogs And A Donkey in the foreground - watercolour - 14¼ x 18¾in.
(Geering & Colyer) **£250**

GRIMSHAW - Moonlit Wooded Street Scene With Two Figures - 51 x 76.5cm.
(Edmiston's) **£30**

ATKINSON GRIMSHAW - Canning Docks, Liverpool By Night - signed - and signed and inscribed on the reverse - 23¼ x 35½in.
(Christie's) £2,600

JOHN ATKINSON GRIMSHAW - Rouen - signed and inscribed - signed, inscribed and dated '93 on the reverse - on board - 6½ x 14½in.
(Sotheby's Belgravia) £150

JOHN ATKINSON GRIMSHAW - Outside The Old Hall, Moonlight - signed and indistinctly dated - board laid on panel - 14½ x 18½in.
(Sotheby's Belgravia) £2,200

LOUIS H. GRIMSHAW - The Tolbooth, Canongate, The Royal Mile; The Royal Mile With A Corner Of Holyrood Palace, Edinburgh - one signed - both on board - each 12 x 16in.
(Sotheby's Belgravia) £3,700 Pair

CHARLES JOSEPH GRIPS - An Interior With A Lady Embroidering - signed and dated 1874 - on panel - 17½ x 13½in.
(Christie's) £2,200

ERNEST GRISET - An Eagle - signed - on board - 24 x 18½in.
(Sotheby's Belgravia) £40

JOHN ATKINSON GRIMSHAW - A November Night - signed and dated 1874 - oil on canvas - 25 x 30in.
(Bonham's) £2,400

A. GROCHPIERRE - Study Of Old Peasant Woman Seated In Cottage - signed and dated 1888 - 30 x 23½in.
(Phillips) £380

GROMAIRE

MARCEL GROMAIRE - Femme Nue Debout - pencil on cloth - signed and dated 1927 - 11¾ x 6¼in.
(Sotheby's) **£260**

R. GRONLAND - Country Scenes - signed - oil - 8 x 12in
(Neale & Son) **£21 Pair**

A. DE GROOTE - Dutch Winter Scene With Skaters And Other Figures in the foreground - signed - oil on panel - 14¾ x 24in.
(Bearnes & Waycotts) **£600**

A. DE GROOTE - Dutch River Scene With A Building, Boats And Figures - signed - oil on panel - 16½ x 23¾in.
(Bearnes & Waycotts) **£640**

JULES DE GROUX - Boats At The Port Of Blankenberghe - oil - signed - 1m. x 1m.24cm.
(Galerie Moderne) **£235**

GRUBACS - Capriccio Views Of Rome And Venice - 17¼ x 23¼in.
(Sotheby's) **£900 Pair**

SCHOOL OF GUARDI - Canal Scene With Buildings And Figures - 20½ x 32in.
(Woolley & Wallis) **£240**

F. GUARDI - The Grand Canal, Venice, with the Rialto Bridge and the Fondaco del Tedeschi - 24 x 29½in.
(Christie's) **£5,500**

F. GUARDI - Piazza San Marco, Venice, with a corner of the Basilica - on panel - 9¼ x 6¼in.
(Christie's) **£4,000**

FRANCESCO GUARDI - An Architectural Capriccio, With A Fountain - 7½ x 6in.
(Christie's) **£12,000**

FRANCESCO GUARDI - The Piazza
San Marco, Venice - 11¼ x 17½in.
(Christie's) **£3,800**

FRANCESCO GUARDI - The Immaculate
Conception - 29 x 22½in.
(Christie's) **£9,500**

FRANCESCO GUARDI - An Architectural
Capriccio, with the courtyard of a palace -
7½ x 6in.
(Christie's) **£15,000**

FRANCESCO GUARDI - The Grand Canal,
Venice, with the Church of Santa Maria
della Salute - 8½ x 14in.
(Christie's) **£30,000**

FRANCESCO GUARDI - A Capriccio
Landscape With a Cypress Tree And A
Tower And Pastoral Figures - on panel -
3¾ x 5¾in.
(Christie's) **£3,800**

FRANCESCO GUARDI - The Bacino Di San
Marco, Venice, looking towards the
Giudecca, with the church of San Giorgio
Maggiore to the left and the Dogana to the
right - 44 x 65¾in.
(Christie's) **£40,000**

FRANCESCO GUARDI - The Entrance To The Grand Canal, Venice, With The Dogana And The Church Of Santa Maria Della Salute - on panel - 9½ x 14in.
(Christie's) **£17,000**

G. GUARDI - River Landscapes, With Towers And Bridges - on paper laid down on panel - 3 x 5in.
(Christie's) **£480 Pair**

RALSTON GUDGEON - Plover - watercolour - 26 x 35cm.
(Edmiston's) **£29**

IL GUERCINO, Studio Of - Samson And Delilah - 66½ x 87in.
(Christie's) **£1,500**

MICHEL MARKINOVITCH GUERMACHEFF - A Snow Covered Landscape At Evening - signed - 18 x 21in.
(Sotheby's) **£280**

LABILLE GUIARD - Portrait Of Robespierre, head and shoulders, Turned To The Right - in a painted oval - 13½ x 11in.
(Sotheby's) **£80**

G. GUIDA - Italianate Peasant Couple Embracing In A Vineyard - oil on canvas - 52 x 36½in.
(John H. Raby & Son) **£2,700**

ALBERT GUILLAUME - Le Commandant - pen and ink and watercolour - signed and inscribed - 5¾ x 4in.
(Sotheby's) **£20**

CONSTANTIN GUYS - Les Cavaliers - pen and ink and wash - 6¾ x 10¼in.
(Sotheby's) **£80**

SEYMOUR JOSEPH GUY - Three Young Children With A Mallard in a landscape - signed - 32 x 45in.
(Sotheby's) **£1,100**

JOSEPH GYSELINCK - Cottage Interior - signed and dated 1867 - oil on panel - 24 x 20in.
(Bonham's) **£2,300**

JOSEPH GYSELINCK - The Young Portraitist - signed and dated 1871 and certified by the Artist on the reverse - on panel - 11¾ x 9½in.
(Christie's) **£1,300**

P. GYSELS - A View Of A Town, A Horsedrawn Wagon By A River in the foreground, Figures Beside Cottages Beyond - on panel - 6½ x 8¼in.
(Sotheby's) **£650**

PEETERS GYSELS - A Village Harbour With Figures And Sailing Vessels, And An Estuary Beyond - on copper - 8¼ x 10¾in.
(Christie's) **£7,500**

BERNARD DE HAAG - Driving The
Herd Home - signed - 23 x 27in.
(Sotheby's) **£300**

REMI VAN HAANEN - A Moonlit River
Landscape With Two Figures In A Boat -
signed - 28 x 35½in.
(Sotheby's) **£400**

CORNELIS VAN HAARLEM - Venus,
Mars And Cupid - signed with monogram
and dated 1604 - 38½ x 52in.
(Christie's) **£9,500**

**CORNELIS CORNELISZ VAN
HAARLEM** - St. John The Baptist
Preaching In The Wilderness - signed
with monogram and dated 1602 -
100 x 180cm.
(Phillips) **£32,000**

CORNELIS VAN HAARLEM - A Hero And
Heroine Of Antiquity - both signed with
monogram and dated 1624 - 34 x 27in
(Christie's) **£7,500 Pair**

HAAS

J. H. L. DE HAAS - Cattle And Landscape - 1869 - on panel - signed on reverse - 44 x 62cm.
(Edmiston's) £350

JAN HACKAERT - A Staghunt In A Forest - 23 x 27½in.
(Christie's) £2,200

HACKER - Portrait Of A Lady, head and shoulders - canvas - on board - 17 x 13in.
(Sotheby's Belgravia) £22

ARTHUR HACKER - Sea Nymphs - signed - 20½ x 10in.
(Sotheby's Belgravia) £260

ARTHUR HACKER - Portrait Of A Young Woman In A White Silk Dress - signed and dated 1892 - oil on canvas - 57¼ x 33½in.
(Bearnes & Waycotts) £210

HADDON - Venice; And Middle Eastern Street Scene - watercolour - 14½ x 21½in. and 29 x 21in.
(Bearnes & Waycotts) £65 Two

DAVID W. HADDON - The Connoisseur - signed - 35¼ x 27¾in.
(Sotheby's Belgravia) £150

JOHAN VAN HAENSBERGEN - A Landscape With Roman Ruins, in the foreground An Old Man Followed By A Boy With A Bundle Of Sticks - on panel - 7½ x 9¾in.
(Sotheby's) £2,200

MAURICE HAGEMANS - Le Depart Du Troupeau - oil on wood - signed - 35 x 28cm.
(Galerie Moderne) £110

ANDERSON HAGUE - A Village Street - heightened with bodycolour - signed - 13 x 19in.
(Sotheby's Belgravia) £38

GEORGE CHARLES HAITE - A View From The Lido Of Murano, Venice - signed - 10 x 14in.
(Sotheby's Belgravia) **£48**

GEORGE E. HALE - Brixham Trawler - watercolour - 9 x 14in.
(G. A. Key) **£22**

W. HALE - Beached Fishing Boats - signed - on board - oil - 7 x 12in.
(Warner, Sheppard & Wade) **£55**

HARRY HALL - 'Thorn', A Chestnut Racehorse In A Landscape - signed and dated 1874 - 29½ x 38¼in.
(Christie's) **£1,100**

FREDERICK HALL - Evening - signed and dated 1886 - 32 x 14½in.
(Sotheby's Belgravia) **£450**

H. HALL - Studies of 'Sophie', A Bay Mare and 'Black Prince', A Black Gelding, Standing In Stables - oil - signed and dated 1867 - 18 x 24in.
(Henry Spencer & Sons) **£220 Pair**

HARRY HALL - 'Rataplan', With Joseph Dawson, On Newmarket Heath - 22½ x 29½in.
(Christie's) **£2,800**

HARRY HALL - 'Blue Gown', With Jockey Up On A Racecourse - 28 x 36in.
(Christie's) **£1,200**

HARRY HALL - A Hackney Showing His Paces - oil on canvas - signed - 23 x 19in.
(J. Francis, T. Jones & Sons) **£95**

HALL

HARRY HALL - 'Auriel', A Bay Racehorse With Jockey Up, With Mr Blake
The Owner, And The Trainer - 24½ x
33in.
(Christie's) **£3,200**

EMIL HALLATZ - Farmyard Scene With
Farmer Forking Hay - signed - oil on
canvas - 20¾ x 30¼in.
(Bonham's) **£1,750**

CHARLES EDWARD HALLE - The
Light From Above - signed and
indistinctly dated - 39½ x 21¼in.
(Sotheby's Belgravia) **£500**

JACQUES HALLET - Seated Nude - oil
on wood - signed - 57 x 59cm.
(Galerie Moderne) **£31**

L. HALLET - Busy Lake Scene - signed -
oil on canvas - 56 x 99 cm
(Galerie Moderne) **£80**

D. HALS - An Interior With Figures
Merrymaking - bears signature - on
panel - 22 x 30in.
(Christie's) **£3,000**

DIRK HALS - Ladies And Gentlemen Making
Music in an interior - signed and dated 1623 -
on panel - 8½ x 12in.
(Christie's) **£9,200**

F. HALS - Portrait Of A Young Man,
half length, Seated, Wearing A Black
Coat And White Collar And Cuffs -
91 x 73cm.
(Phillips) **£2,200**

F. HALS - A Fishwife - 32 x 24¼in.
(Christie's) **£4,500**

HAMILTON - A Blue-Tit And A Goldfinch In A Woody Landscape - on
panel - 13¾ x 18½in.
(Christie's) **£500**

H. D. HAMILTON - Portrait Of Amanda
D'Aranda, bust length, Wearing An
Elaborate Cap - pastel - oval - 11½ x 9in.
(Christie's) **£130**

PHILIPP FERDINAND DE HAMILTON -
A Boar Hunt: The Kill - 13½ x 18in.
(Christie's) **£850**

WILLIAM HAMILTON - The Assassin-
ation Of King Henry IV Of France -
signed - pen and brown ink, brown wash
heightened with white on brown paper -
17¾ x 21½in.
(Christie's) **£90**

EDOUARD JEAN CONRAD HAMMAN -
The Young Minstrel, Playing A Lute For
His Mistress Who Looks On Admiringly -
signed and dated 1852 - on panel - 20 x
15½in.
(Sotheby's) **£800**

THOMAS W. HAMMOND - Leen Side,
Lenton - signed, inscribed and dated 1910 -
charcoal - 13½ x 20in.
(Neale & Son) **£35**

THOMAS W. HAMMOND - The Salutation
Inn, Houndsgate, Nottingham - signed,
inscribed - charcoal - 20½ x 13½in.
(Neale & Son) **£20**

C. HANCOCK - A Terrier In Its
Basket - 17 x 21in.
(Sotheby's Belgravia) **£38**

WILLIAM LEE HANKEY - The Red
Lion, Avebury - signed - 19½ x 23½in.
(Sotheby's Belgravia) **£320**

WILLIAM LEE HANKEY - Algeciras -
signed - 19½ x 23¼in.
(Sotheby's Belgravia) **£420**

GEORGE HANN - Wooded Landscape -
36 x 74cm.
(Edmiston's) **£5**

CHARLES HANNAFORD - Norwich
Flower Market - watercolour - 10 x 14in.
(G. A. Key) **£70**

WILLIAM HANNAN - West Wycombe
Park From The Lake With Venus Temple
And The Willow Bridge - 33½ x 50½in.
(Christie's) **£2,000**

HANSEN

HANS HANSEN - Goats Outside A Farm Building - indistinctly signed and dated 1894 - on panel - 5¾ x 17in.
(Sotheby's) **£120**

G. VAN HANTHORST - Portrait of two children, said to be Prince Edward and Princess Amelia, full length - 66 x 49 ins.
(Christie's, S. Kensington) **£1,300**

JAMES HARDEN - English Setters By A Game Bag - indistinctly signed - 35½ x 27¾in.
(Sotheby's Belgravia) **£75**

HARDIME - A Still Life Of Flowers, Including Roses, Tulips And Chrysanthemums In A Basket On A Ledge - 21¾ x 27¾in.
(Sotheby's) **£600**

DUDLEY HARDY - Study Of A Moroccan Wearing A Fez, head and shoulders - signed and inscribed 'Paris' and dated 1888 - 10 x 6¼in.
(Sotheby's Belgravia) **£28**

FREDERICK DANIEL HARDY - A Visit To Grandma - signed and dated 1892 - 11½ x 15½in.
(Sotheby's Belgravia) **£1,100**

FREDERICK DANIEL HARDY - 'The Gladdened Hearth' - signed and dated 1878 - 71 x 97cm.
(Phillips) **£1,700**

FREDERICK DANIEL HARDY - The Spinning Wheel - signed with initials and dated 1854 - on panel - 9 x 11½ ins.
(Christie's, S. Kensington) **£700**

H. HARDY - Seascapes With Numerous Shipping In Estuaries - 9 x 15in.
(G. A. Key) **£430 Pair**

HEYWOOD HARDY - 'The Glorious Twelfth' - signed and dated 1895 - 74 x 104cm.
(Phillips) **£1,000**

HEYWOOD HARDY - The Mistress Of
The Hunt - signed - 23 x 17½in.
(Christie's) **£2,100**

HEYWOOD HARDY - A Parting Word -
signed and dated 1901 - 30½ x 23½in.
(Christie's) **£2,100**

HEYWOOD HARDY - The Village
Post Office - signed - 19½ x 30½in.
(Christie's) **£2,700**

HEYWOOD HARDY - The Cross Roads -
signed - 17¼ x 23¼in.
(Christie's) **£1,400**

HEYWOOD HARDY - An American
Coaching Scene In An Extensive River
Landscape - signed - 17½ x 32½in.
(Christie's) **£1,900**

HEYWOOD HARDY - At The Farriers -
signed - 19½ x 29½in.
(Christie's) **£2,200**

T. B. HARDY - Shipping In The
Channel - 21 x 33.5cm.
(Edmiston's) **£85**

THOMAS BUSH HARDY - Scarborough,
The Harbour With Fishing Fleet And
Paddle Steamers, And Figures And A
Horse And Cart in the foreground -
signed - inscribed and dated '90 -
watercolour - 9¾ x 13½in.
(Geering & Colyer) **£160**

T. B. HARDY - Fishermen And Boats On
Seashore, village in background and ships
standing off - water colour - signed and
dated 1896 - 30 x 10½in.
(John H. Raby & Son) **£180**

HARLOW

HARLOW - Portrait Of A Young Boy, half length, Wearing A Brown Cloak - on board - 10¼ x 8¼in.
(Sotheby's) **£20**

J. HARMSWORTH - Windy Evening Rural Landscape With Figures In Lane - watercolour - 6 x 11in.
(G. A. Key) **£22**

HENRI-JOSEPH HARPIGNIES - Paysage Au Crepuscule - watercolour - signed - 7¼ x 10¾in.
(Sotheby's) **£240**

HENRI-JOSEPH HARPIGNIES - Le Ruisseau - pen and ink and watercolour - signed and dated '77 - 11¼ x 7¾in.
(Sotheby's) **£650**

C. HARRINGTON - English Wooded Landscape With Two Figures Seated On Bank - watercolour - 7 x 9in.
(G. A. Key) **£40**

CHARLES HARRINGTON - River Landscape With Trees And Bridge in foreground - watercolour - signed - 14½ x 22in.
(Graves Son & Pilcher) **£85**

DANIEL HARRIS OF OXFORD - Braziers, Near Ipsden, Oxford - watercolour heightened with white - 18¼ x 24½in.
(Christie's) **£400**

H. HARRIS - Tintern Abbey and the River Wye in foreground and Brecon Castle with the River Usk - oils on canvas - signed - 16½ x 29in.
(Lalonde Martin) **£120 pair**

HENRY HARRIS of BRISTOL - Tintern Abbey, Monmouth - signed - 18 x 30in.
(Woolley & Wallis) **£180**

HENRY HARRIS of BRISTOL - Landscape With Castle And Figures By A River - signed - 18 x 30in.
(Woolley & Wallis) **£130**

HENRY HARRIS - 'Wooded Landscapes - Thatched Cottage And Two Peasants Near Duck Pond in foreground, and Cattle At Waters Edge' - signed - oils on canvas - pair.
(Lalonde Martin) **£90 pair**

WILLIAM E. HARRIS - Welsh Scene Near Dolgelly - oil - dated 1882 - 11½ x 17½in.
(Charles R. Phillips) **£130**

HARRISON - Study Of Rising Shelldrake - watercolour - 12 x 9in.
(G. A. Key) **£6**

WALTER HARROWING - Portrait Of An Irish Wolfhound - signed and dated 1880 - oil on canvas - 29½ x 24½in.
(Bearnes & Waycotts) **£120**

WALTER HARROWING - A Black Horse In A Stable - signed and indistinctly dated - 22½ x 28¼in.
(Sotheby's Belgravia) **£60**

E. HART - The Resting Place - oil on canvas - signed - 25 x 30cm.
(Galerie Moderne) **£24**

THOMAS HART - Laying Out The Nets - signed - 14 x 24in.
(Sotheby's Belgravia) **£14**

HENRY ALBERT HARTLAND - Criccieth Shore, North Wales - signed - 23¼ x 41½in.
(Sotheby's Belgravia) **£240**

MATTHAUS CHRISTOPH HARTMAN - The Magician's Coup De Grace - on panel - 14¼ x 17in.
(Sotheby's) **£5,800**

SIR GEORGE HARVEY - Three Studies Of A Gentleman - inscribed - on paper - 10 x 7¼in.
(Christie's) **£120**

SIR GEORGE HARVEY - A Study Of A Man Standing With His Hand On His Hip - on paper - 8½ x 7½in.
(Christie's) **£50**

E. W. HASLEHUST - "Princes Street, Edinburgh, looking West" - watercolour - 20½ x 13½in.
(Thomas Love & Sons Ltd) **£30**

HENRY EDGAR HAYES - Far-Away
Thoughts - signed and indistinctly
dated - 24 x 20in.
(Sotheby's Belgravia) £650

RAOUL HAUSSMANN - Interior -
gouache - signed with initials and
dated '57 - 25 x 18½in.
(Sotheby's) £300

CHARLES RICHARDS HAVELL - 'An
Old Favourite' - inscribed on the reverse -
oil on canvas - 24½ x 29½in.
(Bearnes & Waycotts) £270

CECIL HAY - Spode Jug - 60 x 49cm.
(Edmiston's) £24

BENJAMIN ROBERT HAYDON -
Study Of A Mother And Child - pen
and brown ink - 7¼ x 6½in.
(Sotheby's) £40

CLAUDE HAYES - An Extensive Moorland Landscape, with a shepherd, a dog
and a flock of sheep in the foreground -
signed - oil - 36 x 47 in.
(Henry Spencer & Sons) £280

EDWIN HAYES - Off Sheerness -
signed and dated '75 - 7½ x 10½in.
(Sotheby's Belgravia) £150

FREDERICK WILLIAM HAYES - Off
Douglas, Isle Of Man - inscribed on the
reverse - on panel - 7½ x 9¾in.
(Sotheby's Belgravia) £40

F. W. HAYES - Seascape With A Fishing
Boat - oil - 14 x 18in.
(Butler & Hatch Waterman) £50

J. HAYLLAR - Grace - on panel -
arched top - 14 x 18in.
(Sotheby's Belgravia) £200

FRANCIS HAYMAN - Portrait Of A
Gentleman, In A Red Waistcoat And Brown
Coat, Leaning On A Tree Trunk - small
full length - 24 x 17in.
(Christie's) £750

HAYTER - Portrait Of A Gentleman,
half length, Wearing A Coat With A Fur
Collar - 24 x 20in.
(Sotheby's) £90

SIR GEORGE HAYTER - Portrait Study
Of Two Men, Probably The First Baron
Ebury And 14th Earl Of Derby - pencil
and brown wash - 9¼ x 7¾in.
(Christie's) £35

HAYTER

SIR GEORGE HAYTER, After Van Dyck
- The Emperor Theodosius And Saint
Ambrose - on panel - a sketch of a young
man in profile on reverse - 17¼ x 13¼in.
(Christie's) **£110**

WILLIAM HEATH - A River Landscape;
Harvest Time - both signed and dated
1876 - each 15½ x 19½in.
(Sotheby's Belgravia) **£280 Pair**

SIR JOHN HAYTER - Portrait of Queen
Victoria, aged 16, small full length,
Standing In An Interior With Windsor
Castle in the distance And Her Spaniel
'Dash' Beside Her - 20½ x 14½in.
(Christie's) **£1,300**

WILLIAM STANLEY HAYTER -
Figures Fantastiques - pencil and red
gouache - signed - 5¼ x 7½in.
(Sotheby's) **£55**

WILLIAM STANLEY HAYTER -
Figure Studies - pen and coloured inks -
signed and dated 5.11.50 - 18½ x 24½in.
(Sotheby's) **£110 Pair**

T. HEARD - A Paddle Steamer And Sailing
Ships In A Swell - 20 x 30in.
(Woolley & Wallis) **£120**

THOMAS HEARNE - Pontefract -
pencil and grey wash on pink prepared
paper - 5½ x 7½in.
(Christie's) **£140**

HEATH - Rhinoceros Hunting In
Southern Africa - watercolour - 14½ x
20in.
(Christie's) **£70**

FRANK GASCOIGNE HEATH - A
Harbour Scene Entitled 'Old Age
Pensioners' - signed and dated 1912 -
oil on canvas - 49½ x 59in.
(Bearnes & Waycotts) **£380**

GERRIT WILLEMSZ HEDA - A Still
Life Of A Nautilus Cup, A Roemer, And
A Salt, With An Orange And A Lemon In
A Blue And White Porcelain Dish Resting
On A Carpet On A Draped Ledge - on panel
- 25½ x 20in.
(Christie's) **£3,000**

WILLEM CLAESZ. HEDA - A Still Life
With A Leg Of Ham, A Peeled Lemon, Two
Glasses And Pewter Dishes On A Table - on
panel - 23½ x 34½in.
(Christie's) **£5,000**

A. VAN HEDLEGHEN, After VAN HUYSUM - A Flower Piece - 33½ x 19½in.
(Sotheby's Belgravia) **£60**

CORNELIS DE HEEM - Roses, Carnations, Convolvulus, A Poppy, And Honeysuckle in a glass vase on a ledge in a niche - signed - on panel - 16¾ x 13¾in.
(Christie's) **£19,000**

DAVID DAVIDSZ. DE HEEM - A Bunch Of Roses, Grapes and other fruit hanging from a nail - bears Cornelis de Heem signature - 25 x 20in.
(Christie's) **£4,500**

CORNELIS DE HEEM - Grapes, An Orange, A Peeled Lemon, Cherries, Oysters, A Spice Castor And A Glass Of Wine On A Stone Ledge - signed - 10½ x 14in.
(Christie's) **£10,000**

EGBERT VAN HEEMSKERK - A Village Kermesse With Actors, Fiddlers And Numerous Merrymakers - signed and indistinctly dated - 38 x 77in.
(Christie's) **£14,000**

M. VAN HEEMSKERCK - The Judgement Of Paris - on panel - 10¼ x 13¼in.
(Christie's) **£1,900**

THOMAS HEEREMANS - A Winter Landscape with peasants skating on a river outside a town - signed and dated 1686 - on panel - 23 x 32in.
(Christie's) **£6,500**

KARL HEFFNER - An English River Landscape, Possibly The Thames, At Evening - signed - 31 x 47in.
(Sotheby's) **£1,600**

207

KARL HEFFNER - Near Brannenburg,
An Evening Landscape - signed - 12 x
16¼in.
(Sotheby's) **£3,500**
KARL HEFFNER - Eventide - 19 x 31cm.
(Edmiston's) **£900**

ARNOLD HELCKE - A View Of
Richmond Hill - signed and dated
1894 - 107 x 183cm.
(Phillips) **£800**

BARTHOLOMEUS VAN DER HELST -
Portrait Of A Gentleman, half length, in a
dark coat and white neckcloth, holding a
piece of paper, with a landscape beyond -
29 x 24½in.
(Christie's) **£4,500**

B. B. HEMY - Shipping In A Storm -
16½ x 30in.
(Sotheby's Belgravia) **£85**

BERNARD BENEDICT HEMY - A
Harbour Town - signed - 19½ x 26½in.
(Sotheby's Belgravia) **£190**
BERNARD BENEDICT HEMY - On
The Coast - signed and dated 1896 -
on board - 11¾ x 18in.
(Sotheby's Belgravia) **£65**

CHARLES NAPIER HEMY - Burnmouth,
Berwickshire: Fishing Smacks In The
Harbour With Fisherwomen in the fore-
ground - signed and dated 1874 - 29½ x
44½in.
(Christie's) **£1,100**
CHARLES NAPIER HEMY - Off
Brixham - watercolour heightened
with white - signed - inscribed and
dated 1877 - 12½ x 17½in.
(Christie's) **£160**
CHARLES NAPIER HEMY - Wild
Weather - heightened with bodycolour -
signed with initials and dated 1917 -
inscribed on the reverse - 17½ x 26in.
(Sotheby's Belgravia) **£190**
COOPER HENDERSON - A Gentleman
In A Horse-Drawn Gig Attended By His
Groom - 15½ x 23½in.
(Sotheby's) **£200**
CHARLES COOPER HENDERSON -
The Obstinate Horse, A Coach And Four
In A Landscape - 12½ x 23½in.
(Christie's) **£700**

CHARLES COOPER HENDERSON - The York To London Coach Setting Off - 27½ x 35½in.
(Christie's) **£4,500**

CHARLES COOPER HENDERSON - The London To Bristol And Bath Stage Coach - 16½ x 26½in.
(Christie's) **£1,400**

JOSEPH HENDERSON - Coast Scene With Small Boats - 72 x 110cm.
(Edmiston's) **£160**

J. MORRIS HENDERSON - Islands Of Loch Lomond - 50 x 90cm.
(Edmiston's) **£110**

J. MORRIS HENDERSON - Coast Scene With Harbour - watercolour - 34 x 51cm.
(Edmiston's) **£40**

H. HENDRICK - Dunes A Oostduinkerke - on wood - 27 x 30cm.
(Galerie Moderne) **£6**

HENRY W. HENLEY - Near Bettws-Y-Coed - signed - 19¼ x 29½in.
(Sotheby's Belgravia) **£280**

JEAN JACQUES HENNER - Jeune Femme Rousse En Chemise Blanche - signed - 23 x 18½in.
(Sotheby's) **£1,600**

CARSTEN HENRICHSEN - 'Landscape From The Forest Of Sollerod' - signed with monogram and dated 1878 - 69 x 95cm.
(Phillips) **£700**

BARCLAY HENRY - The Galloway Coast - 38 x 58cm.
(Edmiston's) **£70**

E. HENRY - Portrait Of A Man - oil on wood - signed and dated 1856 - 62 x 46cm.
(Galerie Moderne) **£60**

GEORGE HENRY - Portrait Of A Lady, bust length, In Profile - signed - 24 x 18in.
(Christie's) **£75**

GEORGE HENRY - A Promenade, Japan - watercolour - signed - 23 x 19½in.
(Sotheby's) **£320**

WILLIAM HENRY - A Church Interior - heightened with white - signed - 11 x 9¼in.
(Sotheby's) **£20**

WILLIAM HENSEL - The Duke Of
Brunswick At The Duchess Of Richmond's
Ball, on the eve of Waterloo - inscribed on
a label on the reverse - 91½ x 73in.
(Christie's)   **£650**

FREDERICK HENRY HENSHAW -
Tintern Abbey from the Chepstow Road
- signed and dated 1833 - 20 x 28 ins.
(Sotheby's Belgravia)   **£250**

ISAAC HENZELL - A Rest By A Pool -
signed and dated 1869 - 13½ x 17½in.
(Sotheby's Belgravia)   **£500**

ISAAC HENZELL - A Fishergirl -
signed and dated 1875 - 24 x 20in.
(Sotheby's Belgravia)   **£550**

ALBERT HERBERT - On The Sands,
Scheveling - watercolour heightened
with white - signed with monogram
and dated '54 - 14¼ x 25¼in.
(Christie's)   **£380**
ALFRED HERBERT - A Hay Barge
And Other Shipping Off The Isle
Of Sheppey - watercolour - 5½ x
8¾in.
(Christie's)   **£130**

E. B. HERBERTE - The Encounter -
signed and dated 1885 - 19 x 29¼in.
(Sotheby's Belgravia)   **£480**

E. B. HERBERTE - A Coach And Two On A Path By A River - signed and dated 1877 - 18 x 24in.
(Sotheby's Belgravia) **£32**

LEON HERBO - Reclining Female - oil on canvas - signed - 82 x 98cm.
(Galerie Moderne) **£150**

GEORGE EDWARDS HERING - An Extensive Italianate Lake landscape, with peasants resting in the foreground - signed and dated 1845 - 31½ x 45½ in.
(Christie's) **£1,300**

ALFRED HERION - Cattle At Pasture - oil on wood - signed - 48 x 86cm.
(Galerie Moderne) **£94**

LEON L'HERMITE - Le Clocher De Primelle - charcoal and pastel on buff paper - signed - 17¾ x 21 ins.
(Sotheby's) **£420**

WILLEM VAN HERP - The Judgment Of Saint Francis - 33 x 44in.
(Christie's) **£750**

V. HERP - Landscape - oil on canvas - signed - 24 x 30cm.
(Galerie Moderne) **£215**

F. HERRERA - A Religious Procession - 17½ x 28in.
(Christie's) **£700**

HERRING - A Farmyard - bears signature - 13¼ x 18¾in.
(Sotheby's Belgravia) **£260**

HERRING - A Farmyard Scene - bears signature - on board - 9½ x 11½in.
(Sotheby's Belgravia) **£240**

HERRING - A Bay Racehorse And A Groom In A Landscape - bears signature - 34 x 44in.
(Christie's) **£240**

HERRING - A Chestnut Hunter In An Extensive Landscape - 11½ x 14½in.
(Christie's) **£190**

HERRING

BENJAMIN HERRING - A Shorthorn
Cow In A Landscape - signed and
indistinctly dated - 19 x 23in.
(Christie's) £190

J. F. HERRING - Outside A Stable -
bears another signature - circular -
diameter 15½in.
(Sotheby's Belgravia) £350

J. F. HERRING - Three Horses In A Farmyard
with thatched buildings, ducks, pigeons and a
wheelbarrow - on canvas - 10 x 13½in.
(Morphet & Morphet) £570

JOHN FREDERICK HERRING, JNR -
A Mare And Foal In A Paddock - signed -
on panel - 6 x 8in.
(Christie's) £550

JOHN FREDERICK HERRING, JNR -
A Huntsman And Hounds About To
Draw A Covert - 18 x 29in.
(Christie's) £3,600

JOHN FREDERICK HERRING, JNR -
A Carthorse, A Donkey, Goats And
Poultry In A Stable; And Carthorses
And Figures On A Country Road - one
signed and indistinctly dated, the other
signed and dated 1849 - circular - 15½in.
diam.
(Christie's) £2,600 Pair

JOHN FREDERICK HERRING, JNR -
Carthorses Fording A Stream In A Farm-
yard - signed - 13¾ x 19½in.
(Christie's) **£2,500**

JOHN FREDERICK HERRING, JNR -
Busy Farmyards - both signed - each
15½ x 23¼in.
(Sotheby's Belgravia) **£1,600 Pair**

JOHN FREDERICK HERRING, JNR -
Ploughing Time; and The Midday Rest
- signed - 14 x 24in.
(Christie's, S. Kensington) **£3,500 Pair**

JOHN FREDERICK HERRING, JNR -
Horses And Ducks In A Farmyard -
signed with monogram - on board -
7½ x 9½in.
(Christie's) **£900**

JOHN FREDERICK HERRING, JNR -
Landscape With Horses - signed and
dated 1850 - 16in. diameter.
(Bonham's) **£1,100**

J. F. HERRING - Landscape With Pigs,
Cattle, Ducks And Fowl In A Yard Outside A Barn With Figure In Doorway -
oil - 15in. diameter, circular.
(G. A. Key) **£210**

HERRING - Towards The Finishing Post -
inscribed and dated 1847 - 11¼ x 15½in.
(Sotheby's) **£130**

S. HERSZENBERG - Mansion House And
Lawn With Children Playing - 1888 -
27 x 14.5cm.
(Edmiston's) **£400**

LOUIS HERVIEUX - Le Temple - oil -
on canvas - on board - signed - 19½ x
15½in.
(Sotheby's) **£12**

THEODORE BERNARD DE HEUVEL -
The Housekeeping Accounts - signed -
on panel - 24 x 19½in.
(Sotheby's) **£1,200**

YV. HEYMANS - Landscape - oil -
signed - 35 x 57cm.
(Galerie Moderne) **£50**

F. HIDER - Country Scenes - oil paintings
on canvas - signed - 29½ x 19½in
(John H. Raby & Son) **£600 Pair**

ANTHONY HIGHMORE - The
Promenade - watercolour - 3¼ x 5¼in.
(Christie's) **£200**

213

JOSEPH HIGHMORE - Portrait Of Priscilla Edgell, half length, Wearing A Grey Silk Dress And White Headdress, Holding A Garland Of Flowers, In A Landscape - 94 x 81cm.
(Phillips) **£1,500**

HENRY HILES - The Edge Of The Wood - signed - 25 x 30in.
(Buckell & Ballard) **£32.50**

CARL HILGERS - A Village Gathering On A Frozen River - signed and dated 1853 - 16¼ x 23¼in.
(Sotheby's) **£5,800**

HILL - Mother And Child Crossing A Stream - 13¼ x 11in.
(Sotheby's Belgravia) **£55**

DAVID OCTAVIUS HILL - Feu De Joie At Taymouth - 13 x 17½in.
(Sotheby's) **£700**

DAVID OCTAVIUS HILL - Edinburgh From Above The Dean Bridge - 27½ x 53½in.
(Christie's) **£1,000**

WILSON HILL - A Hiker's Path, Grindleford, Derbyshire - signed - board - oil - 17½ x 24in.
(Neale & Son) **£10**

HILLIERS - Beach Scene - oil on canvas - 19½ x 11½in.
(J. Francis, T. Jones & Sons) **£55**

ROBERT ALEXANDER HILLINGFORD - The Friendly Cavalier - signed - 11½ x 15½in.
(Sotheby's) **£220**

ROBERT ALEXANDER HILLINGFORD - Dressing For Action - signed - 17½ x 23in.
(Christie's) **£1,700**

HILLS - An Extensive Wooded Park, Deer in the foreground, A Large Country House Beyond - 15¾ x 23¾in.
(Sotheby's) **£110**

HENRY HILTON - Moorland Near Dolwyddelen - signed - 19½ x 29¼in.
(Sotheby's Belgravia) **£60**

JOHANNES HILVERDINK - The Ferry - signed and dated 1849 - 22 x 29¼in.
(Christie's) **£1,800**

FREDERICK HINES - Hayes Common, Surrey - signed and dated 1875 - 13½ x 11½in.
(Sotheby's Belgravia) **£110**

THEODORE HINES - On A Highland
River; On Loch Katrine, Silverstand -
both signed - inscribed on the reverse -
15½ x 23½in.
(Sotheby's Belgravia) **£220 Pair**

THEODORE HINES - On Loch Ard -
signed - inscribed on the reverse - 19½ x
29½in.
(Sotheby's Belgravia) **£300**

LAURENT DE LA HIRE - The Death Of
Cleopatra - indistinctly signed and dated 16 -
42 x 55in.
(Christie's) **£3,000**

E. HITCHINSON - Mares And Foals In
A Wooded Landscape - signed - 30½ x
46½in.
(Christie's) **£240**

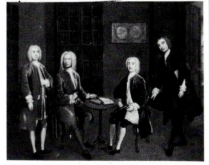

WILLIAM HOARE OF BATH - A Portrait
Group Of Richard Jones, Ralph Allen,
Robert Gay And John Wood, Snr. - oil on
canvas - 39 x 49in.
(Bonham's) **£3,000**

MEINDERT HOBBEMA - A Wooded
River Landscape With Men Hauling In
A Net - on panel - 11½ x 13in.
(Christie's) **£14,000**

W. HODGES - A View Of Rio De
Janiero From The Sea - paper laid down
on canvas - 18½ x 26½in.
(Christie's) **£1,700**

DAVID HODGSON - Cottage At
Whitlingham - signed reverse - oil -
10 x 14in.
(G. A. Key) **£88**

W. HODGSON - A Banquet In A
Mediaeval Hall - heightened with bodycolour - indistinctly signed and dated
'73 - 13½ x 19¾in.
(Sotheby's Belgravia) **£38**

J. JACOB HOEK - A Vegetable Seller,
A Woman Seated Outside A Church,
Surrounded By Piles Of Vegetables,
Baskets Of Fruit On A Trestle Before
Her - signed and dated 1779 - 13½ x
18in.
(Sotheby's) **£3,800**

HOECKE

ROBERT VAN DEN HOECKE - A Battle Between Crusaders And Turks - bears signature and the date 1647 - on copper - 27 x 34in.
(Christie's) **£1,400**

JAKOB HOFF - The Game Of Cards In A Tavern Interior - signed - 16¼ x 20½in.
(Sotheby's) **£400**

HOGARTH - 'The Dull Sermon' - 21½ x 17½in
(Christie's) **£280**

HOGARTH, After - Half length Study Of A Girl - oil - 40.5 x 33cm.
(Phillips in Scotland) **£50**

HOLBEIN - Portrait Of Henry VIII, head and shoulders, In A Red Embroidered Tunic And Black Feathered Hat - in a painted oval - on metal - 8¼ x 7in.
(Sotheby's) **£200**

D. HOLDEN - Highland Stream In Spate - 75 x 49cm.
(Edmiston's) **£80**

EDWARD HENRY HOLDER - Derwentwater, And Falcon Crag From The Bay Near Fernars Crag - signed - signed, inscribed and dated 1906 on the stretcher - 19½ x 29½in.
(Sotheby's Belgravia) **£440**

EDWARD HENRY HOLDER - A Cascade In A Rocky Landscape - signed and dated 1879 - 30 x 40in.
(Christie's) **£720**

EDWIN HENRY HOLDER - Bloody Beck, Harwood Dale, Near Scarborough - signed - inscribed on the reverse - on board - 7½ x 11½in.
(Sotheby's Belgravia) **£38**

EDWARD HENRY HOLDER - Rural Landscape, with a barn and buildings beside a small river; and A Lakeland Landscape, with cattle at the water's edge - both signed - oil on canvas - 49 x 75 cm
(Henry Spencer & Sons) **£480 Pair**

J. HOLDER - The Leddr Bridge - signed and indistinctly dated - inscribed on the stretcher - 23½ x 35¼in.
(Sotheby's Belgravia) **£95**

HENRY JAMES HOLDING - Falls Of The Clyde, At Stonebyres - signed and dated 1871 - signed, inscribed and dated on reverse - 23½ x 37½in.
(Christie's) **£120**

HENRY JAMES HOLDING - Haymaking - signed and dated '71 - watercolour - 12 x 35 ins.
(Christie's, S. Kensington) **£90**

W. F. HOLE - The Arch Of Titus With The Colosseum in distance - watercolour - 18 x 12in.
(G. A. Key) **£30**

HOLLAND - At The Fairground - 16½ x 21½in.
(Christie's) **£300**

JAMES HOLLAND - Venice: The Salute And San Marco From San Giorgio Maggiore - watercolour heightened with white - signed - 19¼ x 23½in.
(Christie's) **£500**

JAMES HOLLAND - The Interior Of Milan Cathedral, With A Procession And Numerous Figures At Prayer - signed and dated 1839 - 100 x 136.5cm.
(Phillips) **£850**

JAMES HOLLAND - Estrella Church, Lisbon - signed twice with monogram - inscribed twice and dated June 27th 1837 - pencil and watercolour heightened with white - 10¼ x 17¼in.
(Christie's) **£1,600**

JAMES HOLLAND - The Ruins Of St. Francisco, Lisbon - signed with monogram - inscribed and dated '37 - pencil and watercolour heightened with white - 10¾ x 8¼in.
(Christie's) **£800**

JAMES HOLLAND - The Old Houses Of Parliament Aflame - a sketch - 16 x 26in.
(Sotheby's Belgravia) **£40**

JOHN HOLLAND - A Mountain Pool - signed - 17 x 26¼in.
(Sotheby's Belgravia) **£30**

S. S. HOLLAND - Summer River Landscapes With Figures And Boats - oil - 11 x 17½in -
(Neale & Son) **£35 Pair**

THOMAS HOLLAND - Convolvulus And Other Flowers On A Ledge - watercolour heightened with white - signed - 10½ x 8½in.
(Christie's) **£100**

JOHN HOLLINS - Portrait Of Lord Brougham, full length, Standing In His Robes - pencil and watercolour - 7¾ x 5¼in.
(Christie's) **£12**

G. O. HOLMES - The Interior Of A Barn, With Two Girls - one carrying a bucket, a sheep-dog stands at their side, and feeding a donkey from a large basket of hay - signed and dated 1879 - 12½ x 16in.
(Henry Spencer & Sons) **£560**

WILFRED HOLMES - Passing The Time Of Day; Old Cottage, New Forest - both heightened with bodycolour - signed - 13¾ x 9¾in.
(Sotheby's Belgravia) **£190 Pair**

LAURITS HOLST - View Of Scarborough Lighthouse With Fishing Boats In A Stormy Sea - signed and dated 1878 - oil on canvas - 17½ x 29½in.
(Bearnes & Waycotts) **£190**

WILLIAM HOLYOAKE - Our Party At The Derby - 23½ x 19½in.
(Christie's) **£800**

MELCHIOR D'HONDECOETER - A Crow Attacked By A Cock With Other Domestic Poultry Nearby In A Wooded Landscape - signed - 52 x 66in.
(Christie's) **£8,500**

MELCHIOR D'HONDECOETER -
Goats, Poultry And Sheep In A Wooded
Farm Landscape - 58½ x 79½in.
(Christie's)   **£11,000**

M. D'HONDECOETER - Domestic Fowl By
A Building In A Landscape - bears signature -
39½ x 36¼in.
(Christie's)   **£3,200**

ABRAHAM HONDIUS - Dogs Attacking A
Bull - signed and dated 1683 - on panel -
15½ x 19in.
(Christie's)   **£750**

ABRAHAM HONDIUS - A Bear Hunt; and
a Wolf Attacking Hounds over a dead roe -
102 x 115 ins.
(Christie's)   **£4,000 Pair**

THIRZE M. HONNSFIELD - Village
Scene With Figures And Duck Pond -
watercolour - 11 x 15in.
(G. A. Key)   **£24**

HONTHORST - Portrait Of A Man In
Black Armour With A White Lace Cravat,
Reputedly King Leopold Of Belgium - oil
on panel - 15½ x 12in.
(Bearnes & Waycotts)   **£150**

W. VAN HONTHORST - Portrait Of A
Lady, Three-Quarter Length, Holding A
Fan And Flowers, A Landscape Beyond -
44½ x 37¼in.
(Sotheby's)   **£440**

DAVID DE HOOCH - An Italianate Rocky
River Landscape With An Artist Sketching
In Front Of A Cascade, And Cattle And
Peasants Beyond - signed - 37 x 46½in.
(Christie's)   **£3,200**

E. B. HOOD - Hills and Glen -
19 x 23.5cm.
(Edmiston's)   **£50**

ERNEST B. HOOD - Demolition - watercolour - 30 x 26cm.
(Edmiston's) £24

ERNEST B. HOOD - November Day, Glasgow - 46 x 68cm.
(Edmiston's) £52

JAMES CLARKE HOOK - The Coral Fisher, Amalfi - signed with monogram and dated 1878 - 31 x 54in.
(Sotheby's Belgravia) £1,000

JAMES CLARKE HOOK - Women Washing On The Beach - signed with monogram and dated 1866 - 27 x 42in.
(Christie's) £600

JOHN HOOPER - Victorian Genre painting of Boy Throwing Snowball - oil on canvas - 11½ x 14½in.
(J. Francis, T. Jones & Sons) £38

JOHN HORACE HOOPER - Country Landscape With Two Figures - signed - oil on canvas - 19¼ x 35½in.
(Bearnes & Waycotts) £500

R. HOPE - Before The Harvest - on board - 7 x 8½in.
(Sotheby's Belgravia) £22

ROBERT HOPE - A Pastoral - signed - 15½ x 19½in.
(Sotheby's Belgravia) £90

ROBERT HOPE - Pomona - signed - 19½ x 15½in.
(Sotheby's) £200

FRANCES ANN HOPKINS - Canadian River Scene with Indians landing on River Bank with Canoes and Raft - watercolour drawing - monogrammed dated 1870 - 17 x 9½in.
(Smith-Woolley & Perry) £420

JOHANNES FRANCISCUS HOPPENBROUWERS and SALOMON LEONARDUS VERVEER - A Gypsy Encampment At Dusk - signed and dated '53 - 15½ x 19in.
(Sotheby's) £950

J. HOPPNER - Portrait Of Lord Keith, half length, In Naval Uniform, Wearing The Star And Order Of The Bath - 29 x 24in.
(Christie's) £240

JOHN HOPPNER - Portrait Of Mary, Lady Gordon - half-length - in a fawn dress and green sash - 29 x 24in.
(Christie's) £1,800

JAN JOSEF HOREMANS, THE YOUNGER - The Interior Of A Money Lenders - signed - canvas - on panel - 15 x 12½in.
(Christie's) £1,300

JAN JOSEPH HOREMANS, THE YOUNGER - The Interior Of A Cobbler's Shop - on copper - 10 x 15in.
(Christie's) £550

JAN JOSEPH HOREMANS, THE ELDER - Figures Outside An Inn - signed - 14¾ x 17¾in.
(Christie's) £1,000

JAN JOSEF HOREMANS, THE ELDER -
Figures Feasting In An Interior - 28 x 35in.
(Christie's) £2,800

GEORGE W. HORLOR - A Setter And
A Pheasant - signed and dated 1869 -
17½ x 23½in.
(Sotheby's Belgravia) £550

GEORGE W. HORLOR - A Study Of Three
Rabbits - circular - inscribed on verso and
dated 1849 - 17in diameter.
(Henry Spencer & Sons) £240

JOSEPH HORLOR - Tantallon Castle,
Scotland - bears another signature and
date - signed and inscribed on the stretcher - 15½ x 23½in.
(Sotheby's Belgravia) £220

JOSEPH HORLOR - Landscape Studies -
oil on millboard - 5½ x 7¾in.
(Bearnes & Waycotts) £150 Pair

JOSEPH HORLOR - A Highland
Drover With His Cattle - signed and
dated 1883 - 33½ x 28½in.
(Sotheby's Belgravia) £250

JOSEPH HORLOR - Village Path;
Fishermen And Their Catch - both
signed - on board - oval - 10¾ x 8¾in.
(Sotheby's Belgravia) £200 Pair

J. HORLOR - Bringing Home The
Sheep - on board - 6¾ x 13¼in.
(Sotheby's Belgravia) £80

JOSEPH HORLOR - Fishermen's
Cottages - signed - 11½ x 19½in.
(Sotheby's Belgravia) **£95**

EDWARD ATKINSON HORNEL - A White
Butterfly - signed and dated 1923 -
19½ x 23½in.
(Sotheby's) **£2,300**

EDWARD ATKINSON HORNEL - Two
Girls Picking Flowers Amidst Blossom -
dated 1917 - 60 x 70cm.
(Edmiston's) **£340**

EDWARD ATKINSON HORNEL - By The
Lake - signed and dated 1917 - on board -
19½ x 15½in.
(Sotheby's) **£1,600**

**HOPKINS HORSLEY HOBDAY
HORSLEY** - Winter - signed on the
stretcher - 26 x 35½in.
(Sotheby's Belgravia) **£1,800**

EDWARD ATKINSON HORNEL -
Brighouse Bay - signed and dated 1920 -
15½ x 19½in.
(Sotheby's) **£1,600**

JOHN CALLCOTT HORSLEY - To
Celia, Valentine's Day - inscribed -
23 x 27¼in.
(Sotheby's Belgravia) **£400**

WARNAAR HORSTINK - A Wooded Landscape With Peasants And Animals On A Path; And A Wooded River Landscape With A Milkmaid And Cattle And Sheep - one signed and dated 1783 - on panel - 14 x 18in.
(Christie's) **£4,200 Pair**

E. HORTON - Cattle Watering - both signed - each 9½ x 13½in.
(Sotheby's Belgravia) **£180 Pair**

E. HORTON - Highland Cattle By A River - signed - 19½ x 29½in.
(Sotheby's Belgravia) **£18**

ELMYR DE HORY - Head Of A Young Girl In The Manner Of Modigliani - 21 x 14¼in.
(Christie's, S. Kensington) **£1,200**

P. HOSIA - A Still Life Of Assorted Flowers In A Glass Vase In A Niche - oil - signed and dated 1810 - 75 x 61cm.
(Phillips in Scotland) **£220**

GERRIT HOUCKGEEST - An Architectural Capriccio, with figures by an ornamental lake - signed with monogram - on panel - 33½ x 45in.
(Christie's) **£900**

GEORGE HOUSTON - Loch Melport - signed - inscribed on the stretcher - 27½ x 35in.
(Sotheby's) **£340**

GEORGE HOUSTON - Cairngow - signed - inscribed and dated 1917 - 27 x 35½in.
(Sotheby's) **£700**

GEORGE HOUSTON - At Inverary - signed - 27½ x 35½in.
(Sotheby's) **£190**

GEORGE HOUSTON - On The River Array - 27½ x 35½in.
(Sotheby's) **£240**

JOHN R. HOUSTON - A Humble Meal - 34 x 44cm.
(Edmiston's) **£115**

ROBERT HOUSTON - A Spring River Landscape - oil - signed and dated 1910 - 50 x 60cm.
(Phillips in Scotland) **£82**

GEORGE HOWARD - Portrait Of Sir Edward Coley Burne-Jones At His Easel - pencil - inscribed and dated '97 - 9¾ x 6½in.
(Sotheby's Belgravia) **£110**

H. HOWARD - Christ Raising Lazarus From The Dead - 26 x 34in.
(Sotheby's) **£70**

J. HOWE - Malcolm Fleming Of Barouchan Mounted On A Chestnut Cob, With John Anderson, His Falconer, In A Woody Landscape - 17½ x 23½in.
(Christie's) **£600**

S. HOWITT - A Partridge - 3½ x 4½in.
(Sotheby's) **£60**

HOWLE - The Ruins Of Lilleshall Abbey - 24½ x 29½in.
(Sotheby's) **£220**

J. VAN HOYEN - The Sail Maker - on wood - signed - 19 x 28cm.
(Galerie Moderne) **£116**

A. HUBERT - Seascape - oil on wood - signed - 20 x 25cm.
(Galerie Moderne) **£4**

R. HUBERT - Cattle At Pasture - on wood - signed - 14 x 19cm.
(Galerie Moderne) **£18**

L. HUBNER - A Still Life Of Fish And Vegetables On A Table - signed - 27¾ x 35¾in.
(Sotheby's) **£250**

223

HUCHTENBURG - A Cavalry Engagement Between Christians And Turks - on panel - 9½ x 11¼in.
(Sotheby's) £180

JAN VAN HUCHTENBURG - A Cavalry Skirmish in an extensive landscape - signed with monogram - 20½ x 24in.
(Christie's) £2,200

JAN VAN HUCHTENBURG - A Cavalry Encampment In A Wooded Valley - signed and indistinctly dated - 20 x 26in.
(Christie's) £3,500

HUDSON - Portrait Of A Gentleman, Possibly William Benson, Esq., half length, Wearing A Brown Coat And Holding A Medal Of Milton - 29 x 24½in.
(Sotheby's) £150

HUDSON - Portrait Of A Gentleman, said To Be The Rt. Hon. Sir Thomas Parker, three-quarter length, Seated, A Parchment In His Right Hand, A Book-case To His Right - 17¾ x 15in.
(Sotheby's) £25

HUET - Two Children In A Garden - inscribed - 13 x 10in.
(Sotheby's) £180

WILLIAM HUGGINS - Donkeys In An Upland Pasture - 29 x 34cm.
(Edmiston's) £175

WILLIAM HUGGINS - Long Sleeping - coloured chalks - signed and dated 1877 - 10 x 15in.
(Sotheby's Belgravia) £850

WILLIAM HUGGINS - A Lion Resting - on panel - 12¾ x 16½in.
(Sotheby's Belgravia) £450

ARTHUR HUGHES - Still Life Of Dead Game - oil on canvas - signed and dated 1876 - 36 x 28in.
(King & Chasemore) £410

WILLIAM HUGHES - Still Lives Of
Fruit And Birds' Nests - both signed
and dated 1861 - on board - 8¾ x 10¾in.
(Sotheby's Belgravia) **£650 Pair**

SIR HERBERT HUGHES-STANTON -
Whitley Woods, Tichfield, Hampshire -
signed and dated 1911 - 19½ x 26½in.
(Sotheby's Belgravia) **£360**

HULK - Cottage Landscapes - both on
board - 18¾ x 15in.
(Sotheby's Belgravia) **£55 Pair**

A. HULK - A Dutch Fishing Boat Off A
Port In A Fresh Breeze - signed - oil -
12 x 18in.
(Warner, Sheppard & Wade) **£85**

A. HULK, JNR - Barges And Other
Shipping In The Thames - each 9½ x
13¼in.
(Sotheby's) **£320 Pair**

ABRAHAM HULK, JNR - Charlwood,
Surrey; Tapsley, Hereford - both
signed - inscribed on the stretcher -
18 x 14in.
(Sotheby's Belgravia) **£130 Pair**

ABRAHAM HULK, JNR - A View Near
Ewhurst, Surrey - signed - inscribed on
the reverse - 39½ x 29½in.
(Sotheby's Belgravia) **£750**

ABRAHAM HULK, JNR - River Landscape With Figures - signed - canvas on board - 19½ x 29½in.
(Bearnes & Waycotts) **£200**

ABRAHAM HULK, JNR - A Windy Day; Fishing In A Pond - both signed - each 7½ x 15½in.
(Sotheby's Belgravia) **£450 Pair**

ABRAHAM HULK, SNR - Dutch Fishing Vessels In A Breeze Offshore - signed - 57.5 x 86.5cm.
(Phillips) **£3,600**

ABRAHAM HULK, SNR - Dutch Fishing Barges And Rowing Boats In Calm Waters - both signed - on panel - 6¼ x 8¼in.
(Sotheby's) **£1,900 Pair**

ABRAHAM HULK, SNR - On The Scheldt; Barges Becalmed Beside A Quay - both signed - on panel - 5½ x 7½in.
(Sotheby's) **£2,600 Pair**

ABRAHAM HULK - Sailing Barges In A Dutch Estuary - oil - on canvas - signed - 16 x 24in.
(King & Chasemore) **£880**

HENDRIK HULK - Dutch River Scene With Fishing Boats - signed and dated 1870 - oil on panel - 12½ x 19½in.
(Bearnes & Waycotts) **£720**

HENDRIK HULK - Dutch Barges And A Rowing Boat In Calm Waters - signed - on panel - 7½ x 12½in.
(Sotheby's) **£550**

FRANK HULME - A Middle Eastern Scene With Ruined Temple in background and Camels And Riders in foreground - signed - watercolour - 13¼ x 8½in.
(Boulton & Cooper) **£19**

FREDERICK WILLIAM HULME - The Village Of Pyrford, Surrey - signed and dated 1859 - oil on canvas - 36 x 28in.
(Bonham's) **£1,100**

FREDERICK WILLIAM HULME - A Wayside Conversation: A Country Road With A Woman Talking To A Game-keeper - signed and dated 1863 - 17½ x 23½in.
(Christie's) **£3,500**

JACOB VAN HULSDONCK - Grapes, Plums, Peaches And Cherries In A Basket On A Ledge - signed on panel - 11½ x 15½in.
(Christie's) **£8,500**

F. DE HULST - A Wooded River Land-scape With A Castle - on panel - 13 x 20½in.
(Christie's) **£2,600**

JEAN CHARLES FERDINAND HUMBERT - Cattle At A Watering Place In A Forest - signed and dated 1854 - 16¾ x 22in.
(Sotheby's) **£350**

ALFRED WILLIAM HUNT - A River Landscape - signed and dated 1860 - 9¾ x 14¼in.
(Sotheby's Belgravia) **£300**

ARTHUR ACKLAND HUNT - The Lion Rock, Dixcart Bay, Sark - signed and inscribed - 10½ x 18½in.
(Sotheby's Belgravia) **£30**

CECIL ARTHUR HUNT - An Italian Lake Landscape - signed - oil - 24 x 32in.
(Warner, Sheppard & Wade) **£48**

CHARLES HUNT - The Amorous Tinker Discovered - signed and dated 1881 - 29 x 44½in.
(Christie's) **£1,100**

EDGAR HUNT - A Goat And Pigeons In A Barn - 61 x 92cm.
(Phillips) **£860**

HUNT

EDGAR HUNT - Feeding Doves - signed
and dated '99 - 24 x 36in.
(Sotheby's Belgravia) **£4,800**

EDGAR HUNT - A Hen And Her
Chicks With Pigeons Outside A Barn -
signed and dated 1918 - 36 x 30cm.
(Phillips) **£1,300**

EDGAR HUNT - Ducks And Hens By A
Farmyard Pond - signed and dated 1925 -
11 x 14¾in.
(Christie's) **£2,100**

EDGAR HUNT - An Interior Of A Barn,
With Donkey, A Cock, Many Hens And
Chickens Pecking Cabbage Leaves On The
Floor - signed and dated 1920 -
21½ x 29½in.
(Henry Spencer & Sons) **£5,200**

W. HUNT - A Farmyard Scene With A Child,
A White Pony And Poultry - signed and dated
1821 - 28 x 36in.
(Warner, Sheppard & Wade) **£2,400**

W. H. HUNT, After - Isabella And The
Pot Of Basil - 25½ x 17½in.
(Sotheby's Belgravia) **£22**

WILLIAM HENRY HUNT - Black
Grapes In A Basket - watercolour -
signed and dated 1827 - 8 x 10in.
(Christie's) **£300**

WILLIAM HENRY HUNT - Plums, Damsons And Grapes On The Ground - watercolour - signed - 12 x 17in.
(Christie's) £75

WILLIAM HOLMAN HUNT - Constantinople - pencil, heightened with white - inscribed and dated January 1856 - on buff paper - 7 x 10in.
(Sotheby's Belgravia) £220

COLIN HUNTER - Off The Scottish Coast - signed and dated 1899 - 34¼ x 59in.
(Sotheby's Belgravia) £180

COLIN HUNTER - The Victory Off Walmer Castle - signed and dated 1903 - 34 x 84½in.
(Sotheby's) £300

COLIN HUNTER - Off The Coast - signed and dated '90 - 15½ x 29½in.
(Sotheby's Belgravia) £20

GEORGE LESLIE HUNTER - Farm Buildings - signed - on board - 19½ x 26½in.
(Sotheby's) £350

GEORGE LESLIE HUNTER - A Village Road, Winter - coloured chalks - signed - 9½ x 6½in.
(Sotheby's) £65

GEORGE LESLIE HUNTER - A Venetian Backwater - pen and ink and watercolour - signed - 10 x 9in.
(Sotheby's) £220

GEORGE LESLIE HUNTER - The Serpentine, Hyde Park - coloured chalks and black ink - signed - 14 x 17in.
(Sotheby's) £160

GEORGE SHERWOOD HUNTER - In The Suppressed Cloisters Of St. Paul's, Rome - signed - inscribed 'Roma' and dated 1876 - 40 x 30in.
(Sotheby's Belgravia)   **£500**

JOHN YOUNG HUNTER - Portrait Of A Lady Wearing A Black Dress, Seated, half length - signed and dated '10 - 39 x 26in.
(Sotheby's Belgravia)   **£18**

LESLIE HUNTER - Apples And Lemon - 29 x 33.5cm.
(Edmiston's)   **£320**

MASON HUNTER - Masted Fishing Boats Leaving Harbour - signed - oil on canvas - 25 x 30in.
(Morphet & Morphet)   **£200**

WILLIAM HUNTER - Head Of A Dog - oil on lined canvas - signed - 32 x 26cm.
(Galerie Moderne)   **£19**

LOUIS BOSWORTH HURT - Loch Clare, Ross-shire - signed and dated 1887 - 23½ x 35½in.
(Sotheby's)   **£500**

LOUIS BOSWORTH HURT - Showery Weather, Waiting For The Drovers - signed and dated 1895 - 36 x 59in.
(Sotheby's)   **£1,000**

L. B. HURT - Lough Derg, Twenty Island - inscribed and dated May 1897 - on paper - 8½ x 17½in.
(Sotheby's Belgravia)   **£60**

J. T. HUTCHINSON - 'Interior Scene', Dog Sat By Door - oil - signed - 15½ x 18¾in.
(J. Entwistle & Co.)   **£19**

J. T. HUTCHINSON - 'Wooded Seashore Scene And River And Woodland Scene With Bridge' - oil - signed - each 23¼ x 11¼in.
(J. Entwistle & Co.)   **£9 Pair**

J. T. HUTCHINSON - 'Memorial To John Ruskin' - oil - signed - 15¼ x 11½in.
(J. Entwistle & Co.)   **£3**

ROBERT GEMMELL HUTCHISON - The Wayside Rest - a sketch - on board - 8 x 6in.
(Sotheby's)   **£110**

ROBERT GEMMELL HUTCHISON -
"Washing Day" - oil - 10 x 10½in.
(Thomas Love & Sons Ltd)   **£550**

R. GEMMELL HUTCHISON - Gruel
Time - pastel - 51 x 36cm.
(Edmiston's)   **£360**

R. GEMMEL HUTCHISON - Two
Children At A Shop Window - 24 x
16.5cm.
(Edmiston's)   **£130**

F. HUYGENS - Dead Birds - oil on
lined canvas - signed - 27 x 35cm.
(Galerie Moderne)   **£40**

HUYSMANS - A Southern Landscape,
in the left foreground Men Beside A
Pool, A Horseman On A Path Beyond -
10½ x 12½in.
(Sotheby's)   **£110**

J. B. HUYSMANS - A Shepherd And
Shepherdess In A Landscape - 19 x 30¾in.
(Christie's)   **£420**

ROBERT GEMMELL HUTCHISON - A
Cottage Interior - oil on canvas - signed -
17 x 13½in.
(King & Chasemore)   **£380**

ROBERT GEMMELL HUTCHISON - 'The
Young Dutchman' - oil on board - signed -
10½ x 8½in.
(King & Chasemore)   **£160**

JAN-BAPTIST HUYSMANS - A Wooded
Landscape With A Horseman On A Path,
A Town Beyond - 18½ x 24½in.
(Christie's)   **£2,800**

JAN-BAPTIST HUYSMANS - A
Mountainous Woody Landscape With
Figures, A River Beyond - 18½ x
24½in.
(Christie's)   **£3,800**

VAN HUYSUM - Mixed Flowers In A Jar On A Ledge, With Insects And Bird Nest - on zinc panel - 24 x 19.2cm.
(Edmiston's) **£430**

VAN HUYSUM - Carnations, An Iris, Peaches, Grapes And Other Fruit On A Marble Ledge - 32½ x 26in.
(Christie's) **£850**

J. VAN HUYSUM - Roses, Tulips, A Sunflower And Other Flowers In A Sculptured Vase With Peaches And A Bird's Nest On A Ledge - bears signature - 38 x 28in.
(Christie's) **£4,800**

A. HYNDMARSH - Highland Cattle Watering - signed - 23½ x 41½in.
(Sotheby's Belgravia) **£50**

L DE LA HYRE - The Adoration Of The Magi - 29¾ x 36in.
(Sotheby's) **£250**

ANDREW HYSLOP - Crofters' Cottages - signed - 13½ x 21in.
(Sotheby's Belgravia) **£80**

HUYSMANS - Portrait Of A Boy, full length, Wearing A Blue Cloak, In A Wooded Landscape - 48 x 39in.
(Christie's) **£350**

IBBETSON - The Sailor's Pleasure; And A Sailor Recreating - watercolour - 7 x 5½in.
(Christie's) **£100 Pair**

J. C. IBBETSON - Pastoral Scene With Figures And Animals By The Riverside - on canvas - 20½ x 17in.
(Worsfolds) **£1,300**

JULIUS CAESAR IBBETSON - A Wooded River Landscape With Cattle And A Man Courting A Shepherdess in the foreground - 25 x 31in.
(Christie's) **£380**

P. A. IMMENRAEDT - A Mountainous Coastal Landscape With Figures in the foreground And A Rocky River Landscape With Figures In A Storm - 15½ x 28½in.
(Christie's) **£1,300 Pair**

JOSEPH MURRAY INCE - Fishing Boats In The Open Sea In A Calm; And Figures By A Windmill - watercolour, one heightened with white - 2¼ x 6¼in.
(Christie's) **£140 Pair**

INDIAN SCHOOL - An Indian Arranging His Long Hair - heightened with bodycolour - 10¾ x 6in.
(Sotheby's) **£30**

FILIPPO INDONI - A Young Girl With A Wayfarer - signed - 30 x 20¼in.
(Sotheby's) £460

FILIPPO INDONI - An Italian Peasant Girl - signed - watercolour - 20 x 12¼in.
(Sotheby's) £85

GEORGE INNESS - 'Viaduct At Laricha, Italy - signed - 46 x 66cm.
(Phillips) £2,200

IGNACIO DE IRIARTE - A Woody River Landscape With Peasants At A Table Outside A Ruin - 43 x 68in.
(Christie's) £2,000

VINCENZO IROLLI - A Busy Market - signed - 18½ x 26½in.
(Sotheby's) £2,700

LOUIS GABRIEL EUGENE ISABEY - La Mort De Virginie - 23¾ x 35¾in.
(Sotheby's) £850

A. ISENBRANDT - Saint Jerome In The Wilderness - on panel - 27½ x 21½in.
(Christie's) £1,200

ISRAELS - A Mother And Her Children By A Gate In The Country - bears signature - 35 x 31in.
(Sotheby's) £850

CAMILLE INNOCENTI - La Donna Espagnola - oil - on panel - signed - 14¼ x 10½in.
(Sotheby's) £460

L. INSTEAD - Stranded - signed - 8½ x 6½in.
(Sotheby's Belgravia) £12

NORTH ITALIAN SCHOOL, 17th Century - Martyrdom of a Bishop and a Deacon - pen and brown ink and wash heightened with white - 42.5 x 30 cm.
(Sotheby's) £95

ITALIAN SCHOOL, circa 1700 - The Holy Family - 16 x 12½in.
(Woolley & Wallis) £230

ITALIAN SCHOOL

ITALIAN SCHOOL, 18th Century -
A Southern Landscape, A Still Life Of
Fruit And Flowers To The Right And
Ruins To The Left - 49 x 69in.
(Sotheby's) **£320**

ITALIAN SCHOOL, 18th Century - The
Taking Down From The Cross - oil on
canvas - 38 x 50in.
(King & Chasemore) **£240**

ITALIAN SCHOOL, 18th Century - The
Taking Down From The Cross - oil on
canvas - 50 x 38in.
(King & Chasemore) **£200**

ITALIAN SCHOOL - The Madonna
And Child With Angels - on gold ground
canvas laid down on panel - 43½ x 25½in.
(Christie's) **£3,200**

**ITALIAN SCHOOL, Late 18th or Early
19th Century** - Pastoral Scenes With
Figures - oil on canvas - 16 x 12¼in.
(Bearnes & Waycotts) **£400 Pair**

ITALIAN SCHOOL, 19th century -
Wine For The Sportsmen - 28¼ x 23¼in.
(Sotheby's) **£450**

ITALIAN SCHOOL, circa 1820 - A
Dominican Preaching To The Crowd By
Trajan's Column - 14¼ x 18¾in.
(Sotheby's) **£500**

ITALIAN SCHOOL, 17th Century -
Adoration Of The Magi - 21¾ x 17¼in.
(Buckell & Ballard) **£1,500**

ITALIAN SCHOOL - A Young Boy
Fishing And Peasant Women By A
Pool - 21 x 44cm.
(Phillips) **£520**

ITALIAN SCHOOL - A Woman In A Red
Robe Seated With A Book - inscribed and
dated 1863 on the reverse - oil - 52 x 37in.
(Warner, Sheppard & Wade) **£160**

ITALIAN SCHOOL, 19th century - Figures
In A Cottage Interior - watercolour -
indistinctly signed - 9½ x 11¾in.
(King & Chasemore) **£120**

ITALIAN SCHOOL - The Holy Family
And St. John - on wood - 1m.06 x 83cm.
(Galerie Moderne) **£500**

ITALIAN SCHOOL - A Pair Of Gouache
Classical Allegorical Scenes - watercolour -
10½ x 22in.
(Woolley & Wallis) **£120 Pair**

FRANZ ITTENBACH - The Virgin And
Child With Lilies In An Extensive Landscape - signed and dated 1853 -
inscribed 'Dusseldorf' on the reverse -
arched top - 42 x 32in.
(Sotheby's) **£4,600**

A. JACKSON - Barn Interiors With
Sheep - signed - oil on board - 10 x 11in.
(Buckell & Ballard)   **£230 Pair**

ALEXANDER YOUNG JACKSON -
View Of The St. Lawrence At St. Fidele -
oil on board - dated 1930 - 8¼ x 10½in.
(Bracketts)   **£5,400**

FREDERICK HAMILTON JACKSON -
By An Italian Lake - heightened with
bodycolour - signed and dated 1893 -
21¼ x 13¾in.
(Sotheby's Belgravia)   **£80**

FREDERICK HAMILTON JACKSON -
Cromer - inscribed and dated Aug '80 on
the reverse - on board - 10 x 18in.
(Sotheby's Belgravia)   **£50**

FREDERICK HAMILTON JACKSON -
Amongst The Clouds - signed and dated
1901 - 16½ x 24¼in.
(Sotheby's Belgravia)   **£300**

FREDERICK HAMILTON JACKSON -
A Cathedral Town, Evening - signed and
dated 1895 - 18 x 26in.
(Sotheby's Belgravia)   **£100**

FREDERICK HAMILTON JACKSON -
Les Bourdes, A Pyrenean Village -
signed and dated 1917 - 18½ x 29½in.
(Sotheby's Belgravia)   **£75**

FREDERICK HAMILTON JACKSON -
A Country Town - signed and dated 1886 -
17¾ x 25¾in.
(Sotheby's Belgravia) £55

FREDERICK HAMILTON JACKSON -
By The Village Pond - heightened with
white - signed and dated 1889 - 17¾ x
25¾in.
(Sotheby's Belgravia) £55

SAMUEL PHILLIPS JACKSON - Boys
Above A Beach - signed - 13 x 22in.
(Sotheby's Belgravia) £60

JACQUE, After - Sheep Watering Under
A Tree - oil - on board - 29.5 x 21.5cm.
(Phillips in Scotland) £42

E. JAFFAY - Accessoires - cartoon -
signed - 44 x 35cm.
(Galerie Moderne) £22

ARMAND JAMAR - Landscape - oil on
canvas - signed - 38 x 47cm.
(Galerie Moderne) £142

ARMAND JAMAR - Marais A Genck -
oil on canvas - signed and dated 1942 -
80cm. x 1m.
(Galerie Moderne) £377

LAJOS JAMBOR - Enjoying A Romance -
signed - signed on the reverse - 29 x 39in.
(Sotheby's) £160

JAMES - Venetian Canal Scene With Boats
And Figures On Quayside - 23 x 34½in.
(Woolley & Wallis) £620

DAVID JAMES - 'Atlantic Breakers,
Pembrokeshire Coast' - signed and
dated 1887 - inscribed on the reverse -
oil on canvas - 24½ x 49¼in.
(Bearnes & Waycotts) £660

DAVID JAMES - Fishing Boats In
Choppy Seas - signed and dated 1879 -
oil on canvas - 29½ x 49½in.
(Bearnes & Waycotts) £320 Pair

STEPHEN JAMES - Broadland Scene
With Wherry Near St. Benets Abbey -
watercolour - 9 x 13in.
(G. A Key) £250

WILLIAM JAMES - A View Of The
Cannareggio, Venice, With San
Geremia - 30 x 50in.
(Christie's) £3,500

WILLIAM JAMES - The Grand Canal,
Venice With The Church Of Santa Maria
Della Carita And Numerous Figures And
Gondolas - 31 x 49in.
(Christie's) £6,000

F. E. JAMIESON - Moored Shipping -
both signed - each 19½ x 29½in.
(Sotheby's Belgravia) £130 Pair

H. JANET - Reading By A Fire -
signed - 15¾ x 12¼in.
(Sotheby's Belgravia) £140

JANSEM

JEAN JANSEM - La Lavandiere - oil - on canvas - signed - 28¾ x 36¼in.
(Sotheby's) **£650**

JOHANNES JANSON — An Extensive Woody Landscape with figures, cattle and sheep on a path by a pond - signed and dated 1783 - on panel - 12¾ x 16¼in.
(Christie's) **£4,200**

PETER JANSON - Dune Landscape With Peasants And Cattle - one dated 1781 - both bear Nasmyth's signature and dated 1830 - on panel - 9½ x 10¾in.
(Christie's) **£2,000 Pair**

MATHURIN JANSSAUD - Concarneau - Retour De Peche - charcoal and pastel - signed - 19¾ x 28¾in.
(Sotheby's) **£340**

JAPANESE SCHOOL - Figures In Palaces And Landscapes - drawings on silk - watercolour - 12 x 16in.
(Woolley & Wallis) **£150 Six**

CHARLES JAQUES - Fowl - oil on panel - 8 x 12 ins.
(Brackett's) **£60**

ALEXEJ VON JAWLENSKY - Der Teddybar - pen and ink and wash - signed and dated 28.1.26 - 5¾ x 4in.
(Sotheby's) **£250**

B. JEGH - Portrait Of A Priest - oil on lined canvas - signed - 54 x 35cm.
(Galerie Moderne) **£50**

H. JEHIN - The Lesson - oil on canvas - signed - 60 x 80cm.
(Galerie Moderne) **£63**

H. JEHIN - Interieur Anime - oil on canvas - signed - 63 x 83cm.
(Galerie Moderne) **£50**

G. H. JENKINS - Fishing Boats, Plymouth - signed - watercolour - 11¾ x 20½in.
(Bearnes & Waycotts) **£110**

THOMAS JENKINS - Portrait Of Thomas Brand - three-quarter length - signed, inscribed and dated 1753 - 45½ x 36in.
(Christie's) **£1,400**

W. JENKINS - Liverpool Docks - bears signature and date - bears inscription on the reverse - 11½ x 23½in.
(Sotheby's Belgravia) **£42**

J. L. JENSEN - Basket Of Flowers - oil - on canvas - 18 x 23in.
(Chrystal Bros. & Stott) **£200**

MAX JENSEN - An Extensive Seascape With Seagulls - signed - 31¼ x 50in.
(Sotheby's) **£170**

AMBROSIM JEROME - Farmyard Scene - signed and dated 1874 - 18 x 24in.
(Elliott & Green) **£240**

AMBROSINI JEROME - Portrait Of King Charles I - oil on canvas - 48½ x 39in.
(Bearnes & Waycotts) **£160**

JERVAS - Portrait Of A Lady, half length, Wearing A Dark Dress - 29½ x 24½in.
(Sotheby's) **£40**

JERVAS - Portrait Of A Lady, three-quarter length, Wearing A Blue Dress, Seated In A Park, Holding A Basket Of Flowers - 49 x 39in.
(Christie's) **£420**

CHARLES JERVAS - Portrait Of A Lady, Possibly Elizabeth, Duchess Of Bridgewater, Reclining Against A Rock In A Landscape - full length - 53 x 61¼in.
(Christie's) **£2,600**

W. JESSUP - The Willow Song, From Othello - signed and dated 1836 - 18 x 14½in.
(Christie's) **£55**

R. JOBLING - 'The Mouth Of The Tyne' - signed and dated 1878 - on canvas - 12½ x 11½in.
(Morphet & Morphet) **£115**

CARL JOHANSSEN - An Extensive Lakeland Scene At Sweden - signed - inscribed 'Are' and dated 1890.
(Sotheby's) **£800**

AUGUSTUS JOHN - 'A Study of Dorelia' - etching - signed - 3¾ x 2¾in.
(King & Chasemore) **£100**

AUGUSTUS JOHN - A Study of a Young Man, Head and Shoulders - etching - signed - 5¾ x 4½in.
(King & Chasemore) **£280**

HARRY JOHNSON - On The Welsh Hills - watercolour - signed and dated 1848 - 17½ x 27¾in.
(Christie's) **£80**

HARRY JOHN JOHNSON - Views Of And Near Istanbul - oils - signed and dated - 19 x 27½in.
(Graves Son & Pilcher) **£900 Pair**

JOHNSON

JOHNSON, Janssens - Portrait Of A Gentleman, half length, Wearing Armour And A White Lace Collar - in a painted oval - 28 x 23in.
(Sotheby's) **£90**

J. S. W. JOHNSON - A Two Decker And Other Shipping, By Moonlight In The Bay Of Naples - signed, indistinctly inscribed and dated 1876 - 29¾ x 39in.
(Christie's) **£250**

SIDNEY YATES JOHNSON - Feeding The Chickens - signed and dated 1906 - 11¾ x 23½in.
(Sotheby's Belgravia) **£85**

ALEXANDER JOHNSTON - The Turning Point - signed - 48 x 38in.
(Christie's) **£850**

SHOLTO JOHNSTON-DOUGLAS - Shipping In The Channel At Dawn - oil - signed with initials - 38.5 x 49.5cm.
(Phillips in Scotland) **£50**

GEORGE WHITTON JOHNSTONE - "On The Earn Near Dalchonzie" - signed - 44.5 x 59.5cm.
(Phillips in Scotland) **£52**

A. JOLI - A North Italian Lake, With A Port And Shipping - 36 x 51½in.
(Christie's) **£2,200**

JONES - Portrait Of A Gentleman, small half length, Wearing A Black Coat - signed and dated 1850 - on board - 10½ x 8½in.
(Christie's) **£35**

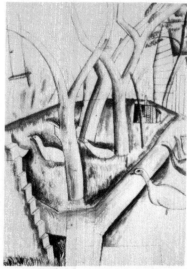

CHARLES JONES - Highland Rovers - signed with monogram and dated - inscribed on the reverse - 23½ x 35¼in.
(Sotheby's Belgravia) **£700**

CHARLES JONES - Winter In The Highlands - signed with initials - signed and dated 1876 on the reverse - 21 x 37in.
(Sotheby's Belgravia) **£700**

CHARLES JONES - Study Of Sheep In A Field - signed with monogram and dated 1889 - 11½ x 19½in.
(Bearnes & Waycotts) **£360**

CHARLES JONES - A Path Through The Hills - signed with monogram - on board - 12 x 17½in.
(Sotheby's Belgravia) **£22**

CHARLES JONES - Sheep In Snowbound Highland Landscape; Highland Landscape In Winter With Sheep and Highland Cattle - signed and dated 1876 and 1865 - 36½ x 21in and 35 x 23½in
(Phillips) **£860 Pair**

DAVID JONES - Geese In A Garden - signed and dated 1924 - pencil and watercolour - 14 x 9¾in.
(Phillips) **£880**

HERBERT JONES - Max - oil on canvas - signed - 51 x 41cm.
(Galerie Moderne) **£115**

J. CLINTON JONES - 'Beddgelert, Early Morning' - signed - oil - 30 x 50in.
(Warner, Sheppard & Wade) **£60**

M. R. JONES - Harvest Field - 1890 - 69 x 90cm.
(Edmiston's) **£122**

P. JONES - Sporting Scenes of a Pointer And Grouse and a Spaniel Retrieving A Mallard - dated 1859 - oils on canvas - 10 x 8in.
(Boulton & Cooper) **£150 Pair**

PAUL JONES - The Rabbiters - signed and dated 1861 - 7½ x 9½in.
(Christie's) **£200**

PAUL JONES - Midday Rest; And The Hare Catcher - both signed and dated 1870 - 7½ x 11½in.
(Christie's) **£800 Pair**

R. JONES - Summer River Scene With Fishermen - signed and dated 1882 - oil on canvas - 12 x 19½in.
(Neale & Son) **£25**

S. JONES - A Wooded Landscape, Two Poachers With Their Bag in the foreground - 7 x 9¾in.
(Sotheby's) **£30**

JOHAN BARTHOLD JONGKIND - Le Chaland, Canal de Willebroeck, Bruxelles - signed and dated 1866 - 13 x 18in.
(Sotheby's) **£23,000**

JOHAN BARTHOLD JONGKIND - Les Patineurs, Scene d'Hiver - signed and dated 1871 - 8¾ x 12¾in.
(Sotheby's) **£19,000**

LUDOLPH DE JONGH - A Lady Playing A Virginal - signed and dated 1651 - 52½ x 40½in.
(Sotheby's) **£4,000**

CORNELIUS JONSON - Portrait Of Sir Richard Browne, BT, In Black Costume With A White Collar - in a painted oval - 29 x 24in.
(Christie's) **£1,000**

JORDAENS

HANS JORDAENS - Moses Striking The Rock - on panel - 72½ x 94½in.
(Christie's) **£3,000**

HANS JORDAENS - David And Goliath - on copper - 27½ x 35½in.
(Christie's) **£1,500**

HANS JORDAENS - The Rape Of Helen - on panel - 23 x 32½in.
(Christie's) **£3,200**

JACOB JORDAENS - Isaac Blessing Jacob - signed and dated - 52 x 67in.
(Christie's) **£6,000**

JACOB JORDAENS and JAN WILDENS - Mercury and Argus - 47¾ x 72¾in.
(Christie's) **£18,000**

Studio of JACOB JORDAENS - Mercury Teaching Cupid To Fish - 63 x 72½in.
(Christie's) **£2,800**

PIO JORIS - In The Garden Of An Italian Town - signed - on panel - 18 x 26½in.
(Sotheby's) **£220**

JOY - Fishing Boats Off The Coast In Choppy Seas - bears signature - 11½ x 19¼in.
(Sotheby's) **£220**

T. M. JOY - 'The Masquerader' - oil -
29½ x 24½in.
(J. Entwhistle & Co)   **£900**

THOMAS MUSGRAVE JOY - Off To
Her First Ball - 23½ x 19½in.
(Sotheby's Belgravia)   **£240**

WILLIAM CANTILOE JOY - Men-O'-War
And Other Vessels In A Stiff Breeze -
signed - 11½ x 17¼in.
(Sotheby's)   **£480**

W. JOY - A River Scene With A Merchantman
And Other Shipping And Small Boats -
25 x 37in.
(Christie's)   **£700**

WILLIAM JOY - Shipping In A Calm Off
Yarmouth - 22½ x 29⅓in.
(Christie's)   **£2,200**

WILLIAM JOY - Fishing Boats Off Shore,
With Fisherfolk On The Beach - 25¾ x 44in.
(Christie's)   **£1,800**

JUEL - Portrait Of A Lady And Gentle-
man, full length, A Landscape With
Waterfall Beyond - 81 x 60in.
(Sotheby's)   **£350**

H. Le JUNE - At Prayer - on panel -
16 x 13.5cm.
(Edmiston's)   **£24**

J. JUNGBLUTH - Cattle At Pasture -
oil on canvas - signed - 70 x 84cm.
(Galerie Moderne)   **£730**

HENRY JUTSUM - The Watermill -
signed and dated 1850 - watercolour -
11 x 16¼in.
(Bearnes & Waycotts)   **£140**

ANDREAS THOMAS JUUEL - Elegant
Figures In The Grounds Of A Danish
Country House - signed and dated 1852 -
22 x 30in.
(Sotheby's)   **£1,600**

K

KADEZ - Portrait Of A Girl In Edwardian Dress On The Edge Of A Wood - 26 x 20½in.
(Buckell & Ballard) £95

FRIEDRICH KAISER - The Kaiser Wilhelm I And His Generals Surveying A Battle - signed - 9 x 13in.
(Sotheby's) £600

CHRISTIAN CORNELIS KANNEMANS - Shipping Becalmed In An Estuary; Barges On A River In A Stiff Breeze - both signed and dated 1844 and 1847 - on panel - 17 x 21¼in.
(Sotheby's) £2,500 Pair

HERMAN TEN KATE - Flowers For Mother - signed and dated 1857 - on panel - 6½ x 8½in.
(Christie's) £950

HERMAN TEN KATE - The Council of War - signed - on panel - 17½ x 24½ ins.
(Christie's) £2500

JAN MARIE TEN KATE - Children Picking Flowers On A Country Lane - signed - on panel - 19½ x 24¾in.
(Christie's) £3,400

JOHAN MARI HENRI TEN KATE - Children With A Goat In A Wood - signed - on panel - 15 x 22cm.
(Phillips) £850

M. TEN KATE - At The Cottage Door - watercolour - 67 x 53cm.
(Edmiston's) £1,000

ANGELICA KAUFFMANN - Valentine, Proteus, Sylvia And Giulia In The Forest - signed and dated 1788 - 61¼ x 85½in.
(Christie's) £3,000

A. KAUFFMAN - The Art of Painting and the Art of Music - a pair - on board 20 x 15 ins.
(Christie's, S. Kensington) £350 Pair

ANGELICA KAUFFMANN - Portrait Of Lady Elizabeth Hamilton, Countess Of Derby, Seated, Her Young Son On Her Lap - 50 x 40in.
(Christie's) **£6,500**

ARCHIBALD KAY - The Chimney Sweep's House, Dorchester, Oxfordshire - signed - on board - 14½ x 9½in.
(Sotheby's) **£160**

ARCHIBALD KAY - Lynn Of The Caillaigh - signed - 20½ x 28¼in.
(Sotheby's) **£170**

ARCHIBALD KAY - Glencoe And Loch Etive From Taynuilt - on panel - 25 x 65.5cm.
(Edmiston's) **£120**

ARCHIBALD KAY - Wooded River Scene With Cattle - 34 x 47cm.
(Edmiston's) **£40**

JAMES KAY - Holiday, Clyde Coast - signed - on board - 11½ x 17½in.
(Sotheby's) **£250**

JAMES KAY - On The Clyde, Cardross - oil - signed - on board - 27.5 x 37.5cm.
(Phillips in Scotland) **£52**

JAMES KAY - Ships On The Clyde At The Broomielaw - watercolour - 44 x 59cm.
(Edmiston's) **£145**

J. KEELHOF - Cattle At Pasture - oil on canvas - signed - 30 x 44cm.
(Galerie Moderne) **£17**

BERNHARD KEIL - A Beggar Woman, suckling her child by a fountain, approached by a pedlar - 55½ x 70in.
(Christie's) **£1,800**

HARRY KEIR - Gypsies - watercolour - 33 x 45cm.
(Edmiston's) **£8**

KEIRINCX

ALEXANDER KEIRINCX - A Wooded River Landscape, Men With Dogs On A Road Emerging From A Dense Wood By The Side Of A River - on panel - 22 x 30in.
(Sotheby's) **£6,500**

J. KELLER - African Landscape - oil on canvas - signed - 32 x 45cm.
(Galerie Moderne) **£2**

ROBERT KEMM, After ROSA BONHEUR - 'Labourage Nivernais': Teams Of Oxen Ploughing - signed and dated Paris 1860 - 51 x 102in.
(Christie's) **£1,000**

ROBERT KEMM - Spanish Girl With Artist Painting Model - 89 x 68cm.
(Edmiston's) **£390**

SYDNEY KENDRICK - Afternoon Tea - signed - 23¾ x 17½in.
(Sotheby's Belgravia) **£320**

SYDNEY KENDRICK - Faith - signed - 23½ x 19½in.
(Sotheby's Belgravia) **£320**

SYDNEY KENDRICK - The Poppy Girl - signed - 33¼ x 25¼in.
(Christie's, S. Kensington) **£950**

WILLIAM KENNEDY - An Arab Grain Market, Tangier - signed - inscribed on the stretcher - 14½ x 23½in.
(Sotheby's Belgravia) **£95**

WILLIAM KENNEDY - Horse And Cart In Front Of Shop - 39 x 60cm.
(Edmiston's) **£190**

J. KENNIS - Le Reverbere - oil on canvas - signed - 60 x 50cm.
(Galerie Moderne) **£110**

KERIN - 'The Bird Fancier', An Elderly Man Wearing A Top Hat Is Feeding A Canary In A Cage - 47 x 32cm.
(Phillips) **£1,700**

ANNY KERNKAMP - A Busy Country Road - on wood - signed - 27 x 36cm.
(Galerie Moderne) **£90**

H. W. KERR - Bust Portrait Of An Elderly Man - watercolour - 14 x 11½in.
(Thomas Love & Sons Ltd) **£70**

J. VAN KESSEL - Swans, Mallards, Herons, A Peacock And Other Birds In A River Landscape - 34½ x 54½in.
(Christie's) **£550**

JAN VAN KESSEL - The Creation Of Eve; God The Father With Eve And The Sleeping Adam - on metal - 34¼ x 44½in.
(Sotheby's) **£3,500**

JAN VAN KESSEL - A Basket Of Roses, A Vase Of Tulips, A Parrot And A Guinea Pig In A Landscape - on panel - 6½ x 8½in.
(Christie's) **£3,200**

TILLY KETTLE - Portrait Of An Artist - half-length - in a blue coat, seated at a table - 29¼ x 24in.
(Christie's) **£600**

HENDRIK KEUN - The Grote Kerk, Haarlem - panel transferred to canvas - 13½ x 21in.
(Christie's) **£1,500**

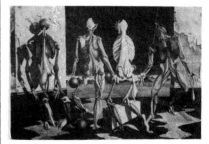

ALEXIS KEUNEN - Resurrection Of The Flesh - oil on canvas - signed and dated 1958.
(Galerie Moderne) **£1,600**

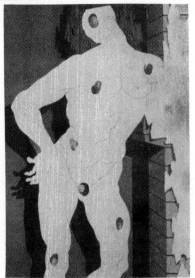

ALEXIS KEUNEN - Tendance A Ne Pas Etre - cartoon - signed and dated 1957 - 86 x 61cm.
(Galerie Moderne) £220

ALEXIS KEUNEN - The Impossible Voyage - cartoon - signed and dated 1957 - 1m.09 x 1m.57cm.
(Galerie Moderne) £345

WILLEM KEY - Portrait Of A Lady, half length, Wearing A Black Dress And White Cap - on panel - 81 x 64cm.
(Phillips) £8,000

KEY - Portrait Of A Lady, Aged 24, small bust length, Wearing Black Costume With White Ruff And Bonnet - bears inscription and dated - on panel - 18 x 14in.
(Christie's) £700

FREDERICK WILLIAM KEYL - Trees Beside A Road Leading To A Village - inscribed - coloured chalk on grey paper - 11 x 21in.
(Christie's) £75

FRIEDRICH WILHELM KEYL - A Bloodhound Bitch With Her Litter - signed and dated 1870 - 21 x 26in.
(Woolley & Wallis) £340

THOMAS KEYSE - Flowers In A Glass Vase - signed and indistinctly dated - oil on canvas - 26¼ x 21¼in.
(Bearnes & Waycotts) £880

NICAISSE DE KEYSER - Young Lovers In Ancient Greece, She Draws His Profile On A Wall Around His Shadow - signed and dated 1869 - 57 x 42in.
(Sotheby's) £600

R. DE KEYSER - The Sailmakers - on wood - signed - 25 x 35cm.
(Galerie Moderne) £23

T. DE KEYSER - Portrait Of A Young Lady, three-quarter length, Wearing A White Ruff And Lace Bonnet, Holding Gloves, Standing By A Table - on panel - 46 x 34½in.
(Christie's) £2,400

THOMAS DE KEYSER - Frans Van Limborch In A Black Doublet And Cloak And A Black Hat, With Gloves In His Hand - inscribed with the sitter's name and age - signed in monogram and dated 1632 - 45¾ x 34in.
(Sotheby's) **£6,000**

KILBURNE - A Lady Doing Embroidery - 10½ x 13¾in.
(Sotheby's) **£25**

GEORGE GOODWIN KILBURNE - 'The Pigeons Of St Marks' - watercolour - signed and dated 1876 - 14½ x 24½in.
(Graves Son & Pilcher) **£550**

GEORGE GOODWIN KILBURNE - The Contented Man - watercolour heightened with white - signed - 9¾ x 14½in.
(Christie's) **£60**

GEORGE GOODWIN KILBURNE - The Proposal -signed - 6 x 9in.
(Christie's) **£250**

GEORGE GOODWIN KILBURNE - Evening - signed - on panel - 11¾ x 6¾in.
(Sotheby's Belgravia) **£460**

GEORGE GOODWIN KILBURNE - A Visitor - watercolour heightened with white - signed - 9¾ x 14½in.
(Christie's) **£70**

ELLA KING - Under Attack - signed and dated 1901 - 10¾ x 13½in.
(Sotheby's Belgravia) **£55**

J. Y. KING - A View Of Oxford From The South West - 37½ x 57in.
(Sotheby's Belgravia) **£500**

JOHN YEEND KING - Harvest Time -
signed - on board - 21 x 17in.
(Christie's) **£240**

HENRY JOHN YEEND KING -
'Sisters' Confidences', Study Of Two
Fair Haired Ladies In Eighteenth
Century Style, Standing On A Stone
Terrace With Azaleas in the fore-
ground - oil - signed - 39½ x 29½in.
(Henry Spencer & Sons) **£1,600**

H. J. KINNAIRD - 'On The Thames
Near Marsh Lock, Henley' -
late 19th century - signed - oil on
canvas - 30 x 50in.
(Lalonde Martin) **£400**

H. J. KINNAIRD - On The Ouse, Sussex;
A Sussex Cornfield - water colours - signed
- 15½ x 7½in
(John H. Raby & Son) **£170 Pair**

JOHN YEEND KING - In The Highlands;
Homewards - both signed - on board -
each 19½ x 14½in.
(Sotheby's Belgravia) **£800 Pair**

JOHN YEEND KING - St. Catherine's
Bay, Jersey - signed and dated May 30th
1913 - on board - 13½ x 20½in.
(Christie's) **£420**

K. G. KIRK - A Wagtail; A Robin; A
Green Woodpecker - gouache - all
signed - each 10¼ x 12½in.
(Sotheby's Belgravia) **£65 Three**

E. M. KISSACK - The Edge Of The Village - signed and dated 1910 - oil - 11½ x 24in.
(Neale & Son) **£18**

ALEXEI KIWSCHENKO - The Sermon - signed and dated 1881 - 25 x 16 ins.
(Christie's, S. Kensington) **£580**

PAUL KLEE - Landschaft Mit Haus - on board - 11 x 13½in.
(Sotheby's) **£11,500**

PIETER LODEWIJK FRANCISCO KLUYVER - An Extensive Wooded Landscape, A Figure On A Path Near Cottages in the foreground, A Town in the distance - signed - oil on panel - 35.5 x 49cm.
(Phillips) **£4,000**

PIETER LODEWYK FRANCISCO KLUYVER - An Extensive Landscape with figures and animals on a path and a windmill - signed - on panel - 14 x 19in.
(Christie's) **£1,600**

KNAPTON - Portrait Of A Young Nobleman - half-length - 30 x 24in.
(Woolley & Wallis) **£650**

WILLIAM KNEEN - The Bridge Over The Thames At Richmond - signed - tempera - 8¾ x 12¾in.
(Geering & Colyer) **£30**

ADOLPHUS KNELL - Numerous Fishing And Other Vessels Off A Moonlit harbour - signed - oil on board - 19½ x 26½in.
(Geering & Colyer) **£210**

W. A. KNELL - Fishermen Bringing In Their Catch - canvas - on panel - oval - 3½ x 7¾in.
(Sotheby's Belgravia) **£100**

KNELL

W. A. KNELL - Salvaging A Wreck - on board - 7 x 11¾in.
(Sotheby's Belgravia) £60

WILLIAM ADOLPHUS KNELL - On The Lagoon; The Rialto Bridge, Venice - one signed - all on board - one arched top - 5½ x 11½in.
(Sotheby's Belgravia) £400 Three

WILLIAM ADOLPHUS KNELL - A Man-Of-War And Other Shipping At Sunset - signed and dated 1882 - 9½ x 13¼in.
(Sotheby's Belgravia) £450

WILLIAM ADOLPHUS KNELL - 'At The Mouth Of The Harbour' - signed - watercolour - 10 x 14¼in.
(Bearnes & Waycotts) £250

WILLIAM ADOLPHUS KNELL, SEN - Vessels Off Portsmouth - watercolour - signed - 9¾ x 19in.
(Christie's) £420

WILLIAM CALLCOTT KNELL - Early Morning, Fishing Boats Laying To Mouth Of The Thames - signed and dated 1863 - signed and inscribed on the reverse - 14 x 24in.
(Christie's) £800

KNELLER - Portraits Of The Duke Of York and The Duke Of Marlborough - oval - 30½ x 26in.
(Woolley & Wallis) £300 Pair

SIR GODFREY KNELLER - Study Of The Head Of A Child - black chalk heightened with white on brown paper - 10½ x 9¼in.
(Christie's) £350

SIR GODFREY KNELLER - Portrait Of The Rt. Hon. James Craggs In A Blue Coat And White Cravat, Standing Near A Table - three-quarter length - signed and inscribed - 49 x 39½in.
(Christie's) £550

WALTER HOLMES KNEWSTUB - Still Life Of Apples And A Blue And White And Earthenware Vase - heightened with bodycolour - signed - 11 x 13in.
(Sotheby's Belgravia) £130

WALTER HOLMES KNEWSTUB - Still Life Of A Jug And Fruit - heightened with white - signed with monogram - 9½ x 11½in.
(Sotheby's Belgravia) £100

ADAM KNIGHT - Lundgate Tower, Rye - watercolour - 9 x 13in.
(G. A. Key) £9

ADAM KNIGHT - Fishing Villages -
signed - oil - 11½ x 8½in
(Neale & Son) **£18 Pair**

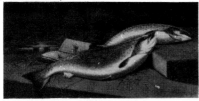

A. R. KNIGHT - Still Life Of Salmon,
with Fishing Rod And Flies - on board -
11½ x 23¼in.
(Sotheby's Belgravia) **£40**

G. KNIGHT - Shipping Off A Pier -
canvas - on board - 9 x 13in.
(Sotheby's Belgravia) **£48**

J. KNIGHT - A Fishing Boat Off The
Coast - 8 x 14in.
(Sotheby's Belgravia) **£75**

JOHN BUXTON KNIGHT - By The
Paddock, Greatham Hall - coloured
chalks - signed - on canvas - 13¾ x
20¼in.
(Sotheby's Belgravia) **£42**

DAME LAURA KNIGHT - 'Plaiting
Her Hair' - signed - pastel - 13½ x 10in.
(Buckell & Ballard) **£170**

WILLIAM HENRY KNIGHT - 'The
Apple' - signed with initials and dated
1861 - on panel - 29 x 25cm.
(Phillips) **£800**

HENRI KNIP - The Windmill - oil on
canvas - signed - 37 x 56cm.
(Galerie Moderne) **£12**

KOEKKOEK

KOBELL - Cattle, Sheep, A Shepherd And
A Shepherdess In A Wooded Evening
Landscape - bears signature - 19½ x 26¾in.
(Sotheby's) **£620**

KOBELL - A Rustic Family Resting With
Their Animals In A Wooded River Land-
scape - on metal - 15 x 18¼in.
(Sotheby's) **£220**

LUDVIG KOCH - The Battlefield -
charcoal heightened with white
chalk on buff paper - signed -
inscribed and dated 1926 - 14 x 20in.
(Sotheby's) **£50**

HENRY KOEHLER - The Girl Groom -
pencil, watercolour and gouache -
signed - 17½ x 22in.
(Sotheby's) **£190**

KOEKKOEK - Dutch Coastal Scene
With Fishing Boats - signed - oil on
canvas - 11½ x 15½in.
(Bearnes & Waycotts) **£440**

BAREND CORNELIS KOEKKOEK - A
Dutch Wooded Landscape With Travellers,
Cattle And Donkeys By The Edge Of A
Stream - signed - on panel - 18½ x 15in.
(Sotheby's) **£13,000**

BAREND CORNELIS KOEKKOEK -
A Winter Landscape, With Figures By A
Castle - signed with initials - on panel -
4¾ x 3¾in.
(Sotheby's) **£1,800**

BAREND CORNELIS KOEKKOEK -
A Wooded Landscape With Figures And
Cattle, A River in the distance to the
left, A Country House On A Hill to the
right - signed and dated 1842 - 29 x 37in.
(Sotheby's) **£17,000**

H. B. KOEKKOEK - Rocky coastline
with bathers and figures on beach;
and companion - signed - inscribed
on reverse - on board - 10 x 15 ins.
(Phillips) **£400 Pair**

KOEKOEK

HENDRIK PIETER KOEKOEK A
View Near Sheire, Surrey - signed -
13½ x 23½in.
(Sotheby's) **£1,000**

HERMANUS KOEKKOEK - Shipping
Scenes Off the Dutch Coast with fishing
vessels and figures on the shore - signed -
14 x 22in
(Christie's) **£12,000 Pair**

HERMANUS KOEKKOEK, JNR -
Figures And Fishing Boats Off The
Coast - signed - 12½ x 19¾in.
(Sotheby's) **£1,300**

HERMANUS KOEKKOEK, JNR -
Vessels In A Heavy Sea - signed - on
panel - 4¼ x 6in.
(Sotheby's) **£400**

HERMANUS KOEKKOEK, JNR - A
Coastal Scene With A Fishing Boat
Leaving Harbour, A Paddle Steamer
Dropping Anchor And Figures On
A Jetty - signed - 32½ x 51in.
(Christie's) **£7,500**

HERMANUS KOEKKOEK, JNR -
Barges And Small Boats In An Estuary -
signed - 14 x 22in.
(Sotheby's) **£3,000**

HERMANUS KOEKKOEK, SNR -
Shipping At The Mouth Of A River In
A Stiff Breeze - signed and dated
1861 - 14¾ x 21¾in.
(Sotheby's) **£4,800**

HERMANUS KOEKKOEK, SNR -
Fishing Vessels In A Swell Off A Coastline, Figures Unloading Their Boat in
the foreground - signed - 39.5 x 55cm.
(Phillips) **£5,200**

HERMANUS KOEKKOEK - Sailing
Vessels Offshore In A Calm - signed -
14½ x 23in.
(Christie's) **£8,500**

JAN HERMANUS KOEKKOEK - An
Estuary With Dutch Shipping In Breezy
Weather - signed and dated 1838 -
on panel - 15½ x 21in.
(Christie's) **£3,600**

**HERMANUS KOEKKOEK & EUGENE
VERBOECKHOVEN** - Fishing Boats
With Cattle And A Castle On The Bank
Nearby - oil - on panel - signed and
dated 1838 - 12 x 14½in.
(King & Chasemore) **£1,100**

M. A. KOEKKOEK - An Extensive Woody Landscape With Peasants By A Windmill - 22½ x 20¼in.
(Christie's) **£1,300**

MARINUS ADRIANUS KOEKKOEK - A Wooded River Landscape With A Cottage And Cattle - signed and dated 1860 - on panel - 11½ x 15½in.
(Christie's) **£2,000**

OSKAR KOKOSCHKA - Florenz; Ausblick Vom Mannelli Turm - signed with initials - 33½ x 43¼in.
(Christie's, New York) **£71,200**

PIOTR KONCHALOVSKY - Forest Landscape - oil - on canvas - signed on the reverse - 7¼ x 10¾in.
(Sotheby's) **£22**

J. KONIG - The Entombment - on copper.
(Christie's) **£380**

JACOB KONINCK THE ELDER - A Mountainous River Landscape With A Fortified Town, A Bridge And A Fisherman in the foreground - signed - on panel - 15 x 29in.
(Christie's) **£3,800**

RUDOLF KONOPA - Pont-Aven - brush and ink and gouache on board - signed and dated 1909 - 20½ x 14¾in.
(Sotheby's) **£65**

SIPKE KOOL - Washing The Baby - signed - on panel - 13½ x 18½in.
(Sotheby's) **£720**

A. KOROS - Blackhaired Beauty - 50 x 40cm.
(Edmiston's) **£2**

FRANZ XAVIER KOSLER - The Waterseller - signed and dated 1902 - 25 x 17½in.
(Christie's) **£2,200**

G. HUGO KOTSCHENREITER - The Coachman's Yarn - signed and dated '81 - 10¾ x 8¾in.
(Christie's, S. Kensington) **£360**

KOUCHAKOWILCH - The Hay Cart - oil on canvas - signed - 51 x 35cm.
(Galerie Moderne) **£10**

M. KOZAROOFF - Tolstoy In Readiness For His Flight - signed and indistinctly dated - 39¾ x 23¾in.
(Sotheby's) **£30**

VINCENZ KREUZER - Figures By A
Church, A Castle On A Hilltop Beyond -
signed - on panel - 9 x 11in.
(Sotheby's) £580

KRIEGER - Portrait Of A Boy
Reading A Book On Butterflies -
pastel - signed - 19 x 16in.
(Graves Son & Pilcher) £300

WILHELM KUHNERT - A Lion And
Lioness - signed - 15½ x 23in.
(Christie's) £3,400

WILHELM KUHNERT - Studies Of An
East African Ibex - pencil - signed -
inscribed and dated 2.8.05 - 8 x 11in.
(Sotheby's) £450

WILHELM KUHNERT - An Orangoutang
- pen and black ink - signed - 9¾ x 10½in.
(Sotheby's) £360

HANS SUSS VON KULMBACH - A
Bishop Saint, In A Gold-Embroidered
Blue Chasuble, Holding A Pastoral Staff
And A Book With A Green Cover - gold
ground - on panel - 15¼ x 14¼in.
(Sotheby's) £4,500

BORIS KUSTODIEV - Women In The
Fields - pencil and watercolour -
signed with initials - 13 x 8¼in.
(Sotheby's) £58

JEAN LOUIS VAN KUYCK - The Back
Yard - signed and authenticated on the
reverse by the artist's son - on panel -
11½ x 15¼in.
(Sotheby's) £520

L

**CHARLES FRANCOIS LACROIX, called
LACROIX DE MARSEILLES** - An Italianate
Rocky River Landscape, with an angler and
other figures in the foreground, a capriccio
view of the Pont du Gard and a castle beyond
- 39 x 49¼in.
(Christie's) **£4,200**

LADBROKE - A Woodland Scene In
Summer With Two Men Standing in
the foreground - oil - 24½ x 30½in.
(Henry Spencer & Sons) **£520**

J. B. LADBROKE - A Woodland Scene -
oil on canvas - 18 x 24in.
(King & Chasemore) **£500**

JOHN BERNEY LADBROKE - A Wooded
Landscape With Youths By A Pond -
signed with monogram - 19 x 23½in.
(Christie's) **£300**

R. LADBROOKE - A Wooded Landscape
With Old Church Ruins - oil - 7 x 9in.
(G. A. Key) **£30**

R. LADBROOKE - Classic Norwich
School Picture Of A Clay Lump Cottage
And Treed Landscape - 28 x 36in.
(G. A. Key) **£510**

EDWARD LADELL - Still Life Of
Fruit And A Glass - signed with
monogram - 9½ x 11½in.
(Sotheby's Belgravia) **£3,900**

EDWARD LADELL - Still Life With
Wine Glass, Fruit And Jewel Casket -
signed with monogram oil on canvas -
14 x 12in.
(Bonham's) **£4,200**

LADELL

EDWARD LADELL - A Still Life Of Prawns, A Blue And White Jar, A Roehmer And Lemons - signed with monogram - 9¼ x 11½in.
(Christie's) **£950**

ELLEN LADELL - Grapes, Peaches, Raspberries And A Glass Of Wine On A Ledge - signed - 10 x 12in.
(Christie's) **£550**

PIETER VAN LAER - The Crucifixion - on panel - 33½ x 26½in.
(Christie's) **£800**

PAULUS CORNELIUS LAFARGUE - A View Of The Hague, Holland - signed and dated 1784 - oil - 10½ x 14in.
(Henry Spencer & Sons) **£750**

J. LAGOOR - A Wooded Landscape With Deer - on panel - 8½ x 10½in.
(Christie's) **£2,600**

RAFF LAGYE - Landscape - oil on canvas - signed - 52 x 82cm.
(Galerie Moderne) **£75**

LAIRESSE - The Triumph Of Bacchus - 38 x 60in.
(Christie's) **£800**

GERARD DE LAIRESSE - Venus And Adonis - signed with initials - 42½ x 47in.
(Christie's) **£5,000**

EDWARD LAIT - Harvest Time; Outside A Cottage - both heightened with bodycolour - signed - each 5½ x 11½in.
(Sotheby's Belgravia) **£85 Pair**

JACQUES DE LAJOUE - The Swing - signed - 34½ x 53½in.
(Christie's) **£6,000**

S. LALEAGNY - The Story Teller - signed - 26 x 37in.
(Christie's) **£4,800**

LALLEMAND - Still Life Of Vegetables - on wood - signed - 40 x 45cm.
(Galerie Moderne) **£35**

ALEX. LALLEMAND - Landscape - cartoon - signed - 40 x 30cm.
(Galerie Moderne) **£2**

K. LALLEMAND - Still Life Of Apples - on wood - signed - 39 x 46cm.
(Galerie Moderne) **£50**

CECIL LAMBERT - Mountain Cottage Scenes - both signed - each 17½ x 31½in.
(Sotheby's Belgravia) **£230 Pair**

GEORGE WASHINGTON LAMBERT - A Still-Life of Two Dead Grouse - signed and dated 1907 - 14 x 23½in.
(Henry Spencer & Sons) **£850**

GEORGE WASHINGTON LAMBERT - Portraits of Mr and Mrs John Proctor - 28 x 22in
(Henry Spencer & Sons) **£6,700 Pair**

GEORGE WASHINGTON LAMBERT - A
Group Portrait Of Miss Alison Preston And
John Proctor with a pony on Mearbeck Moor
Yorkshire - signed and dated 1909 -
39 x 49in.
(Henry Spencer & Sons) £9,200

J. B. LAMBRECHTS - An Italianate Landscape with Travellers on a Road and
Fishmonger; and An Italianate Landscape
with Numerous Peasants by a Fountain - on
copper - 9 x 12in
(Christie's) £4,000 Pair

JAN BAPTISTE LAMBRECHTS - A
Musical Party On A Terrace - 17¼ x 28in.
(Sotheby's) £2,800

JAN BAPTIST LAMBRECHTS -
Figures At Table In An Interior -
indistinctly signed with monogram -
26½ x 21½in.
(Christie's) £2,000

GEORGE WASHINGTON LAMBERT - A
Full Length Portrait of Miss Alison Preston
wearing a black evening gown and white
gloves - 83 x 41in.
(Henry Spencer & Sons) £3,600

CRISTOFFEL VAN DER LAMEN -
Elegant Figures And Musicians In A
Palatial Interior - on panel - 29 x 41½in.
(Christie's) £2,800

CHRISTOFFEL JACOBSZ VAN DER LAMEN - An Open Air Banquet, A Party Of Ladies And Gentlemen Seated Around A Laden Table In The Open, Served By Pages, An Old Man At The Head Of The Table - on panel - 17¼ x 24¾in.
(Sotheby's) £7,000

EMILE LAMMERS - The Old Bridge - oil on canvas - signed - 1m. x 1m. 20cm.
(Galerie Moderne) £35

AUGUSTUS OSBORNE LAMPLOUGH - On The Banks Of The Nile - signed - 13¼ x 18½in.
(Sotheby's Belgravia) £65

GEORGE LANCE - Fruit And Flowers On A Mossy Bank - 35 x 27½in.
(Christie's) £900

GEORGE LANCE - Still Life Of Fruit, Filberts And A Butterfly In Wooded Landscape - signed with monogram - 23½ x 18½in.
(Buckell & Ballard) £925

CORNELIS JOSEPH d'HEUR, After NICOLAS LANCRET - 'Le Midi'; And 'L'Apres-Dinee' - on panel - 13¾ x 16¼in.
(Sotheby's) £2,700 Pair

ANDREA LANDINI - A Good Story - signed - 28½ x 36in.
(Christie's) £5,000

LANDSEER - An Aerie With Eagles, Perched In A Rocky Landscape - heightened with gum arabic - 10 x 13½in.
(Sotheby's) £30

LANDSEER - The Donkey Race - indistinctly signed - on panel - 9½ x 10¾in.
(Sotheby's Belgravia) **£25**

E. LANDSEER - Study Of Dogs In A Stable Interior - oil - bears signature - paper laid down on panel - 40 x 50cm.
(Phillips in Scotland) **£150**

SIR E. LANDSEER - A Stag Attacked By A Deerhound - 21¼ x 25½in.
(Sotheby's Belgravia) **£70**

SIR EDWIN LANDSEER - Sketch Of A Goat - signed with initials - 4 x 6½in.
(Christie's) **£50**

E. LANE - The Park - cartoon - signed - 46 x 55cm.
(Galerie Moderne) **£18**

J. VAN DER LANEN - A Woody River Landscape With Peasants And Sheep - on panel - 11 x 17½in.
(Christie's) **£1,500**

IDA VAN LANGENHOVE - Still Life Of Game Birds And Fruit - oil on canvas - signed - 42 x 60cm.
(Galerie Moderne) **£25**

GEORGE NASMYTH LANGLANDS - Tympendean Ford - signed - 13½ x 20½in.
(Sotheby's Belgravia) **£100**

WILLIAM LANGLEY - Cattle Watering, Sunset - signed - 19½ x 29½in.
(Sotheby's Belgravia) **£40**

WILLIAM LANGLEY - Sand Dunes - signed - 15½ x 23½in.
(Sotheby's Belgravia) **£90**

WILLIAM LANGLEY - Another Cottage On A Bend Of A River - signed - 15½ x 23¼in.
(Sotheby's Belgravia) **£70**

WILLIAM LANGLEY - By A Mountain Stream - signed - 15½ x 23½in.
(Sotheby's Belgravia) **£150**

J. LANGLOIS - Trapped - signed - 11¾ x 19½in.
(Sotheby's Belgravia) **£73**

M. LANGLOIS - On Watch - 11½ x 16in.
(Sotheby's Belgravia) **£45**

MARK W. LANGLOIS - Tossing Pancakes - inscribed - 20¼ x 16in.
(Sotheby's Belgravia) **£85**

MARK W. LANGLOIS - 'The Village Optician' - signed - oil on canvas - 35½ x 27¼in.
(Bearnes & Waycotts) **£440**

POLIDORO LANZANI, After - The Holy Family in a Landscape - on panel - 8¼ x 12 ins.
(Christie's) **£3,000**

J. LAPORTE - A Horse Fair On A Village Green - 60 x 120in.
(Christie's) **£2,600**

GEORGE LARA - Peasants And Horses Outside A Farmhouse - 19½ x 29½in.
(Christie's) **£1,000**

GEORGE LARA - A Wooded Landscape With Figures And Horses Outside A Farm; And A Wooded Landscape With A Horse And Cart Outside A Farm - both bear signatures - 9½ x 13½in.
(Christie's) **£600 Pair**

NICOLAS DE LARGILLIERRE - Portrait Of A Gentleman Holding A Gun In His Left Hand, A Dog At His Side, With A Dead Pheasant And A Landscape Beyond - 53½ x 41in.
(Christie's) **£5,000**

NICOLAS DE LARGILLIERRE - Portrait Of A Lady Resting Her Right Hand On An Overturned Pitcher, A Wooded Landscape Beyond - 53½ x 41in.
(Christie's) **£5,000**

N. DE LARGILLIERRE - Portrait Of A Lady, Seated three-quarter length, Wearing An Embroidered Blue Dress And A Pink Cloak - 40 x 31in.
(Christie's) **£1,000**

MIKHAIL LARIONOV - La Fiancee - oil - on board - signed with initials - 12¾ x 16in.
(Sotheby's) **£440**

LARKIN - Portrait of Sir Charles Montague, half-length, wearing armour inscribed and inscribed with coat-of-arms - 42 x 34½ ins.
(Christie's, S. Kensington) **£550**

L. LAROY - Vieille Ferme - on wood - signed - 20 x 30cm.
(Galerie Moderne) **£43**

C. J. LAUDER - Looking Towards Montreaux - watercolour - 27 x 39cm.
(Edmiston's) **£14**

MARIE LAURENCIN - Femme Aux Cheveux Boucles - pencil - 3¼ x 2¾in.
(Sotheby's) **£180**

LAURI - Syrinx Fleeing From Pan, In A Wooded Landscape - 13½ x 18¾in.
(Sotheby's) **£90**

F. LAURI - The Agony In The Garden - inscribed 'Albano' on the reverse - 11½ x 8½in.
(Christie's) **£160**

LAVERY - Portrait Of Mme. Rohll - 32 x 23cm.
(Edmiston's) **£17**

SIR JOHN LAVERY - Portrait Of John T. Laing Esq - signed - 77½ x 39in.
(Sotheby's) **£260**

DAVID LAW - A River Landscape - signed - 16¼ x 27¼in.
(Sotheby's Belgravia) **£65**

G. E. LAW - Wooded Scene With Houses - 15 x 23cm.
(Edmiston's) **£15**

LAWRENCE - The Duke Of Wellington On Horseback - on panel - 63½ x 41½in.
(Christie's) **£300**

LAWRENCE, After - Portrait Of The Duke Of Wellington, half length, Wearing A Black Cloak, A White Waistcoat And A White Stock - 29½ x 24½in.
(Sotheby's) **£30**

LAWRENCE

SIR THOMAS LAWRENCE, After -
Portrait Of Miss Coker - 7½ x 6in.
(Sotheby's) **£55**

BENJAMIN WILLIAMS LEADER - A
View Of A Village In The Swiss Alps
With A Lake in the foreground -
signed - 47 x 67cm.
(Phillips) **£540**

SIR THOMAS LAWRENCE - Portrait Of A
Lady Said To Be Miss Sweeting, Later Mrs.
Alnutt In A White Dress, standing in a land-
scape - three-quarter length - inscribed on
reverse - 49½ x 39½in.
(Christie's) **£6,500**

FREDERICK WILFRED LAWSON - A
Study For Imprisoned Spring - signed
and inscribed - 15½ x 11½in.
(Sotheby's Belgravia) **£90**

P. J. LEA - Landscape With Cattle At
Riverside - signed - oil on canvas - 10
x 8in.
(Staniland's) **£130**

B. W. LEADER - Llanberis, North
Wales - signed - 15 x 23¼in.
(Buckell & Ballard) **£120**

BENJAMIN WILLIAMS LEADER -
The Sand Dunes Near Cromer,
Norfolk - oil - signed - 15½ x 20½in.
(Henry Spencer & Sons) **£320**

BENJAMIN WILLIAMS LEADER -
A Path To The Valley Burrows Wood -
signed and dated 1909 - inscribed on
the stretcher - 17½ x 14in.
(Sotheby's Belgravia) **£1,000**

BENJAMIN WILLIAMS LEADER -
Evening On The Lugwy Near Bettws-
Y-Coed - signed and dated 1863 -
inscribed on the stretcher - 27¼ x 41½in.
(Sotheby's Belgravia) **£700**

C. LEADER - By The Ford - 19 x 29in.
(Sotheby's Belgravia) £150

BENJAMIN WILLIAMS LEADER -
Stokesay Castle, Shropshire - signed and
dated 1872 - inscribed on the stretcher -
30 x 40in.
(Sotheby's Belgravia) £2,600

BENJAMIN WILLIAMS LEADER -
'The Road Over The Common' -
signed and dated 1878 - 51 x
76.5cm.
(Phillips) £2,100

LEAKEY - Portrait Of A Country
Gentleman, A Hunt in the distance - oil on
canvas - 50 x 40in.
(King & Chasemore) £85

BENJAMIN WILLIAMS LEADER - On
The Conway, North Wales - signed and
dated 1908 - inscribed on the stretcher -
11¾ x 17½in.
(Sotheby's Belgravia) £500

EDWARD LEAR - Nenares - watercolour heightened with white - signed
with monogram - inscribed on the
reverse and dated 1875 - 9½ x 15in.
(Christie's) £950

BENJAMIN WILLIAMS LEADER - A
Welsh Lake And Mountain Landscape
With Birch Trees in foreground And A
Cottage on the far side - 19¾ x 23¼in.
(Buckell & Ballard) £110

EDWARD LEAR - 'Cella - A View Of
The Coast' - watercolour - 4 x 8in.
(Bearnes & Waycotts) £380

LEAR

EDWARD LEAR - Temples By A River In Southern India - watercolour - 5¼ x 10½in.
(Christie's) **£250**

EDWARD LEAR - A Waterfall - signed and dated 1837 - pencil heightened with white on grey paper - 4¾ x 6¾in.
(Christie's) **£320**

EDWARD LEAR - Valetta, From Inland Near Casal Luca - extensively inscribed, numbered and dated 1866 - pencil, pen and brown ink and watercolour heightened with white - 8½ x 17¼in.
(Christie's) **£650**

EDWARD LEAR - Keswick - inscribed - numbered and dated 1836 - pencil and watercolour heightened with white on buff paper - 7¼ x 10¼in.
(Christie's) **£750**

EDWARD LEAR - Crummock Water - inscribed, numbered and dated 1836 - pencil on grey-green paper - 7 x 10½in.
(Christie's) **£300**

JOHN HENRY LEATHERBROW - Vegetable Picking - heightened with body-colour - 9¾ x 13¾in.
(Sotheby's Belgravia) **£14**

CHARLES LEBON - Paysage Enneige - oil on canvas - signed - 94 x 99cm.
(Galerie Moderne) **£597**

CHARLES LEBON - The Old Thatched Cottage - oil on wood - signed and dated 1937 - 38 x 46cm.
(Galerie Moderne) **£240**

F. R. LEE and T. S. COOPER - At The Ford - bears signature and dated - 25 x 31in.
(Sotheby's Belgravia) **£700**

FREDERICK RICHARD LEE - A Watermill, With Children And A Donkey On A Path, And A Sailing Barge On A River Beyond - signed with initials and dated 1825 - 35½ x 48in.
(Christie's) **£400**

FREDERICK RICHARD LEE - Figures By A Lake - 10 x 14¾in.
(Sotheby's Belgravia) **£200**

FREDERICK RICHARD LEE - The Breakwater At Plymouth Looking East - signed and dated 1862 - 28 x 36in.
(Sotheby's Belgravia) **£2,600**

SYDNEY LEE - The House Of Mystery, Barnard Castle - signed - 13¾ x 9½in.
(Sotheby's Belgravia) **£16**

WILLIAM LEE-HANKEY - Town Square With Figures Outside A Street Cafe - signed - 19¾ x 23½in.
(Phillips) **£290**

C. VAN LEEMPUTTEN - Domestic Fowl In An Extensive Landscape; A Threat To The Brood - both on panel - 9½ x 12½in.
(Sotheby's) **£1,100 Pair**

CORNELIUS VAN LEEMPUTTEN - Matinee d'Avril Campine - oil on canvas - signed and dated 1895 - 64 x 84 cm.
(Galerie Moderne) **£786**

CORNELIUS VAN LEEMPUTTEN - King Of The Farmyard - signed - on panel - 6¾ x 9¼in.
(Sotheby's) **£280**

J. L VAN LEEMPUTTEN - Poultry In Farmyard, With Extensive Landscapes Beyond - both signed and one dated 1867, the other 1868 - on panel - 13 x 19in.
(Christie's) **£1,100 Pair**

WILLEM VAN LEEN - Roses, Tulips, Carnations And Other Flowers In A Vase On A Ledge - signed - on panel - 19 x 14in.
(Christie's) **£13,000**

A. DE LEEUW - Winter Landscape With Horse, Skaters And A Group Of Figures in the foreground - oil on canvas - 27 x 47in.
(Bearnes & Waycotts) **£580**

ALEXIS DE LEEUW - A Winter Landscape with peasants and a sledge - signed and dated 1864 - 22 x 33½in.
(Christie's) **£1,600**

267

CLAUDE LEFEBVRE - Portrait Of A Gentleman, In A Brown Doublet And Breastplate With A Feathered Hat By His Side - 109 x 88cm.
(Phillips) £750

CHARLES LEFEVRE - A View Over Florence From The South, Woodcutters in the foreground - signed and inscribed 'Florence' and dated 1856 - 35 x 65in.
(Sotheby's) £2,600

R. LE FEVRE - Portrait Of A Lady And Her Young Daughters, Seated On A Sofa - 38½ x 31¼in.
(Sotheby's) £350

FRANZ LEFLER - An Allegorical Scene Representing Hunting - signed - 14½ x 42in.
(Sotheby's) £1,000

GEOFFREY R. LEFTWAY - Playing Hard To Get - signed - 19½ x 15½in.
(Sotheby's Belgravia) £90

FERNAND LEGER - Composition Avec Buste - signed and dated '29 - 25½ x 36in.
(Sotheby's) £38,000

FERNAND LEGER - Une Figure Et Une Fleur - signed and dated - signed titled and dated on the reverse - 19¾ x 25½in.
(Sotheby's) £15,500

ALEXANDER LEGGETT - The Moorland Spring - 23½ x 19½in.
(Christie's) £380

W. F. LEGGETT - A View Of St Pauls From The River - watercolour and pastel - 8 x 10in.
(G. A. Key) £26

CHARLES HENRI JOSEPH LEICKERT - A Frozen River Landscape With Skaters Near A Cottage - signed - 48 x 77.5cm.
(Phillips) £1,000

CHARLES HENRI JOSEPH LEICKERT - A Frozen River Landscape with figures on the ice - signed - on panel - 5½ x 8½in.
(Christie's) £1,100

CHARLES HENRI JOSEPH LEICKERT - A Frozen River Landscape with figures and a windmill - signed - 8 x 10in.
(Christie's) **£1,000**

R. J. LEIGH - A Country Spring Scene, With Apple Blossom in the foreground - oil on canvas - 19½ x 23½in.
(Hollingsworths) **£35**

EDMUND BLAIR LEIGHTON - Vows - signed and dated 1906 - 31½ x 38½in.
(Sotheby's Belgravia) **£420**

FREDERICK LORD LEIGHTON - Amarilla - 50 x 29½in.
(Sotheby's Belgravia) **£5,000**

R. P. LEITCH - Autumn Landscapes - both heightened with white - 6¼ x 9½in.
(Sotheby's) **£30 Pair**

WILLIAM LEIGHTON LEITCH - The Bridge At Pau - signed and dated 1839 - watercolour - 8 x 12in.
(Christie's, S. Kensington) **£280**

WILLIAM LEIGHTON LEITCH - Italian Estuary Scene With Old Buildings, Boats and Figures - watercolour - 4 x 7in.
(G. A. Key) **£30**

WILLIAM LEIGHTON LEITCH - A Scottish Mansion With An Important Glass Conservatory, Figures In The Garden in the foreground - heightened with white - signed with monogram - 4¾ x 13¼in.
(Sotheby's) **£90**

FRANZ LEITGEB - The Old Bavarian; A Glass Of Beer - both signed - on panel - 10¼ x 8¼in.
(Sotheby's) **£750 Pair**

M. LELVA - 'Gotterville Bretague' - signed and dated 1957 - oil - 13 x 22in.
(Warner, Sheppard & Wade) **£5**

LELY - Portrait Of A Lady, three-quarter length, Wearing A Brown Dress With Blue Cloak, Seated In A Wooded Landscape - 49 x 38½in.
(Christie's) £200

LELY, After - Portrait Of Anna Maria Brudenell, Countess Of Shrewsbury, half length, Wearing A Brown Dress - in a painted oval - 24 x 19in.
(Sotheby's) £50

LELY, School - Portrait Of A Lady, three-quarter length, Seated, Wearing A Brown Dress - 46 x 36½in.
(Sotheby's) £90

P. LELY - Portrait Of A Lady, three-quarter length, Seated Wearing A Brown Dress, A Rose In Her Right Hand - 45 x 35in.
(Sotheby's) £320

SIR P. LELY - Portrait Of Anne, Duchess Of York, half length, In A Cartouche - 29 x 24in.
(Sotheby's) £100

LEMAIN - Wild and Domestic Duck By A Stream - oil - 11 x 17in.
(G. A. Key) £60

ARTHUR LEMON - Old Duke, A Study Of A Working Horse - on board - 9 x 11¾in.
(Sotheby's Belgravia) £50

F. LENOIR - Barges In A Dutch Canal - signed - 26½ x 21¼in.
(Sotheby's) £240

MARCEL LENOIR - Torse Couche - charcoal - signed twice and inscribed - 7½ x 15in.
(Sotheby's) £5

COLLE LEONE - Piazzetta San Marco And The Scuola Grande Di San Marco By Moonlight - both signed and dated 1876 - 17 x 24¼in.
(Sotheby's) £400 Pair

AUGUSTE LEPERE - Paris - Au Bord De La Seine - pencil - 5 x 9¼in.
(Sotheby's) £28

EUGENE LEPOITTEVIN - Paul Potter's Studio - 36 x 30in.
(Sotheby's) £650

A. LESLIE - Thaden Woods, Epping, Essex - signed - 13½ x 17¼in.
(Sotheby's Belgravia) £170

CHARLES LESLIE - Adour De L'Espoune Pres Campan, Haute Pyrenees - signed and dated 1870 and inscribed on the reverse - 14¼ x 22¼in.
(Christie's) £170

CHARLES LESLIE - Mountain River Scenes - both bear another signature and dated - inscribed on the stretchers - each 11¼ x 23¼in.
(Sotheby's Belgravia) £340 Pair

EMMANUEL LEUTZE - Prayer Discovered - signed and dated '50 - 18½ x 14½in.
(Sotheby's) £300

LUIGI LEVI, called ULVI LEIGI - Marina A Costiglioncello - signed and signed and inscribed on the reverse - on panel - 6¾ x 10¼in.
(Sotheby's) £350

LUCIEN LEVY-DHURMER - Fantasmagorie - signed - 62 x 81in.
(Sotheby's) £1,100

LUCIEN LEVY-DHURMER - L'Odalisque - signed - 42 x 78in.
(Sotheby's) £2,900

C. J. LEWIS - Figures Outside Cottages - both heightened with bodycolour - each 7½ x 10in.
(Sotheby's Belgravia) £75 Pair

JOHN FREDERICK LEWIS - Lilium Auratum - signed and dated 1871 - watercolour heightened with white - 21½ x 13¾in.
(Christie's) £25,000

JOHN FREDERICK LEWIS - Waiting
For The Ferry, Upper Egypt - signed
and dated 1859 - on panel - 13 x 31¾in.
(Christie's) **£7,500**

JOHN FREDERICK LEWIS - Balkan
Girl Kneeling - pencil and watercolour
heightened with white on grey paper -
13½ x 10in.
(Christie's) **£120**

JOHN FREDERICK LEWIS - A Spanish
Gypsy Family With A Donkey And A
Dog Beneath Trees - watercolour -
19 x 24in.
(Henry Spencer & Sons) **£400**

S. VAN DER LEY - A Street Bazaar
In Khartoum - signed and inscribed on
the reverse - on panel - 12 x 10in.
(Sotheby's) **£250**

OTTO LEYDE - Portrait Of A Young
Girl, half length - heightened with
white - signed with monogram and
dated 1869 - oval - 23½ x 18½in.
(Sotheby's Belgravia) **£18**

PAUL JOSEPH LEYENDECKER - Playing
With Poodle - signed and dated 1869 - on
panel - 12 x 9in.
(Christie's) **£1,000**

HENRI LEYS - The Study - oil on
canvas - 32 x 40cm.
(Galerie Moderne) **£70**

LEON LHERMITTE - Les Moissonneurs -
charcoal and blue crayon on grey paper -
heightened with white gouache - signed
with initials - 8 x 6½in.
(Sotheby's) **£300**

CHARLES SILLEM LIDDERDALE -
Portrait of a young woman - oil on
canvas - signed with monogram and
dated '79 - 24 x 20 ins.
(King & Chasemore) **£350**

LIERIS

J. VAN LIERIS - Vase Trimmed With
Flowers - oil on canvas - signed and
dated 1887 - 46 x 32cm.
(Galerie Moderne) **£63**

L. LIESZBOVSKA - The Marsh - oil on
canvas - signed - 75cm. x 1m.62cm.
(Galerie Moderne) **£133**

A. VAN LIEVEN - Landscape - oil on
wood - signed - 44 x 52cm.
(Galerie Moderne) **£22**

A. LIGHT - A Dismasted Sailing Ship In
A Stormy Sea, Hailing A Passing Companion Ship - signed and dated 1849 - oil
on canvas - 23½ x 37⅓in.
(Bearnes & Waycotts) **£300**

D. LIGHTFOOT - Punt On River With
Village in background - oil - 13 x 21in.
(G. A. Key) **£10**

J. VAN DEN LINDLAR - Landscape -
oil on canvas - signed - 48 x 70cm.
(Galerie Moderne) **£75**

JOHANNES LINGELBACH - A Market
Scene In Rome With Peasants Selling
Fruit And Vegetables; And A Market
Scene In Rome With A Quack Doctor
Selling His Wares - one signed - 20½ x
24½in.
(Christie's) **£11,000 Pair**

JOHANNES LINGELBACH - A Market
Scene In Rome with a quack doctor
selling his wares - signed - 20½ x 24½in.
(Christie's) **£6,000**

JOHANNES LINGELBACH - A Market
Scene In Rome with peasants selling fruit
and vegetables - 20½ x 24½in.
(Christie's) **£5,500**

THE SCHOOL OF LINGELBACH - An
Italianate Port With Classical Ruins And
A Large Crowed In Festive Spirit And
In Numerous Pursuits - 46 x 67in.
(Buckell & Ballard) **£4,200**

J. LINNELL - A Landscape With Cattle And
Figures - oil on board - signed - 19½ x 9½in.
(J. Francis, T. Jones & Sons) **£82**

JOHN LINNELL - A Thames Sailing Barge Aground Near Westminster Bridge - signed - inscribed and dated 1806-7 - black chalk heightened with white on brown paper - 11¾ x 9½in.
(Christie's) £150

JOHN LINNELL - Stacking Barley Near Witley, Surrey - signed and dated 1863 - watercolour heightened with white - 8½ x 14in.
(Christie's) £450

JOHN LINNELL - Barges On The Thames Near A Waterman's Hut - black chalk heightened with white on grey-blue paper - 7½ x 16¼in.
(Christie's) £75

JOHN LINNELL - The Harvest Field - bears signature - 15½ x 26in.
(Christie's) £700

J. LINNELL, SNR - Bringing In The Cattle - 18 x 28½in.
(Sotheby's Belgravia) £300

JOHN LINNELL, SNR - A Portrait Of Catherine Babington, Nee Brooke, half length - signed with initials and dated 1824 - on panel - 21 x 16.5cm.
(Phillips) £620

WILLEM LINNIG - Rehearsing A Song - signed and dated 1850 - on panel - 16 x 12½in.
(Sotheby's) £750

WILLEM LINNIG - A Rustic Family Enjoying A Good Meal - signed and dated 1840 - on panel - 24 x 19½in.
(Sotheby's) £1,300

W. LINTON - Peasants And Cattle In A Mountainous Woody Landscape - 18½ x 28in.
(Christie's) £260

LIONEL - Belaugh Church From The River - oil - 10 x 18in.
(G. A. Key) £30

H. LITS - The Farmyard - on wood - signed - 21 x 30cm.
(Galerie Moderne) £16

LITTLEWOOD - Extensive Wooded Landscape With Drover And Cattle - oil - 16 x 24in.
(G. A. Key) £24

E. LITTLEWOOD - A Woodland Road Near Buildings - signed - 17 x 23½in.
(Sotheby's) £140

EDWARD LITTLEWOOD - Piggins Ferry, Norwich And Old Tollgate House, Dereham Road, Norwich - oval - oils - 10 x 8in
(G. A. Key) £105 Pair

LIZARS

WILLIAM HOME LIZARS - Aurora, Phaeton And The Seven Heliades - signed on reverse - 28½ x 35in.
(Christie's) £280

ROBERT MALCOLM LLOYD - Fishing Boats In Squally Weather - watercolour - both signed and indistinctly inscribed - 14 x 21in.
(Christie's) £90 Pair

STUART LLOYD - Autumn Evening Near Hillingford Church - signed - oil - 20 x 36in.
(Warner, Sheppard & Wade) £90

W. STUART LLOYD - Dartmouth Castle; Carnarvon Castle - both heightened with bodycolour - signed - 15½ x 23¼in.
(Sotheby's Belgravia) £260 Pair

A. LOCATELLI - Two Horsemen and Others on a road leading up a slope to a Villa outside which are several figures - 38 x 28 ins.
(Sotheby's) £1,500

A. LOCATELLI - Italianate Woody Landscape With Shepherds - 19½ x 38½in.
(Christie's) £2,000 Pair

LOCATELLI - Figures In A Wooded River Landscape, A Castle in the distance - 47 x 36in.
(Woolley & Wallis) £480

ANDREA LOCATELLI - A Waterfall With An Artist Sketching; and Peasants On A Rocky Path - canvas laid down on panel - 24 x 8in.
(Christie's) £900 Pair

J. LOCHHEAD - The Village School - oil - 13 x 9½in.
(Thomas Love & Sons Ltd) **£50**

GEORGE EDWARD LODGE - Grouse On The Alert - heightened with bodycolour - signed - 10¾ x 17in.
(Sotheby's) **£780**

GEORGE EDWARD LODGE - Pheasant; Black Game - both signed - grisaille - 13¼ x 20in.
(Sotheby's) **£200 Pair**

GUSTAVE LOISEAU - A Normandy Landscape - signed and dated 1901 - 15¾ x 19¾in.
(Henry Spencer & Sons) **£1,350**

K. LOMAS - Flowers And Birds - on glass - signed - 60 x 29cm.
(Galerie Moderne) **£12**

GEORGE EDWARD LODGE - A Golden Eagle - heightened with bodycolour - signed - 6½ x 4½in.
(Sotheby's) **£160**

GEORGE EDWARD LODGE - Blackcock - heightened with bodycolour - signed - 11¼ x 17¼in.
(Sotheby's) **£800**

JOHN ARTHUR LOMAX - St. Valentine's Day - signed - on panel - 15½ x 11½in.
(Sotheby's Belgravia) **£900**

275

LOMAX

JOHN ARTHUR LOMAX - A Print
Collector - watercolour - signed J. A. L. -
6 x 4in.
(Stewart & Gore) **£60**

LOWRY LOMAX - A Yarmouth Beach Scene
- oil on panel - signed - 25 x 15in.
(J. Francis, T. Jones & Sons) **£75**

L LOMBARD - Portrait Of A Bearded
Man, bust length, Wearing A Black
Hat And Doublet - on panel - 18½ x
17¼in.
(Christie's) **£950**

LOMBARD SCHOOL, circa 1650 - Recto:
The Rest On The Flight; Verso: Male
Nude - drawn with the brush in brown
wash over black chalk, heightened with
white 9recto); red chalk (verso) - 290 x
430cm.
(Sotheby's) **£121**

D. DE LONCIN - Vase Of Flowers - oil
on canvas - signed - 70 x 49cm.
(Galerie Moderne) **£265**

E. LONG - Figures And Geese On
Village Green And Autumn Twilight
Scene - watercolours - 7 x 10in.
(G. A. Key) **£20 Pair**

P. LONGHI - A Concert - 39 x 32in.
(Christie's) **£900**

D. DE LONCIN - Vase Of Flowers -
oil on canvas - signed - 75 x 60cm.
(Galerie Moderne) **£200**

D. DE LONCIN - Vase Trimmed With
Flowers - oil on wood - signed - 24 x
18cm.
(Galerie Moderne) **£25**

D. DE LONCIN - Pint Pot Trimmed With
Flowers - oil on wood - signed - 27 x
22cm.
(Galerie Moderne) **£40**

DANIEL DE LONCIN - Vase Of Flowers
- oil on canvas - signed - 56 x 46cm.
(Galerie Moderne) **£220**

EDGAR LONGSTAFFE - A Waterfall -
signed with monogram and dated 1881 -
13½ x 11½in.
(Sotheby's Belgravia) **£140**

EDGAR LONGSTAFFE - Kilchurn Castle; Ben Cruachan, Loch Awe - both signed with initials - each 11¾ x 23¾in.
(Sotheby's Belgravia)　　　**£130 Pair**

CARLE VAN LOO - The Toilet Of Esther - signed and dated 1736 - on panel - 18 x 15in.
(Christie's)　　　**£4,200**

CARLE VAN LOO - 'La Sultane': a lady in oriental costume seated, playing a lute - 48½ x 38in.
(Christie's)　　　**£22,000**

JEAN BAPTISTE VAN LOO and STUDIO - Portrait Of Frederick, Prince Of Wales, Wearing The Order Of The Garter - three-quarter length - 48 x 39in.
(Christie's)　　　**£550**

JAN LOOTEN - A Rocky Wooded River Landscape with a hawking party crossing a bridge - signed and dated 1661 - 46½ x 71in.
(Christie's)　　　**£6,000**

A. LORENZ - Norwegian Fjords - signed - 38½ x 28in.
(Christie's)　　　**£500 Pair**

F. DI LORENZO - The Madonna And Child In The Clouds surrounded by cherubim - on panel - 27½ x 28½in.
(Christie's)　　　**£4,500**

LORENZO LOTTO, after - Two Studies of a Herald - pen and brown ink and wash - 18 x 18.5 cm.
(Sotheby's)　　　**£55**

LOTTO

LORENZO LOTTO - Portrait of a Gentleman wearing a black cap and coat and holding a pomegranate - 30¾ x 23½ ins.
(Christie's) **£2,800**

EMILE CHARLES JOSEPH LOUBON - Figures in the Grounds of an Italian Villa; and A Lake in the Grounds of a Villa, with figures in a rowing boat - one signed and dated 1838 - 12½ x 20 ins.
(Christie's) **£2600 Pair**

THOMAS LOUND - Crowland Abbey - pencil and watercolour - 11½ x 19in.
(Christie's) **£380**

THOMAS LOUND - Bacton Abbey, Norfolk - pencil and watercolour - 13¼ x 18¾in.
(Christie's) **£160**

M. LOUS - A Moroccan Street - signed - on board - 11¾ x 8 ins.
(Sotheby's) **£90**

PHILIPP JAMES DE LOUTHERBOURG - An Italianate Landscape, With Peasants And Cattle Fording A River; And An Italianate Landscape With Peasants And Cattle in the foreground And Buildings Beyond - 16 x 20½in.
(Christie's) **£1,900 Pair**

MAURICE LOUTREUIL - Portrait De Dame - oil - on canvas - 25¼ x 17¾in.
(Sotheby's) **£140**

MAURICE LOUTREUIL - Portrait
d'Homme - oil - on canvas - 25¼ x 21¼in.
(Sotheby's) **£130**

CHARLES FREDERICK LOWCOCK -
In the Tepidarium - signed - 18 x 8 ins.
(Christie's, S. Kensington) **£170**

CHARLES FREDERICK LOWCOCK -
The Toilet - signed - on panel - 12¾ x
5¾in.
(Sotheby's Belgravia) **£190**

CHARLES LOWCOCK - A Study Of A
Spirit - oil on panel - 10 x 6in.
(Henry Spencer & Sons) **£760**

C. J. LUAMTICK - The Baby Sitter -
signed and inscribed on the reverse -
canvas laid on panel - 10 x 8½in.
(Sotheby's Belgravia) **£120**

A. D. LUCAS - Still Life of Flowers -
oil on canvas - signed and dated - 10 x 8
ins.
(A. Sharpe & Partners) **£460**

THOMAS LUNY - Smugglers Landing
Barrels At A Cove - signed and dated
1803 - oil on canvas - 18¾ x 23¼in.
(Bearnes & Waycotts) **£1,350**

ALBERT DURER LUCAS - The
Milkmaid's Nosegay - signed and dated
1878 - 15¼ x 11½in.
(Sotheby's Belgravia) **£580**

J. S. LUCAS - Portrait Of Dante, head
and shoulders - 29 x 24in.
(Sotheby's Belgravia) **£25**

JOHN SEYMOUR LUCAS - The New
Spinet - signed and dated 1916 - 27 x
35½in.
(Christie's) **£1,100**

LUCAS LUCAS - A Bay Horse In A
Stable - 19½ x 25¼in.
(Sotheby's Belgravia) **£110**

T. LUCAS - Fishing Vessels On The
Strand By Night With Figures in the
foreground - signed - oil on canvas -
23 x 15in.
(Smith-Woolley & Perry) **£60**

THOMAS LUNY - Viscount Pellew's
Ship 'Culloden' Calling At Tristan Da
Cunha - signed and dated 1821 - oil
on canvas - 19¼ x 26½in.
(Bearnes & Waycotts) **£640**

MAXIMILIEN LUCE - Nu Assis -
cartoon - signed - 55 x 46cm.
(Galerie Moderne) **£53**

LUFTSCHOSER - The Pipers Lovesong -
pastel - 12 x 11in.
(G. A. Key) **£13**

ALOIS DE LUG - Philippina Welser
Pleading With Emperor Ferdinand -
signed and dated - 68 x 94½in.
(Christie's) **£700**

EVARISTE VITAL LUMINAIS - Two
Ladies In A Carriage Drawn By Donkeys,
recto; A Figure Study, verso - inscribed
'Petit Gris Et Petit Loup' and dated -
on panel - 6½ x 9¼in.
(Sotheby's) **£350**

THOMAS LUNY - 'The Vixen' Off Sambro
Lighthouse, Nova Scotia, December 28th,
1797 - signed and dated 1822 - inscribed
on a label on the reverse - on panel - 9 x
11½in.
(Christie's) **£650**

THOMAS LUNY - The Battle Of The Nile - signed and dated 1802 - 22 x 34in
(Christie's) **£3,200 Pair**

T. LUNY - A Coastal Scene With Men Ashore And Others Handling A Fishing Boat in foreground - 19th century - oil on wood panel - signed - 9½ x 12¾in.
(Foll & Parker) **£190**

LUTI - Jacob And Rachel At The Well - 14 x 18½in.
(Christie's) **£500**

I. LUTTICHUYS - Portrait Of A Man, In Black Costume And Bands - in a painted oval - on panel - 14 x 11½in.
(Christie's) **£280**

J. LYNN - The British Man-O-War 'Repulse' In A Choppy Sea - oil on canvas - 24 x 36in.
(Bonham's) **£1,000**

J. LYNN - Sailing Vessels Under Full Sail - 19½ x 23in.
(Christie's) **£400**

C. DE LYON - Portrait Of A Gentleman, Small half length, In Black Gold Embroidered Costume, Holding Gloves - on panel - 13 x 10in.
(Christie's) **£1,600**

CORNEILLE DE LYON - Portrait of a Man, small bust length, in a black doublet - on panel - 6½ x 5in.
(Christie's) **£3,800**

LYSS - A Reveller Attended By Nymphs - 20 x 16in.
(Christie's) **£1,000**

MAAS - A Wooded Italianate Landscape With A Riding Party And
Peasants By A River, A Town Beyond -
37 x 44¾in.
(Christie's) **£750**

DIRK MAAS - A Scene Outside A
Stable, A Man On Horseback, Drinking
From A Tankard, A Manservant Beside
Him And, Seated On The Ground, A
Woman With A Spindle - signed and
dated 1682 - on panel - 15¼ x 17¾in.
(Sotheby's) **£2,000**

DIRK MAAS - An Alpine River Landscape With Travellers On A Path And
Buildings Beyond - indistinctly signed -
on panel - 9½ x 12in.
(Christie's) **£6,000**

ANDREW MacCALLUM - 'The Landmark
To The Double Tide, That Purpling Rolls
On Either Side' - watercolour - signed -
inscribed 'Corinth' and dated 1874 - 17 x
53¾in.
(Christie's) **£70**

NORMAN M. MacDOUGALL - Landscape And Loch With Cottage - dated
1911 - 34 x 50cm.
(Edmiston's) **£46**

NORMAN M. MacDOUGALL - Wooded
Country Road - 50 x 74cm.
(Edmiston's) **£140**

MacGEORGE - The Old Jetty,
Grangemouth - watercolour - 22 x 29cm.
(Edmiston's) **£10**

WILLIAM STEWART MacGEORGE -
On A Dutch Canal - signed - on board
- 9¾ x 13½in.
(Sotheby's) **£260**

SARA MacGREGOR - The Lavender
Beads - signed and dated 1912 -
39¼ x 22½in.
(Sotheby's) **£900**

SARA MacGREGOR - Boy In A Fez - on board - 15½ x 11¼in.
(Sotheby's) **£100**

BARBARA MACKAY - Self-Portrait, with still life - signed and dated '90 - 38 x 51in.
(Sotheby's) **£440**

J. MACKAY - A Wayside Inn, In A Sunlit Rural Setting - watercolour - signed and dated 1906 - 10¾ x 15½in.
(Hollingsworths) **£20**

WILLIAM DARLING MACKAY - On The Tyne, East Linton - oil - signed and dated '73/'74 - 69.5 x 128.5cm.
(Phillips in Scotland) **£190**

DUNCAN MacKELLAR - Lady With Cat At An Open Fire - 35 x 45cm.
(Edmiston's) **£85**

D. MacKENZIE - 'Loch Ard', Highland Landscapes with Figures - signed - oil on canvas - 12 x 18in.
(Morphet & Morphet) **£125 Pair**

D. MacKENZIE - 'Loch Long', Highland Landscapes with Figures - signed - oil on canvas - 20 x 30in.
(Morphet & Morphet) **£140 Pair**

SHEILA MacKENZIE - Still Life Of A Vase Of Flowers - on board - 31¾ x 26½in.
(Sotheby's Belgravia) **£40**

CHARLES RENNIE MacKINTOSH - Bouquet Of Flowers - watercolour - 30.5 x 26.5cm.
(Edmiston's) **£510**

CHARLES RENNIE MacKINTOSH - Bouquet Of Flowers - watercolour - 27 x 24.5cm.
(Edmiston's) **£330**

J. MacLAREN - Collecting mussels - oil - signed - 23 x 28cm.
(Phillips in Scotland) **£55**

ALEX MacLEAN - Seascape - oil - signed - 23½ x 41½in.
(John H. Raby & Sons) **£95**

ALEX MacLEAN - View Of The Sea - oil - signed - 14 x 10in.
(John H. Raby & Sons) **£67.50**

K. MACLEAY - Portrait Of Egerton Eastwick, Son Of Edward Backhouse Eastwick - arched top - 29 x 24in.
(Sotheby's) **£350**

MACLEAY

M. MACLEAY - By A Scottish Loch -
34½ x 56in.
(Sotheby's) **£250**

MACLISE - The Sanctuary - 25 x 37in.
(Sotheby's Belgravia) **£32**

DANIEL MACLISE - The Meeting Of
Henry VIII And Anne Boleyn At
Hampton Court - 51 x 61in.
(Sotheby's Belgravia) **£1,100**

DANIEL MACLISE - A Terrier On A
Lead - pencil and watercolour heightened
with white on grey paper - inscribed - 5¾
x 6¼in.
(Christie's) **£45**

W. RUSSELL MACNEE - "Pitroddie" -
watercolour - 14½ x 21in.
(Thomas Love & Sons Ltd) **£75**

SIR WILLIAM MacTAGGART - Carol
Singers - signed and dated '57 - on board -
23½ x 19½in.
(Sotheby's) **£120**

JOHN MacWHIRTER - Bringing Home
The Sheep - signed - 23½ x 41½in.
(Sotheby's) **£200**

JOHN MacWHIRTER - Girgenti, Sicily -
signed with initials - 23½ x 35½in.
(Sotheby's) **£340**

JOHN MacWHIRTER - Silver Strand,
Loch Katrine 'So wondrous wild, the
whole might seem, The Scenery of a
fairy dream' Lady of the Lake - signed -
37 x 62½in.
(Christie's) **£680**

WILLES MADDOX - Flora With A
Companion - signed and dated 1849 -
oak panel - 10½ x 15½in.
(Woolley & Wallis) **£400**

ADRIEN MADIOL - An Interior - oil on
wood - signed - 27 x 21cm.
(Galerie Moderne) **£11**

NICOLAES MAES - Portrait Of A
Gentleman, Standing, small three-
quarter length, Leaning Against A
Pediment - signed with monogram -
25¼ x 21in.
(Christie's) **£1,200**

NICOLAES MAES - Portrait Of A Small Boy, half length, in green and white dress, and dark green cloak, wearing a plumed hat, holding a branch of a lemon tree, with peaches on a plinth - 27 x 24in.
(Christie's) **£13,000**

THE MASTER OF THE MAGDALEN LEGEND - The Virgin And Child - on panel - 9¼ x 6in.
(Sotheby's) **£6,000**

GIROLAMO DI MAGGIO - The Madonna And Child, Saint Peter, Saint John The Baptist And A Donor - inscribed - on panel - 33 x 53½in.
(Christie's) **£6,000**

JAMES CHARLES MAGGS - The Brighton To London Coach At A Halt Outside The Foxhound Inn - signed - oil on canvas - 24 x 36in.
(Bonham's) **£910**

JOHN CHARLES MAGGS - 'The Hero' - The Bristol To Birmingham Coach Passing Through A Village - signed and dated 1878 - 36 x 66.5cm.
(Phillips) **£500**

JOHN CHARLES MAGGS - 'The Bath Coach', in a winter landscape - on canvas - signed and dated 'Bath 1873' - 18 x 31½ ins.
(King & Chasemore) **£580**

A. MAGNASCO - An Italianate Coastal Landscape With Classical Ruins, And Peasants Playing Cards in the foreground - 66½ x 92½in.
(Christie's) **£4,200**

A. MAGNASCO - An Italianate Coastal
Landscape With Classical Ruins, And
Beggars And Other Figures in the fore-
ground - 66½ x 92½in.
(Christie's) **£4,800**

ALESSANDRO MAGNASCO - Three Men
With Bundles Resting At The Foot Of A
Wooded Slope, A Young Woman Seated
By A Path Above Them; In The Left
Background A Church And Houses - 86¼
x 67in.
(Sotheby's) **£38,000**

ALESSANDRO MAGNASCO - A Wooded
Italianate River Landscape With
Washerwomen, and buildings beyond -
45 x 56in.
(Christie's) **£6,500**

ALESSANDRO MAGNASCO - A Rocky
Wooded Landscape, with figures - shaped
corners - 17¼ x 11¾in.
(Christie's) **£3,000**

CAMILLE MAGNUS - Landscape - oil on
lined canvas - signed - 23 x 34cm.
(Galerie Moderne) **£28**

ARISTIDE MAILLOL - Portrait
d'Elisa - signed - 23½ x 19in.
(Sotheby's) **£9,000**

CORNELIS JOHANNES MAKS - The Picador - oil - on panel - signed - 15¾ x 19¾in.
(Sotheby's) **£480**

CHRISTIAN MALI - A River Landscape, With Cattle Watering Near A Town - signed and inscribed 'Munchen' - 22 x 44½in.
(Christie's) **£9,000**

R. MALLETT - River And Lake Scenes Near Norwich - oils - 6 x 8in
(G. A. Key) **£26 Pair**

J. VAN MANDER - The Feeding Of The Five Thousand - on panel - 19 x 24in.
(Christie's) **£850**

K. VAN MANDER - The Worship Of The Golden Calf - on copper - 10 x 23in.
(Christie's) **£450**

WILLIAM HENRY MANDER - On The Lledr - signed - inscribed on the reverse - 11½ x 17½in.
(Sotheby's Belgravia) **£380**

WILLIAM HENRY MANDER - 'In The Gwynant Valley' - signed - oil on canvas - 19½ x 29½in.
(Bearnes & Waycotts) **£780**

WILLIAM HENRY MANDER - A Waterfall - canvas laid on board - 17¼ x 23¼in.
(Sotheby's Belgravia) **£400**

WILLIAM HENRY MANDER - Views In The Lledr Valley, Near Dolwydellan, North Wales - both signed - signed and inscribed on the reverse - 16 x 23½in.
(Christie's) **£1,200 Pair**

W. H. MANDER - Wooded River Landscape - canvas - 10 x 15½in.
(Morphet & Morphet) **£150**

W. MANDER - Landscape near Bont ddu - signed - oil on canvas - 24 x 16 ins.
(Hall, Wateridge and Owen) **£80**

ALEXANDER MANN - On The Sea Shore - signed - inscribed Tangier - dated 1891 - 16¼ x 20¼in.
(Sotheby's Belgravia) **£200**

ALEXANDER MANN - Ebb Tide, On The Ald - signed and dated 1894 - 20¾ x 33¼in.
(Sotheby's Belgravia) **£45**

ALEXANDER MANN - Cigarera - signed - on panel - 9¼ x 5¼in.
(Sotheby's Belgravia) **£22**

MANNERS

VIOLET MANNERS, DUCHESS OF RUTLAND - Studies Of Marion Terry, Actress Sister Of Ellen Terry, Head And Shoulders - both pencil - signed with monogram - inscribed and dated 1879 - 9¼ x 6in.
(Sotheby's Belgravia) **£95 Pair**

P. MANZONI - A Woodland Scene, With A Male Figure - signed - oil on canvas - 38¾ x 29¼in.
(Geering & Colyer) **£270**

L. MARCANIS - The Skaters - oil on canvas - signed - 39 x 50cm.
(Galerie Moderne) **£86**

ALEX. MARCETTE - The Boats - oil on lined canvas - signed - 26 x 33cm.
(Galerie Moderne) **£25**

VINCENTE MARCH - The Fruit Seller - signed and inscribed 'Roma' and dated '84 - on panel - 12 x 18in.
(Christie's) **£2,600**

JEAN MARCHAND - Charette Devant Une Eglise; Le Cheval - each pencil - 10¼ x 8¼in. and 7¼ x 9in.
(Sotheby's) **£30 Two**

JEAN MARCHAND - Le Danseur Turc - oil - on canvas - signed - 21 x 17¼in.
(Sotheby's) **£220**

SCHOOL OF THE MARCHES, Early 15th Century - The Virgin, Bust Length, In Prayer - gold ground - on panel - 14 x 9in.
(Sotheby's) **£3,000**

VICTOR MARECHAL - Nature Morte Aux Fruits Et Au Pichet - oil - on canvas - signed - 11¾ x 9¼in.
(Sotheby's) **£110**

S. MARESCA - Portrait Of An Old Peasant Woman, half length - signed - oil on canvas - 15½ x 10in.
(Geering & Colyer) **£55**

JACOPO MARIESCHI - A View Of The Arsenal, Venice, with figures in the Campo dell' Arsenale - 24 x 37½in.
(Christie's) **£4,500**

M. MARIESCHI - The Rialto Bridge, Venice, From The North, With The Palazzo Dei Camerlenghi And The Fabbriche Vecchie Di Rialto - 28 x 44in.
(Christie's) **£4,800**

M. MARIESCHI - The Piazza San Marco, Venice, with figures - 24 x 38in.
(Christie's) **£4,500**

M. MARIESCHI - The Bacino, Venice, With The Library, And The Church Of Santa Maria Della Salute - 22 x 23in.
(Christie's) **£2,800**

MICHELE MARIESCHI - The Bacino, Venice, with the Island of San Giorgio - 22½ x 34in.
(Christie's) **£2,800**

MARIESCHI - Le Sattere, Venice, With The Church Of Santo Spirito - 18½ x 27½in.
(Christie's) **£3,200**

MICHELE MARIESCHI - The Courtyard Of The Doge's Palace, Venice - 46¼ x 71in.
(Christie's) **£55,000**

ALESSANDRO MARINI - The Poetry Reading - signed and indistinctly dated - on panel - in a painted oval - 16½ x 20½in.
(Sotheby's) **£350**

MARINUS - The Tax Gatherers - on panel - 39 x 29in.
(Christie's) **£4,200**

Wm. MARJORAM - Norfolk Wherry Near Cantley - 6in. oval.
(G. A. Key) **£25**

ALBERT ERNEST MARKES - Shipping Off The Coast - both heightened with white - each 6¼ x 14¾in.
(Sotheby's Belgravia) **£200 Pair**

289

CARL MARKO, The Younger - A Mediterranean Sunlit Coastal Scene With Figure On A Sandy Path in the foreground - signed and dated 1855 - oil on panel - 10¾ x 14in.
(Bonham's) **£2,000**

HENRY STACY MARKS - "Charity - Say Not Unto Thy Neighbour, Go And Come Again, And Tomorrow I Will Give; When Thou Hast It By Thee." - A Medieval Town, With An Old Blind Man Playing A Pipe Outside A Baker's Shop - oil - signed, inscribed on verso and dated 1864 - 33½ x 43½in.
(Henry Spencer & Sons) **£1,000**

JEAN-LOUIS DE MARNE - A Wooded River Landscape, With Figures And Animals in the foreground And A Church Beyond - 12½ x 16in.
(Christie's) **£1,700**

WILLIAM MARLOW - Ruined Classical Building and Figures - signed with initials - watercolour - 15½ x 13¼in.
(Woolley & Wallis) **£210**

P. MARNEY - A Market Stall, Rouen - signed - 15½ x 11½in.
(Sotheby's) **£170**

PAUL MARNY - Sligny - heightened with bodycolour - signed - 6¼ x 18in.
(Sotheby's Belgravia) **£80**

PAUL MARNY - Montreuil-Sur-Mer - signed and inscribed - 25¼ x 15½in.
(Sotheby's) **£130**

PAUL MARNY - View Of Angor, Brittany - signed - watercolour - 20 x 35¼in.
(Bearnes & Waycotts) **£280**

ALBERT MARQUET - Port d'Hambourg - signed - 25¾ x 31in.
(Sotheby's) **£16,000**

THOMAS FALCON MARSHALL - The Midday Hour - signed and dated 1855 - 18 x 25in.
(Christie's) **£1,900**

ALBERT MARQUET - Collioure - signed - 19½ x 24in.
(Sotheby's) **£7,000**

W. MARSDEN - His Majesty's Dogs - signed - 15½ x 19½in.
(Sotheby's Belgravia) **£35**

B. MARSHALL - Horse And Trainer On Newmarket Heath - oil - 26 x 34in.
(G. A. Key) **£195**

HENRY MARTENS - The First Bombay European Regiment And Two Mounted Officers Of The Bombay Light Cavalry In India - 20¼ x 29½in.
(Christie's) **£1,100**

MARTIN - Belshazzar's Feast - 11½ x 15½in.
(Christie's) **£140**

J. MARTIN - The Destruction Of Pompeii And Herculaneum - watercolour - 26 x 38in.
(Christie's) **£240**

J. MARTIN - The Burning Of Rome - 30½ x 42½in.
(Christie's) **£140**

BEN MARSHALL - 'Muly Moloch', A Chestnut Colt Being Rubbed Down On Newmarket Heath, With Portraits Of Trotter, Hardy And Thompson To The Left - signed and dated 1803 - 40 x 50in.
(Christie's) **£55,000**

R. MARSHALL - In Aberdeenshire - signed - 13½ x 23½in.
(Sotheby's Belgravia) **£140**

JOHN MARTIN - Belshazzar's Feast - signed and dated 1820 - 63 x 98in.
(Christie's) **£22,000**

MARTIN

JOHN MARTIN - The Wye, Looking Towards Chepstow - signed and dated 1844 - watercolour - 11¾ x 24¾in.
(Christie's) **£2,000**

JOHN MARTIN - A Wooded Landscape - signed and dated 1845 - canvas on board - 13¼ x 17¾in.
(Christie's) **£500**

HENRI MARTIN - Le Pont - oil - on canvas - signed - 17¼ x 9¼in.
(Sotheby's) **£500**

S. MARTIN - A Foxhunting Scene 'Fairly On Him' - signed - inscribed and dated 1904 - oil on canvas - 19¼ x 29½in.
(Bearnes & Waycotts) **£200**

W. MARTIN - Shipping Off The Coast - both on board - 11½ x 19½in.
(Sotheby's Belgravia) **£95 Pair**

M. MARTINO - Venetian Scenes - both signed - oval - 11¾ x 8½in.
(Sotheby's) **£50 Pair**

F. MARVEY - A Dangerous Step - signed - 11½ x 8½in.
(Sotheby's) **£700**

C. MASKELL - Landscape - oil on lined canvas - monogrammed - 23 x 31cm.
(Galerie Moderne) **£63**

CHARLES M. MASKELL - Suffolk Cottages With Figures And Ducks On Pond - oil - 16 x 20in.
(G. A. Key) **£72**

FRANK H. MASON - This Fleet Majestical - heightened with bodycolour - signed - 19¾ x 24½in.
(Sotheby's Belgravia) **£110**

FRANK H. MASON - The Last Of The Emden - watercolour - 36 x 53cm.
(Edmiston's) **£18**

FRANK H. MASON - Vessels Off A Quay In A Stiff Breeze - pen and brown ink and watercolour heightened with white - signed - 5½ x 10¼in.
(Christie's) **£140**

FRANK H. MASON - Motor Boat In A Stormy Sea - watercolour - 25 x 17.5cm.
(Edmiston's) **£26**

FRANK H. MASON - The Aftermath Of The War At Sea - watercolour and crayon - 36 x 48cm.
(Edmiston's) **£22**

FRANK H. MASON - Merchantmen In A Breeze Near A Lighthouse - pen and brown ink and watercolour heighted with white - signed - 6¼ x 8¾in.
(Christie's) **£85**

FRANK H. MASON - HMS Euryalus Passing The Kahet Station, Suez Canal - heightened with bodycolour - signed - 13¼ x 19¾in.
(Sotheby's Belgravia) **£110**

FRANK H. MASON - A sailing yacht in an offshore scene - oil on canvas - signed and dated 1944 - 20 x 24 ins.
(King & Chasemore) **£260**

GEORGE HEMMING MASON - An Italian Landscape: Evening - 15½ x 30in.
(Christie's) **£250**

POMPEO MASSANI - What The Butler Saw - signed - 12 x 8¼in.
(Sotheby's) **£650**

JEAN EUGENE JULIEN MASSE - Au Bord Du Lac - signed and dated 1897 - 16 x 21½in.
(Sotheby's) **£350**

Q. MASSYS - Saint Jerome in his study - 52 x 40 ins.
(Christie's, S. Kensington) **£750**

E. MASTERS - A Village In Kent - inscribed on the stretcher - 19½ x 29¼in.
(Sotheby's Belgravia) **£1,300**

E. MASTERS - Branscombe, Devon - signed with initials and dated 1880 - inscribed on the stretcher - 19½ x 29¼in.
(Sotheby's Belgravia) **£1,100**

GIOVANNI ANDREA DONDUCCI, Called IL MASTELLATA - Christ And The Adulteress - 36½ x 27in.
(Sotheby's) **£4,000**

THE MASTER OF 1518, Circle Of - The Circumcision - on panel - 21 x 17in.
(Christie's) **£650**

AGOSTINO MASUCCI - The Penitent Magdalen - inscribed with the artist's name and date 1735 on the reverse - 25 x 19in.
(Christie's) **£1,300**

KAOMUNA F. MATANIA - A Present From Caesar - signed and inscribed on the reverse - 40 x 55in.
(Sotheby's Belgravia) **£900**

MATHES - Hide And Seek - indistinctly signed and dated - inscribed 'Munchen' - 26 x 20½in.
(Sotheby's) **£320**

HENRI MATISSE - Prima Vere Poupre - signed - 23¼ x 28½in.
(Sotheby's) **£38,000**

HENRI MATISSE - Le The Du Matin - signed - 13 x 22in.
(Christie's, New York) **£55,000**

HENRI MATISSE - Paysage, Environs De Nice - signed - 14½ x 17¾in.
(Sotheby's) **£40,000**

BARTHOLOMEUS MATON - Portrait Of A Lady Aged 67, three-quarter length, seated wearing a fur-lined cloak and white head-dress - signed and bears date 1654 - 39 x 33in.
(Christie's) **£1,100**

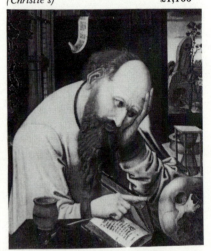

Q. MATSYS - Saint Jerome In His Study - on panel - 24½ x 20in.
(Christie's) **£2,400**

MATTEIS - An Old Testament Subject, Two Leaders Meeting - 22¼ x 28in.
(Sotheby's) **£200**

J. A. MATTLINGS - Continental Street Scenes With Figures - oils - 10 x 7in.
(G. A. Key) **£54 Pair**

CHIARA MAYER - A Greek Wedding Dance In The Village Of Belgraden Near Constantinople - watercolour and pastel - signed - inscribed and dated 1797 - 14 x 21¼in.
(Sotheby's) **£280**

J. B. DEL MAZO - Portrait Of A Boy, bust length, Wearing A Dark Doublet And White Collar - 14¼ x 12½in.
(Christie's) **£950**

S. MAZZOLINI - Spare A Penny Sir?; A Bunch Of Violets? - one indistinctly signed and dated '80 - each 18 x 13¾in.
(Sotheby's) **£180 Pair**

WALTER McADAM - "Glen Affric" - oil - 28 x 32½in.
(Thomas Love & Sons Ltd) **£250**

W. McALPINE - A Shipwreck Off The Coast - 23½ x 41½in.
(Sotheby's Belgravia) **£160**

McBEY - River With Town In Distance - watercolour - 22 x 33cm.
(Edmiston's) **£10**

JAMES McBEY - Ingatestone, Essex - signed and dated 1931 - watercolour drawing - 23 x 38in.
(Edmiston's) **£100**

SAMUEL McCLOY - Sheltering From The Rain - signed and dated 1873 - 8¾ x 6in.
(Sotheby's Belgravia) **£96**

ARTHUR DAVID McCORMICK - The Last Drop - signed - 17½ x 13½in.
(Sotheby's) **£240**

ARTHUR DAVID McCORMICK - The Connoisseur - signed - 23½ x 17½in.
(Sotheby's) **£600**

NONI McCRONE - "Evening, Bennybeg" - oil - signed with a monogram - on board - 40.5 x 50.5cm.
(Phillips in Scotland) **£12**

HORATIO McCULLOCH - By The Side Of A Loch - signed and dated 1863 - 14½ x 17¾in.
(Sotheby's) **£480**

HORATIO McCULLOCH - Scene In Marquis Of Breadalbane's Deer Forest, Black Mount, Argyllshire - oil - 72 x 132cm.
(Phillips in Scotland) **£100**

McEVOY

AMBROSE McEVOY - A Portrait Of A Girl - pastel - watercolour - 14 x 11½in.
(Henry Spencer & Sons) **£150**

W. McEVOY - View Of Dublin Bay From The Three Rock Mountain - signed - oil on canvas - 23½ x 41¼in.
(Bearnes & Waycotts) **£600**

WILLIAM McEVOY - A River Scene - signed - 23½ x 41½in.
(Sotheby's Belgravia) **£170**

TOM McEWAN - The Good Book - 33 x 27cm.
(Edmiston's) **£175**

TOM McEWAN - News From the Outer World - 74 x 56 ins.
(Edmiston's) **£310**

J. M. McGEEHAN - The Jam Stealers - signed - 19½ x 29½in.
(Sotheby's) **£780**

J. M. McGEEHAN - Learning To Walk - signed - 19½ x 26in.
(Sotheby's) **£400**

J. McGHIE - End Of The Day - 60 x 90cm.
(Edmiston's) **£30**

JOHN McGHIE - Full Length Portrait Of Elizabeth Jardine Tonner - oil - signed and dated 1898 - 107.5 x 61cm.
(Phillips in Scotland) **£55**

ROBERT McGREGOR - A Young Girl Playing With A Bird - signed - on board - 8 x 5½in.
(Sotheby's) **£160**

ROBERT McGREGOR - Field Workers - signed - on panel - 8½ x 11½in.
(Sotheby's) **£220**

ROBERT McGREGOR - The Little Help - signed with initials - 13½ x 9½in.
(Sotheby's) **£320**

JAMES McINTYRE - The Lass That Loves A Sailor - watercolour - signed - 4½ x 8¼in.
(Christie's) **£95**

CHARLES McKINLEY - Rural Land-scapes - both signed - 16 x 24in.
(Sotheby's Belgravia) **£90 Pair**

G. M. McLAREN - Extensive Wooded Landscape - 40 x 56cm.
(Edmiston's) **£20**

JOHN McWHIRTER - Scott's House At Abbotsford With Angler And Rainbow - watercolour - 23 x 14.5cm.
(Edmiston's) **£70**

RICARDO MEACCI - The Virgin Mary - heightened with gold - signed - arched top - 14 x 7in.
(Sotheby's Belgravia) **£70**

J. B. MEAD - Rural Landscape With Shepherd And Sheep - signed - dated 1911 - oil - 23½ x 35½in.
(Charles R. Phillips) **£475**

WILLIAM McTAGGART - The Press Gang - 24½ x 20in.
(Sotheby's Belgravia) **£700**

ARTHUR MEADOWS - An Extensive Venetian Scene - signed and dated 1897 - on canvas - 23½ x 41½in.
(King & Chasemore) **£800**

ARTHUR JOSEPH MEADOWS - 'The Thames Near Benfleet, Essex' - signed and dated 1875 - 23 x 46cm.
(Phillips) **£420**

WILLIAM McTAGGART - 'Herding Ai Ma Lam And Euwe For Her Puir Mammie' - My Boy Jamie - signed with monogram - 17¾ x 13½in.
(Sotheby's) **£950**

ARTHUR JOSEPH MEADOWS - Jesuits Church, Venice - signed and dated 1898 - inscribed on the reverse - 11½ x 19½in.
(Sotheby's Belgravia) **£850**

MEADOWS

ARTHUR JOSEPH MEADOWS - Barraque Near Calais - signed and dated 1872 - 13¾ x 23½in.
(Sotheby's Belgravia) **£900**

W. MEADOWS - Venetian Scene - oil - on canvas - 41½ x 29¾in.
(D. M. Nesbit & Co.) **£410**

W. MEADOWS - Venetian Canal Scenes - 17 x 31¼in.
(Sotheby's Belgravia) **£150 Pair**

GEORGE MEARS - HMS Minotaur - signed and dated '84 - 17¼ x 29¼in.
(Sotheby's Belgravia) **£460**

GEORGE MEARS - The "Queen" At Full Steam - oil - signed and dated '92 - 23½ x 35½in.
(Graves Son & Pilcher) **£240**

HENRY MEASHAM - Summer On The Moors - signed and dated 1880 - watercolour - 9 x 15in.
(Neale & Son) **£26**

H. MEDDLYCOTT - Limehouse - watercolour - 9 x 15in.
(G. A. Key) **£70**

THE REV. SIR HUBERT JAMES MEDLYCOTT - Sunset On San Georgio - signed and dated 1891 - inscribed and dated on the reverse - 8½ x 14¼in.
(Sotheby's Belgravia) **£35**

WALTER MEEGAN - Whitby Harbour - signed - 9½ x 13½in.
(Sotheby's Belgravia) **£160**

BAREND VAN DER MEER - Apples, Grapes And Other Fruit On A Stone Ledge - 21 x 32in.
(Christie's) **£1,000**

FRANZ MEERTS - The Prayer - on wood - signed - 38 x 38cm.
(Galerie Moderne) **£76**

MEIJER - Dutch Fishing Boats Moored Off The Coast - 13½ x 17in.
(Sotheby's) **£400**

JEAN LOUIS ERNEST MEISSONIER - Study Of An Hussar On A White Charger With A Study Of The Charger's Head - signed with monogram - on panel - 14¼ x 17½in.
(Christie's) **£5,000**

JEAN CHARLES MEISSONIER - A Garden At Antibes - signed and dated 1869 - 18 x 32in.
(Sotheby's) **£2,800**

JEAN CHARLES MEISSONIER - A Knight Of The Road - signed and dated 1889 - 22½ x 16in.
(Christie's) **£1,300**

JEAN LOUIS ERNEST MEISSONIER -
Artist And Drunkard - signed - 7½ x 7in.
(J. Francis, T. Jones & Sons) **£70**

LUIS EUGENIO MELENDEZ - A Still
Life Of Fruit, Pears And Plums On A
Table, A Covered Red Earthenware
Jug Behind - signed with initials - 15½
x 13½in.
(Sotheby's) **£36,000**

LUIS EUGENIO MELENDEZ - A Still
Life With Lemons And Oranges - signed
with initials - 19 x 14in.
(Sotheby's) **£31,000**

MELENDEZ - A Still Life Of Fruit,
Including Peaches, Pears, A Melon And
Figs - canvas - on panel - 19¼ x 23in.
(Sotheby's) **£300**

JOSEPH MELLOR - A Welsh River
Landscape - signed and dated 1853
on the reverse - 13½ x 20¾in.
(Sotheby's Belgravia) **£80**

W. MELLOR - A Welsh Mountain
Stream - 17¾ x 13½in.
(Sotheby's Belgravia) **£80**

WILLIAM MELLOR - Wooded River
Scene With A Figure On A Bridge -
signed - oil on canvas - 35 x 27¼in.
(Bearnes & Waycotts) **£420**

WILLIAM MELLOR - River Landscape
with sheep - signed - 20 x 30 ins.
(Christie's, S. Kensington) **£250**

WILLIAM MELLOR - Derwentwater,
Cumberland - signed - on canvas
11½ x 19½in.
(Morphet & Morphet) **£200**

WILLIAM MELLOR - On The River Llugwy,
North Wales - signed and inscribed on verso -
20 x 30in.
(Henry Spencer & Sons) **£250**

WILLIAM MELLOR - Wooded River Landscapes in Borrowdale, Cumberland, and
Langdale, Westmorland - signed - on canvas -
16 x 12in.
(Morphet & Morphet) **£450 Pair**

WILLIAM MELLOR - Mountain Scene
Near Capel Curig - signed - oil - 30 x 20in.
(John H. Raby & Sons) **£390**

F. MELON - Village Of Chassepierre -
oil on canvas - signed - 40 x 50cm.
(Galerie Moderne) **£18**

A. MELVILLE - In The Hills - inscribed -
11½ x 18½in.
(Sotheby's Belgravia) **£10**

ARTHUR MELVILLE - Figure Of A
Young Lady Feeding Ducks By A
Stream - oil - signed and dated 1877 -
59.5 x 84cm.
(Phillips in Scotland) **£440**

HARDEN SIDNEY MELVILLE -
Carting Lumber - signed - 29 x 49in.
(Sotheby's Belgravia) **£260**

MEMLINC, Circle Of - The Annunciation
- on panel - 17 x 13in.
(Christie's) **£12,000**

J. MENARD - Seascape - oil on canvas -
signed - 25 x 40cm.
(Galerie Moderne) **£50**

F. MENGALLI - The Entertainer -
signed - 32 x 44in.
(Christie's, S. Kensington) **£950**

MORTIMER MENPES - Portrait Of
Claude Menpes, Seated, small three-
quarter length - inscribed on reverse -
grisaille - mixed media - on board -
10 x 13in.
(Christie's) **£90**

FERNAND MERCHE - Le Moulin -
oil - on canvas - signed - 22¾ x 28¼in.
(Sotheby's) **£160**

L. MERCIER - The Fight - enamel -
signed - 34 x 44cm.
(Galerie Moderne) **£270**

PHILIP MERCIER - Two Little Boys
Playing with a Duelling Pistol - 29 x
24¼ ins.
(Sotheby's) **£900**

PHILIPPE MERCIER - Portrait Of A
Girl, half length, At A Window -
29 x 24½in.
(Christie's) **£350**

A. MERTENS - A Pitcher Trimmed
With Roses - oil on canvas - signed -
50 x 70cm.
(Galerie Moderne) **£18**

W. MERTENS - A Still Life With A
Lobster On A Dish, A Bowl Of Straw-
berries And A Basket Of Cherries, Grapes
And Peaches On A Draped Table - signed -
32 x 45in.
(Christie's) **£8,500**

SALAMON MESDACH - Portrait Of A Lady, standing, three-quarter length, in a black dress and white ruff with gold necklace - on panel - 44½ x 33in.
(Christie's) **£3,000**

HENDRIK MESDAG - The Departure Of The Fishermen - oil on wood - signed - 40 x 60cm.
(Galerie Moderne) **£472**

SIDNEY HAROLD METEYARD - 'Then A Drink In A Crystal Beaker For Me Did She Mingle' - tempera and gold - inscribed - on panel - circular - diameter 11¼in.
(Sotheby's Belgravia) **£700**

SIDNEY HAROLD METEYARD - Design For Stained Glass - black chalk - 38 x 10¾in.
(Sotheby's Belgravia) **£55**

GABRIEL METSU - The Expulsion Of Hagar
- signed - 45 x 34½in.
(Christie's) **£15,000**

MICHELE MEUCCI - Still Lives Of Song
Birds - both signed - inscribed 'Firenze'
and dated 1876 - on board - oval - each
8½ x 6¾in.
(Sotheby's) **£220 Pair**

ADAM FRANS VAN DER MEULEN -
A Wooded Landscape With A Huntsman
Saluting A Nobleman With His Retinue
Nearby - 45 x 65in.
(Christie's) **£6,000**

ADAM FRANS VAN DER MEULEN -
Elegant Horsemen Resting Outside A
Tavern And Drinking, A Wagon Train
In The Right Distance - signed and
dated 1659 - 21¼ x 26in.
(Sotheby's) **£7,000**

EDMOND VAN DER MEULEN -
Visitors To The Pantry - signed -
78¾ x 59in.
(Sotheby's) **£700**

WILHELM ALEXANDER MEYERHEIM -
Welcoming The Hussars - signed and dated
1866 - 16¾ x 21¾in.
(Christie's) **£1,900**

WILHELM ALEXANDER MEYERHEIM -
The Young Wood Gatherers By A Horse
Drawn Sledge In A Frozen River Land-
scape - signed and dated 1851 - 20 x
27in.
(Sotheby's) **£3,200**

ALBERT MEYERING - A Wooded
Italianate Landscape, with travellers on a
road by a torrent - signed - 27 x 22in.
(Christie's) **£2,000**

ISIDORE MEYERS - Sheep At Pasture -
oil on wood - signed - 15 x 23cm.
(Galerie Moderne) **£157**

MICALI - The Cat's Clever Escape -
signed - 15½ x 20in.
(Sotheby's) **£220**

T. MICHAU - A Wooded Landscape
With Travellers On A Road - on panel -
10 x 13¾in.
(Christie's) **£3,000**

MICHEL - Extensive Landscape Under A
Cloudy Sky - 22 x 28in.
(Woolley & Wallis) **£180**

EMILE FRANCOIS MICHEL -
Pecheurs De Crevis Au Bord De L'Ain -
signed and dated '97 - on panel - 19 x
26in.
(Sotheby's) **£550**

EDWARD MIDDLEDITCH - Tree In
Blossom, 1956 - on board - 50½ x 40¼in.
(Phillips) **£240**

C. MIDDLETON - Stepping Stones Over
A Stream In Wooded Glade - oil - 21 x 29in.
(G. A. Key) **£520**

J. MIDDLETON - On Loch Achray -
both signed and dated 1895 - both
inscribed on the stretcher - 11½ x
17½in.
(Sotheby's Belgravia) **£65 Pair**

JAN MIEL - The Adoration Of The Magi -
28½ x 23½in.
(Christie's) **£1,500**

JAN MIEL - 17th Century Landscape -
tondo on copper - 15 ins. diam.
(A. Sharpe & Partners) **£200**

J. MIEL - A Peasant Family - 17 x 15in.
(Christie's) **£420**

FRANS VAN MIERIS THE YOUNGER -
The Oyster Eaters - bears signature and the
date 1719 - on panel - 15½ x 13¼in.
(Christie's) **£3,200**

WILLEM VAN MIERIS - A Family Group
on a Terrace: a lady seated in the centre,
holding a baby, her husband standing to the
right; to the left, two boys one playing with
a dog, and another resting his hand on a
book - signed and dated 1728 - 34 x 36½in.
(Christie's) **£5,500**

WILLEM VAN MIERIS - The Interior Of An Inn, with a young Savoyard displaying a puppet case - on panel - 29½ x 19in.
(Christie's) **£1,800**

ABRAHAM MIGNON - Swags Of Fruit And Flowers Suspended In A Niche, surrounding a casement with a landscape beyond - signed - on panel - 15½ x 24in.
(Christie's) **£24,000**

AURELIANO MILANI - The Worship of the Golden Calf - on panel - 15 x 22 ins.
(Christie's) **£3,000**

THOMAS ROSE MILES - A Stormy Day At Dover - signed and inscribed - 42¾ x 33½in.
(Christie's, S. Kensington) **£360**

ALESSANDRO MILESI - The Fisherman's Return - signed and inscribed Venezia - 36½ x 50½in.
(Christie's) **£8,000**

SIR JOHN EVERETT MILLAIS - The Storming Of A Town - pen and sepia ink - signed - 13¼ x 19in.
(Sotheby's Belgravia) **£250**

SIR JOHN EVERETT MILLAIS - Ariel Sings, 'The Tempest', Act I, Scene 2 - pencil - signed with initials - 6½ x 4½in.
(Sotheby's Belgravia) **£360**

J. MILLAR - Portrait Of A Gentleman Seated By A River With His Dog - full length - 29 x 24in.
(Christie's) **£550**

JOHN MILLER - Cinerarias - 52 x 71cm.
(Edmiston's) **£38**

MILLET - A Classical Landscape With Figures Preparing For The Sacrifice Of A Bull - 37½ x 45in.
(Christie's) **£1,100**

MILLET - Christ And The Woman Of Samaria - 38 x 35½in.
(Christie's) **£400**

FRANCISQUE MILLET - A Classical
Landscape with Joshua returning from the
Promised Land - on paper laid down on
canvas - 17¼ x 23½in.
(Christie's) **£55,000**

FRANCISQUE MILLET - Mercury discovers
Herse Returning From the Festival Of
Minerva - 29½ x 47½in.
(Christie's) **£18,000**

JEAN-BAPTISTE MILLET - A Field In
Winter - pen and ink and watercolour -
signed - 5¾ x 8in.
(Christie's) **£60**

J. F. MILLET - A Southern Landscape,
Figures Conversing On A Path in the
foreground, A Shepherd With A Flock
Near Classical Buildings To The Right -
17¼ x 22½in.
(Sotheby's) **£420**

FRANK MILLON - A View Of Ghent
From The River - heightened with
bodycolour - inscribed on the reverse -
circular - 11in. diameter.
(Sotheby's) **£25**

JOSEPH MILNE - Stirling From The River
Forth - signed - 15½ x 23¼in.
(Sotheby's) **£130**

VICTOR MARAY MILTON - A Volume
On The Index - signed - 18 x 13in.
(Christie's) **£1,700**

HENDRICK VAN MINDERHOUT - An
Extensive Italianate River Landscape, with
sheep and horses by ruined buildings -
signed and dated 1653 - 62 x 81in.
(Christie's) **£8,500**

IL MAESTRO DELL A MISERICORDIA -
The Crucifixion - on the reverse, a bust of
an angel in a quatrefoil design, a fragment -
on gold ground, on panel - 16¾ x 10¼in.
(Christie's) **£4,800**

JOHN CAMPBELL MITCHELL - The
Village Of Findhorn By The Sea - signed
and dated 1919 - oil on canvas - 17½ x
29½in.
(Bearnes & Waycotts) **£125**

WILLIAM MITCHELL - Portrait Of The Four-Masted Sailing Ship 'Falls Of Bruar' Off The Fastnet Light - signed - inscribed and dated 1898 on the reverse - oil on canvas - 23½ x 35½in.
(Bearnes & Waycotts) **£420**

WILLIAM MITCHELL - 'A Four-Masted Fellow Close Hauled, Head Reaching In A Cape Sea' - signed and dated 1898 - inscribed on the reverse - oil on canvas - 19½ x 29½in.
(Bearnes & Waycotts) **£250**

GIOVANNI MOCHI - A Melon Vendor, Santiago, Chile - a market scene, with many figures - signed - 17 x 14in.
(Henry Spencer & Sons) **£500**

AMEDEO MODIGLIANI - L'Italienne - signed.
(Sotheby's) **£22,000**

JEAN BAPTISTE VAN MOER - A Mediterranean Harbour Scene With Numerous Figures - signed - 25½ x 48in.
(Christie's) **£2,600**

CLAES CORNELISZ. MOEYAERT - Manoah's Sacrifice - signed with monogram and indistinctly dated 16 . . - 39½ x 52in.
(Christie's) **£2,000**

JAN CORNELISZ MOEYAERT - Saint John The Baptist Preaching In The Wilderness - bears indistinct signature - 40 x 58in.
(Christie's) **£1,000**

JOHN MOGFORD - Kynance Cove, Lizard, Cornwall - signed and inscribed on reverse - 12 x 24½ ins.
(Sotheby's) **£120**

JOHN MOGFORD - Becalmed, Scotch Herring Boats Off The Isle Of Arran - signed and dated 1875 - 35½ x 59½in.
(Sotheby's Belgravia) **£750**

JOHN MOGFORD - A Coastal Scene - signed and dated 1878 - 9 x 13¾in.
(Sotheby's) **£70**

GERALD EDWARD MOIRA - Zephyr
And Aurora - signed and dated 1907 -
36½ x 38in.
(Sotheby's Belgravia)   **£600**

MOITROUX - Allegorie - oil on canvas -
signed and dated 1921 - 1m. x 80cm.
(Galerie Moderne)   **£300**

MOLA - Bacchanalian Scenes: A Satyr
Giving Wine To A Child, Other Children
Asleep To The Left; A Woman Pouring
Wine, Another Asleep in the foreground,
Women Dancing Beyond - oval - each
27½ x 22in.
(Sotheby's)   **£1,550 Pair**

PIER FRANCESCO MOLA - Saint Jerome
In The Wilderness - 25 x 19½in.
(Christie's)   **£3,800**

PIER FRANCESCO MOLA - The Rest On
The Flight Into Egypt, with angels -
28¾ x 24¼in.
(Christie's)   **£2,200**

MOLA - Saint John The Baptist, In A
Landscape - 36 x 28in.
(Christie's)   **£550**

MOLA - Venus Discovered By Pan -
on panel - oval - 9 x 12in.
(Sotheby's)   **£100**

J. H. MOLE - Hayfields And Wooded Landscape - signed and dated 1849 - 13¼ x 8in.
(John H. Raby & Son)   **£48**

JOHN HENRY MOLE - A Rural Scene
With A Girl On A Pathway Approaching
A Woman Outside A Cottage - signed
and dated 1868 - 5½ x 8¾in.
(King & Chasemore)   **£210**

MOLENAER - Paris Street Scene - 51 x
72cm.
(Edmiston's)   **£37**

J. M. MOLENAER - The Flower Seller -
on panel - 12½ x 8½in.
(Christie's)   **£1,200**

307

J. M. MOLENAER - A Man And Woman With Their Son In A Cottage Interior - on panel - 34 x 27.5cm.
(Phillips) **£650**

KLAES MOLENAER - A Landscape With Washerwomen By A Pond, and peasants on a country road nearby - signed and dated 1651 - on panel - 13½ x 19in.
(Christie's) **£4,800**

KLAES MOLENAER - A Winter Landscape with a horse-drawn sledge on a bridge, and numerous figures on a frozen waterway, cottages nearby - signed - on panel - 13½ x 18in.
(Christie's) **£10,000**

KLAES MOLENAER - Fishermen Loading Their Boats By a House - signed and dated 1670 - 31 x 26in.
(Christie's) **£6,000**

KLAES MOLENAER - Peasants Outside An Inn By A River - signed - 31 x 26in.
(Christie's) **£7,000**

K. MOLENAER - A Winter Landscape, With Horsemen And Figures On A Path - on panel - 10½ x 14½in.
(Christie's) **£1,700**

ANTONIO MOLINARI - The Death Of Cleopatra - inscribed on the reverse Molinari AE49B - 57 x 45in.
(Christie's) **£1,600**

JEAN PETER MOLLER - A Scandinavian Farmstead - signed with initials - dated 1846 - 24¼ x 31¾in.
(Sotheby's) **£400**

FRANS DE MOMPER - A Winter Landscape with figures skating on a frozen waterway with a town beyond - signed with initials - 18½ x 27in.
(Christie's) **£20,000**

JOOS DE MOMPER - Soldiers Playing Skittles Outside A Fort At The Foot Of A Cliff, A Port In A Bay Beyond; Two Officers On A Road in the foreground And A Boy With A Dog - on panel - 24½ x 32¾in.
(Sotheby's) **£4,500**

JOOS DE MOMPER II - A Rocky Landscape with travellers and cattle on a road - on panel - 13¾ x 18½in.
(Christie's) **£4,000**

JOOS DE MOMPER, THE YOUNGER - Saint John The Baptist Preaching In The Wilderness - on panel - 24½ x 19in.
(Christie's) **£4,500**

JOOS DE MOMPER THE YOUNGER - A Winter Landscape with peasants and travellers on a village road - on panel - 21½ x 34in.
(Christie's) **£30,000**

HUGH MONAHAN - Pale Brents, Over The Sea - signed and dated 1948 - 19½ x 29½in.
(Sotheby's) **£200**

MONAMY - British Men-O'-War And Other Shipping In A Calm - bears Van De Velde signature and dated - 14½ x 18½in.
(Christie's) **£1,100**

P. MONAMY - A Man-O'-War Firing A Salute; and A Man-O'-War In A Rough Sea - canvas on panel - 22 x 9½in.
(Christie's) **£380 Pair**

PETER MONAMY - A Frigate In Breezy Weather With Men - O'-War beyond - signed - 11½ x 16½in.
(Christie's) **£600**

P. MONAMY - Shipping In A Calm Sea
With A Flagship And Royal Barge - oil
on canvas - 21¼ x 31in.
(Bearnes & Waycotts)   **£360**

PETER MONAMY - English And Dutch
Sailing Ships In A Squall - signed -
23 x 34¾in.
(Christie's)   **£3,000**

PETER MONAMY, ITALIAN SCHOOL,
19th century - 'The Albemarle 80/90 Guns';
Flagship of Admiral of the Fleet, Sir John
Leake, K.T. - signed and dated 1725 - on
canvas - 40 x 50in.
(King & Chasemore)   **£3,000**

E. MONDY - Cattle In A Landscape,
signed and dated 1875 - 11 x 14½in.
(Sotheby's Belgravia)   **£50**

MONET - Landscape - on wood - signed -
30 x 40cm.
(Galerie Moderne)   **£21**

CLAUDE MONET - L'Entree Du Petit
Bras A Vetheuil - signed - 33½ x 35½in.
(Christie's, New York)   **£116,500**

CLAUDE MONET - La Prairie De
Limetz, Pres Giverny - stamped with
signature - 25½ x 36¼in.
(Sotheby's)   **£20,000**

LOUIS DE MONI - A Girl And A
Masquerader, A Girl About To Splash
Water From A Copper Bowl On To A
Man In Brown Carnival Dress Holding
A Comic Mask Before His Face -
signed - on panel - 11¼ x 9¾in.
(Sotheby's)   **£4,400**

WILTON MONLEY - Loch Scene
With Cattle - 89 x 68cm.
(Edmiston's) £28

FANNY MOODY - 'Wake Up' -
coloured chalks - signed - on grey
paper - 12½ x 17 ins.
(Sotheby's, Belgravia) £50

FANNY MOODY - Sharing - signed -
18½ x 27½in.
(Sotheby's Belgravia) £650

MOORE - Fishing Fleet Off The Coast -
oil - 9 x 17in.
(G. A. Key) £30

JEAN-BAPTISTE MONNOYER - A
Rose, Tulips And Other Flowers In A
Basket On A Table; And Dahlias, A
Tulip, Convolvulus, A Crown Imperial
Lily, And Other Flowers In A Basket
On A Table - 29 x 24¼in.
(Christie's) **£7,500 Pair**

ALFRED MONTAGUE - Coastal Scene
with Fishing Boats Off A Jetty - signed and
dated 1867 - oil - 11¾ x 17¾in.
(Neale & Son) £115

FANNY MOODY - A Cat Under Attack -
17½ x 13½in.
(Christie's) £150

BARLOW MOORE - The Yacht
'Miranda' Crossing From Dover To
Ostend, 29 June, 1880 - pen and
ink and watercolour heightened with
white on buff paper - signed and
dated 1880 - 10 x 13½in.
(Christie's) £250

BARLOW MOORE - The Latona Working
Out Of Portsmouth Harbour - pen and
ink and watercolour - signed and dated
1891 - 19 x 25in.
(Christie's) £320

BARLOW MOORE - The Latona Under
Spinnaker - pen and ink and watercolour -
signed - 14½ x 20¾in.
(Christie's) £70

CLAUDE T. STANFIELD MOORE -
Shipping In The Pool Of London - oil on
canvas - signed and dated '80 - 13 x 17in.
(King & Chasemore) £370

EDWIN MOORE - The Terrace, Haddon
Hall - signed - inscribed and dated -
watercolour heightened with white -
11½ x 18in.
(Christie's) £200

HENRY MOORE - Rochester Castle,
Evening - signed and dated 1867 - 6 x
12¾in.
(Sotheby's Belgravia) £65

HENRY MOORE - Open Sea -
signed and dated - 17½ x 29½in.
(Sotheby's Belgravia) £170

HENRY MOORE - Every Cloud Hath
Its Silver Lining - signed and dated 1870 -
38 x 71in.
(Christie's) £950

HENRY MOORE - A Choppy Sea, With
A Steamship On The Horizon - signed
with initials and dated Sept. 2nd, 1886 -
21 x 31in.
(Christie's) £250

HENRY MOORE - Seascape With
Fishing Smacks Off The Dutch Coast -
signed - 7 x 12in.
(Buckell & Ballard) £67.50

HENRY MOORE - Fishing Boats
Becalmed - watercolour - 7 x 11in.
(G. A. Key) £22

J. MOORE - Fine Seascape With
Numerous Boats, Barges And Figures Off
The Coast - oil - 23 x 35in.
(G. A. Key) £1,900

J. C. MOORE - Portrait Of A Young
Girl - head and shoulders, heightened
with bodycolour - 12½ x 9½in.
(Sotheby's Belgravia) £14

SIR A. MOR - Portrait Of King
Philip II Of Spain, three-quarter length,
In Black Doublet With Gold Buttons,
Yellow Sleeves And Hose - inscribed -
44½ x 35½in.
(Christie's) £1,500

J. MORE - A Capriccio View Of The
Falls At Tivoli - 50 x 40in.
(Christie's) £340

ADRIEN MOREAU - A Table - pen and ink and watercolour - heightened with white gouache - signed - 4 x 5½in.
(Sotheby's) £70

J. MOREAU - A View Of Goldrill Crag, Cumberland; A View Of Stockley Bridge, Borrowdale - both signed and inscribed on the reverse - on board - each 8½ x 10½in.
(Sotheby's) £220 Pair

JAN EVERT MOREL - An Extensive Dutch River Landscape - signed - on panel - 9½ x 15in.
(Christie's) £850

JAN EVERT MOREL - A Woody Landscape With Peasants And Cattle By A Stream - signed - on panel - 19 x 23¼in.
(Christie's) £2,300

PIERRE MOREL - Couloir Des Loges - heightened with bodycolour - inscribed - 8½ x 6in.
(Sotheby's) £20

MORGHEN AND DOMENICO MORELLI - Prince Demidoff And Princess Matilda Bonaparte On The Road From The Villa At San Donato To The Farms At Florence - inscribed on the reverse - 22 x 35in.
(Sotheby's) £350

E. MORGAN - A Canal running through a City - watercolour - dated 1873 - 7¼ x 11 ins.
(Jackson-Stops & Staff) £28

FRED MORGAN - The Apple Pickers - signed - 29 x 41in.
(Christie's) £500

OWEN BAXTER MORGAN - Minding The Sheep; Evening - both heightened with bodycolour - signed - 9 x 13¾in.
(Sotheby's Belgravia) £32 Pair

DAVID MORIER - Frederick The Great On Horseback with a battle beyond - 50 x 58in.
(Christie's) £4,000

MORLAND - A Gipsy Encampment - signed - oil on panel - 19 x 22½in.
(Bearnes & Waycotts) £110

MORLAND, After - A Peasant Woman With Child In Conversation With Shepherd Boy - oil on canvas - 22½ x 17in.
(Boulton & Cooper) £80

SCHOOL OF MORLAND - The Warrener - 17¾ x 23½in.
(Henry Spencer & Sons) £230

G. MORLAND - A Winter Landscape With A Horse And Cart And A Cart By A Beyond - signed - on panel - 6¾ x 10½in.
(Christie's) £260

G. MORLAND - Farmyard Scene With A Man And Girl Feeding Pigs - on wood panel - 12 x 17in.
(Morphet & Morphet) £210

G. MORLAND - Cottager With Pigs - oil on canvas - signed and dated 1786 - 23½ x 18½in.
(J. Francis, T. Jones & Sons) £200

GEORGE MORLAND - Pigs In Stable Interior - signed - 24 x 34in.
(Woolley & Wallis) £250

GEORGE MORLAND - A Farmyard, With Pigs At A Trough And Two Peasants Nearby - 18 x 23½in.
(Christie's) £850

MORLAND

G. MORLAND - Stable Interior With Figures And Horses, - bears signature - 24 x 36in.
(Woolley & Wallis) **£125**

HENRY MORLEY - Hoeing - signed - 11½ x 15¾in.
(Sotheby's Belgravia) **£90**

FEDERICO MORONI - Il Musicano Negro - pen, brush and indian ink - signed - 13¼ x 5¼in.
(Sotheby's) **£20**

C. MORRIS - The Evening Fisherman; The Rustic Cottage - both bear signatures - each 4½ x 6½in.
(Sotheby's) **£120 Pair**

C. MORRIS - Landscape With Sheep And Village - oil on canvas - signed - 29 x 19in.
(J. Francis, T. Jones & Sons) **£30**

GARMAN MORRIS - Scarborough - watercolour - circular - 29cm. diam.
(Edmiston's) **£19**

GARMAN MORRIS - Yarmouth Fishing Smack - watercolour - 11 x 5in.
(G. A. Key) **£2**

J. MORRIS - Herders, Sheep And Cattle In Highland Landscape - oil - 25 x 19in.
(G. A. Key) **£130**

J. W. MORRIS - Highland Sheep Studies - oils - signed - 24 x 17½in.
(Graves Son & Pilcher) **£140 Pair**

PHILIP RICHARD MORRIS - Amongst The Corn Stooks; On The Moors; A Country Path - all signed with initials - on board - 3½ x 4½in.
(Sotheby's Belgravia) **£110 Three**

PHILIP RICHARD MORRIS - The Farewell; The Return - one heightened with bodycolour - both signed - each 14¼ x 11¼in.
(Sotheby's Belgravia) **£170 Pair**

PHILIP RICHARD MORRIS - The Premiere Communion, Dieppe - signed - 39 x 32in.
(Christie's) **£170**

R. MORRIS - Highland Cattle - signed - 16 x 24in.
(Sotheby's Belgravia) **£20**

W. W. MORRIS - Terriers With A Dead Rabbit - signed and dated 1861 - 27 x 35¼in.
(Christie's) **£480**

G. MORTIMER - Man And Workhorses In Wooded Country Lane - oil - 10 x 14in.
(G. A. Key) **£42**

G. MORTIMER - A Gypsy Encampment - oil - 7 x 9in.
(G. A. Key) **£12**

JOHN HAMILTON MORTIMER and THOMAS JONES - The Death Of Orpheus - 59 x 55in.
(Christie's) **£1,900**

G. MOSTAERT - The Crucifixion - on panel - 49½ x 38in.
(Christie's) **£1,000**

GILLIS MOSTAERT - A Village Kermesse With Peasants Feasting And Dancing, Beggars Receiving Food And Travellers Arriving At An Inn - on panel - 16½ x 23in.
(Christie's) **£38,000**

TOM MOSTYN - Portrait Of A Gentleman, Standing, full length, In A Landscape, In Van Dyck Costume - signed - 90 x 57in.
(Christie's) **£160**

GEORGE WILLIAM MOTE - Coney Hurst Hill, Surrey - signed and dated 1880 - inscribed on the stretcher - 23½ x 35½in.
(Sotheby's Belgravia) **£750**

GEORGE WILLIAM MOTE - A Rest On A Path, Springtime - signed and dated 1876 - 19½ x 23½in.
(Sotheby's Belgravia) **£240**

ANNIE W. MOTTRAM - A Parrot In A Cage - signed and dated 1916 - inscribed on the reverse - 23 x 19½in.
(Sotheby's Belgravia) **£40**

CHARLES SIM MOTTRAM - Expectation - heightened with body-colour - signed and dated '98 - 10¼ x 7¼in.
(Sotheby's Belgravia) **£12**

DE MOUCHERON - A Wooded River Landscape With Figures in the fore-ground - 13½ x 18in.
(Christie's) **£1,000**

H. MUFFREY - An Amusing Visitor - signed - on panel - 15 x 18½in.
(Sotheby's) **£600**

JOHN MUIRHEAD - A Summer Morning - 31 x 40cm.
(Edmiston's) **£70**

JOHN MUIRHEAD - A Village Street - signed - 7¼ x 5¼in.
(Sotheby's Belgravia) **£12**

S. A. MULHOLLAND - Morning On The Thames - signed - inscribed on the reverse - 23¼ x 35¼in.
(Sotheby's Belgravia) **£330**

315

MULLER

MULLER - Young Boys Fishing On A
Loch - 27¼ x 35¼in.
(Sotheby's Belgravia) £260

C. F. MULLER - The Three Masted
Schooner - Airey Of Liverpool - oil - on
glass - 18 x 20in.
(G. A. Key) £30

L. MULLER - Horses Drawing A Loaded
Haycart With Figures - on panel - 6½ x
4½in.
(Worsfolds) £250

RICHARD MULLER - Der Zaun -
pencil - signed and dated 1936 - 9½ x 7in.
(Sotheby's) £240

WILLIAM JAMES MULLER - The Carpet
Bazaar, Cairo - signed - on panel - 9½ x
6½in.
(Sotheby's) £80

WILLIAM JAMES MULLER - Horses In
A Stable, Turkey - watercolour - 21½ x
15¾in.
(Christie's) £150

WiLLIAM JAMES MULLER - Hampstead
Heath - black chalk and watercolour
heightened with white on buff paper -
4¾ x 7¼in.
(Christie's) £150

WILLIAM JAMES MULLER - The
Bacino, Venice, At Dusk - pencil and
watercolour - 4¾ x 14¼in.
(Christie's) £800

WILLIAM JAMES MULLER - A Dance
At Xanthus - signed and dated 1844 -
inscribed on reverse - on panel - 15 x
24in.
(Christie's) £1,000

WILLIAM JAMES MULLER - Interior
Of The Temple Of Osiris At Philae -
29 x 52in.
(Christie's) £5,800

WILLIAM JAMES MULLER - The Good
Samaritan - signed and dated 1843 -
21½ x 33in.
(Christie's) £480

MULREADY - A Convivial Evening,
Tavern Interior With Figures Drinking
At The Foot Of A Staircase - oil on
panel - 8 x 10½in.
(Neale & Son) £105

AUGUSTUS MULREADY, Attributed to -
Schoolboys and Master - oil on canvas -
10 x 11½in.
(J. Francis, T. Jones & Sons) £42

WILLIAM MULREADY - A Boy
Stealing Apples From A Fruitstall At
Night - 16½ x 13½in.
(Christie's) £250

WILLIAM MULREADY - The Young
Pugilists - signed with initials - on
board - 6 x 8½in.
(Christie's) £280

J. MUNDELL - Summer And Autumn -
both signed - each 10 x 18in.
(Sotheby's Belgravia) **£380 Pair**

MUNNINGS - Still Life Flower Pot On
Table - watercolour - 7 x 11in.
(G. A. Key) **£15**

SIR A. J. MUNNINGS - Racehorse Being
Whipped By A Jockey - oil on board -
10 x 8in.
(King & Chasemore) **£220**

HUGH MUNRO - Harbour Scene -
40 x 51cm.
(Edmiston's) **£20**

LUDWIG MUNTHE - A Winter Landscape
At Sunset - signed - 17½ x 23½in.
(Christie's) **£2,200**

F. DE MURA - Achilles In His Tent -
bears Tiepolo signature - 30 x 50in.
(Christie's) **£600**

MURILLO - The Immaculate Conception -
81½ x 52in.
(Christie's) **£550**

MURILLO, After - Madonna And Child
With Attendant Angels - oil on canvas -
49½ x 39¼in.
(Bearnes & Waycotts) **£160**

SCHOOL OF MURILLO - El Pescederido -
the study of a boy holding large crab, many
fish at his feet, figures at the edge of the sea
in the distance, a town beyond - 45 x 58in.
(Henry Spencer & Sons) **£1,500**

A. H. HALLAM MURRAY - Venice,
San Michele - 7 x 10in.
(Sotheby's Belgravia) **£16**

SIR DAVID MURRAY - Near Cardonald
- heightened with white - signed and
dated '69 - inscribed on the mount -
10½ x 16¾in.
(Sotheby's Belgravia) **£40**

SIR DAVID MURRAY - Highland
Cattle By A Rocky Outcrop -
signed - 23½ x 35¼in.
(Sotheby's Belgravia) **£85**

SIR DAVID MURRAY - A Mist Coming
On - signed and dated 1873 - 13½ x
20¼in.
(Sotheby's Belgravia) **£50**

W. MURRAY - Study Of A Hunter And A
Dog - oil on canvas - 28 x 36in.
(King & Chasemore) **£360**

F. MUSCHAMP - A Moonlit Pool -
signed - 22 x 18½in.
(Sotheby's Belgravia) **£30**

F. MUSCHAMP - Wooded Waterfalls -
one signed and dated 1886 - each 30 x
25in.
(Sotheby's Belgravia) **£120 Pair**

SYDNEY MUSCHAMP - A Pause In The
Melody - signed - 15¾ x 23½in.
(Sotheby's Belgravia) **£140**

AUGUSTE MUSIN - Seascape - on wood
- signed - 10 x 14cm.
(Galerie Moderne) **£85**

FRANCOIS MUSIN - A Beach Scene
At Dusk, With Fisherfolk Near Smacks
in the foreground And A Man-O'-War
Anchored Offshore Beyond - signed -
46 x 67cm.
(Phillips) **£1,250**

HERONOMUS VAN DER MY - Elegant
Company And A Negro Servant Taking
Refreshment In The Grounds Of A
Country House - signed - oil on canvas -
17 x 13½in.
(Bonham's) **£3,500**

S. MYLES - A Riverside Village - signed -
16½ x 20½in.
(Sotheby's Belgravia) **£50**

MYRIAM - Vase Trimmed With Roses -
oil on canvas - signed - 50 x 40cm.
(Galerie Moderne) **£14**

N

MATTHYS NAIVEU - A Man Reading Outside A Tavern - indistinctly signed with initials and dated - on panel - 12½ x 9½in.
(Christie's) **£1,400**

MATTHYS NAIVEU - Interior With A Woman Spinning - signed indistinctly - dated 1668 - on panel - 19 x 14in.
(Sotheby's) **£8,000**

M. NAIVEU - A Fruit Vendor, A Basket Of Fruit On Her Arm, A Couple Conversing Beyond; A Wine Seller, A Dog Beside Him, A Boat On A Canal To The Left - each 18 x 15in.
(Sotheby's) **£440 Pair**

NAPIER - The County of Peebles In Full Sail, the first of Craig's fleet of four-masted sailing ships - 24½ x 33½in.
(Sotheby's) **£650**

FILIPPO NAPOLITANO - The Massacre Of The Innocents; And The Martyrdom Of Saint Catherine - on slate - 10½ x 13½in.
(Christie's) **£700 Pair**

MARIOTTO DI NARDO - The Agony In The Garden - on gold ground, on panel - cusped top - 14½ x 6in.
(Christie's) **£9,500**

NASMYTH - Figures In A Wooded Landscape, A Town, Loch And Mountains In The Distance - 18 x 24in.
(Woolley & Wallis) **£720**

NASMYTH - River Scene - on panel - oil on canvas - 5 x 7¾in.
(Bearnes & Waycotts) **£110**

ALEXANDER NASMYTH - A View Of Inverary Castle And Town From The East With Deer in the foreground - 43½ x 58in.
(Christie's) **£4,200**

ALEXANDER NASMYTH - A Croft By A Loch - 17½ x 23in.
(Sotheby's) **£450**

ALEXANDER NASMYTH - Dalmahoy Hills Near Edinburgh showing Lennox Castle Tower - indistinctly signed - on panel - 17¾ x 23½in.
(Sotheby's) **£2,000**

ALEXANDER NASMYTH - A Wooded
Rocky River - 17¼ x 23¼in.
(Sotheby's) **£380**

MARGARET NASMYTH - A Distant View
Of London From Twickenham - signed and
dated 1856 - 17½ x 23in.
(Sotheby's) **£2,000**

P. NASMYTH - A Wooded Landscape
With Figures On A Path By A Cottage -
on panel - 10½ x 14¾in.
(Christie's) **£1,300**

PATRICK NASMYTH - A Mother And Child
On A Path By A Stream - oil on panel -
10 x 12in.
(King & Chasemore) **£1,200**

PATRICK NASMYTH - Peasants And Cattle
On A Country Path - oil on panel - signed -
12 x 16in.
(King & Chasemore) **£1,900**

NATTIER - A French Prince On
Horseback Wearing Armour And The
Order Of The Saint Esprit With A Page
In Attendance, In A Landscape - arched
top - 54 x 43½in.
(Christie's) **£850**

**JEAN-BAPTISTE NATTIER, called
NATTIER THE ELDER** - Cleopatra; And
Porcia, Wife Of Decimus Junius Brutus -
42 x 54in.
(Sotheby's) **£2,500 Pair**

NATTIER

J. M. NATTIER - Portrait Of A Lady
As Diana, Seated, In A River Landscape
- 35½ x 52½in.
(Christie's) **£1,200**

EDUARD NAVENE - A Man And Woman
In Balkan Costume - one signed - 17 x
11in.
(Sotheby's) **£50 Pair**

JOHN PRESTON NEALE - New Hall,
Yorkshire - signed - inscribed on the
reverse - dated 1825 - 6¼ x 8¾in.
(Sotheby's) **£70**

**NEAPOLITAN SCHOOL, Early 19th
Century** - An Extensive View Of The
Bay Of Naples With Vesuvius in the
distance - gouache - 16¼ x 24½in.
(Sotheby's) **£110**

NEAPOLITAN SCHOOL, 19th Century -
Views In The Bay Of Naples - each
10 x 15in.
(Sotheby's) **£250 Four**

PEETER NEEFFS THE YOUNGER - The
Interior of Antwerp Cathedral, at night -
signed and dated 1616 - on panel -
15 x 22½in.
(Christie's) **£3,000**

AERT VAN DER NEER - A Wooded
Winter Landscape, with figures sledging
and playing golf on a frozen waterway, with
houses nearby and a church with windmills
in the distance - signed with two monograms
- 45½ x 64in.
(Christie's) **£10,000**

AERT VAN DER NEER - An Extensive
Wooded Winter Landscape, with numerous
figures on a frozen waterway, and buildings
and a church in the distance - signed with
two monograms - on panel - 20 x 28¾in.
(Christie's) **£62,000**

E. J. NEIMANN - An Extensive River
Landscape With Thatched Cottages in
the left foreground - signed - on canvas -
30 x 50in.
(Morphet & Morphet) **£500**

ANTAL NEOGRADY - Watering
The Garden - oil - on board - signed and
indistinctly dated - 20¼ x 29½in.
(Sotheby's) **£190**

NOEL LAURA NESBIT - The Vision -
inscribed on exhibition label on reverse -
watercolour - 24 x 18 ins.
(Christie's, S. Kensington) **£110**

JOHN NESBITT - A Fishing Village -
signed and dated 1875 - 13 x 19¾in.
(Sotheby's Belgravia) **£25**

NESFIELD - Aqua Claudius, Near
Tivoli - signed with initials - inscribed
and dated 1828 - 7½ x 5¼in.
(Sotheby's) **£18**

WILLIAM ANDREWS NESFIELD -
The Falls Of Foyers - watercolour -
signed with initials and dated 1827 -
44½ x 27½in.
(Christie's) **£120**

NETHERLANDISH SCHOOL - The
Castle Of Laarne Near Ghent, With
Figures And Cattle in the foreground -
indistinctly signed and dated 1741 -
on panel - 15½ x 20¼in.
(Christie's) **£1,000**

SOUTH NETHERLANDISH SCHOOL -
The Adoration Of The Kings - dated 1515 -
on panel - 36½ x 23in.
(Sotheby's) **£8,000**

G. NETSCHER - Lady Artist In Red
Dress - on panel - 15 x 11in.
(Worsfolds) **£4,000**

A. NEUHUYS - Interior With Mother
Spinning And Child In Cot - 31 x 39cm.
(Edmiston's) **£600**

ALGERNON NEWTON - A Scene At
Goathland, Near Whitby Entitled
'Spring Evening' - signed with monogram
and dated 1943 - oil on canvas - 15¼ x
23½in.
(Bearnes & Waycotts) **£100**

PIETER PIETERSZ. DE NEYN -
Horsemen Charging Past A Cottage Among
Trees On The Bank Of A River Across
Which Other Soldiers Are Fleeing, Some
On Horseback - signed and dated 1626 -
on panel - 12¼ x 22¼in.
(Sotheby's) **£3,800**

RICHARD HENRY NIBBS - 'Shipping
In The Pool Of London', An Extensive
View Of The Thames - oil - on canvas -
signed and dated 1882 - 18 x 48in.
(King & Chasemore) **£850**

RICHARD HENRY NIBBS - 'Brigantine Off
Dungeness' - signed - watercolour -
23 x 35in.
(King & Chasemore) **£240**

RICHARD HENRY NIBBS - Below
London Bridge - 9¼ x 22¼in.
(Sotheby's Belgravia) **£55**

NICHOLSON

FRANCIS NICHOLSON - The Sinking
Of The River Nidd, Yorkshire -
watercolour - signed - inscribed and
dated 1809 on the reverse - 29¾ x 25¼in.
(Christie's) **£240**

FRANCIS NICHOLSON - Falls On The
River At Asseharborberg, And A House
Beyond - 11¾ x 17½in.
(Sotheby's) **£75**

FRANCIS NICHOLSON - London
Bridge, With St. Paul's Cathedral,
Beyond - etched outline and water-
colour - 11¾ x 16½in.
(Christie's) **£600**

FRANCIS NICHOLSON - St. Paul's
Cathedral From The Embankment Near
The Adelphi - etched outline and water-
colour - 11¾ x 16½in.
(Christie's) **£350**

GEORGE W. NICHOLSON - A Coastal
Scene With Fisherfolk On The Beach In
A Storm And A Village On A Cliff -
signed - 30 x 40in.
(Christie's) **£260**

P. W. NICHOLSON - Donald Clark's
House - watercolour - dated 1883 -
22 x 37.5cm.
(Edmiston's) **£10**

AUGUSTO NICODEMO - The Lambton
Family in Italy: William Lambton and his
wife Anne with their four children and a
dog - signed and dated '1797 in Napoli' -
30½ x 38½in.
(Christie's) **£4,500**

NICOL - Study Of A Young Boy In A
Cap - oil - bears signature and dated -
on panel - 23.5 x 19cm.
(Phillips in Scotland) **£5**

ERSKINE NICOL - Insolvent - signed and
dated 1862 - 19½ x 25½in.
(Sotheby's) **£1,050**

JOSEPH NICOLLS - A View Of Old
Westminster Bridge With Boats in the foreground And Westminster Abbey beyond -
31¼ x 59in.
(Christie's) **£5,000**

EDMUND JOHN NIEMANN - Richmond
Castle - signed - 30 x 50in.
(Christie's) **£500**

EDMUND JOHN NIEMANN - A View
Of Cliveden On The Thames With
Figures And Eel Traps Near A Weir in
the foreground - signed - dated and
inscribed - 61 x 107cm.
(Phillips) **£2,400**

EDMUND JOHN NIEMANN - An
Extensive View Of The River Tay -
signed - 76 x 128cm.
(Phillips) **£800**

EDMUND JOHN NIEMANN - View Of
The River At Richmond, Yorkshire - signed
and inscribed - 19½ x 35½in.
(Christie's, S. Kensington) **£200**

EDMUND JOHN NIEMANN - A
Mediterranean Coastal Landscape With
Peasants On A Path - signed and dated
'53 - 13½ x 17½in.
(Christie's) **£400**

E. J. NIEMANN - A Rocky Shore Scene
With Figures And Beached Fishing
Boats in the foreground - signed - on
canvas - 8 x 9¾in.
(King & Chasemore) **£380**

POLLOCK S. NISBET - The Cathedral,
Iona - 80 x 58cm.
(Edmiston's) **£38**

POLLOCK SINCLAIR NISBET - A Cafe,
Algiers - signed - 14 x 9¼in.
(Sotheby's Belgravia) **£3**

POLLOCK S. NISBET - Street Scene
Near The Alhambra - signed - 17¼ x
14in.
(Sotheby's) **£220**

JOHN NIXON - Shipping On The
Thames - West Thurrock - watercolour -
signed with initials - inscribed and
dated 1801 - 5½ x 8¾in.
(Christie's) **£85**

JOHN NIXON - A Flower Seller On
The Steine At Brighton - inscribed -
watercolour - 5¼ x 3¼in.
(Christie's) **£55**

JOHN SARGENT NOBLE - Shooting
Blackcock - signed - 23½ x 31½in.
(Christie's) **£250**

ROBERT NOBLE - Wooded River Scene -
Evening - 69 x 89cm.
(Edmiston's) **£150**

J. B. NOEL - Farmyard Scene With
Figures - signed and dated 1900 -
24 x 36in.
(Woolley & Wallis) **£170 Pair**

JULES NOEL - Unloading The Day's
Catch - signed - on panel - 19 x 15in.
(Sotheby's) **£1,000**

NOEL

JULES NOEL - Sailing Boats Reached By A Jetty - signed and inscribed 'Normandy' and dated 1875 - on panel - 8½ x 6½in.
(Sotheby's) **£600**

JAN VAN NOORDT - Portrait Of A Lady, half length, in a black dress, standing before a landscape - 32 x 25½in.
(Christie's) **£1,100**

PIETER VAN NOORT - Christ And The Pharisees - signed with initials and indistinctly dated - on panel - 12½ x 16½in.
(Christie's) **£480**

BENGT NORDENBERG - The Family Bible Reading - signed - inscribed 'Dusseldorf' and dated 1852 - 37¼ x 49½in.
(Sotheby's) **£11,000**

ORLANDO NORIE - Types Of The British Army, Mounted And Dismounted - signed - watercolour heightened with white - 14 x 28½in.
(Christie's) **£500**

ORLANDO NORIE - Mounted Dragoon Officer - watercolour - 22.5 x 17.5cm.
(Edmiston's) **£105**

ORLANDO NORIE - Mounted Group - Group Scots Grays Skirmishing - watercolour - 33 x 50cm.
(Edmiston's) **£200**

E. G. A. NORMAN - Falstaff Asleep - signed - on panel - 13½ x 22¼in.
(Sotheby's Belgravia) **£100**

PARSONS NORMAN - A Broadland Landscape - watercolour - 12 x 8in.
(G. A. Key) **£22**

PARSONS NORMAN - Coastal Scene With Lighthouse - watercolour - 10 x 6in.
(G. A. Key) **£20**

JOHN WILLIAM NORTH - A Woman Seated Beneath A Pergola In A Garden In Summer - watercolour - 12 x 17½in.
(Christie's) **£350**

JOHN WILLIAM NORTH - A Sweet Meadow In England - 34½ x 41½in.
(Christie's) **£550**

J. NORTHCOTE - Portrait Of An Officer, Standing, three-quarter length, With An Oriental Attendant Holding A Parasol, In A Landscape - 48½ x 39½in.
(Christie's) **£380**

NORWICH SCHOOL - 'The Reapers' - oil on canvas - 24 x 20in.
(Southam & Sons) **£70**

NORWICH SCHOOL - Wooded River Scene With Figures - oil - 11 x 16in.
(G. A. Key) **£36**

NORWICH SCHOOL, early 19th century - Rural Landscape With A Girl Carrying Sticks And Accompanied By A Dog, in the foreground; a man with cattle and sheep beneath large old oak trees in the distance, a thatched cottage beyond - 16½ x 13in.
(Henry Spencer & Sons) **£200**

Z. NOTERMAN - Monkey Musicians - signed and dated 1877 - on panel - 14½ x 17½in.
(Sotheby's) **£400**

PHILIPPE NOYER - Haute Ecole - oil on canvas - signed and dated Paris '58 - 39 x 19¼in.
(Sotheby's) **£440**

E. NOYER - View Of A Port - oil on canvas - signed - 50 x 70cm.
(Galerie Moderne) **£50**

ELIZABETH NUTT - November on the North West Arm, Nova Scotia - signed and dated 1922, signed again twice, inscribed and dedicated and dated 1922 on the stretcher - 20¼ x 24 ins.
(Christie's) **£58**

CARLO FRANCESCO NUVOLONE - Laban Searching For The Images Of His Gods - 55 x 70¼in.
(Sotheby's) **£2,400**

C. NYPELS - Seascape - oil on canvas - signed - 54 x 73cm.
(Galerie Moderne) **£204**

JOHN WRIGHT OAKES - 'Sketch On The Coast' - signed with monogram - dated 1873 - oil on panel - 11½ x 17½in.
(Bearnes & Waycotts) **£380**

JOHN WRIGHT OAKES - A Boat By A Pool, A Haywain Nearby - water-colour - signed and dated '63 - 21½ x 30in.
(Christie's) **£25**

J. M. OAKLEY - City Of London From Tower Bridge - oil - signed - 34 x 43.5cm.
(Phillips in Scotland) **£9**

EVANS OBBIE - Nude Woman - oil on board - signed - 7½ x 11½in.
(J. Francis, T. Jones & Sons) **£16**

J. OCHTERVELT - The Flirtation - on panel - 14½ x 13in.
(Christie's) **£550**

O'CONNOR - Crossing A Bridge - 9¾ x 15¾in.
(Sotheby's Belgravia) **£75**

JAMES ARTHUR O'CONNOR - The Valley Of Rocks Near Mettlach - bears photograph of signature inscription, and date on the stretcher - 5½ x 6¾in.
(Christie's) **£65**

JAMES ARTHUR O'CONNOR - A Coastal View Near Dublin; A Lake View At Sunset - on board - each 2¾ x 4in.
(Sotheby's) **£320 Pair**

OGG

A. C. A. OGG - Sea And Rocks - 33 x 45cm.
(Edmiston's) £28

MARCO D'OGGIONO - Venus In A Grotto; In The Background A Rocky Sea Coast With Distant Mountains - 21 x 17½in.
(Sotheby's) £6,500

EMMA SOPHIA OLIVER - The Vale Of Dedham, Sportsmen Shooting With Spaniels in the foreground - signed - inscribed and dated 1859 - watercolour heightened with white - 11¾ x 18½in.
(Christie's) £250

WILLIAM OLIVER - A View On The River Moselle Near Pommera - signed - inscribed and dated 1852 - 18½ x 31½in.
(Christie's) £2,200

WILLIAM OLIVER - The Fisherman's Daughter - signed - 36 x 28in.
(Christie's) £480

WILLIAM OLIVER - In The Summer Of Life - signed - 40 x 13½in.
(Sotheby's Belgravia) £500

WILLIAM OLIVER - Roses - signed - 17¼ x 23¼in.
(Sotheby's Belgravia) £800

OOST

WILLIAM OLIVER - The Love Letter -
signed and dated 1858 - 17½ x 13¼in.
(Sotheby's Belgravia)   **£550**

GEORGE BERNARD O'NEILL -
'Grandma's Attorney' - signed -
51 x 44cm.
(Phillips)   **£1,100**

HENRY O'NEILL - Portrait Of The
Artist's Mother, half length, In Dark Dress
With A Lace Collar - 29 x 24½in.
(Christie's)   **£45**

UMBERTO ONGANIA - Piazza San
Marco, Venice - 7½ x 12in.
(Sotheby's)   **£40**

GUY ONKELINX - Bords De La Meuse
A Godinne - cartoon - signed - 50 x 41cm.
(Galerie Moderne)   **£10**

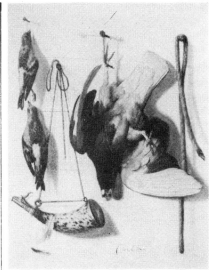

JACOB VAN OOLEN - A Trompe-L'Oeil
Still Life Of Birds, Suspended On A
White Wall Are Two Finches, A Hunting-
Horn, A Pigeon And A Length Of Tow -
signed - 22¾ x 18in.
(Sotheby's)   **£5,800**

VAN OOST - Portrait Of A Lady, Aged
24, bust length - inscribed - 20 x 16in.
(Christie's)   **£200**

JACQUES VAN OOST THE YOUNGER -
The Mystic Marriage Of Saint Catherine -
canvas laid down on board - 45¾ x 39½in.
(Christie's)   **£1,600**

OOST

Y. VAN OOST - Portrait Of A Magistrate - oil on canvas - 1m.29 x 1m.02cm.
(Galerie Moderne) £377

JACOB CORNELISZ. VAN OOSTZANEN - Saint Andrew; And Saint Jerome - on panel - 12 x 5½in.
(Christie's) £7,500 Two

GEORGE WILLEM OPDENHOFF - Unloading The Day's Catch - signed - on panel - 15½ x 19¾in.
(Sotheby's) £750

OPIE - Portrait Of A Lady With Her Two Children - 29 x 24in.
(Sotheby's) £65

OPIE - Portrait Of Victorian Gentleman - oil - 24 x 20in.
(G. A. Key) £20

MORITZ DANIEL OPPENHEIM - Portrait Of Mayer Karl Von Rothschild, half length, Wearing A Grey Coat, Brown Waistcoat And Dark Cravat - signed with monogram and dated 1837 - 19½ x 15¼in.
(Christie's) £950

RIMINALDI, ORAZIO - Daedalus and Icarus - 52 x 39 ins.
(Christie's) £2,000

ORIENTAL SCHOOL - Figures Tilling The Fields - a gouache painting - 14½ x 18in.
(King & Chasemore) £120

JAMES ORROCK - Lumley Castle,
Chester-Le-Street, County Durham -
signed and dated 1877 - 13½ x 20½in.
(Sotheby's Belgravia) **£120**

JAMES ORROCK - Hindhead From The
Hog's Back - heightened with bodycolour - signed - inscribed and dated
1910 - 36 x 52in.
(Sotheby's Belgravia) **£90**

JAMES ORROCK - Deer In The Park
At Arundel - watercolour - signed -
inscribed and dated 1871 - 18¼ x
29¼in.
(Christie's) **£170**

JAMES ORROCK - Kilchurn Castle,
Loch Awe - pencil and watercolour
heightened with white - inscribed -
13¼ x 18¾in.
(Christie's) **£65**

BUCKLEY ORSEY - Interior With Sheep
Shearers - oil on canvas - signed - 29 x 19in.
(J. Francis, T. Jones & Sons) **£160**

GIUSTINA ORSINI - Views Of The Bay
Of Naples With Figures And Fishing
Boats in the foreground - both signed -
13 x 39in.
(Christie's) **£600 Pair**

GUISTINA ORSINI - Views Of The Bay Of
Naples, with many figures and fishing
vessels in the foreground - buildings and
Mount Vesuvius in the distance - signed -
13 x 39in
(Henry Spencer & Sons) **£680 Pair**

**JAN FRANS VAN BLOEMEN, called
ORIZZONTE** - An Italianate Wooded
Landscape With Classical Figures By A
Fountain; And An Italianate Wooded
River Landscape With Classical Figures
in the foreground, A House And A
Tower Beyond - 54 x 39in.
(Christie's) **£6,500 Pair**

JAMES ORROCK - Caernarvon Castle
And Town - pencil and watercolour -
signed - 11½ x 18¾in.
(Christie's) **£140**

MARTIN RICO Y ORTEGA - A Venetian Canal Scene - signed - 27½ x 17¼in.
(Christie's) **£5,000**

FRANCOIS AUGUSTE ORTMANS - A Cow On A Forest Path - stamped with the artist's vente mark - 21½ x 18in.
(Sotheby's) **£300**

VAN OS - A River Landscape, Fishermen in the foreground, A Herdsman With Animals By A Cottage To The Left - 11 x 13in.
(Sotheby's) **£520**

JAN VAN OS - Dutch Fishing Boats And Sailing Vessels In A Calm Offshore - signed - 14½ x 18in.
(Christie's) **£15,000**

JAN VAN OS - A View Of A Riverside Village, Figures, Animals And Moored Barges in the foreground - signed - on panel - 20¾ x 27¾in.
(Sotheby's) **£4,800**

JAN VAN OS - Roses, A Crown Imperial Lily, Dahlias and other flowers, with fruit on a ledge - signed on panel - 24¾ x 19in.
(Christie's) **£32,000**

WALTER OSBORNE - Portrait Of Miss Cecilia Armstrong Of Tipperary, Ireland, three-quarter length, Seated, Wearing A Low-Cut Black Dress With Puff Sleeves - 49¼ x 39¼in.
(Sotheby's) **£70**

SAMUEL WILLIAM OSCROFT - Spring - watercolour - signed, reverse with signed artists label - 14 x 9in.
(Neale & Son) **£18**

PHIL OSMOND - Conway Bay And Gemmaes, Anglesey - watercolours - 10 x 14in.
(G. A. Key) **£20 Pair**

VAN OSTADE - An Interior Scene With Figures At A Table Smoking Clay Pipes And A Cat Sitting In A Bowl On The Floor - oil on panel - 12½ x 9¾in.
(Geering & Colyer) **£380**

FRANZ OSTUCKENBERG - 19th century - A Hunter In A Stable With Terrier - oil on canvas - signed - 29 x 25½in.
(J. Francis, T. Jones & Sons) **£100**

C. W. OSWALD - A Highland Torrent -
signed - 17¾ x 31½in.
(Sotheby's Belgravia) **£48**

J. H. OSWALD - Shipping In The Forth
Estuary Off Bowness - oil - signed with
initials - on board - 12.5 x 20cm.
(Phillips in Scotland) **£22**

RUDOLF RITTER VON OTTENFIELD -
A Mounted Officer And His Soldiers,
In A Landscape - signed and dated 1894 -
on panel - 8¼ x 6¼in.
(Sotheby's) **£650**

OTTO DIDRIK OTTESEN - Still Life
Of Roses And Forget-Me-Nots - signed
and dated 1876 - 9 x 11in.
(Sotheby's) **£500**

BENJAMIN JOHN OTTEWELL - The
Dee At Allan-A-Quoich - signed and
dated Sept., 1894 - 23½ x 17½in.
(Sotheby's Belgravia) **£40**

JOHANNES DIRCKSZ. OUDENROGGE -
A Wooded River Landscape, With Figures
And Cattle And A Village Beyond - on
panel - 23 x 32½in.
(Christie's) **£1,300**

ROLAND OUDOT - Le Sarcophage -
oil - on canvas - on board - signed - 17¼ x
21in.
(Sotheby's) **£280**

JURIAAN OVENS - A Nautilus Cup,
A Goblet, A Lobster In A Chinese
Dish, Bread And A Lobster Claw On A
Silver Plate, On A Table Covered With
A White Cloth, With A Landscape In
The Background - 38 x 32in.
(Christie's) **£2,500**

JURIAAN OVENS - A Nautilus Cup, A
Goblet, A Lobster In A Chinese Dish,
Bread And A Lobster Claw On A Silver
Plate, on a table covered with a white cloth,
with a landscape in the background -
38 x 32in.
(Christie's) **£2,800**

C. OVERY - Still Life Of Summer Fruits
In Basket On A Table - oil - 11 x 17in.
(G. A. Key) **£38**

SAMUEL OWEN - Shipping Scenes -
signed - watercolour - 5¼ x 8¾in.
(Bearnes & Waycotts) **£520 Pair**

OWEN

SAMUEL OWEN - Shipping In The Channel, North Foreland - signed - pencil and watercolour - 8¼ x 6¾in.
(Christie's) **£460**

OWEN - Ships In A Bay With Figures On The Shore - 7½ x 10½in.
(Sotheby's) **£70**

OWEN - Shipping In A Calm Bay, A Sailing Barge in the foreground - 8 x 11¼in.
(Sotheby's) **£110**

W. H. OXLEY - Landscape With Sheep And Drover - oil - 15 x 20in.
(G. A. Key) **£22**

MATTEO PACETTI - Views Of The Bay Of Naples, With Numerous Figures And Vesuvius Beyond - both signed and dated Rome 1830 - 25 x 33½in.
(Christie's) **£2,000 Pair**

FERDINAND PACHER - The Loser - signed - on panel - 6½ x 8¼in.
(Sotheby's) **£700**

ALESSANDRO VAROTARI, Attributed To, Called IL PADOVANINO - An Extensive Landscape With Putti Playing Amongst Trees in the foreground, Farm Buildings And A Castle Keep In The Distance - 94 x 150cm.
(Phillips) **£1,100**

J. VAN PAEMEL - A Wooded Landscape With Peasants On A Bridge; And An Extensive Wooded Landscape With Peasants On A Path - one signed and dated 1795 - on panel - 18½ x 24in.
(Christie's) **£4,800 Pair**

HENRY PAGE - I Saw Three Ships Come Sailing By; Beneath The Sea - three on one mount - gouache and gold - one inscribed - one signed and inscribed on the reverse - 4¼ x 3¾in.
(Sotheby's Belgravia) **£85 Three**

SIDNEY PAGET - A Landscape With A Girl In A Muddy Lane - signed and dated 1882 - 19 x 29in.
(Woolley & Wallis) **£120**

GIOACCHINO PAGLIEJ - Awaiting the next dance - signed - 36 x 22 ins.
(Christie's, S. Kensington) **£480**

GEORGE PAICE - Racehorse 'Cloister' In A Stable - signed and dated '94 - oil - 9½ x 12½in.
(Warner, Sheppard & Wade) **£20**

HARRY SUTTON PALMER - A Drover On His Way Home - signed and dated 1872 - 9 x 13in.
(Sotheby's Belgravia) **£70**

HARRY SUTTON PALMER - 'Windermere' - watercolour - signed - 13½ x 19 ins.
(King & Chasemore) **£190**

HARRY SUTTON PALMER - Bolton Abbey From The River - signed and dated '81 - watercolour - 10 x 14in.
(Woolley & Wallis) **£225**

HARRY SUTTON PALMER - Corn Stooks In The Lake District - watercolour - signed and dated '76 - 4¼ x 6in.
(Christie's) **£42**

HARRY SUTTON PALMER - 'The Esk At Egton Bridge' - watercolour - signed and dated '81 - 14 x 21in.
(King & Chasemore) **£210**

SAMUEL PALMER - Papigno On The Nar, Below The Falls Of Terni - signed and dated 1871 - pencil and brown wash - 8¼ x 7¼in.
(Christie's) **£600**

W. J. PALMER - Broadland Scenes - watercolours - 4 x 13in
(G. A. Key) **£12 Pair**

PANNINI - Classicial Landscape With Figures And Ruined Buildings - 24½ x 48¾in.
(Woolley & Wallis) **£820**

SCHOOL OF PANNINI - Figures In A Ruined Classical Landscape - 22 x 32in.
(Woolley & Wallis) **£420**

SCHOOL OF PANNINI - Figures And Cattle In Groups Around Classical Ruins - 34½ x 35½in.
(Buckell & Ballard) **£900**

PANNINI

G. P. PANNINI - Figures Among Classical Ruins Including Trajan's Column, The Pantheon And The Equestrian Statue Of Marcus Aurelius - 38½ x 48½in.
(Christie's) **£3,800**

G. P. PANNINI - Diogenes Throwing Away His Cup, with figures and classical ruins - 56 x 48¾in.
(Christie's) **£10,000**

GIOVANNI PAOLO PANNINI - A Capriccio View Of Roman Ruins With The Colosseum And The Temple Of Faustina - signed and dated Roma 1739 - 29¼ x 39¼in.
(Christie's) **£11,000**

G. P. PANNINI - Classical Ruins With Figures Beneath An Arch; And Soldiers And Other Figures Talking By Classical Ruins - one bears initials - 28 x 49½in. and 27 x 49½in.
(Christie's) **£3,800 Two**

GIOVANNI PAOLO PANNINI - The Interior Of An Imaginary Picture Gallery, with the artist finishing a copy of the Aldobrandini Wedding - 66¾ x 88¾in.
(Christie's) **£170,000**

ANTONIO PAOLETTI - The Violinist - signed and inscribed 'Venezia' - on panel - 8¾ x 13½in.
(Sotheby's)   **£1,300**

JAMES PARDON - Portrait Of An Artist, small full-length, Seated In A Wooded Landscape - signed - 26½ x 21½in.
(Christie's)   **£260**

JAMES STUART PARK - Geraniums - signed twice - 19½ x 23½in.
(Sotheby's)   **£90**

JAMES STUART PARK - Yellow Roses - signed - 14½ x 11½in.
(Sotheby's)   **£110**

JAMES STUART PARK - Pink Roses - signed - 27 x 23½in.
(Sotheby's)   **£170**

J. STUART PARK - Pink And White Roses - oval - 57 x 71cm.
(Edmiston's)   **£190**

STUART PARK - "Clematis" - oval - oil - 24 x 19½in.
(Thomas Love & Sons Ltd)   **£125**

STUART PARK - "Study Of Red And White Mixed Flowers" - oval - oil - 23½ x 19½in.
(Thomas Love & Sons Ltd)   **£285**

HENRY H. PARKER - On The Lledr, North Wales - signed - and signed and inscribed on the reverse - 19 x 31½in.
(Christie's)   **£1,600**

HENRY H. PARKER - The Ride Home - signed - inscribed on the reverse - 23½ x 35½in.
(Sotheby's Belgravia)   **£650**

HENRY H. PARKER - 'The Last Load', a rural landscape with farm labourers harnessing a team of cart horses in the foreground - 23 x 41in.
(Henry Spencer & Sons)   **£1,000**

HENRY H. PARKER - 'A Bend On The Avon' - signed - watercolour - 21 x 29½in.
(Warner, Sheppard & Wade)   **£150**

JOHN PARKER, Attributed To - Portrait Of Elizabeth Darcy, Aged 20, three-quarter length, Wearing A Black Dress With White Lace Collar And Cuffs, Standing Before A Pillar - inscribed and dated 1634 - 52½ x 41½in.
(Christie's) £9,500

JOHN PARKER, Attributed To - Portrait Of Richard Evelyn, Aged 48, three-quarter length, Wearing Black Costume And White Collar And Cuffs, Standing By A Table Holding A Stick - inscribed and dated 1635 - 95½ x 35½in.
(Christie's) £3,200

JOHN PARKER, Attributed To - Portrait Of Eleanor Evelyn, three-quarter length, Wearing A Black Dress, With White Collar And Cuffs, Holding A Rose - 44 x 33in.
(Christie's) £6,500

R. H. PARKER - ' The Fisherman's Return' - on canvas - 25 x 30in.
(Morphet & Morphet) £110

PARKMAN - 'Temple Church And Shakespeare Inn, Victoria Street, Bristol - signed - watercolour - 12 x 10in.
(Lalonde Martin) £70

WILLIAM PARS - A Mountain Lake In Italy - inscribed 'Cozens' on the reverse - watercolour - 11¼ x 18in.
(Christie's) £900

ANNIE M. PARSONS - Loch Leven - watercolour - 25 x 55cm.
(Edmiston's) £8

ALFRED WILLIAM PARSONS - Old Farm, Arundel, Sussex - signed - 17½ x 11½in.
(Sotheby's Belgravia) £45

JULES PASCIN - Le Village Cubain - pencil, pen and brush and indian ink - 7¼ x 10in.
(Sotheby's) £320

JULES PASCIN - Figures - brush and ink and wash - 9½ x 8¼in.
(Sotheby's) £180

JULES PASCIN - Au Restaurant - pen
and ink - 10¼ x 13¼in.
(Sotheby's) **£300**

JULES PASCIN - Femme Assise - pen
and ink - 12¾ x 9in.
(Sotheby's) **£320**

PASINI - Fishing Boats In The Bay Of
Naples - signed - on panel - 11¾ x 17¾in.
(Sotheby's) **£140**

DANIEL PASMORE - At The Well - signed
with monogram and dated 1855 - 7¾ x
7¾in.
(Sotheby's Belgravia) **£360**

DANIEL PASMORE - The Courtship -
signed and dated 1877 - on panel - 12 x
10 ins.
(Christie's, S. Kensington) **£350**

DANIEL PASMORE - The Courtship -
signed and dated 1883 - 16½ x 13½in.
(Christie's) **£480**

MRS J. F. PASMORE - The Flower
Seller - signed and dated 1877 -
17½ x 13¼in.
(Sotheby's Belgravia) **£200**

CHARLES H. PASSEY - In Wharfdale,
Near Otley; and Near Harrogate,
Yorkshire - signed and inscribed on
reverse - 27¾ x 36in.
(Christie's, S. Kensington) **£380 Pair**

CHARLES H. PASSEY - Extensive
Wooded Landscape With Sheep - oil -
28 x 36in.
(G. A. Key) **£46**

PATCH - A Scene From A Play Probably
'The Alchemist' - 29 x 23½in.
(Christie's) **£850**

T. PATCH - A View Of Genoa With
Shipping And Figures in the foreground -
30 x 54in.
(Christie's) **£2,800**

PATEL - Figures In Classical Landscape
With Ruined Buildings - 18½ x 26¼in.
(Woolley & Wallis) **£820**

JOACHIM PATENIER, Circle Of - A
Landscape With The Rest On The Flight -
on panel - 21¾ x 31¼in.
(Sotheby's) **£6,000**

J. B. PATER - Fetes Champetres -
17½ x 21in.
(Christie's) **£2,400 Pair**

JEAN-BAPTISTE PATER - A Lady
Crowned As Flora in a pastoral landscape -
on copper - 13½ x 17½in.
(Christie's) **£3,800**

J. P. PATER - The Declaration Of
Love: Elegant Figures In A Landscape -
12½ x 16in.
(Christie's) **£6,500**

J. N. PATON - Excelsior, 'A youth who bore
'mid snow and ice, A banner with a strange
device . . . ' - bears signature - arched top -
23¾ x 15½in.
(Sotheby's) **£320**

RICHARD PATON - A Naval
Engagement Between English And
French Fleets - 63 x 125cm.
(Phillips) **£1,500 Pair**

WALLER HUGH PATON - Rannoch Moor - heightened with bodycolour - signed and dated 20 July 1870 - 5¾ x 9¾in.
(Sotheby's) **£80**

WALLER HUGH PATON - Study Of A Croft - on board - unframed - 6 x 9in.
(Sotheby's) **£70**

WALLER HUGH PATON - Anglers Near A Shaded Stream In Summer - watercolour heightened with white - signed - inscribed 'Dohar' and dated 11th June 1874 - 9¼ x 14in.
(Christie's) **£160**

JAMES McINTOSH PATRICK - Wades Bridge, Glen Lethnot, Edzell, Near Strathmore - signed and dated '35 - inscribed on the reverse - on board - 11¼ x 15½in.
(Sotheby's) **£110**

A. PATTERSON - Crossbill And Crested Grebe With Young - pen and ink drawings - 5 x 7in.
(G. A. Key) **£15 Pair**

JOSEPH PAUL - Large Broadland Landscape with Distant View Of Norwich - oil - 48 x 39in.
(G. A. Key) **£180**

JOHN PAUL - Saint John's Gate, Clerkenwell - 24½ x 29in.
(Christie's) **£300**

JOHN PAUL - The Thames At Westminster Bridge From The Lambeth Shore With Figures in the foreground - 19 x 35¼in.
(Christie's) **£420**

JOHN PAUL - A View On The River Thames, With Lambeth Palace And Saint Paul's Cathedral in the distance - 23¼ x 39½in.
(Christie's) **£2,400**

J. PAULMAN - Harvest Time; A Rainy Day - both signed - each 15½ x 23½in.
(Sotheby's Belgravia) **£260 Pair**

P. PAULUS - The Chateau - oil on canvas - signed - 80 x 60cm.
(Galerie Moderne) **£600**

PAULSEN

FRITZ PAULSEN - Portraits Of A Young Boy And Girl - both signed and dated 'London 1875' - canvas laid on board - 15 x 12¼in.
(Sotheby's) **£320 Pair**

H. PAUWELS - The Lady Farmer - oil on canvas - signed - 53 x 36cm.
(Galerie Moderne) **£15**

EUGENE PAVY - Study Of A Cavalier Drinking - oil on panel - signed - 10 x 7½in.
(King & Chasemore) **£200**

PAYNE - A Wooded River Scene With Figures And A Cottage - 11 x 15¼in.
(Sotheby's) **£15**

PAYNE - Fishing From A Punt - 13 x 19in.
(Sotheby's Belgravia) **£75**

PAYNE - Haddon Hall, Derbyshire, an evening scene with cattle - oil - 19 x 30in.
(Neale & Son) **£110**

DAVID PAYNE - Gypsies' Tent - signed - inscribed and dated 1877 on the reverse - 17¼ x 29¼in.
(Sotheby's Belgravia) **£800**

DAVID PAYNE - Going To The Hayfield - signed - inscribed on the reverse - 12½ x 17½in.
(Sotheby's Belgravia) **£280**

DAVID PAYNE - A Trent Scene - signed - inscribed on the reverse - dated 1877 - 20 x 30in.
(Sotheby's Belgravia) **£600**

DAVID PAYNE - On The Trent Near Castle Donnington - signed and dated 1876 - 15½ x 25½in.
(Sotheby's Belgravia) **£550**

HARRY PAYNE - 4th Incustrian Hussars On Patrol - signed and dated 1895 - oil on canvas - 17½ x 23½in.
(Charles R. Phillips) **£320**

W. PAYNE - Castle Near A Lake; A Mountain River - 9½ x 14½in.
(Sotheby's) **£65 Pair**

WILLIAM PAYNE - A Castle On An Island In An Estuary; And A Netsman In A River - the second bears initials - pencil and watercolour - 7¼ x 11½in.
(Christie's) **£50 Pair**

WILLIAM PAYNE - Cascades In The Lake District - both signed - watercolour - 8½ x 5¾in. and smaller.
(Christie's) **£240 Two**

WILLIAM PAYNE - Views Of Villages
In The Lake District - both signed -
watercolour - 4½ x 6¾in. and smaller.
(Christie's) **£320 Two**

PEACOCK - Head Of A Young Woman -
17½ x 13½in.
(Sotheby's Belgravia) **£12**

JAMES PEALE - Washington And His
Generals At Yorktown, 1781 - signed and
dated York 178? - 25 x 33¾in.
(Christie's) **£180,000**

F. PEARSON - Evening, Yorkshire - signed -
watercolour - 19 x 11½in.
(Neale & Son) **£10**

W. H. PEARSON - Woolwich Reach On
An Ebb Tide - heightened with white -
signed and inscribed - 10¼ x 27in.
(Sotheby's Belgravia) **£70**

W. H. PEARSON - 'Off Calais - Seascape
With French Fishing Boats and Brig In
Full Sail' - signed - 19th century -
watercolour - 12 x 24in.
(Lalonde Martin) **£110**

MAX-HERMANN PECHSTEIN - Der
Boxer - pencil, pen and indian ink -
signed with initials - 6½ x 8¼in.
(Sotheby's) **£220**

J. PEEL - Ovington On Tees - oil painting
on canvas - signed - 47½ x 29½in.
(John H. Raby & Son) **£1,275**

JAMES PEEL - Gathering Wood; In
The Hills - both signed - one with
initials and dated 1868 - both inscribed
on the reverse - each 14 x 23¼in.
(Sotheby's Belgravia) **£950 Pair**

JAMES PEEL - At Barrow On Trent;
The Trent Near Ingleby - both signed -
both inscribed on the reverse - one on
the stretcher - each 9½ x 15½in.
(Sotheby's Belgravia) **£900 Pair**

JAMES PEEL - A Lane Near Fringle,
Devon - signed - inscribed on the reverse -
19 x 29in.
(Sotheby's Belgravia) **£1,200**

JAMES PEEL - An Extensive Landscape
With Wells Cathedral in the distance -
bears another monogram - on panel - 8 x
12½in.
(Sotheby's Belgravia) **£220**

JAMES PEEL - Ingleby, Trent - signed -
17½ x 28½in.
(Sotheby's Belgravia) **£380**

B. PEETERS - Sailing Vessels Off A
Rocky Shore, With A Castle - bears
initials - on panel - 7 x 10in.
(Christie's) **£1,400**

BONAVENTURA PEETERS - Fishermen In
A Rowing Boat, with other vessels nearby
and a woman watching from the shore -
signed with initials - on panel - 18½ x 27½in.
(Christie's) **£3,800**

GILLIS PEETERS - A River Landscape,
with a dairy maid, and figures in a sailing
boat - signed with initials and dated 1641 -
on panel - 18¾ x 27¾in.
(Christie's) **£3,500**

THOMAS KENT PELHAM - The
Fisherwife - signed - 15¼ x 11½in.
(Sotheby's Belgravia) **£300**

G. PENCZ - Portrait Of A Lady Standing,
three-quarter length, Wearing A Black
Dress And Holding A Book, A Hilly
River Landscape With A Castle Beyond -
on panel - 35½ x 26½in.
(Christie's) **£3,000**

EDWIN AARON PENLEY - A Mountainous Lake Scene - heightened with bodycolour - signed twice - once with monogram - inscribed Cheltenham and dated 1862 - 7¼ x 18½in.
(Sotheby's Belgravia) **£45**

EDWIN A. PENLEY - Loch Tay. Looking West; And Sound Of Kerrara - watercolour heightened with white - both signed - inscribed and dated 1890 - 7¼ x 18½in.
(Christie's) **£80 Pair**

STANLEY PENN - The Langdale Pikes - signed - 19½ x 29¼in.
(Sotheby's Belgravia) **£120**

HENRY PENNELL - A River Landscape - signed - inscribed on the reverse - 23 x 39in.
(Sotheby's Belgravia) **£500**

EDWARD PENNY - A Butcher Disputing With A Blacksmith - 20½ x 16½in.
(Christie's) **£100**

EDWIN PENNY - 'Study Of A Golden Eagle' watercolour - signed - 9¾ x 14½in.
(Lalonde Martin) **£80**

SAMUEL JOHN PEPLOE - A Perthshire Landscape - signed - 15½ x 17¼in.
(Sotheby's) **£1,200**

SAMUEL JOHN PEPLOE - Rhum And Skye - 35 x 45cm.
(Edmiston's) **£750**

SAMUEL JOHN PEPLOE - Apples And Oranges - signed - 23½ x 32½in.
(Sotheby's) **£3,000**

SAMUEL JOHN PEPLOE - Corn Stooks - signed - on board - 11¼ x 14½in.
(Sotheby's) **£1,100**

R. PERCY - Harvest Time; By A Pond - both signed - 19½ x 29½in.
(Sotheby's Belgravia) **£460 Pair**

R. PERCY - Summer Landscapes - oil on canvas - 14½ x 19½in.
(Buckell & Ballard) **£26 Pair**

S. R. PERCY - 'A Ford On The Llyngwy' - signed - canvas - 20 x 30in.
(Morphet & Morphet) **£180**

SIDNEY RICHARD PERCY - The Oncoming Storm - signed - 12 x 16in.
(Christie's) **£220**

PERCY

SIDNEY RICHARD PERCY - A Moonlit Lake Scene - signed - on board - 7 x 10in.
(Christie's) **£200**

SIDNEY RICHARD PERCY - An Extensive Mountainous Landscape With Peasants Harvesting - signed and dated '69 - 37 x 59½in.
(Christie's) **£3,600**

SIDNEY RICHARD PERCY - A Highland River Landscape With Peasants And Cattle in the foreground - signed and dated 1877 - 23¼ x 37½in.
(Christie's) **£2,800**

SIDNEY RICHARD PERCY - Ferrying Sheep - signed and dated '68 - 8½ x 13½in.
(Sotheby's Belgravia) **£1,300**

SIDNEY RICHARD PERCY - A Highland Lochside Scene, With Figures And Cattle in the foreground - signed and dated 1865 - on canvas - 24 x 36in.
(King & Chasemore) **£3,400**

ARTHUR PERIGAL - Caderedris, North Wales - watercolour - 31 x 47cm.
(Edmiston's) **£64**

ARTHUR PERIGAL - Bringing Home The Sheep - signed and dated 1865 - on board - 9 x 13½in.
(Sotheby's) **£280**

PERIGNON - A Study Of Mixed Flowers - paper laid down on canvas - 18½ x 14in.
(Christie's) **£500**

R. F. PERLING - Highland Landscapes With Red Deer And Sheep Dogs - signed - on porcelain - 9 x 10½in.
(Morphet & Morphet) **£140 Pair**

FELIX PERRET - Beside The Pool - signed and dated 1872 - inscribed 'Rio De Janeiro' - 64¼ x 40½in.
(Sotheby's) **£1,000**

G. S. PERRIMAN - Fantasy - signed and dated 1939 - on board - 12 x 37in.
(Sotheby's Belgravia) **£85**

JEAN-BAPTISTE PERRONEAU - Portrait Of Jacques Cazotte, half length, in a red coat and waistcoat, with lace cravat and cuffs and a grey wig, his hat under his left arm - signed - 35 x 28¼in.
(Christie's) **£80,000**

WILLIAM PERRY - Waiting For The Boats - signed and dated '60 - 34½ x 24¼in.
(Sotheby's Belgravia)   **£280**

GUSTAVE JOSEPH PERSIN - Playing Patience - signed and dated 1861 - on panel - 14 x 10½in.
(Sotheby's)   **£550**

B. PERSON - Cargo Vessel With Tugs - 49 x 70cm.
(Edmiston's)   **£18**

CHARLES EDWARD PERUGINI - 'Justine' - oil on canvas - 10½ x 8¼in.
(Bearnes & Waycotts)   **£240**

W. PETCH - Cottages at Staveley - watercolours - 10 x 14in.
(G. A. Key)   **£32 Pair**

GEORGE PETER - Alpine Landscape with cattle - signed and dated 1886 - 28½ x 39½in.
(Christie's, S. Kensington)   **£1,000**

H. PETERSEN - The Cumberland Off The Coast - signed - indistinctly inscribed and dated 1881 - 17¾ x 24¾in.
(Sotheby's Belgravia)   **£620**

IVAN A. PETERWIN - Haymakers Resting, Near Farm Buildings - signed and dated 1892 - on panel - 5 x 7½in.
(Sotheby's)   **£600**

PETHER - A Continental Lake Scene, Moonlight - on panel - 13½ x 17¼in.
(Sotheby's Belgravia)   **£300**

A. PETHER - 'Moonlight Fishing' - oil on canvas.
(Southam & Sons)   **£75**

ABRAHAM PETHER - A Wooded River Landscape With Peasants And Cattle in the foreground And Cottages Beyond; And A Wooded River Landscape With Travellers On A Path - both signed - 16 x 24½in.
(Christie's)   **£1,700 Pair**

ABRAHAM PETHER - A Moonlight River Scene, With Sheep And A Heron - on panel - 5¾ x 7¼in.
(Christie's)   **£150**

PETHER

HENRY PETHER - The Thames At Greenwich By Moonlight - signed - 23 x 35¼in.
(Christie's) **£1,800**

HENRY PETHER - Windsor Castle By Moonlight From The Thames, With Barge Horses in the foreground - signed - 23 x 35¾in.
(Christie's) **£1,700**

HENRY PETHER - The Doge's Palace, And The Riva Degli Schiavoni, Venice, By Moonlight - signed - 23½ x 35½in.
(Christie's) **£2,400**

SEBASTIAN PETHER - A Moonlight River Landscape with figures in a boat - signed with initials - oil on wood panel - 5½ x 8 ins.
(Geering & Colyer) **£165**

SALVATORE PETRUOLO - An Italian Fishing Boat in a Calm - signed and dated 1885 - on canvas - 27½ x 41¾in.
(King & Chasemore) **£460**

AUGUST VON PETTENKOFEN - Man With Ruff - signed with initials - on panel - 10¼ x 6½in.
(Christie's) **£1,300**

AUGUST VON PETTENKOFEN - Portrait Of A Girl, Bust Length - oval - 21 x 17in.
(Christie's) **£1,000**

JOHN PETTIE - The Herbalist - signed - 28 x 20in.
(Sotheby's) **£340**

PETTITT - Loch Katrine - 1876 - 36 x 61 cm.
(Edmiston's) £56

CHARLES PETTITT - A Woody River Landscape, With Fishing Boats - 20 x 28in.
(Christie's) £280

JOSEPH PAUL PETTITT - Bolton Abbey; The Strid, Wharfedale, Yorkshire - both signed and dated '72 - each 18 x 14in.
(Sotheby's Belgravia) £550 Pair

CHARLES PHILIPON - Le Marriage; Franchissant La Marne - pen and ink and coloured crayons - one signed and the other signed and dated '52 - one 8 x 12in. and the other 11½ x 7¼in.
(Sotheby's) £25 Two

JOHN PHILLIP - Spanish Girl With Fan - on panel - 59 x 50cm.
(Edmiston's) £380

T. PHILLIPS - Portrait Of John Chaloner, half length, Wearing Van Dyck Style Costume - bears inscription - 29 x 24in.
(Christie's) £95

THOMAS PHILLIPS - Portrait Of Mary Anne Dunn, Wife Of Francis William, Afterwards 6th Earl Of Seafield, Seated, three-quarter length, With A Landscape Beyond - signed and inscribed on the reverse - 49½ x 39½in.
(Christie's) £220

PHILLIPS - Art And Liberty - 21 x 15½in.
(Sotheby's Belgravia) £40

L. PHILPOT - Still life, mixed flowers in a glass vase - oil on canvas - signed - 24 x 18 ins.
(Jackson—Stops & Staff) £42

JEAN PICART-LEDOUX - La Tour Au Bord D'Un Lac - charcoal and watercolour - signed - 10¼ x 14¼in.
(Sotheby's) £30

PABLO PICASSO - Le Hibou Sur La Chaise - signed - dated 1947 on the reverse - 28¾ x 23½in.
(Sotheby's) £50,000

PABLO PICASSO - Buste De Femme - signed - on board laid down on panel - 30¼ x 22½in.
(Christie's, New York) **£194,100**

PABLO PICASSO - Verre - signed and inscribed - canvas on panel - 9 x 11½in.
(Sotheby's) **£13,500**

ANTON PICK - A View Of The Konigssee by Berchtesgaden - signed - 20 x 36½in.
(Sotheby's) **£580**

GEORGE PICKERING - Mill At Bonsale Dale, Derbyshire - inscribed and numbered 15 on the reverse - 11¾ x 16¾in.
(Sotheby's) **£85**

HENRY PICKERING - Portrait Of Sir Wolstan Dixie, 4th Baronet And His Family - signed and dated 1755 - 111 x 159in.
(Christie's) **£4,800**

J. L. PICKERING - 'Under A Northern Sky' - signed - oil - 50 x 36in.
(Warner, Sheppard & Wade) **£70**

W. H. PIGOTT - Bringing Home The Flock - 13 x 19in.
(Sotheby's Belgravia) **£70**

SIDNEY PIKE - Rounding Up The Sheep - watercolour - 10 x 14in.
(G. A. Key) **£32**

WILLIAM H. PIKE - 'In The Village Of Hessenford, Cornwall' - signed and inscribed on the reverse - oil on canvas - 20 x 30in.
(Bearnes & Waycotts) **£340**

HENRY PILLEAU - Venice - heightened with bodycolour - signed with monogram - 7¼ x 4¾in.
(Sotheby's Belgravia) **£60**

PILLEMENT - A River Landscape, A Fisherman And Washer Women in the foreground - on panel - 9 x 11in.
(Sotheby's) **£500**

JEAN BAPTISTE PILLEMENT - An Italianate Coastal Landscape With Fishermen in the foreground And Moored Sailing Vessels Beyond - 17½ x 26in.
(Christie's) **£2,600**

J. B. PILLEMENT - A Decorative
Panel, Depicting Rustic Lovers In A Land-
scape In A Pendant Cartouche With A
Decorative Floral Surround - 66 x 37½in.
(Christie's) **£480**

WILMOT PILSBURY - 'A Footbridge' -
signed and dated 1896 - watercolour -
7 x 11in.
(Warner, Sheppard & Wade) **£15**

JEAN BAPTISTE PILLEMENT - Shipwrecked Sailors On A Rock, A Sailing
Boat Nearby - signed and dated 1786 -
20 x 29in.
(Christie's) **£2,500**

PINTURICCHIO, Circle Of - The Virgin
And Child With The Infant Saint John
The Baptist - on gold ground panel -
circular - 24½in. diam.
(Christie's) **£2,800**

PINTURICCHIO - The Madonna And
Child - on panel - 21 x 15in.
(Christie's) **£800**

JEAN-BAPTISTE PILLEMENT - A Rocky
Coastal Landscape, with men salvaging
wreckage - signed and inscribed '14 v.81' -
21¼ x 31¾in.
(Christie's) **£6,000**

GEORGE JOHN PINWELL - Study For
'The Fiddler And Flower Girl' - pencil
and watercolour heightened with white -
signed with monogram - 4¾ x 6in.
(Christie's) **£100**

DOMENICO PIOLA, Circle Of - The
Holy Family With The Infant Baptist -
39 x 29in.
(Sotheby's) **£800**

JEAN-BAPTISTE PILLEMENT - A Rocky
River Landscape, with washerwomen and a
rustic bridge; and A Rocky Wooded Landscape, with peasants caught in a storm - one
signed - 20 x 24in.
(Christie's) **£8,500 Pair**

ANTOINE PIOTROWSKI - An Officer
In A Horse Drawn Cart Passing Peasants
On A Country Road - signed - inscribed
'Paris' and dated 1883 - 16¾ x 26in.
(Sotheby's) **£1,300**

PIRE

MARCEL PIRE - Still Life Of Fish - oil on canvas - signed - 73 x 92cm.
(Galerie Moderne) **£204**

VIVIAN PITCHFORTH - Shipping near a pier - pencil and watercolour - signed - 16¼ x 22¾ ins.
(Sotheby's) **£90**

CAMILLE PISSARRO - Cour De La Maison De Piette A Montfoucault - signed and dated 1876 - 25½ x 21¼in.
(Sotheby's) **£40,000**

CAMILLE PISSARRO - Baigneuses - signed and dated 1896 - 28¾ x 36¼in.
(Sotheby's) **£83,000**

CAMILLE PISSARRO - Paysage A Eragny, Le Pre - signed and dated '97 - 25½ x 36¼in.
(Sotheby's) **£58,000**

HENRIE PITCHER - Portrait Of A Scotsman, head and shoulders - signed and dated 1902 - 19¾ x 15½in.
(Sotheby's Belgravia) **£18**

WILLIAM PITT - Lane at Kingston, South Devon and Kingston Church - a pair - one signed with mongram and dated 1865 - both signed, inscribed and dated on the reverse - 19 x 8 ins.
(Christie's, S. Kensington) **£580 Pair**

WILLIAM PITT - On the Thames, Ditton Hampden - signed with monogram and dated 1882 - signed, inscribed and dated on the reverse - 11½ x 21½ ins.
(Christie's, S. Kensington) **£440**

PLATZIER - Peasants Making Music And Drinking, Outside An Inn - on panel - 7½ x 10¾in.
(Sotheby's) **£280**

ROWLAND PLUMBE - Children In Wooded Landscapes, One With Sea In The Distance - signed - 36 x 28in
(Woolley & Wallis) **£155 Pair**

N. POCOCK - River Scene With A Paddle Steamer And Numerous Figures On The River Banks - oil on canvas - 19½ x 29½in.
(Bearnes & Waycotts) **£2,500**

NICHOLAS POCOCK - The Engagement Between The Frigates 'La Nymphe' and 'Cleopatre' - signed and dated 1795 - 25¼ x 36¼in.
(Christie's) **£2,400**

NICHOLAS POCOCK - 'Capture Of 'La Virginie' French Frigate of 44 Guns By H.M. Ship 'Indefatigable', Commanded By Sir Edward Pellew By Moonlight, April 21st, 1797' - signed and dated 1797 - oil on canvas - 25¼ x 36¼in.
(Bearnes & Waycotts) **£800**

NICHOLAS POCOCK - 'The Avon With Shipping 1771' - signed - watercolour - 15½ x 22¼in.
(Bearnes & Waycotts) **£1,400**

NICHOLAS POCOCK - The Avon Gorge, Looking Towards The Hot Wells - signed and dated 1786 - watercolour - 16 x 20½in.
(Christie's) **£600**

E. POCOCKE - Bishop Bridge, Norwich - watercolour - 5 x 7in.
(G. A. Key) **£12**

EDWARD CHARLES POCOCKE - Fore Street, Ipswich - watercolour - 3 x 5in.
(G. A. Key) **£15**

POELENBERG - Nymphs Dancing By A Ruin In An Italianate Landscape - on panel - 11 x 13¼in.
(Christie's) **£550**

CORNELIS VAN POELENBERG - The Flight Into Egypt - on panel - 8 x 10in.
(Christie's) **£1,400**

POELEMBURG

CORNELIS POELEMBURG - Festival Of Venus, A Landscape With Numerous Terrestrial And Celestial Figures - on keyed oak panel with three seals with coronets - 52.5 x 45cm.
(Edmiston's) **£2,100**

CHARLES POERSON - Ceres With A Satyr, Reclining On A Sheaf Of Corn, A Sickle In Her Hand, And Kneeling Beside Her A Satyr, In The Background A Fountain And Standing Corn - on panel - circular - diameter 5in.
(Sotheby's) **£1,900**

CHARLES H. POINGDESTRE - 'Cintella On The Sabine Mountains' - signed and dated 1879 - 46 x 73cm.
(Phillips) **£450**

EUGENE LE POITTEVIN - L'Attente - oil on canvas - signed - 46 x 56cm.
(Galerie Moderne) **£200**

IVAN POKITONOV - A Peasant Woman Sewing - signed and dated '82 - on panel - 4¾ x 4¼in.
(Sotheby's) **£1,350**

P. POLAEN - Fishing Boats - 44 x 65cm.
(Edmiston's) **£10**

POLLARD - The Bristol To London Mail Arriving At An Inn At Night - 12½ x 20½in.
(Christie's) **£400**

ALFRED POLLENTINE - The Rialto, Venice - signed and dated - 29 x 49cm.
(Phillips) **£540**

SILVIO POMA - A Village On Lake Como - signed - oil on panel - 12 x 18in.
(Bonham's) **£480**

PONTORMO - Seated Male Nude - red chalk - 41.5 x 26.5 cm; and another attributed to Vouet
(Sotheby's) **£35 Two**

JAMES POOLE - A View In The Lake District, Derwentwater - signed and dated 1832 - and signed and inscribed on the reverse - 18 x 25in.
(Christie's) **£420**

PAUL FALCONER POOLE - The Fisherman's Daughter - watercolour heightened with white - signed - 21 x 13¾in.
(Christie's) **£105**

LIUBOV POPOVA - Les Arbres recto - brush and indian ink and penil - Tete d'Homme verso - pencil - 14 x 8¾in.
(Sotheby's) **£160**

LIUBOV POPOVA - Composition - black and purple gouache au pochoir - 9¾ x 7⅛in.
(Sotheby's) **£220**

JAN PORCELLIS - Dutch Fishing Boats In A Choppy Sea - signed with initials - 13½ x 22in.
(Christie's) **£8,000**

JEAN PORTAELS - Study Of A Nude - oil on lined canvas - 75 x 35cm.
(Galerie Moderne) **£43**

LOUIS PORTAELS - The Undergrowth - oil on wood - signed and dated 1868 - 66 x 54cm.
(Galerie Moderne) **£220**

LODEWYK TOEPUT, IL POSSOSERRATO - Saint Martin, Dividing His Cloak With The Beggar - 103 x 75½in.
(Christie's) **£2,200**

GEORGE HENRY LA PORTE - A Huntsman And Hounds Negotiating A Hedge - oil on canvas - 24½ x 29½in.
(King & Chasemore) **£620**

H. PORTEMAN - Grand Place A Bruxelles - on wood - signed - 24 x 30cm.
(Galerie Moderne) **£20**

VAN PORTEN - Dutch Harbour Scene - 30 x 46cm.
(Edmiston's) **£160**

GERARD PORTIELJE - Les Nouvelles De La Ville - signed and inscribed on the reverse - on panel - 6½ x 8½in.
(Sotheby's) **£1,700**

ALVARO DI PIETRO, called ALVARO PORTOGHESE - Head Of Saint Cosmas - on panel - 10½ x 8in.
(Christie's) **£1,260**

FRANS POST - Brazilian Peasants Feasting And Merrymaking In A Village with an extensive landscape beyond - signed and dated 164(or5)3 - on panel -19 x 26½in.
(Christie's) **£175,000**

GERMAIN POSTELLE - A Village Scene With A Clock Tower Incorporating A Clock Face, Sportsmen Resting in the foreground - signed and dated 1826 - 26 x 32in.
(Sotheby's) **£600**

LASLETT JOHN POTT - A Dampening Response - signed and dated 1880 - 22 x 27in.
(Christie's) **£350**

LASLETT JOHN POTT - The Invitation -
signed - 35 x 23½in.
(Sotheby's Belgravia) **£1,300**

N. POUSSIN - The Flight Into Egypt -
22 x 28in.
(Christie's) **£6,500**

POWELL - A Yacht Off The Coast -
9¼ x 13½in.
(Sotheby's Belgravia) **£130**

C. M. POWELL - Dutch Shipping In A
Squall, Men-O'-War Beyond - 14 x 19in.
(Christie's) **£950**

C. M. POWELL - Dutch Fishing Boats
Offshore In A Calm - signed - 14 x 19in.
(Christie's) **£1,700**

GEORGE HYDE POWNALL - Victoria
Embankment, By Night - signed -
inscribed on the reverse - on board - 5½
x 9in.
(Sotheby's Belgravia) **£55**

POYNTER - Salome - 31¼ x 19in.
(Sotheby's) **£40**

SIR EDWARD JOHN POYNTER -
Hardran Force - heightened with bodycolour - signed with monogram and
dated 1874 - 19¼ x 12¼in.
(Sotheby's Belgravia) **£160**

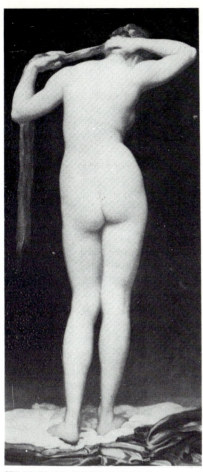

SIR EDWARD JOHN POYNTER - A
Lady At Her Toilet - 21½ x 10in.
(Christie's) **£1,600**

SIR EDWARD JOHN POYNTER -
Jessica - signed with monogram and
dated 1870 - watercolour - 11½ x
8 ins.
(Christie's) **£300**

F. POZZETTI - A Harbour Scene -
with a palace by the waterside and
sailing boats in the foreground -
watercolour - signed - 11½ x 18in.
(Christie's, New York) **£100**

JONATHAN PRATT - A Sister of
Mercy - signed with monogram -
on board - 11½ x 8¾ ins.
(Christie's) **£200**

C. PRATT - The Love Letter - 36 x 30in.
(Sotheby's Belgravia) **£110**

H. L. PRATT - 'Tamworth, On The River
Tame' - oil on canvas laid on board -
signed and dated 1854 - 21½ x 30in.
(King & Chasemore) **£210**

WILLIAM PRATT - Hauling In The Nets -
signed - 25½ x 31½in.
(Sotheby's) **£400**

357

PRAX

VALENTINE PRAX - Le Buveur - pen and indian ink, gouache and oil - on board - signed - 24¼ x 19¼in.
(Sotheby's) **£300**

ANDREA PREVITALI - Portrait Of A Young Man, small bust length, wearing a black cap and ermine-trimmed coat - inscribed on the reverse - on panel - 12 x 10in.
(Christie's) **£20,000**

EDWARD PRICE - Landscape - oil on lined canvas - signed and dated 1855 - 23 x 33cm.
(Galerie Moderne) **£110**

G. K. PRIECHENFRIED - A Quiet Hour - signed - on panel - 17 x 13in.
(Christie's) **£1,000**

E. PRIESTLEY - Village Scenes With Figures - oil - signed - 19½ x 29½in.
(Henry Spencer & Sons) **£170 Pair**

BERTRAM PRIESTMAN - A Dock Scene - signed and dated IV '14 - 15½ x 19½in.
(Sotheby's Belgravia) **£180**

LUCIANO PRINA - The Old Bridge - oil on canvas - signed - 46 x 55cm.
(Galerie Moderne) **£10**

LEON PRINTEMPS - A Veiled Nude - crayon - signed and dated 1919 - 60 x 41cm.
(Galerie Moderne) **£60**

EDWARD PRITCHETT - 'The Church Of S.S. Giovanni E. Paolo, Venice' - 25 x 36cm.
(Phillips) **£1,400**

EDWARD PRITCHETT - A View On The Grand Canal, Venice, With Figures in the foreground And The Piazza San Marco And The Doge's Palace Beyond - 33 x 46.5cm.
(Phillips) **£1,200**

EDWARD PRITCHETT - Venice: The Doge's Palace From The Dogana - pencil and watercolour - 9½ x 13½in.
(Christie's) **£550**

EDWARD PRITCHETT - The Rialto
Bridge, Venice - 9½ x 13½in.
(Christie's) **£650**

DOD PROCTER - Study Of A Nude
Girl - signed - oil on panel - 17½ x
14¼in.
(Bearnes & Waycotts) **£140**

S. PROUT - The Ship Inn - bears monogram - 11¼ x 17¼in.
(Sotheby's) **£50**

SAMUEL PROUT - Hulks Converted
To Domestic Use - pen and brown ink
and watercolour - 7¾ x 10¾in.
(Christie's) **£280**

SAMUEL PROUT - Boatman Under
The Arches - pencil - inscribed 'Paris'
under mount - 4¼ x 7¾in.
(Sotheby's) **£20**

SAMUEL PROUT - Launceston -
pencil and watercolour - 13 x 20¼in.
(Christie's) **£110**

SKINNER PROUT - Flemish Street Scene
With Street Traders In The Foreground And
Church Spire In The Far Distance - late 19th
century watercolour - signed - 14 x 10in.
(Lalonde Martin) **£100**

SKINNER PROUT - 'Aborigines Encampment' and 'Settlers Encampment' -
Australian Bush Scenes At Night - 19th
century watercolours - 10 x 14⅓in
(Lalonde Martin) **£2,900 pair**

JOHN SKINNER PROUT - King Charles
Tower, Chester - signed and dated 1858
- watercolour heightened with white -
16¾ x 12½in.
(Christie's) **£160**

JOHN SKINNER PROUT - A Figure
By A Mill In A Mountain Landscape -
watercolour heightened with white -
signed - 14¾ x 19½in.
(Christie's) **£180**

ALFRED PROVIS - A Mother And Child
In A Cottage Interior - 7 x 9½in.
(Christie's) **£300**

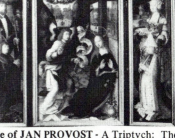

Circle of **JAN PROVOST** - A Triptych: The
Annunciation, flanked by Saint Matthew
with a donor, and Saint Catherine with the
donor's wife; on the reverse, Saint
Christopher carrying the Christ Child, and
Saint Anthony Abbot - the wings inscribed
with coats-of-arms - on panel - central
compartmen 47½ x 31in - wings
48½ x 14in.
(Christie's) **£22,000**

DOMENICO PULIGO - Portrait Of A Young
Man, half length, in black costume and hat,
holding a letter - oval - on panel - 25 x 19in.
(Christie's) **£5,500**

359

PRYCE

G. WILLIS PRYCE - Bridges, Llandrindod, Wales - both signed - each 8 x 12in.
(Sotheby's Belgravia) **£70 Pair**

LUCIEN PRZEDIORSKI - Decorating The Hat - signed - dated 1870 and inscribed 'Paris' - 23¼ x 19¼in.
(Sotheby's) **£650**

PULIGO - The Madonna And Child, And The Infant Saint John The Baptist - on panel - 28½ x 23in.
(Christie's) **£850**

SCIPIONE PULZONE, IL GAETANO - Salome With The Head Of Saint John The Baptist - signed and dated 1571 - 27½ x 35in.
(Christie's) **£550**

P. A. PUMFREY - Still Life in 17th Century Dutch Style, Flowers In An Alcove - signed - 24 x 20in.
(Woolley & Wallis) **£100**

IVAN PUNI - Two Studies for 'The Musician' - each pencil - one stamped with the signature - the second inscribed Paris - 2¾ x 3¾in.
(Sotheby's) **£150 Two**

MARG. PUTSAGE - Vase Trimmed With Flowers - cartoon - signed - 30 x 40cm.
(Galerie Moderne) **£6**

LEO PUTZ - Die Badende - oil - on canvas - signed - 33¾ x 47¼in.
(Sotheby's) **£580**

A. PYNACKER - Peasants Outside A Cavern In A Rocky Landscape - bears signature - on panel - 12 x 9in.
(Christie's) **£2,800**

GEORGE PYNE - Rugby School - signed and dated 1859 - pencil and watercolour - 6¼ x 8in.
(Christie's) **£350**

GEORGE PYNE - A Jacobean Country House - signed and dated 1835 - watercolour - 7½ x 10½in.
(Christie's) **£100**

JAMES BAKER PYNE - Lyons From The Saone - indistinctly signed - circular - diameter 24in.
(Sotheby's Belgravia) **£320**

JAMES BAKER PYNE - Bristol Harbour - heightened with bodycolour - signed - dated 1835 - 13 x 19in.
(Sotheby's Belgravia) **£700**

JAMES BAKER PYNE - A Farmstead In The Hills - signed and dated 1842 - 10¾ x 17¼in.
(Sotheby's Belgravia) **£100**

JAMES BAKER PYNE - Lago Maggiore - signed and dated 1868 - 24 x 32¾in.
(Sotheby's Belgravia) **£800**

JAMES BAKER PYNE - A View of Sand's-End, Yorkshire - signed and dated 1846 and numbered - 26½ x 36 ins.
(Christie's) **£1600**

PYNE - Entrance to Harbour (Venetian Scene) - dated 1834 - watercolour - 9¾ x 13¼ ins.
(J. Entwistle & Co.) **£275**

WILLIAM HENRY PYNE - A Boy Playing A Drum In The Garden Of A Country House - signed and dated 1793 - pen and grey ink and watercolour - 11¾ x 15in.
(Christie's) **£300**

LAM QUA - Portrait of Leonard Millett, small half length, wearing naval uniform - inscribed and dated Canton October 1843 - 9 x 7½ ins.
(Christie's) **£400**

HRH QUEEN VICTORIA - Portrait Of A Lady By A Vase Of Flowers, half length - signed with initials - 7 x 5½in.
(Sotheby's Belgravia) **£75**

JOSEPH QUINAUX - The Washerwomen - oil on canvas - 35 x 45cm.
(Galerie Moderne) **£57**

ALFRED ROBERT QUINTON - A Farmstead Looking Over A River Landscape - signed - 20½ x 14in.
(Sotheby's Belgravia) **£110**

ALFRED ROBERT QUINTON - The Church Gate, Welford On Avon, Gloucestershire - heightened with bodycolour - signed - 7½ x 10½in.
(Sotheby's Belgravia) **£30**

EDWARD QUITTON - The Botany Lesson - signed and dated Anvers 1876 - on panel - 26 x 19 ins.
(Christie's) **£800**

ARTHUR RACKHAM - 'Taught Them To
Fly Kites' - watercolour and pen and ink -
signed, inscribed and dated '04 -
16½ x 12½in.
(King & Chasemore)   **£120**

ARTHUR RACKHAM - Portrait Of The
Artist's Daughter: Beryl Decides To
Dress Arabella Stuart Like The Little
Elizabethan Lady - signed and inscribed
on the reverse - pen and black ink and
watercolour - 12½ x 9½in.
(Christie's)   **£850**

ARTHUR RACKHAM - A Silhouette:
Ding, Dong, Bell,
Pussy's In The Well! - signed - pen and
black ink, black wash - 7 x 10in.
(Christie's)   **£320**

ARTHUR RACKHAM - 'Die Blatter
Fielen, Der Rabe Schrie Hohl ....' -
signed with monogram - inscribed and
dated 1910 - pen and black ink and
watercolour - 18¾ x 12¼in.
(Christie's)   **£950**

ARTHUR RACKHAM - 'She Did Not Go
Once But Many Times Backwards And
Forwards To The Well' - watercolour and
pen and ink - signed, inscribed and dated
1900 - 20½ x 11½in.
(King & Chasemore)   **£240**

W. LESLIE RACKHAM - Spring At
Acle And St. Benets Abbey By Moon-
light - oil - 8 x 12in.
(G. A. Key)   **£70**

W. LESLIE RACKHAM - Broadland
Scenes With Wherrys And Yachts - water-
colours
(G. A. Key)   **£36 Pair**

JAMES RADFORD - Bow Bridge, Near
Totnes, Devon - signed and dated 1844 -
25 x 36in.
(Sotheby's Belgravia)   **£700**

HENRY RAEBURN - Man With A
White Necktie - oil on canvas - 61 x
51cm.
(Galerie Moderne)   **£240**

SIR HENRY RAEBURN - Portrait Of
Mrs Walter Learmouth, half length,
Wearing A White Dress Standing In A
Landscape - 29½ x 24½in.
(Christie's)   **£1,800**

L. RAINER - In The Crypt - heightened
with bodycolour - bears signature -
23¼ x 19¼in.
(Sotheby's Belgravia)   **£15**

RAMSAY - Portrait Of A Lady, Seated,
three-quarter length, In A White Dress
And Black Shawl, In A Landscape -
39 x 29in.
(Christie's)   **£150**

A. RAMSAY - Portrait Of A Gentleman,
three-quarter length, Wearing A Green
Coat And Blue Gold Embroidered Vest -
49 x 39in.
(Christie's)   **£450**

JEAN P. RAMSAY - The Red Jacket -
heightened with bodycolour - signed -
inscribed and dated 1944 - 15½ x 20½in.
(Sotheby's Belgravia)   **£50**

JEAN P. RAMSAY - The Thermopylae,
Red Jacket, Leander and Another In
Open Seas - all heightened with body-
colour - each 7½ x 11in.
(Sotheby's Belgravia)   **£130 Four**

AUBREY RAMUS - Descending Mists -
signed - 19 x 29in.
(Sotheby's Belgravia)   **£28**

S. RANFLE - A Country Woman With Three
Children Beneath A Wayside Shrine - signed
and dated 1839, Wien - watercolour - 12¾ x
10½in.
(Warner, Sheppard & Wade)   **£32**

SCOTT RANKIN - Study Of A Terrier -
oil - 14½ x 10½in.
(Thomas Love & Sons Ltd)   **£5**

RAPHAEL, After - Madonna Of The
Goldfinch - oil on panel - 41½ x
29¾in.
(Bearnes & Waycotts)   **£240**

RAPHAEL, After - The Transfiguration -
16½ x 12½in.
(Sotheby's)   **£120**

RAPPINI

R. RAPPINI - By Eastern Waters - both
heightened with bodycolour - signed -
each 10½ x 14½in.
(Sotheby's Belgravia) **£25 Pair**

CARL RASMUSSEN - Young Fisherlads
On The Coast At Sunset - signed and
dated 1874 - 16¾ x 29in.
(Sotheby's) **£450**

RATHBONE - An Autumn River Landscape - 9 x 11¼in.
(Sotheby's) **£220**

J. RATHBONE - A Woodland Road
Beside A Stream - on panel - 5½ x 7in.
(Sotheby's) **£160**

JOHN RATHBONE - Wooded River
Landscapes - both signed with initials -
on panel - 5 x 4in.
(Christie's) **£310 Pair**

J. G. RAVEN - Landscape With Cottage
And Figures Near Warboys - oil -
16 x 24in.
(G. A. Key) **£50**

JOHN SAMUEL RAVEN - Harlech
Castle - signed with monogram and dated
1873 - 35 x 59in.
(Sotheby's Belgravia) **£350**

JOHN SAMUEL RAVEN - Winter Landscape With Five Figures - signed - oil on
canvas - 6¼ x 8½in.
(Bearnes & Waycotts) **£250**

AUGUSTE RAVIER - Coucher De
Soleil - oil on panel - signed - 7¾ x 12¼in.
(Sotheby's) **£600**

AUGUSTE RAVIER - Environs De
Morestel Du Haut De La Colline A Bour-
denou - oil on canvas - signed - 9¼ x
10¼in.
(Sotheby's) **£360**

LOUISE RAYNER - Great St. Mary's
Church And Market Place, Cambridge -
signed - 14½ x 21¾in.
(Bonham's) **£1,200**

LOUIS RAYNER - Minster Street,
Salisbury - watercolour heightened
with white - signed - 13¾ x 10in.
(Christie's) **£1,100**

S. RAYNER - The Crypt Of Four Crosses Abbey - gouache - 19¾ x 30½in. *(Sotheby's Belgravia)* **£22**

SAMUEL RAYNER - The Tomb Of Catherine Parr, Sudeley Castle - signed with monogram and dated 1859 - on panel - 15½ x 21½in. *(Christie's)* **£180**

G. RECCO - Crabs And Fish With An Owl In A Landscape - 58 x 44⅛in. *(Christie's)* **£1,300**

GIUSEPPE RECCO - A Still Life, With An Eel In A Bowl Of Water And Other Fish On A Ledge - signed with initials - 28¾ x 39¼in. *(Christie's)* **£4,000**

ARTHUR W. REDGATE - Family Affection; Cattle By A River - both signed - one inscribed on the reverse - 7½ x 11½in. *(Sotheby's Belgravia)* **£180 Pair**

ARTHUR W. REDGATE - Harvest Time - signed - 19½ x 29½in. *(Sotheby's Belgravia)* **£270**

ARTHUR W. REDGATE - A Welcome Refreshment - signed - 19½ x 29½in. *(Sotheby's Belgravia)* **£320**

REDGRAVE - Roslin Castle - on board - 19 x 23¼in. *(Sotheby's Belgravia)* **£35**

REDMORE - Coastal Scenes, With Sailing Barges And Rowing Boats, And Harbour Buildings in the distance - oil - 8½ x 12in. *(Henry Spencer & Sons)* **£190 Pair**

E. REDMORE - Off The Dutch Coast - signed with red monogram - 29 x 55cm. *(Edmiston's)* **£260**

HENRY REDMORE - Fishing Smacks, A Man-O'-War And Other Shipping At Anchor, With Fishermen in the foreground - signed and dated 1869 - 24.5 x 38.5cm. *(Phillips)* **£1,150**

HENRY REDMORE - Two Men O' War Becalmed In Estuary - signed and dated 1856 - 24 x 18in. *(Dee & Atkinson)* **£2,400**

HENRY REDMORE - Shipping off the Coast - signed - 24 x 42 ins. *(Woolley & Wallis)* **£440**

HENRY REDMORE - Men-O'-War And Other Vessels Offshore - signed and dated 1853 - 13 x 18½in. *(Christie's)* **£260**

REDNER - The Chorus Girl - signed and dated 1931 - 18¾ x 22¾in. *(Sotheby's)* **£40**

REDPATH

ANNE REDPATH - Before The Voyage; The Discovery - all signed - on board - each 34 x 46in.
(Sotheby's) £220 Three

ANNE REDPATH - Fighting At Sea; On The Quayside - both signed - on board - each 34 x 33½in.
(Sotheby's) £220 Pair

ANNE REDPATH - The White Gloxinia - signed - 34 x 44in.
(Sotheby's) £950

L. E. REED - A View Of Newton Abbot From Orwell Hill - signed and dated 1837 - 23½ x 35½in.
(Christie's) £350

C. REEVES - 'To The Rescue', Farmyard Scene with Terrier and Cockerel defending his Young - signed and dated '92 - on canvas - 14 x 18in.
(Morphet & Morphet) £360

JEAN-BAPTISTE REGNAULT - Cupid And Psyche - on panel - 23 x 18½in.
(Christie's) £1,000

FLORA M. REID - Two Women Digging Potatoes - oil on canvas - dated 1883 - 27 x 18in.
(Bracketts) £270

H. REID - 'An Early Naval Engagement' - signed - oil - on metal panel - 10 x 14in.
(Butler & Hatch Waterman) £50

R. PAYTON REID - 'Addio Mia Bella Napoli' - signed and dated '03 - signed and inscribed on reverse - 15¼ x 11¼in.
(Christie's) £240

DAVID REID-HENRY - Kudu; The Kill - both signed - 14 x 18in.
(Sotheby's Belgravia) £250 Pair

DAVID REID-HENRY - An Elephant - signed - 14 x 18in.
(Sotheby's Belgravia) £80

RAMSAY RICHARD REINAGLE - Westminster Abbey From Green Park - 16½ x 20¼in.
(Christie's) £1,400

RAMSAY RICHARD REINAGLE - Fishermen Hauling In A Net Off The Italian Coast - watercolour - signed and dated 1812 - 37½ x 55in. *(Christie's)* **£500**

CHRISTIAN REK - A Priest Playing A Cello - signed - on panel - 7 x 5in. *(Sotheby's)* **£200**

STUDIO OF REMBRANDT - Bust Portrait Of A Man In A Reddish Brown Coat And Cap - on panel - 10¾ x 8½in. *(Sotheby's)* **£2,000**

GUIDO RENI - Rosa De Tivoli - oil on canvas - signed - 1m.05 x 86cm. *(Galerie Moderne)* **£377**

GEORGE MELVIN RENNIE - Iona And The Sound Of Mull - signed - 29 x 38½in. *(Sotheby's)* **£520**

GEORGE MELVIN RENNIE - "Loch Hourne" - oil - 20 x 30in. *(Thomas Love & Sons Ltd)* **£45**

PIERRE-AUGUSTE RENOIR - Fruits, Oranges Et Citrons - stamped with signature - 7½ x 12½in. *(Sotheby's)* **£7,000**

PIERRE-AUGUSTE RENOIR - Vase De Fleurs - signed - 16¼ x 15in. *(Christie's, New York)* **£71,200**

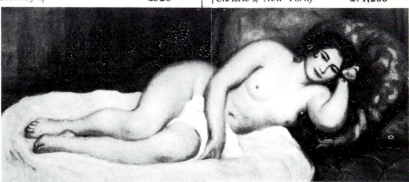

PIERRE-AUGUSTE RENOIR - Baigneuse Couchee - signed and dated - 25¾ x 61¼in.   *(Christie's, New York)*   **£388,200**

PIERRE-AUGUSTE RENOIR - Les
Environs De Varengeville - signed -
19¾ x 25in.
(Sotheby's) **£36,000**

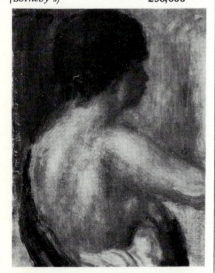

PIERRE-AUGUSTE RENOIR - Petit Nu
Assis - signed - 7¼ x 5¼in.
(Sotheby's) **£10,000**

PIERRE-AUGUSTE RENOIR - Nature
Morte Aux Pommes Et Poires - signed -
7½ x 10¾in.
(Sotheby's) **£15,700**

PIERRE-AUGUSTE RENOIR - La Jeune
Fille Au Banc - signed - 25¼ x 20½in.
(Sotheby's) **£125,000**

GERHARDT VON RENTENR - 'The
Casket' - signed with initials and dated
1836 - 17½ x 15½in.
(Warner, Sheppard & Wade) **£1,700**

REVERENZ - The Prioress - indistinctly
signed - inscribed 'Munchen' and dated
1874 - on panel - 15¼ x 9in.
(Sotheby's) **£80**

ANTONIO REYNA - A Venetian
Canal Scene With Numerous Gondolas -
signed and inscribed - 26.5 x 47cm.
(Phillips) **£1,300**

ANTONIO REYNA - Capriccio Views Of
Venice With Figures And Shipping - both
signed and one inscribed Venezia - 10½ x
18½in.
(Christie's) **£2,600 Pair**

ANTONIO REYNA - A View Of San
Trovaso, Venice, With The Boat Yard -
signed - 11¼ x 19½in.
(Christie's) **£1,100**

REYNOLDS, After - Late 18th century -
Portrait Of A Gentleman In Red Surcoat -
oil - on canvas - 20 x 26in.
(Butler & Hatch Waterman) **£60**

REYNOLDS, After - Portrait Of A
Lady Wearing A Pink Dress And Holding
A Dove - oil on canvas - 34¾ x 26¾in.
(Bearnes & Waycotts) **£210**

STUDIO OF SIR JOSHUA REYNOLDS -
Portrait Of The Countess Of Dartmouth,
three-quarter length, In Peeress's Robes,
Standing Near A Chair, Holding A
Coronet - 49 x 39in.
(Christie's) **£750**

SIR J. REYNOLDS - A Child Seated
Beside A Lamb At A Spring, oil on
canvas - 27½ x 35½in.
(Bearnes & Waycotts) **£75**

SIR JOSHUA REYNOLDS - Portrait Of Mrs
Richard Hoare, Seated, In A White Dress,
With Her Son Henry On Her Lap - half
length - 29 x 24½in.
(Christie's) **£3,800**

SIR JOSHUA REYNOLDS - Portrait Of A
Lady, Apparently Mrs. Trecothick -
93 x 57in.
(Christie's) **£6,000**

SIR JOSHUA REYNOLDS - A Family
Distinction, With An Ayah; Traditionally
identified As Lord Clive And His Family -
55 x 67½in.
(Christie's) **£105,000**

SIR JOSHUA REYNOLDS - Portrait Of
Elizabeth Bridget Morris, Later Mrs.
Lockwood, half length, Wearing A Pink
And White Dress With A Blue Mantle -
29½ x 24½in.
(Christie's) **£650**

SIR JOSHUA REYNOLDS - The Nativity -
arched top - 35¼ x 19½in.
(Christie's) **£2,600**

REYNOLDS
SAMUEL WILLIAM REYNOLDS -
Windsor Castle From The River - inscribed
on a label on reverse - on board -
11¾ x 18½in.
(Christie's) **£350**

FELICE A. REZIA - Views in Rouen -
a pair - signed and dated 1878 - on
paper laid on panel - 13½ x 11 ins.
(Christie's, S. Kensington) **£500 Pair**

SCHOOL OF THE MIDDLE RHINE,
Second Half Of The 15th Century -
The Flagellation - Christ Bound To A
Column, Beaten By Three Men - on
panel - 43½ x 34½in.
(Sotheby's) **£6,000**

SCHOOL OF THE UPPER RHINE,
Late 15th Century - St. Anthony Abbot
Holding A Staff Surmounted By A Tau-
Cross, A Bell And A Book, Beside Him
A Hog With A Bell On Its Collar - gold
ground - on panel - 13¾ x 8in.
(Sotheby's) **£1,600**

J. N. RHODES - Evening Landscape With
A Young Boy Leading A White Horse -
signed and dated 1831 - oil on canvas -
9 x 14in.
(Morphet & Morphet) **£140**

RIAR - Landscape - on paper - signed -
12 x 18cm.
(Galerie Moderne) **£5**

ARTURO RICCI - Twixt Love And
Riches - signed - inscribed - oil on canvas
- 17 x 24in.
(Bonham's) **£3,300**

M. RICCI - The Rehearsal Of An Opera -
16½ x 22in.
(Sotheby's)   **£8,500**

S. RICCI - Hercules And Omphale -
73 x 53in.
(Christie's)   **£5,500**

S. RICCI, After Tintoretto - The
Adoration Of The Golden Calf - 41 x 31in.
(Christie's)   **£1,400**

ALFRED WILLIAM RICH - A River
Landscape With A Windmill - water-
colour - signed - 4½ x 6½in.
(Christie's)   **£38**

FRANK RICHARDS - Head Study Of A
Girl - signed with monogram - inscribed
and dated '88 - 10½ x 9in.
(Sotheby's Belgravia)   **£20**

JOHN RICHARDS - River Landscapes
With Figures And Cattle - bodycolour ·
oval - 8½ x 10¾in.
(Christie's)   **£200 Pair**

JOHN INIGO RICHARDS - A View Of Old
Westminster Bridge With The Royal Barge
And Other Boats in the foreground -
23 x 43½in.
(Christie's)   **£4,200**

W. RICHARDS - 'Queen's View Killie-
crankie' and 'Brig o'Teith, Doone' -
signed - oil on canvas - 19½ x 29½in.
(Bearnes & Waycotts)   **£140 Pair**

RICHARDSON - Portrait Of A Gentleman, half length, Wearing A Turban -
pencil and white chalk on blue paper -
6 x 4½in.
(Sotheby's)   **£70**

RICHARDSON - St. Giles Cathedral,
Edinburgh - bears initials - 13½ x 9½in.
(Sotheby's)   **£20**

RICHARDSON - Portrait Of John Parker Of
Woodthorpe As A Boy - 27½ x 22in.
(Woolley & Wallis)   **£300**

CHARLES RICHARDSON - On The
Moor At Bocklesbury - signed - 6 x 8¼in.
(Sotheby's Belgravia)   **£38**

EDWARD RICHARDSON - Lake Scenes
With Castles - signed - watercolour -
8¼ x 12in.
(Bearnes & Waycotts)   **£100 Pair**

JOHN RICHARDSON - Boats In A
Harbour - oil on canvas - signed and
dated 1906 - 51 x 76cm.
(Galerie Moderne)   **£47**

JONATHAN RICHARDSON - Portrait Of
Lady Mary Wartley Montague, in Landscape
Background - three-quarter length -
48 x 37in.
(Woolley & Wallis)   **£660**

THOMAS MILES RICHARDSON, JNR -
Fisherfolk Near A Boat On The Shore -
watercolour heightened with white -
oval - signed and dated 1882 - 9½ x
13½in.
(Christie's)   **£280**

THOMAS MILES RICHARDSON, JNR -
A Street In A German Town - heightened
with bodycolour - signed with initials -
9¼ x 13in.
(Sotheby's)   **£150**

RICHARDSON

THOMAS MILES RICHARDSON, JNR - Durham - watercolour heightened with white - signed and dated 1859 - 16¼ x 24¾.
(Christie's) **£750**

THOMAS MILES RICHARDSON, SNR - Fishermen By The Shore Of A North Italian Lake - watercolour heightened with white - signed - 7½ x 19½in.
(Christie's) **£340**

THOMAS MILES RICHARDSON - 'Off The Italian Coast' - watercolour - signed and indistinctly dated - 12½ x 26½in.
(King & Chasemore) **£145**

WILLIAM RICHARDSON - A View On The Thames - signed and dated 1851-2 - 36 x 66½in.
(Sotheby's Belgravia) **£600**

HERMAN RICHIR - Woman In A Red Jacket - oil on canvas - signed - 80 x 60cm.
(Galerie Moderne) **£150**

RICHMOND - Portrait Of A Gentleman, Seated, half length - 30 x 25in.
(Sotheby's Belgravia) **£50**

SIR WILLIAM BLAKE RICHMOND - Studies Of A Sleeping Dog - pen and brown ink, brown wash - 5¼ x 8¼in.
(Christie's) **£20**

SIR WILLIAM BLAKE RICHMOND - The Entombment - gouache and gold - arched top - 12 x 24¼in.
(Sotheby's Belgravia) **£30**

RICHTER - Portrait Of German Peasant Lad - oil - 28 x 14in.
(G. A. Key) **£50**

H. DAVID RICHTER - Springtime - Flowers And Still Life - 100 x 75cm.
(Edmiston's) **£150**

J. G. RICHTER - The Doge's Palace, Venice From The Bacino Looking Towards The Grand Canal - 28 x 43½in.
(Christie's) **£1,200**

J. A. RIDDEL - Two Goats In A Landscape - 49 x 60cm.
(Edmiston's) **£164**

P. RIDEOUT - Old Time Coaching Scenes - oils - 7 x 14in.
(G. A. Key) **£54 Pair**

PHILIP H. RIDEOUT - Before The Hunt; Taking A Fence; In Full Cry - all signed and dated 1890 - one 11½ x 19½ - two 11¾ x 15½in.
(Sotheby's Belgravia) **£150 Three**

PHILIP H. RIDEOUT - A Coach And
Four - signed and indistinctly dated -
9¾ x 13½in.
(Sotheby's Belgravia) **£55**

PHILIP H. RIDEOUT - A Coach-And-
Four In A Country Lane - signed and
dated 1890 - on board - 5¼ x 8½in.
(Sotheby's Belgravia) **£40**

P. H. RIDEOUT - A Coaching Scene - oil on
board - signed and dated 1903 - 14 x 6½in.
(J. Francis, T. Jones & Sons) **£40**

S. RIER - Vase Trimmed With Flowers -
oil on lined canvas - signed - 29 x 23cm.
(Galerie Moderne) **£20**

RIGAUD - Portrait Of Louis XIV,
bust length, Dressed In Armour -
oval - 13 x 10½in.
(Sotheby's) **£80**

PIETER DE RING - A Bowl Of Strawberries,
grapes, a pewter plate and a gold watch on a
table - signed with initials - 20½ x 18in.
(Christie's) **£10,000**

ALICE RISCHGITZ - The Young
Draughtsman - signed - 15¾ x 11¼in.
(Sotheby's) **£120**

LEOPOLD RIVERS - Wooded Landscape
With Boy And Donkey Coming Up Hill From
Cottage By Man Bundling Brushwood -
signed - 19½ x 29½in.
(Phillips) **£300**

BRITON RIVIERE - Collies - black
chalk and watercolour heightened with
white on grey paper - signed with monogram - 17¾ x 23¼in.
(Christie's) **£50**

BRITON RIVIERE - Head Study Of A
Lion - black and brown chalks - signed
with monogram - 21 x 24in.
(Sotheby's Belgravia) **£80**

BRITON RIVIERE - Endymion, 'Ah,
well-a-day, Why Should our young
Endymion pine away' - Keats - signed
and dated '80 - 40¾ x 56¼in.
(Sotheby's Belgravia) **£1,500**

BRITON RIVIERE - 'Una And The
Lion' - signed and dated 1882 - 106
x 150cm.
(Phillips) **£1,900**

C. W. ROBB - Still Life Of Fish And A
Rod In A Cove - signed and indistinctly
dated - 12¾ x 20in.
(Sotheby's Belgravia) **£32**

ROBERT

HUBERT ROBERT - Roman Ruins With
An Equestrian Statue - oval - 19¾ x
24½in.
(Sotheby's) **£9,500**

HUBERT ROBERT - A Wooded Landscape,
with a woman seated by a fallen tree playing
with her children; and A Landscape Garden,
with a woman and children seated by a
statue, a fountain beyond - ovals -
18½ x 14½in.
(Christie's) **£20,000 Pair**

L L-ROBERT - L'Arrivee Des Moisson-
neurs Dans Les Marais Pontins, Rome:
Le Retour Du Pelerinage A La Madone
De L'Arc, Naples - both inscribed on
the reverse - both on metal - 12 x 14½in.
(Sotheby's) **£1,200 Pair**

DAVID ROBERTS - The Interior Of The
Church Of SS. Giovanni E Paolo, Venice -
inscribed - pencil and watercolour on
buff paper - 9¾ x 7in.
(Christie's) **£280**

DAVID ROBERTS - A View Of The
Houses Of Parliament From Across The
Thames - 69 x 58.5cm.
(Phillips) **£850**

DAVID ROBERTS - A Herdsman With
Cattle In An Extensive Landscape - signed
and dated 1838 - 10¾ x 23½in.
(Christie's) **£600**

EDWIN ROBERTS - The Bashful Lover,
Or Faint Heart - signed - inscribed on
the reverse - 35½ x 27½in.
(Sotheby's Belgravia) **£2,100**

EDWIN ROBERTS - A Hard Case -
signed with monogram and dated 1870 -
23 x 19½in.
(Sotheby's Belgravia) **£900**

EDWIN ROBERTS - Soldier's Return -
signed - 17½ x 13½in.
(Sotheby's Belgravia) **£550**

LARPORT ROBERTS - Wooded Landscape With Figures On Path - oil -
20 x 30in.
(G. A. Key) **£20**

LARPORT ROBERTS - Golden Eve,
Millers Dale, Derbyshire - oil - 30 x 20in.
(G. A. Key) **£28**

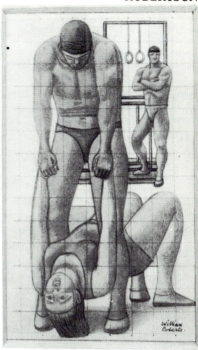

WILLIAM ROBERTS - The Acrobats -
signed - pencil and wash - 7¼ x 4¼in.
(Bonham's) **£140**

G. ROBERTSON - Portrait Of A Girl With
Bouquet of Flowers - oil on canvas - signed -
36 x 33in.
(J. Francis, T. Jones & Sons) **£80**

TOM ROBERTSON - A Scottish Harbour -
signed and dated 1886 - 7½ x 13½in.
(Sotheby's) **£60**

TOM ROBERTSON - On The Banks Of A
Loch - signed - 27½ x 35½in.
(Sotheby's) **£160**

TOM ROBERTSON - Loch Leven,
Argyllshire - signed and with artist's
original label on the reverse - oil on
canvas - 17½ x 23½in.
(Geering & Colyer) **£310**

ROBINS

THOMAS ROBINS THE YOUNGER -
Studies Of Canary Bindweed, Scarlet
Honeysuckle, Anthericum, Monarda
And Butterflies - pencil and water-
colour heightened with white on pre-
pared paper - 22½ x 17½in.
(Christie's)   **£600**

THOMAS ROBINS THE YOUNGER -
Studies Of Melissa Grandiflora,
Peruvian Scilla, Philadelphus And
Butterflies - pencil and watercolour
heightened with white on prepared
paper - 22¼ x 17½in.
(Christie's)   **£500**

T. S. ROBINS - Sailing Ships At Sea -
inscribed - bears initials - 8½ x 13½in.
(Sotheby's)   **£25**

THOMAS SEWELL ROBINS - Sailing
Barges And A Fishing Boat In A Calm -
signed and dated 1853 - oil on canvas -
11 x 16in.
(King & Chasemore)   **£520**

THOMAS SEWELL ROBINS - Fishing
Boats Going Out Of Loom Harbour -
signed and dated 1857 - watercolour
heightened with white - 18½ x 25¾in.
(Christie's)   **£600**

THOMAS HEATH ROBINSON - A
Village Cricket Match - signed with
initials and dated 1951 - 20½ x 27¾in.
(Sotheby's Belgravia)   **£80**

THOMAS HEATH ROBINSON -
Shakespeare At The Globe - signed with
initials and dated 1952 - 19¾ x 27¾in.
(Sotheby's Belgravia)   **£65**

THOMAS HEATH ROBINSON - Under
Queensberry Rules - signed with initials
and dated 1951 - 20¾ x 27½in.
(Sotheby's Belgravia)   **£75**

THOMAS HEATH ROBINSON - Sir
Walter Raleigh And Queen Elizabeth I -
signed with initials and dated 1952 -
20½ x 27½in.
(Sotheby's Belgravia)   **£65**

THOMAS HEATH ROBINSON -
Beaten To The South Pole -
signed with initials and dated 1953 -
20½ x 27¾in.
(Sotheby's Belgravia)   **£50**

ROELAND ROGHMAN - A Wooded River Landscape with a traveller and peasants by a bridge - signed - 45½ x 67in.
(Christie's) **£12,000**

WILLIAM HEATH ROBINSON - The Vicar's Temptation - signed and signed again on the back - pen and black ink and watercolour heightened with white - 16¾ x 12½in.
(Christie's) **£380**

GEORGE FENNEL ROBSON - A Bridge Over A River In The Highlands - watercolour - 8¼ x 10¼in.
(Christie's) **£70**

CLARENCE ROE - A Rocky Gorge - signed - 35½ x 23½in.
(Sotheby's Belgravia) **£42**

R. E. ROE - Fishing Smacks And A Sailing Vessel By The Entrance To A Small Harbour With Lighthouse - signed - oil on canvas - 8¼ x 12¼in.
(Smith-Woolley & Perry) **£74**

JEAN ALPHONSE ROEHN - The Scolding, Two Figures In An Elegant Interior - signed - on panel - 18 x 15in.
(Sotheby's) **£2,500**

WILLEM ROELOFS - A Woody Landscape With Children Fishing By A Cottage - signed and dated 1848 - on panel - 12¼ x 16¼in.
(Christie's) **£700**

JEAN ROGER - Busy Street - cartoon - signed - 40 x 33cm.
(Galerie Moderne) **£6**

ROELAND ROGHMAN - A Scandinavian River Landscape with figures by a bridge and log cabins beyond - 46 x 67in.
(Christie's) **£20,000**

FRANZ WOLFGANG ROHRICH, After Cranach - A Portrait Of The Brandenberg Children, The Boy, half length, Wearing A Red Cap And Coat With An Ermine Collar, The Girl, three-quarter length, Wearing A Brocade Dress - signed Rohrich - bears Cranach monogram - on panel - 22 x 16in.
(Christie's) **£2,600**

A. ROLAND - The Babes In The Wood - oil on canvas - signed - 77 x 51cm.
(Galerie Moderne) **£53**

ALEXANDER F. ROLFE - Portrait Of William Davies - signed and dated 1847 - 40 x 50in.
(Sotheby's) **£750**

HENRY LEONIDAS ROLFE - Salmon And Trout; An Otter And A Salmon - both signed - one twice and one dated 1865, the other 1866 and 1867 - 17½ x 29½in.
(Sotheby's) **£750 Pair**

HENRY LEONIDAS ROLFE - Still Life Of Game Birds, And Salmon And Trout - signed - signed and dated 1869 - 24 x 36in.
(Sotheby's) **£620 Pair**

H. L. ROLFE - Hen Partridge, With Chicks - 13½ x 23in.
(Sotheby's) **£200**

E. ROLLETT - Villagers In A Wooded Lane - signed - oil - 33 x 21in.
(Warner, Sheppard & Wade) **£50**

V. ROLYAT - Scottish Lake And Mountain Scenes - oil - one signed - 23 x 35in.
(Henry Spencer & Sons) **£260 Pair**

G. ROMANINO - Figures In An Interior, An Old Woman Selling A Chicken To A Cavalier To The Right, Two Women Embracing To the Left - on panel - 9 x 16½in.
(Sotheby's) **£500**

E. ROMANO - Tower Bridge - signed - 13¾x 9¾in.
(Sotheby's) **£70**

GIULIO ROMANO - Virgin And Child St. Elizabeth And The Infant St. John - on panel - 27 x 23in.
(Buckell & Ballard) **£2,000**

GIULIO ROMANO, After - Lucretia, half length, Turned To The Left, In Green Drapery - 25½ x 19½in.
(Sotheby's) **£400**

S. ROMBOUTS - A Wooded Landscape, With Figures On A Road - 41 x 51in.
(Christie's) **£1,100**

W. ROMEYN - A Herdsman And Animals, Resting By A Barn, Other Animals Grazing Beyond - bears signature - on panel - 12 x 17in.
(Sotheby's) **£220**

G. ROMNEY - Portraits Of Samuel And Mary Walker - with label of Eade & Saunders, No. 10 Great Castle Street, Cavendish Square - 30 x 26in.
(Woolley & Wallis) **£170 Pair**

G. ROMNEY - Portrait Of Maria Pelham Carleton, daughter of the first Lord Dorchester, and afterwards Lady Bolton - 67½ x 46in.
(Christie's) **£2,800**

GEORGE ROMNEY - Portrait Of Master Wallace, half length, Wearing A Buff Jacket And Red Cloak - 29 x 24in.
(Christie's) **£12,000**

GEORGE ROMNEY - Portrait Of Mrs Richard Wilbraham Bootle, In A White Dress, With A Greyhound - standing, three-quarter length - 50½ x 40in.
(Christie's) **£5,000**

G. ROMNEY - Portrait Of A Lady, seated three-quarter length, Wearing A White Dress - 50 x 40in.
(Christie's) **£170**

ROMNEY - Portrait Of A Lady, Said To Be The Honourable Mrs. Beresford, head and shoulders - 17 x 13in.
(Sotheby's) **£110**

HENRIETTA RONNER - 'Around The Kettle' - signed and dated 1895 - oil on panel - 10¼ x 13½in.
(Bearnes & Waycotts) **£3,100**

HENRIETTE RONNER-KNIP - Studies Of Long Haired Cats - signed and dated '93 - on panel - 15 x 18in.
(Sotheby's) **£6,200**

THOMAS MATTHEWS ROOKE - Spinning Wool, Le Hon - signed - inscribed and dated 1892 - 13 x 8¼in.
(Sotheby's Belgravia) **£28**

MICHAEL ANGELO ROOKER - Travellers And Shepherds Resting Near Buildwas Abbey - signed and dated 1765 - watercolour - 5¼ x 7¼in.
(Christie's) **£1,100**

WILHELM ROOS - Portrait Of A Gentleman - signed and dated 1838 - 11¼ x 9in.
(Sotheby's) **£48**

KAREL ROOSEN - Winter Landscape - oil on canvas - signed - 55 x 35cm.
(Galerie Moderne) **£95**

ALBERT ROOSENBOOM - Portrait Of A Man - oil on canvas - signed - 76 x 65cm.
(Galerie Moderne) **£34**

NICHOLAS JAN ROOSENBOOM - A Dutch Winter Landscape With Figures Skating On A Frozen River - signed - on panel - 8¼ x 11½in.
(Sotheby's) **£2,700**

M. VAN ROOY - The Accessories - oil on canvas - signed - 60 x 50cm.
(Galerie Moderne) **£50**

ROPER

C. ROPER - An Alpine Waterfall with figures and chalet - signed and dated 1883 - oil - 31 x 25½in.
(Neale & Son)   **£105**

ROSA - Italian harbour scene with figures and sailing vessels - 40 x 69 ins.
(Christie's, S. Kensington) **£1,100**

PACECCO DE ROSA - The Triumph Of David; David With Goliath's Head, Surrounded By Warriors - 48¼ x 87½in.
(Sotheby's)   **£2,000**

S. ROSA - A Ravine With Fallen Trees And A Group Of Figures in the foreground - oil on canvas - 24½ x 18½in.
(Bearnes & Waycotts)   **£270**

S. ROSA - Mountainous Landscape With Figures - oil on canvas - 18 x 14¼in.
(Bearnes & Waycotts)   **£270**

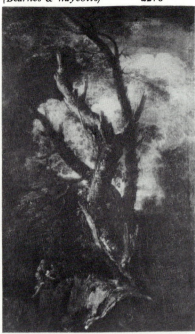

SALVATOR ROSA - A Landscape with a soldier and another figure by a blasted tree - 37 x 24in.
(Christie's)   **£1,000**

A. ROSANBURGER - Beach Scene With Figures - oil on canvas - signed - 25 x 15in.
(J. Francis, T. Jones & Sons)   **£130**

A. ROSE - Landscape - oil on wood - signed and dated 1919 - 23 x 34cm.
(Galerie Moderne)   **£6**

ALEXANDER ROSELL - Our Young Apprentice - signed - 21 x 29½in.
(Sotheby's Belgravia)   **£450**

JAMES ROSS - A Hunting Party At A
Ruined Castle - signed - 16 x 23in.
(Christie's) **£720**

DANTE GABRIEL ROSSETTI -
Portrait Study Of Mrs William Morris,
Seated, three-quarter length - red
chalk on grey paper - 18 x 14¾in.
(Sotheby's Belgravia) **£190**

DANTE GABRIEL ROSSETTI -
Portrait Of Fanny Carnforth, Seated -
pencil - 15 x 13in.
(Sotheby's Belgravia) **£480**

H. ROTTENHAMMER - The Madonna
And Child, Surrounded By Angel
Musicians - on metal - 8 x 6¾in.
(Sotheby's) **£320**

J. ROTTENHAMMER - Saint John The
Evangelist; And Saint Matthew And
The Angel - on panel - 7½ x 3½in.
(Christie's) **£480 Pair**

CECIL ROUND - 'A Mackerel Day'
Petit Tor, And Oddicombe Bay, Torquay
- signed and dated 1881/2 - inscribed on
the reverse - oil on canvas - 19½ x 29½in.
(Bearnes & Waycotts) **£145**

FRANK ROUSSE - Harbour Scene With
Shipping - watercolour - 11 x 19in.
(G. A. Key) **£14**

KER-XAVIER ROUSSEL - Les Deux
Arbres - charcoal and white chalk on
brown paper - 8¼ x 10¼in.
(Sotheby's) **£40**

PIERRE ROUSSEL - Yvonne Brodant
Dans L'Atelier - oil - on canvas -
signed - 35¾ x 28½in.
(Sotheby's) **£300**

GIL ROUX - Le Prunier - oil - on
paper - on board - signed and dated '61 -
13 x 16¼in.
(Sotheby's) **£60**

ROUX, after Boucher - A Couple In A
Garden, The Man Holding A Basket Of
Fruit - oil on canvas - 28 x 36in.
(King & Chasemore) **£500**

MRS ROWAN - Three Flower Pieces -
heightened with bodycolour, on grey
paper - all signed and dated 1883-1889 -
each 15 x 10½in.
(Sotheby's) **£25 Three**

CHARLES ROWBOTHAM - Near Savona,
Coast Of Genoa - watercolour heightened
with white - signed - inscribed on the
reverse and dated 1898 - 10¾ x 15¾in.
(Christie's) **£45**

CLAUDE ROWBOTHAM - Griande,
Lago Di Como; And Pallanza, Lago
Maggiore - watercolour - signed -
the first inscribed and both dated 1905 -
7¾ x 18½in.
(Christie's) **£100 Pair**

T. L ROWBOTHAM - A Castle By A
Bridge - pencil and watercolour - 7½ x
10¼in.
(Christie's) **£25**

TOM ROWDEN - 'Glen Turrett,
Perthshire - Highland River Landscape With
Cattle in foreground' - signed and dated '99
- watercolour - 12 x 19in.
(Lalonde Martin) **£22**

S. GRANT ROWE - Pastoral - 44 x 59cm.
(Edmiston's) **£240**

W. H. P. ROWLAND - On The Barn
Water, Oxon - signed - inscribed on the
stretcher - 11½ x 17in.
(Sotheby's Belgravia) **£80**

ROWLANDSON

THOMAS ROWLANDSON - Study Of A Classical Figure - pen and grey ink and watercolour - 7¼ x 4½in.
(Christie's) £28

THOMAS ROWLANDSON - A Landscape With Monks By A Wayside Shrine - pen and grey ink and grey, blue and pale brown wash, watermark - 10¼ x 14in.
(Christie's) £75

THOMAS ROWLANDSON - View From The Inn At Lynton - inscribed on the reverse - pen and grey ink and watercolour, watermark - 5¾ x 9½in.
(Christie's) £300

THOMAS ROWLANDSON - Travelling In Holland - pen and ink, grey, pale blue, brown and pink wash - 7½ x 11¾in.
(Christie's) £650

THOMAS ROWLANDSON - The Old Nurse And Her Pets, Or The Female Penitentiary - pen and ink and watercolour - 13 x 10½in.
(Christie's) £1,400

MARY ROWLEY - A Swiss Girl - signed with monogram - 13½ x 10½in.
(Sotheby's Belgravia) £55

HARRY ROWNTREE - The Calm Before The Storm - signed - 9 x 12½in.
(Sotheby's Belgravia) £40

HERBERT ROYLE - 'Farm Nr. Nesfield' - oil painting - signed - 24 x 14in.
(Dacre, Son & Hartley) £150

LOUIS ROYONT - The Sailmaker - cartoon - signed and dated 1940 - 56cm. x 1m.
(Galerie Moderne) £142

RUBENS, Studio Of - Alexander Crowning Roxana - 81½ x 66½in.
(Christie's) £3,800

RUBENS - A Bacchanal - on panel - 20 x 30in.
(Christie's) £480

RUBENS - The Holy Family With Saints John The Baptist, Elizabeth, Jerome, Anthony Abbot And Francis, God The Father Above - 17¾ x 11¾in.
(Sotheby's) £280

SIR P. P. RUBENS, Studio Of - Two Horsemen In Armour Attacking A Lion With Lances, A Fallen Man Beneath Them; To The Right A Lion Seizing A Man On A Rearing Horse, A Leopard Lying In The Right Foreground - 87 x 136in.
(Sotheby's) £3,800

SIR PETER PAUL RUBENS AND STUDIO - The Triumph of Divine Love - a cartoon for a tapestry - 153 x 190in.
(Christie's) **£22,000**

RUBENS - The Holy Family With Saint Elizabeth And The Infant Saint John The Baptist - on metal - 15 x 12½in.
(Sotheby's) **£200**

C. RUDELL - A Busy Quay Scene - oil on canvas - signed - 50 x 60cm.
(Galerie Moderne) **£65**

JACOB VAN RUISDAEL and ADRIAEN VAN DER VELDE - An Extensive Woody Landscape with a herdsman driving cattle along a path - signed with Ruisdael monogram - 17½ x 15½in.
(Christie's) **£4,500**

JACOB VAN RUISDAEL - A Mountainous Landscape With a Blasted Tree By a Cornfield - signed - 21¾ x 26¾in.
(Christie's) **£30,000**

JACOB VAN RUISDAEL - A Wooded River Landscape - signed with monogram - 28 x 30in.
(Christie's) **£6,000**

HORACE VAN RUITH - A Young Girl Reading A Book With Apple - signed - oil on canvas - 23 x 19in.
(Smith-Woolley & Perry) **£210**

P. RULOFS - Landscape - oil on canvas - signed - 80 x 64cm.
(Galerie Moderne) **£17**

C. F. RUMP - Scene Near Ranworth, With Figures And Wherry - oil - 14 x 21in.
(G. A. Key) **£92**

C. F. RUMP - Open Landscape With Figures On A Path - oil - 8 x 11in.
(G. A. Key) **£25**

C. F. RUMP - Sheep And Shepherd In Country Lane - watercolour - 9 x 15in.
(G. A. Key) **£20**

RUOPPOLO - A Monkey With Grapes, And Other Fruit And Flowers In A Formal Garden; And A Peacock With Roses, And Other Flowers In A Sculptured Vase - 51½ x 37¾in.
(Christie's) **£6,500 Pair**

JOHN RUSKIN - Study Of Shipping - inscribed 'same as 28th in position' - dated 30th Dec. 1876 - pencil - 5¼ x 5¼in.
(Christie's) **£90**

FREDERICK RUSSEL - Farmyard Scene With Windmill And Figures - watercolour - 12 x 18in.
(G. A. Key) **£30**

RUSSIAN SCHOOL, circa 1890 - Cherubs In Allegorical Poses Representing Poetry, Painting, Sculpture And Music - 56¼ x 18½in.
(Sotheby's) **£500 Four**

KARL ANDREAS RUTHART – A Boar Hunt - 26½ x 33½in.
(Christie's) **£2,200**

JACOB SALOMONSZ. VAN RUYSDAEL - Two Cows And Several Sheep By A Wooded Bank Beside A Road On Which Are A Sheep And A Goat, Two Figures In The Right Background - inscribed - on panel - 14½ x 19¾in.
(Sotheby's) **£2,500**

SALOMON VAN RUYSDAEL - A Wooded River Landscape with cattle on a ferry, fishermen, and the Castle of Nijenrode beyond - signed - on panel - 28¼ x 34¾in.
(Christie's) **£60,000**

SALOMON VAN RUYSDAEL - A Wooded River Landscape, with peasants and cattle in a punt, men fishing and sailing barges beyond - signed with initial and monogram and dated 1637 - on panel - 17½ x 31½in.
(Christie's) **£4,200**

D. RYCKAERT - Two Young Men At Study, One Seated Writing At A Desk, Another Holding A Drawing, Paintings Hanging On A Wall Behind - on panel - 13¾ x 9¾in.
(Sotheby's) **£1,400**

JACOBUS RYCKAERT - A Frozen River Landscape, Figures On The Bank And Skating On The Ice - signed - on panel - 10 x 16in.
(Sotheby's) **£650**

OLIVER RYHS - In A Venetian Courtyard - signed and numbered OPCXVI - 10 x 13in.
(Sotheby's Belgravia) **£450**

P. A. RYSBRACK - An Extensive Classical Landscape, With Figures On A Road - 28¾ x 38in.
(Christie's) **£600**

P. SADLER - His Sunday Best - signed -
15¼ x 11½in.
(Sotheby's Belgravia) **£45**

WALTER DENDY SADLER - Village
Gossips - signed - 33½ x 47½in.
(Sotheby's Belgravia) **£850**

HERMAN SAFTLEVEN - Saint Paul
And Saint Barnabas At Lystra - on
panel - 13¼ x 26½in.
(Christie's) **£1,800**

HERMAN SAFTLEVEN - An
Extensive Mountainous River Landscape
With Numerous Figures And Boats in
the foreground And Town Beyond -
signed with monogram and dated 1670 -
on panel - 16.5 x 23cm.
(Phillips) **£11,000**

GIOVANNI CAMILLO SAGRESTANI -
The Madonna And Child Appearing To
A Saint - inscribed 'Sagrestani' -
black and white chalk on grey pre-
paration - watermark an encircled
Fleur-de-Lys - 37.6 x 24.9cm.
(Christie's) **£44**

LOUDON SAINTHILL - Three
Figures - pen and ink and watercolour -
signed and dated - 20 x 16½in.
(Sotheby's) **£200**

THE MASTER OF SAINT GUDULE -
Saint Jerome Reading In His Study, The
Penitent Saint Jerome Beyond - on panel -
22½ x 16in.
(Christie's) **£30,000**

A. SALOMON - Allegory - oil on canvas -
signed and dated 1802 - 97 x 65cm.
(Galerie Moderne) **£125**

J. SALT - A Venetian Capriccio - signed -
13 x 17in.
(Sotheby's Belgravia) **£140**

J. SALT - Backwaters, Venice - both
signed - each 23½ x 13½in.
(Sotheby's Belgravia) **£320 Pair**

J. SALT - A Venetian Capriccio - signed -
13½ x 17¼in.
(Sotheby's Belgravia) **£130**

JAMES SALT - Venetian Canal Scene; and
companion - signed - 13½ x 23in
(Phillips) **£320 Pair**

FRANK SALTFLEET - At Close Of Day,
with team returning homeward - signed -
watercolour - 9½ x 13½in.
(Neale & Son) **£26**

**GIOVANNI BATTISTA SALVI, IL
SASSOFERRATO** - The Madonna And
Child In Glory - 28¼ x 22in.
(Christie's) **£8,500**

F. SALVIATI - Portrait Of A Gentleman,
Standing, three-quarter length, In A
White And Gold Doublet And Black
Cloak With Green Lining, Against An
Architectural Background, With Classical
Ruins In A Landscape Beyond - on
panel - 43½ x 33in.
(Christie's) **£2,200**

B. SALVIATZ - Venetian Canal Scene With Boats And Figures - watercolour - 12 x 7in.
(G. A. Key) **£26**

PAUL SANDBY - Bothwell Castle - signed - inscribed and dated 1800 on the back of the mount - pencil, grey-brown, brown and ochre wash heightened with white on light brown paper - 7½ x 10½in.
(Christie's) **£220**

PAUL SANDBY - An Imaginary Landscape With An Erupting Volcano And Cattle Near A River - pencil and watercolour heightened with white on blue paper - 7¾ x 9¼in.
(Christie's) **£50**

ROBERT SANDERSON - "Immigrant Farmers" - oil - signed - 29.5 x 24.5cm.
(Phillips in Scotland) **£135**

JOACHIM VON SANDRART - Mountainous River Landscapes, Fishermen And Other Figures On A Path, Boats In The River Beyond - signed with monogram - on metal - 5½ x 8in.
(Sotheby's) **£2,600 Pair**

PIERO SANSALVADORE - An Impression Of Piccadilly - signed - on panel - 4¼ x 3¼in.
(Sotheby's) **£100**

JAMES SANT - An English Rose - signed with monogram - 62 x 43 ins.
(Christie's, S. Kensington) **£420**

J. SANT - Portrait Of A Young Girl, Said To Be Miss Sharp, Daughter Of The Reverend Samuel Sharp, Of America - on panel - oval - 24 x 19½in.
(Christie's) **£160**

SANT - A Girl Reading By A Window - 11¼ x 15in.
(Sotheby's Belgravia) **£70**

GERRIT VAN SANTEN - The Battle Of Vuchterheide Between French And Dutch Cavalry, February 5th, 1600 - 35½ x 54in.
(Christie's) **£3,500**

A. SANTI - Old Man With Pipe - 69 x 49cm.
(Edmiston's) **£7**

F. SANTORO - Roman Scenes - dated 1875 - on panel - 31 x 20cm
(Edmiston's) **£240 pair**

RUBENS SANTORO - A Venetian Backwater - signed - on panel - 7¼ x 10½in.
(Christie's) **£1,600**

CHATIN SARACI - Still Life With A Bowl Of Fruit - oil - on canvas - signed and inscribed indistinctly - 27½ x 35½in.
(Sotheby's) **£100**

V. SARONI - Reclining Nude - 48 x 68cm.
(Edmiston's) **£10**

DEL SARTO - Saint John The Baptist - on panel - 36½ x 24in.
(Christie's) **£1,200**

FRANCIS SARTORIUS - Six Huntsmen In An Extensive Landscape - signed and dated 1774 - 34½ x 48in.
(Christie's) £5,500

JOHN NOST SARTORIUS – Tally-Ho - signed and dated 1818 - 16½ x 23½in.
(Christie's) £1,500

SASSOFERRATO, After - The Madonna In Prayer - 26 x 19¼in.
(Sotheby's) £80

GIOVANNI BATTISTA SALVI, Called IL SASSOFERRATO - The Madonna And Child - 74 x 62cm.
(Phillips) £1,600

GIOVANNI BATTISTA SALVI, IL SASSOFERRATO - The Madonna, head and shoulders - 18½ x 14½in.
(Christie's) £3,200

ROELANDT SAVERY - A Rocky Landscape With The Entrance To A Mine, A Man Axing Felled Trees in the foreground - on panel - 7 x 10¾in.
(Sotheby's) £15,000

ROELANDT SAVERY - Foxes Attacking a Cow, with a charging bull and other animals in a wooded landscape - signed - 42½ x 62½in.
(Christie's) £4,800

H. SCHAFER - The Market Square, Ratisbon, Bavaria - oil on canvas - initialled and dated 1884 - 29 x 19 ins.
(Jackson-Stops & Staff) **£420**

HENRY SCHAFER - Evreux, Normandy; And Inside The Cathedral Of St. Lawrence, Nuremberg - pencil and water-colour heightened with white - both signed and inscribed - 17¾ x 13¾in.
(Christie's) **£100 Pair**

HENRY THOMAS SCHAFER - The Wreath - signed and dated 1877 - 35 x 46½ ins,
(Christie's, S. Kensington) **£1,600**

HENRY THOMAS SCHAFER - River Landscapes - both signed - on panel - 9 x 13 ins.
(Christie's) **£280 Pair**

W. SCHAFER - Flemish Tower And Cathedral - 29 x 24cm.
(Edmiston's) **£190**

GODFRIED SCHALCKEN - A Scene In A Brothel - signed - on panel - 15 x 12in.
(Sotheby's) **£35,000**

G. SCHALCKEN - A Boy Blowing On A Firebrand, Holding A Candlestick - on panel - 13 x 10½in.
(Christie's) **£220**

FRANZ SCHAMS - 'Irresistible Charms' - signed and dated 1852 - on panel - 57.5 x 47cm.
(Phillips) **£1,700**

HENDRICUS JOHANNES SCHEERES - Preparing The Vegetables - signed - on panel - 13½ x 17½in.
(Sotheby's) **£1,250**

ARY SCHEFFER, After - The Arrest Of Charlotte Corday - inscribed - 17½ x 13¼in.
(Sotheby's) **£90**

JEAN SCHELLEKENS - The Windmill - oil on canvas - signed and dated 1886 - 40 x 60cm.
(Galerie Moderne) **£141**

PETRUS VAN SCHENDEL - Seascape With Fishing Boats - oil on wood - signed - 40 x 52cm.
(Galerie Moderne) **£785**

PETRUS VAN SCHENDEL - A Market Scene In Amsterdam, At Night - signed and inscribed on a label on the reverse - on panel - 30½ x 44in.
(Christie's) **£4,800**

ALEXANDER SCHETKAY - Swiss Or Austrian Scene - signed and inscribed - watercolour - 29 x 31cm.
(Edmiston's) **£95**

SCHIANCHI

H. SCHIANCHI - A View Of St. Peter's, Rome - indistinctly signed and inscribed 'Roma' - on panel - 8¼ x 13¾in.
(Sotheby's) £320

ANDREA SCHIAVONE, After - Marius listening to the Sibyllic Oracles - on panel - 6¾ x 9 ins.
(Christie's) £2,600

SCHIDONE - The Young Saint John The Baptist, Seated, Covered By Red Drapery - 40 x 21in.
(Sotheby's) £240

EDUARD SCHLEICH - A Busy Track - oil on canvas - signed - 45 x 65cm.
(Galerie Moderne) £115

HENRI GUILLAUME SCHLESINGER - The Youthful Proposal - signed - 29 x 23½in.
(Christie's) £850

A. SCHMIDT - The News - oil on canvas - signed - 49 x 39cm.
(Galerie Moderne) £666

HERMANN SCHNEIDER - 'The Unequal Couple' - signed - on panel - 78.5 x 58cm.
(Phillips) £2,000

WILHELM SCHNEIDER - Stanislas, King Of Poland - oil - on board - signed - 46 x 38in.
(Stewart & Gore) £65

MATTHYS SCHOEVAERDTS - A Wooded Landscape With The Virgin And Child - on copper - 6½ x 8¾in.
(Sotheby's) £3,500

K. SCHOFIELD - Broadland Scene With Man On Punt - oil - 11 x 17in.
(G. A. Key) £30

JOHANN HEINRICH SCHONFELDT -
The Triumph Of David; A Procession Of
Women With Musical Instruments, Headed
By David Holding The Head Of Goliath,
In The Centre Dancing Boys And An Old
Man - 50 x 81in.
(Sotheby's) **£3,000**

OTTO MARSEUS VAN SCHRIEK -
A Still Life Of A Lizard, A Grass Snake,
A Snail, A Grasshopper, A Butterfly And
Moths Amongst Daisies, Forget-Me-Nots
And Other Flowers At The Base Of A
Tree, In A Landscape - 28 x 22cm.
(Phillips) **£2,000**

FLORIS VAN SCHOOTEN - A Woman
Preparing Fish At A Table Laden With
A Side Of Meat, Vegetables, Pans And
Earthenware Jugs, A Boy Holding A Ball
Close By - signed with initials - 35 x 46½in.
(Christie's) **£10,000**

HENRY SCHOUTEN - Hens And A
Cock - oil on canvas - signed - 80 x 59cm.
(Galerie Moderne) **£566**

PIETER SCHOUTEN - Sheep In A Pen -
oil on canvas - signed - 60 x 90cm.
(Galerie Moderne) **£251**

A. SCHOTH - Continental Harbour
Scenes - signed - each 9¾ x 17½in.
(Sotheby's) **£650 Four**

BENNO SCHOTZ - Sketch For Bronze
Tree - pen and ink - 23 x 16cm.
(Edmiston's) **£20**

AXEL THORSEN SCHOVELIN - A Danish
Landscape with Houses under Trees - signed -
oil - 20 x 30in.
(Warner, Sheppard & Wade) **£210**

ALBERT FRIEDERICH SCHROEDER -
A Merry Company - signed - on panel -
20½ x 16½in.
(Christie's) **£2,200**

SCHULMAN

DAVID SCHULMAN - A Shepherd And Sheep Near A Farmhouse - signed - 23½ x 31½in.
(Sotheby's) £450

FELIX SCHURIG - Furtive Romance - signed and dated '76 - 30¼ x 24½in.
(Sotheby's) £600

CLAUDE SCHURR - Audierne - Voiliers Au Port - oil - on canvas - signed - 19¼ x 25in.
(Sotheby's) £120

CORNELIS SCHUT - The Madonna And Child - on panel - 24½ x 18¾in.
(Christie's) £1,700

FRANZ WENZEL SCHWARZ - A Farm Courtyard With A Young Bull And Two Farmers - signed - on panel - 25¼ x 30½in.
(Sotheby's) £1,250

HENDRIK WILLEM SCHWEICKHARDT - A Winter Landscape With Figures Skating On A Frozen Waterway - signed - on panel - 11 x 15in.
(Christie's) £6,000

HENRY SCOTT - A Good Wind - signed - 19¾ x 29½in.
(Sotheby's Belgravia) £170

JOHN SCOTT - Good Morrow - heightened with bodycolour - signed - 14¼ x 10¼in.
(Sotheby's Belgravia) £32

MAXWELL SCOTT - Highlanders, Loch Etive - 49 x 73cm.
(Edmiston's) £42

PETER SCOTT - Black Duck Flushed - signed and dated 1946 - on board - 10 x 14in.
(Sotheby's) £360

ROBERT BAGGE SCOTT - Fishing Boat Off Great Yarmouth - watercolour and pencil - 9 x 13in.
(G. A. Key) £18

SEPTIMUS EDWIN SCOTT - The Victoria Cross - signed - canvas laid on board - 21 x 17½in.
(Sotheby's Belgravia) £160

TOM SCOTT - Autumn Landscape - signed and dated '10 - 10¼ x 13in.
(Sotheby's Belgravia) £50

SCOTTISH SCHOOL - Portrait Of A Gentleman, three-quarter length, Wearing a Kilt - 55½ x 43½in.
(Christie's) £260

EDWARD SEAGO - India Water Carrier - pen and wash - 14 x 21in.
(G. A. Key) £50

SELLAER - The Personification Of Charity - 63 x 47½in.
(Christie's) £220

CHARLES A. SELLAR - An Old Garden Near Stratford - signed - 35½ x 23½in.
(Sotheby's Belgravia) £350

HENRY COURTNEY SELOUS - Figures In A Mountain Pass - signed and dated 1850 - 24 x 17½in.
(Woolley & Wallis) £180

SEM - Napoleon III En Habit Anglais; Napoleon III - Avant Pendant Et Apres La Deuxieme Empire - pencil - both signed and one dated '60 - 21¼ x 15in. and 15 x 21¼in.
(Sotheby's) £22 Two

EISMAN SEMENOWSKI - Robbing the Orchard - signed and dated Paris 1886 - on panel - 21½ x 15 ins.
(Christie's) £650

SEMENOWSKI

EISMAN SEMENOWSKI - 'The Blonde' -
signed - oil on panel - 12¼ x 9¼in.
(Bearnes & Waycotts) **£460**

JACQUES ALBERT SENAVE -
Peasants With Animals In A Farmyard -
signed and dated 1791 - 20¾ x 25in.
(Sotheby's) **£3,000**

R. SENET - The Grand Canal With
The Salute On The Left Bank - 8¼ x
15in.
(Sotheby's) **£30**

GEORGE HARCOURT SEPHTON -
A Double Portrait of Winifred And
Christina Roberts As Children, Both
With Long Fair Hair And Wearing
White Dresses - oil - signed and
inscribed on verso and dated 1900 -
39½ x 48in.
(Henry Spencer & Sons) **£320**

L SERGENT - A Cavalry Engagement -
100 x 140cm.
(Edmiston's) **£380**

DOMINIC SERRES - The Arrival Of H.R.H.
Prince William Henry At Martinique In April
1783 - signed and dated 1791 - 70 x 48in.
(Christie's) **£12,000**

DOMINIC SERRES - Men-O'-War On A
Calm Sea - signed - pen and grey ink,
grey wash - 5¾ x 9in.
(Christie's) **£280**

JOHN THOMAS SERRES - British
Men-O'-War And Other Shipping Off
A Coastal Town - signed - 45 x 72cm.
(Phillips) **£950**

PAUL SERUSIER, circa 1900-10 - La
Rousse - oil - on canvas - signed with
initials - 20 x 15¼in.
(Sotheby's) **£1,500**

W. SETTLE - A Busy Day On The Firth Of
Forth - both on board - each 8 x 15¾in -

(Sotheby's) **£1,000 Pair**

WILLIAM FREDERICK SETTLE - A
Grimsby Yawl And Other Shipping Off-
Shore In A Calm - watercolour heightened
with white - signed with monogram and
dated 87 - 8½ x 13in.
(Christie's) **£140**

F. VAN SEVERDONK - "Combat Des Conquest" - signed - oil - on panel - inscribed on rear - 6½ x 9¾in.
(Charles R. Phillips) **£510**

WILLIAM A. SEXTIE - 'Geheimniss', With T. Cannon Up - signed and dated 1882 - 36 x 46in.
(Christie's) **£1,800**

SEYMOUR - Study Of A Racehorse With Jockey Up - oil - 41 x 56.5cm.
(Phillips in Scotland) **£95**

J. SEYMOUR - Full Cry; and The Kill - 33½ x 48in
(Christie's) **£2,800 Pair**

J. SEYMOUR - Coast Scenes - 14 x 30cm.
(Edmiston's) **£60 Pair**

G. SHALDERS - 'Storm In The Glen' - signed - on canvas - 12 x 16in.
(Morphet & Morphet) **£200**

GEORGE SHALDERS - A Woody Landscape With Peasants Harvesting; and An Extensive Woody River Landscape With Peasants And Cattle By A Farmstead - both signed and dated '59 - 11½ x 19½in.
(Christie's) **£2,700 Pair**

GEORGE SHALDERS - A Mountainous Lake Landscape, With Cattle And Sheep - signed and dated 1871 - 21½ x 35½in.
(Christie's) **£280**

W. SOMMERVILLE SHANKS - Chez Nous (6 Park Circus) - 60 x 50cm.
(Edmiston's) **£85**

DOROTHEA SHARPE - Beach Scene With Children On Rocks - oil on board - 11½ x 15½in.
(Bearnes & Waycotts) **£150**

DOROTHEA SHARPE - Beach Scene With A Rowing Boat, A Bathing Hut And Figures - oil - 11¼ x 15¼in. - with another sketch on the reverse.
(Bearnes & Waycotts) **£140**

DOROTHEA SHARPE - Sketch on Porthmeor - signed - on panel - 11¾ x 15¾ ins.
(Sotheby's, Belgravia) **£140**

BYAM SHAW - Truly The Light Is Sweet - dated 1901 - on panel - 40 x 30cm.
(Edmiston's) **£550**

CHARLES J. SHAW - A Scene In North Wales With Cattle And Drover - signed - oil - 20½ x 28½in.
(Neale & Son) **£80**

CHARLES L. SHAW - After A Storm, A Moorland Landscape With A Pedlar Walking Along a Muddy Path in the foreground, Cottages And Trees in the distance - oil - signed and dated 1889 - 15½ x 26in.
(Henry Spencer & Sons) **£150**

JOSHUA SHAW - A River Landscape, With A Ruined Castle, And Children And Two Donkeys in the foreground - 37½ x 50½in.
(Christie's) **£3,200**

JOHN BYAM LISTON SHAW - The Captive - pen and ink - signed and inscribed - 12½ x 15in.
(Sotheby's Belgravia) **£10**

WALTER SHAW - 'After The Storm' - signed and dated 1887 - oil on canvas - 27¼ x 49¼in.
(Bearnes & Waycotts) **£190**

SHAW

WALTER SHAW - The Lion Rock, Near
Newquay, Cornwall - oil - 25 x 39in.
(G. A. Key) **£30**

W. R. B. SHAW - Outside The Royal Oak;
Outside The Crown - one signed and
dated 1868 - 11¼ x 9¼in.
(Sotheby's Belgravia) **£550 Pair**

SHAYER - Bringing Home The Day's
Catch - 17½ x 25½in.
(Sotheby's Belgravia) **£10**

SHAYER - A Beach Scene, With A Woman
And A Boy With A Donkey, Many Baskets,
Bundles And Fish At Their Feet, Further
Figures And Boats in the distance -
19 x 23in.
(Henry Spencer & Sons) **£210**

SHAYER - "Cattle With Manger And
Farm Buildings" - traces of signature -
on panel - 22 x 26½in.
(Charles R. Phillips) **£500**

W. SHAYER - At The Water Trough -
17¾ x 22in.
(Sotheby's Belgravia) **£400**

W. SHAYER - Coastal Scene With Ponies
And Fisherfolk - oil on canvas - 36 x
27¾in.
(Bearnes & Waycotts) **£440**

W. SHAYER - Interior Of A Farm Shed
With Cattle And Poultry - signed - oil
on canvas - 24 x 29in.
(Bearnes & Waycotts) **£230**

WILLIAM SHAYER - A Gipsy Encampment In A Woodland Scene - signed and
dated '53 - on canvas - 12 x 10in.
(King & Chasemore) **£440**

WILLIAM SHAYER, SNR - Men ploughing In An Extensive Landscape - signed
and dated 1855 - 27½ x 35½in.
(Christie's) **£1,300**

WILLIAM SHAYER, SNR - Milking
Time - signed - 27½ x 35½in.
(Christie's) **£3,000**

WILLIAM SHAYER, SNR - The Sailor's
Home, Shirley, Near Southampton -
signed and signed and inscribed on an
old label on the reverse - on panel - 13½ x
17½in.
(Christie's) **£1,800**

WILLIAM SHAYER, SNR - A Coast
Scene, The Isle Of Wight - signed and
dated 1854 - 21¼ x 29¼in.
(Sotheby's Belgravia) **£2,000**

WILLIAM J. SHAYER - Rustics, A Horse
And Dogs By A Gate - signed and dated
1887 - on board - 9½ x 12in.
(Sotheby's) **£500**

WILLIAM SHAYER, SNR - A Wooded
Landscape With Tinkers On A Path -
signed - 61 x 51cm.
(Phillips) **£750**

WILLIAM SHAYER, SNR - Coming
Back From Market - signed - 23¼ x
19¼in.
(Sotheby's Belgravia) **£3,000**

THOMAS F. N. SHEARD - Rehearsing
For The Fete De Dieu - signed - 16 x 10in.
(Sotheby's Belgravia) **£150**

SHEE - Portrait Of George Bushell, half
length, Wearing Naval Uniform - 27 x
12½in.
(Sotheby's) **£80**

SHEE

ARCHER SHEE - Portraits Of Young Boys, half length, Wearing Dark Coats, Yellow Waistcoats And Black Cravats - each 29½ x 24½in.
(Sotheby's) **£300 Two**

SIDNEY SHELTON - Embroidering - signed - 19½ x 15½in.
(Sotheby's Belgravia) **£55**

ERNEST H SHEPARD - 'Blister' - A Study of the Artist's Dog - pencil and wash drawing - inscribed and dated Christmas 1954 - 5 x 4½in.
(King & Chasemore) **£220**

ERNEST H SHEPARD - 'Dogs Through The Ages' - famous personalities and their canine associates - 15½ x 21½in.
(King & Chasemore) **£90**

ERNEST H SHEPARD - 'The Nativity' - pen and ink and watercolour - 5¾ x 8¼in.
(King & Chasemore) **£35**

W. SHEPPARD - Margate Harbour - oil - on board - signed - 72 x 39in.
(Stewart & Gore) **£38**

WILLIAM SHEPPARD - Coastal Scenes Off Plymouth - watercolours - 5 x 7in.
(G. A. Key) **£22 Pair**

DANIEL SHERRIN - Figures On Sandy Beach With Dunes in foreground and distant Mountains - signed - 47 x 75cm.
(Phillips) **£440**

DANIEL SHERRIN - A Snowy Wooded Landscape At Sunset, With Sheep - signed - oil on canvas - 20 x 30in.
(Geering & Colyer) **£85**

DANIEL SHERRIN - River Scene - signed - oil on canvas - 19½ x 29½in.
(Bearnes & Waycotts) **£240**

JOHN SHERRIN - Still Life Of Apples And A Plum By A Bank - heightened with bodycolour - signed - 11¾ x 16in.
(Sotheby's Belgravia) **£130**

HENRY SHIRLEY - The Bird Trap - inscribed on the reverse - 13½ x 22½in.
(Sotheby's Belgravia) **£400**

CAPTAIN THE HON. F. W. J. SHORE - The Bazaar, Umballa - heightened with white - signed with monogram - dated 1878 - 15½ x 23½ ins.
(Sotheby's) **£20**

J. SIBERECHTS - A Farmyard With Peasant Women Softing Vegetables, A Youth By A Carthorse, A Woman Drawing Water And An Extensive Landscape Beyond - 54¼ x 50¼in.
(Christie's) **£8,500**

JAN SIBERECHTS - A Wooded Landscape with peasant women going to market and a boy herding cows on a flooded road - signed and inscribed 'Au Anvers, 1671' - 27½ x 39in
(Christie's) **£13,000**

SICILIAN SCHOOL, Late 15th Century - The Madonna And Child Flanked By Angels, Surmounted By The Crucifixion, With Predella Scenes Showing The Pieta, The Agony In The Garden And The Good Shepherd - on panel - 36 x 22in.
(Christie's) **£2,000**

SICKERT - The Old Middlesex 30 x 40cm.
(Edmiston's) **£32**

HENRI EUGENE AUGUSTIN LE SIDANER - Mother And Child - signed - oil on canvas - 22½ x 26¾in.
(Bearnes & Waycotts) **£240**

ADOLFO LOZANO SIDRO - 'At The Ball' - signed - oil on panel - 8½ x 6½in.
(Bearnes & Waycotts) **£170**

LUDWIG BLUME SIEBERT - Guess Who - signed and inscribed - on panel - 11 x 15 ins.
(Christie's, S. Kensington) **£820**

AUGUSTUS SIEGEN - Eastern Scene With Mosques And Figures - oil - 16 x 12in.
(G. A. Key) **£290**

MARTINO DI BARTOLOMMEO DA SIENA - Angels Blowing Trumpets (a fragment) - on gold ground panel - 8¾ x 5½in.
(Christie's) **£1,500**

SIENESE SCHOOL

SIENESE SCHOOL - The Madonna
And Child - on panel - 16½ x 8½in.
(Christie's) **£1,200**

ROSA SIGNORINI - An Italian Landscape; And A Capriccio Harbour Scene
At Sunrise - painted under glass -
signed - 7½ x 11¼in.
(Geering & Colyer) **£980 Pair**

R. SIMKIN - The 6th Dragoon Guards -
signed - 8½ x 12½in.
(King & Chasemore) **£300**

DE SIMONE - The Newton Hall And SS
Roma In Full Steam - both heightened
with bodycolour - inscribed - each 15 x
25¼in.
(Sotheby's Belgravia) **£80 Pair**

A. de SIMONE - Landscapes With
Rivers in foreground - oil - 30 x 20in.
(Thomas Love & Sons Ltd) **£40 Pair**

SIMPSON - Landscape With Lake in
foreground - oil - 7½ x 11in.
(Thomas Love & Sons Ltd) **£9**

WILLIAM SIMPSON - Some Well-Known
Members Of The Bench - indistinctly
signed - 9½ x 17in.
(Sotheby's Belgravia) **£220**

SIMONINI - A Cavalry Engagement -
21½ x 28½in.
(Christie's) **£800**

F. SIMONINI - A Cavalry Engagement,
A Man In Yellow On Horseback
Threatening A Swordsman Wearing Red
And Blue - oval - 23¾ x 29in.
(Sotheby's) **£480**

M. SIMONS - A Still Life With A Crayfish
And Fruit - inscribed - 23¼ x 32½in.
(Sotheby's) **£3,800**

WILLIAM SIMSON - Study Of A
Stag's Head - watercolour heightened
with white on grey paper - signed -
inscribed, numbered, dated Oct. 13,
1845 - signed again with initials -
8½ x 11½in.
(Christie's) **£55**

LOUIS DE SILVESTRE, THE YOUNGER -
Portrait Of A Lady In A Brown Velvet
Dress Holding A Book - 28½ x 23½in.
(Sotheby's) **£1,300**

OTTO LUDWIG SINDING - The First
Sight Of The Sun: Peasants On A
Mountain Summit In Winter - signed
and dated 1885 - 92 x 134in.
(Christie's) **£1,000**

ANDRE SINET - Portrait Of A Lady -
oil on canvas - signed - 32 x 24cm.
(Galerie Moderne) **£20**

HENRY SINGLETON - Captain Faulknor
On The 'Zebra' Storming Port Royal,
Martinique, 1794 - 19½ x 25½in.
(Christie's) **£550**

HENRY SINGLETON - The Death Of
Captain Alexander Hood Following The
Engagement Between His Ship 'Mars' And
The French Ship 'Hercule', April 21, 1798
- 19½ x 24¾in.
(Christie's) **£350**

J. SINGLETON-COPLEY - Group Of
Musicians - oil - 8 x 6in.
(G. A. Key) **£310**

SIRANI - Lucretia - 48 x 39in.
(Christie's) **£900**

SIRANI - Venus Reclining, On A Bed
Covered With Grey Drapery, Holding A
Mirror In Her Left Hand - in a painted
circle - 58½ x 58½in.
(Sotheby's) **£300**

ALFRED SISLEY - Bords Du Loing -
signed and dated '92 - 23¾ x 28¾in.
(Sotheby's) **£48,000**

NOEL SLANEY - The Kitchen Chair -
64 x 41cm.
(Edmiston's) **£5**

J. F. SLATER - Stormy Coast Scene -
69 x 90cm.
(Edmiston's) **£36**

MARY SLEWERS - A Panoramic View
Of Edinburgh, Seen From Portobello To
Canongate Church - pencil with grey
wash - a key in the lower margin -
signed - inscribed and dated 1822 - 11½ x
32in.
(Sotheby's) **£28**

P. VAN SLINGELAND - An Old Man
And Boy At A Fireside - bears signature -
on panel - 16½ x 12½in.
(Christie's) **£2,000**

JAN SLUYTERS - Reclining Woman
Reading - pencil, coloured crayons and
watercolour - signed - 10 x 13½in.
(Sotheby's) **£390**

JOHN SMART - Arnprior - signed, inscribed
and dated 1895 on the reverse - on board -
11½ x 17½in.
(Sotheby's) **£60**

JOHN SMART - Tattie Hawks - signed and
dated 1881 - 12½ x 19¼in.
(Sotheby's) **£65**

FRANZ SMEERS - Reading - oil on
canvas - signed - 50 x 40cm.
(Galerie Moderne) **£235**

JOHN SMELLIE - Stonehaven Beach -
watercolour - 18 x 23cm.
(Edmiston's) **£50**

J. SMETHAM - Madonna And Child
With Angels - on panel - 7¾ x 6¼in.
(Sotheby's Belgravia) **£18**

JAMES SMETHAM - The Rose Of Dawn -
signed - signed and inscribed on an old
label on the reverse - 24 x 13¾in.
(Christie's) **£300**

JAMES SMETHAM - Caedmon Singing
To The Abbess Hilda At Whitby - on
panel - 7 x 9½in.
(Christie's) **£280**

LOUIS SMETS - A Winter Landscape
With Figures On A Frozen Canal Near
Houses - signed and dated XX on
panel - 19 x 26¼in.
(Sotheby's) £2,300

LOUIS SMETS - A Frozen River
Landscape with numerous figures - signed -
23 x 30½in.
(Christie's) £1,800

JOHN SMIBERT - Portrait Of Edward
Nightingale; And Portrait Of Eleanor
Nightingale - one signed, and the other
signed with initials - inscribed and dated
1727 - 49½ x 39½in.
(Christie's) £6,000 Pair

ROBERT SMIRKE - The Hunch-Back And
The Tailor; and The Christian Merchant -
21¾ x 18in
(Christie's) £550 Pair

SMIT - Dutch Sailing Vessels Offshore -
on panel - 12½ x 16½in.
(Christie's) £1,500

AERNOUT SMIT - Dutch Shipping
In A Choppy Sea Offshore - 46½ x
58½in.
(Christie's) £3,200

ARTHUR REGINALD SMITH - A View
On The Yorkshire Moors - signed - 12¼ x
17¾in.
(Sotheby's Belgravia) £40

CAMPBELL LINDSAY SMITH - Study Of A Girl Looking Out To Sea - oil - signed - 35.5 x 27.5cm.
(Phillips in Scotland) **£40**

CARLTON ALFRED SMITH - Daily Bread - signed and dated - watercolour heightened with white - 17¾ x 25¾in.
(Christie's) **£250**

DENZIL SMITH - Shipping Off A Continental Town - on board - 8½ x 11in.
(Sotheby's Belgravia) **£120**

SMITH OF CHICHESTER - A Shepherd With His Sheep In A Winter Landscape - on board - 10¾ x 14¾in.
(Sotheby's) **£140**

G. SMITH of CHICHESTER - Wooded classical landscape with figures by a river - on copper - 6½ x 9¼ins.
(Christie's, S. Kensington) **£500**

GEORGE SMITH OF CHICHESTER - A Wooded Landscape With A Cottage By A River - signed and dated 1754 - 16 x 24½in.
(Christie's) **£1,800**

GEORGE SMITH OF CHICHESTER - A Winter Landscape With Two Peasants Walking Towards A Cottage - 16½ x 24in.
(Christie's) **£1,600**

JAMES BURRELL SMITH - A Rocky Coast - heightened with bodycolour - signed and dated 1869 - 8¾ x 16½in.
(Sotheby's Belgravia) **£38**

JOHN BRANDON SMITH - The Falls Of Aysgarth - signed and dated 1870 - 29½ x 49½in.
(Christie's) **£420**

JOHN BRANDON SMITH - A Waterfall; And A Torrent - both signed and dated 1891 - 17¾ x 13½in.
(Christie's) **£900 Pair**

MILLER SMITH - Country Girl Seated On Bench Outside Cottage - oil - 27 x 22in.
(G. A. Key) **£72**

R. DUMONT SMITH - Still Life Of Fruit On A Table - signed - 15½ x 19½in.
(Sotheby's Belgravia) **£140**

WILLIAM SMITH - A Spaniel With A Rabbit In An Extensive Landscape - signed and dated 1848 - 11½ x 19½in.
(Christie's) **£200**

WILLIAM J. SMITH - Trefiew, North Wales - watercolour heightened with white - signed and inscribed beneath the mount and on the reverse - 14¾ x 21½in.
(Christie's) **£22**

WILLIAM SMITH - Dover Mail Coach
Passing Two Rustics - 24 x 36in.
(Woolley & Wallis) **£720**

WILLIAM COLLINGWOOD SMITH -
Porta Paradiso, Venice - heightened with
bodycolour - signed - oval - 7¼ x 11¼in.
(Sotheby's Belgravia) **£35**

EUGENE SMITS - The Mandolin - oil on
wood - signed - 26 x 21cm.
(Galerie Moderne) **£470**

SMYTHE - The Woodland Cottage, a
winter scene by moonlight - signed - panel
- 9½ x 7 ins.
(Neale & Son) **£36**

E. R. SMYTHE - Donkey's Head - black
ink drawing - 9 x 6in.
(G. A. Key) **£28**

E. R. SMYTHE - The Wayside Drink,
Figures, Horse And Dog Outside A
Cottage - oil - 15in. diameter circular.
(G. A. Key) **£280**

EDWARD ROBERT SMYTHE - A
Horse-Drawn Sled In A Winter Landscape
- signed - 11½ x 19½in.
(Christie's) **£360**

EDWARD ROBERT SMYTHE - A Pony And
Sheep In A Woodland Landscape - oil on
canvas - 12 x 16in.
(King & Chasemore) **£750**

H. B. D. SMYTHE - Cattle And Sheep
In A Landscape - signed - on panel -
11½ x 13¾in.
(Sotheby's Belgravia) **£200**

PAUL SMYTH - Rehearsal At Blickling -
oil - 16 x 20in.
(G. A. Key) **£22**

TOM SMYTHE - An Extensive View Of
Southwold; Southwold, A View Of The
Beach With Figures Beside A Breakwater
- oil - on canvas - both signed and
inscribed 'Ipswich' - 10½ x 20½in.
(King & Chasemore) **£2,900 Pair**

THOMAS SMYTHE - A Village Scene, With
Many Farm Labourers, Women And Children
Watching A Punch And Judy Show - signed -
on panel - 11¾ x 26in.
(Henry Spencer & Sons) **£2,000**

J. G. SNAPE - 'Coastal Scene, Pendennis
Castle From Swan Pool, Falmouth' -
signed - 19th century - oil on canvas -
12 x 18in.
(Lalonde Martin) **£10**

PEETER SNAYERS - The Entry Of The Archduke Leopold William Into a Town - signed - 30 x 46¾in.
(Christie's) **£12,000**

J. HERBERT SNELL - Extensive Landscape with distant view of Windsor Castle - signed - 20 x 30 ins.
(Christie's, S. Kensington) **£440**

F. SNYDERS - A Fox Hunt, Dogs Chasing Two Foxes in the foreground Of A Hilly Landscape - 42½ x 63½in.
(Sotheby's) **£1,600**

FRANS SNYDERS - Dead Game And Birds, A Lobster, Bunches Of Grapes And Delftware On A Table - 32½ x 46½in.
(Christie's) **£7,000**

FRANS SNYDERS - A Carcass Of Meat, A Spaniel, Two Greyhounds, Dead Game, And A Basket Of Fruit, With A Landscape Beyond - 94 x 86in.
(Christie's) **£4,500**

FRANS SNYDERS - Dead Game And Birds, A Lobster, Bunches Of Grapes And Delftware on a table - 32½ x 46½in.
(Christie's) **£3,200**

A. SODAR - Landscape - oil on canvas - signed - 35 x 45cm.
(Galerie Moderne) **£116**

SOLARIO, after - Virgin Mary holding Baby Jesus - oil painting - 7½ x 6 ins.
(Jackson-Stops & Staff) **£140**

ANDREA SOLDI - Portrait Of An Architect, three-quarter length, Wearing A Blue Coat And Yellow Waistcoat And Holding Architectural Plans - signed and dated 1758 - 38 x 32in.
(Christie's) **£6,000**

F. SOLDWEDELL - Ship In The Arctic; Two Penguins - pencil and watercolour - both signed - 9¼ x 8in. and 9¾ x 8¾in.
(Sotheby's) **£40 Two**

F. SOLDWEDELL - The Fisherman - pencil and watercolour - signed - 12¼ x 17¾in.
(Sotheby's) **£60**

FRANCESO SOLIMENA - Madonna
And Child With Attendant Putti
And A Saint In Adoration - 76 x
62.5cm.
(Phillips) **£460**

FRANCESCO SOLIMENA - The
Personification of Faith - a sketch for the
decoration of a spandrel - 19½ x 30in.
(Christie's) **£3,500**

FRANCESCO SOLIMENA - An
Allegory Of Fortitude, Time And
Religion - 19½ x 23½in.
(Christie's) **£1,100**

SIMEON SOLOMON - Sleep - red chalk -
signed with monogram - inscribed and
dated 1891 - 15¼ x 13in.
(Sotheby's Belgravia) **£420**

SOLOMON JOSEPH SOLOMON - Portrait
Of A Girl In Black - signed with monogram
- on board - 14 x 10in.
(Christie's) **£120**

ABRAHAM SOLOMON - Art Critics In
Brittany - signed and dated 1860 - 29 x
23in.
(Christie's) **£1,600**

S. J. SOLOMON - A Young Girl Reading
In An Interior - 23½ x 18in.
(Sotheby's Belgravia) **£200**

F. SOLYAKOV - Village Girls Merrymaking, A Snow-covered Village
Beyond - signed and dated 1914 -
53¾ x 81 in.
(Sotheby's) £3,200

JORIS VAN SON - A Still Life Of Fruit,
Peaches And An Orange In A Silver Tazza
In A Stone Niche And, Below, Grapes,
Peaches And A Medlar - 15¼ x 11¼in.
(Sotheby's) £4,000

ELIZABETH SONREL - Trois Genies
Fantastiques - gouache - signed and
inscribed and dated Noel 1926 - 9¼ x
12¼in.
(Sotheby's) £190

HENRI SOMM - La Matelotte - pen and
indian ink and watercolour - signed -
9¾ x 8in.
(Sotheby's) £300

HENRI SOMM - L'Elegante Au Rideau -
pen and indian ink and wash - signed -
9½ x 7½in.
(Sotheby's) £70

HENRI SOMM - L'Elegante Au Marche
Aux Fleurs - pen and indian ink - signed -
9½ x 7½in.
(Sotheby's) £110

HENRI SOMM - L'Elegante A l'Exposi-
tion De Tableaux - pencil and watercolour
- signed - 9¾ x 6in.
(Sotheby's) £320

THOMAS JAMES SOPER - A View
From Limmick Road, Holmwood - signed
- 19½ x 23½in.
(Sotheby's Belgravia) £130

THOMAS JAMES SOPER - In Rustic
Devon - signed - 12½ x 17½in.
(Sotheby's Belgravia) **£120**

RAFFAELLO SORBI - Replenishing
The Wine - signed - on panel - 4¾ x 3¼in.
(Sotheby's) **£400**

JAN SOREAU - Grapes, Peaches And
Plums In A Basket And In An Early 17th
century Wan-Li Bowl, and mixed flowers in
a Netherlandish roehmer on a table strewn
with grapes, cherries and wild strawberries -
on panel - 28¾ x 40¼in.
(Christie's) **£48,000**

HENDRIK MAERTENSZ SORGH - A
Market Scene, A Vegetable Seller Seated
Surrounded By Piles Of Vegetables Of
All Kinds And Fruit In Baskets, Pointing
To A Man And Woman Who Are Putting
A Bunch Of Carrots In A Wheelbarrow -
signed indistinctly - 18½ x 24½in.
(Sotheby's) **£5,500**

G. SORMAIRY - The Promenade, Venice;
Fishing In The Lagoon - heightened with
white - both signed - 17¼ x 9¾in.
(Sotheby's) **£80 Pair**

R. S. SOTT - In The Rough - signed and
dated 1905 - 50 x 33in.
(Sotheby's) **£220**

SOUTH AMERICAN SCHOOL - The
Madonna And Child Adored By Saints -
on panel - 16¼ x 25½in.
(Sotheby's) **£10**

JEAN SOUVERBIE - Ceres - oil - on
canvas - signed and dated '63 - 19¼ x
23½in.
(Sotheby's) **£780**

JEAN SOUVERBIE - La Nuit - oil - on
canvas - signed and dated '58 - 16½ x
25in.
(Sotheby's) **£600**

PAUL CONSTANT SOYER - Baby's
Bedtime - signed - on panel - 14 x 11in.
(Sotheby's) **£1,150**

G. M. SOYTE - Saint Agatha, after
Sebastiano del Piombo; The Virgin,
after Carlo Dolci - oval - on panel -
each 8½ x 6¾in.
(Sotheby's) **£110 Pair**

V. SOZONOV - South Of France -
31 x 38cm.
(Edmiston's) **£9**

MARCELLO SOZZI - La Poesia - watercolour - circular - 17in. diameter.
(Geering & Colyer) **£42**

SPANISH SCHOOL - Saint Helen; And
Saint Sebastian - on gold ground panel -
dated 1530 - 52 x 23½in.
(Christie's) **£1,300 Two**

SPANISH SCHOOL, 19th Century -
A View Of Seville - 21 x 29in
(Christie's) **£460**

SPANISH SCHOOL, 18th century -
'Pisces' - February Scene - 37 x 54in.
(Chrystal Bros. & Stott) **£950**

RICHARD PHENE SPEARS - Broadway,
Worcester - signed and inscribed - 10¼ x
13¼in.
(Sotheby's Belgravia) **£25**

CHARLES SPENCELAYH - 'The
Music Lesson' - signed - 31 x 41cm.
(Phillips) **£650**

CHARLES SPENCELAYH - Just Ripe -
signed - indistinctly inscribed on the
stretcher - 15½ x 11½in.
(Sotheby's Belgravia) **£750**

CHARLES SPENCELAYH - Two
Minutes' Silence - signed - 25½ x 17½in.
(Christie's) **£700**

WALTER SPINDLER - Portrait Of Sarah Bernhardt, three-quarter length, Seated, Wearing A White Dress - signed, inscribed and dated 1891 - 56 x 43½in.
(Christie's) **£2,000**

FRANK SPENLOVE SPENLOVE - Venice - signed - on panel - 7¾ x 4½in.
(Sotheby's Belgravia) **£140**

C. SPERA - An Italianate Landscape, With Classical Ruins And Soldiers Playing Cards in the foreground - 66½ x 92½in.
(Christie's) **£4,200**

THOMAS SPINKS - Wooded River Landscapes - both signed and one dated 1875 - 20 x 36in.
(Christie's, S. Kensington) **£480 Pair**

J. J. SPOHLER - A Summer River Landscape, A Barge And Other Boats By A Wharf in the foreground - bears signature - 11¼ x 17½in.
(Sotheby's) **£1,750**

JAN JACOB SPOHLER - A Frozen River Landscape, A Windmill And Other Buildings To The Left - signed - 24¼ x 33½in.
(Sotheby's) **£7,200**

JAN JACOB COENRAAD SPOHLER - A Dutch Canal Scene - signed - on panel - 11 x 8½in.
(Sotheby's) **£1,700**

W. SPILSBURY - Christians Thrown To The Tiger In A Roman Arena - signed and dated 1883 - oil on canvas - 29 x 48½in.
(Bearnes & Waycotts) **£140**

JACOB VAN SPREEUWEN - Interior
Of A Kitchen, A Woman Peeling Parsnips;
A Cabbage And A Marrow At Her Feet,
A Metal Jug And An Earthenware Pot
Beside Her On A Table - 26 x 29¼in.
(Sotheby's) **£2,000**

L. R. SQUIRRELL - Grey Day At Durham
- watercolour - 10 x 15in.
(G. A. Key) **£26**

N. SSAMOKISCH - A Battle Scene With A
Bugler, Cavalry And A Gun Team - signed
and dated 1885 - 39 x 60in.
(Warner, Sheppard & Wade) **£2,100**

L. VAN STAATEN - Dutch Canal Scene
With Sailing Barges And Windmill
Beyond - signed - watercolour - 14½ x
21¼in.
(Charles R. Phillips) **£100**

NICOLAS DE STAEL - Rectangles
Jaunes Et Verts - signed - 51 x 38in.
(Christie's, New York) **£51,800**

HENDRIK STAETS - Men-O'-War In A
Heavy Swell - signed with monogram -
33½ x 43in.
(Christie's) **£3,000**

GEORGE STAINTON - 'Off Dover,
Laying-Too For Pilot' and 'Cullercoats' -
signed - inscribed and signed on
reverse - 38 x 57cm.
(Phillips) **£620 Pair**

A. VAN STALBEMT - A Rocky Woody
Landscape With A Man On A Path; And
A Wooded Landscape With Travellers
On A Path - one bears initials - on panel -
circular - 8in. diameter.
(Christie's) **£2,600 Pair**

A. VAN STALBEMT - Pastoral Figures
Feasting In A Wooded Landscape - on
panel - 17 x 26½in.
(Christie's) **£1,600**

ADRIAEN VAN STALBEMT - A Wooded
Mountainous Landscape with a gypsy telling
a traveller's fortune near a stream, and a
walled monastery on a hill beyond - signed
and dated 1604 - on copper - 10¼ x 14½in.
(Christie's) **£11,000**

ADRIAEN VAN STALBEMT - The
Israelites Building The Tabernacle -
on copper - 15 x 20in.
(Sotheby's) **£11,500**

STANFIELD - Shipping Off A Port -
5¾ x 8¼in.
(Sotheby's) £95

CLARKSON STANFIELD - Small
Vessels In A Choppy Sea - signed and
dated 1853 - watercolour - 8¼ x 10¾in.
(Bearnes & Waycotts) £100

GEORGE CLARKSON STANFIELD - A
Town On The Rhine With Timber Mer-
chants Under A Bridge And A Castle
Beyond - signed and dated 1863 - 26 x
39½in.
(Christie's) £6,200

GEORGE CLARKSON STANFIELD -
The Lucerne Bridge - 19¼ x 29¼in.
(Sotheby's Belgravia) £450

W. C. STANFIELD - Busy Estuary Scene -
33 x 49in.
(Woolley & Wallis) £320

WILLIAM CLARKSON STANFIELD -
Vessels Offshore In A Choppy Sea -
signed and dated 1821 - 9 x 13in.
(Christie's) £520

CHARLES J. STANILAND - Imitation,
The Sincerest Flattery - signed on panel -
12 x 7in.
(Sotheby's Belgravia) £110

CALEB ROBERT STANLEY - A Rural
Scene - signed and dated 1834 - on
board - 21 x 16½in.
(Sotheby's Belgravia) £950

ELOISE HARRIET STANNARD -
Strawberries, Raspberries In Basket With
Flowers On Slab - oil - dated 1882 -
10 x 12in.
(G. A. Key) £875

ELOISE HARRIET STANNARD -
'Summer' Strawberries On Cabbage
Leaf With Woodbine - oval - dated
1866 - oil - 10½ x 13½in.
(G. A. Key) £1,075

SYLVESTER STANNARD - 'By A Woodman's Cottage Near Stratford On Avon' - signed - watercolour - 13 x 21in.
(Bearnes & Waycotts) **£120**

L. H. STANNERS - British Destroyer Under Steam - oil on canvas - signed - 23 x 14½in.
(J. Francis, T. Jones & Sons) **£16**

ELOISE HARRIET STANNARD - Duckling - signed and dated 1894 - 17 x 15in.
(Sotheby's) **£1,000**

HENRY STANNARD - Fieldfare Thrushes In A Winter Landscape - signed - 18½ x 13½in.
(Sotheby's) **£40**

HENRY SYLVESTER STANNARD - Children Picking Flowers Outside A Cottage - 9¾ x 13¼in.
(Sotheby's Belgravia) **£110**

HENRY SYLVESTER STANNARD - Barrington Near Burford - signed and inscribed on the reverse - 11 x 15½in.
(Sotheby's) **£80**

JOSEPH STANNARD - Fishermen And Their Boats On The Shore - signed twice with monogram and dated 1839 - black chalk and touches of coloured chalk on grey paper - 5½ x 8½in.
(Christie's) **£240**

JOSEPH STANNARD - Horses And A Cart By A Fishing Boat At Low Tide - coloured chalks on buff paper - 6¾ x 10½in.
(Christie's) **£260**

JOSEPH STANNARD - Study Of A Fisherman - signed with initials - pencil and watercolour on oatmeal paper - 4½ x 3½in.
(Christie's) **£85**

JOSEPH STANNARD - The Watermill - signed with initials - 10 x 13½in.
(Christie's) **£350**

LILIAN STANNARD - 'A Peaceful Walk - Summer Garden Scene - watercolour - 9¾ x 14in.
(Lalonde Martin) **£14**

L SANDYS STANYON - The Newark, Leicestershire - signed - 15½ x 23½in.
(Sotheby's Belgravia) **£320**

MASSIMO STANZIONE - Saint John The Baptist In The Wilderness - 56 x 46in.
(Christie's) **£1,600**

WILLIAM STAPLETON - Fishing Boats On The Shore At Low Tide - pencil and watercolour - 17½ x 30½in.
(Christie's) **£38**

JAMES STARK - A Wooded River Scene, With Cattle Standing In The Water, And Figures On A Rustic Bridge in the distance - 11½ x 15¼in.
(Henry Spencer & Sons) **£200**

J. STARK - An East Anglian Canal
Scene - signed - on panel - 14 x 19in.
(King & Chasemore)   **£380**

JAMES STARK - A Wooded Landscape,
With A Stream - 17½ x 23½in.
(Christie's)   **£4,500**

**JACOBUS NICHOLAS BARON TJARDA
VAN STARKENBORGH** - Peasants And A
Haycart by a trough on a mountain pass -
signed - 16¼ x 23in.
(Christie's)   **£1,100**

ALBERT STARLING - Cwmerra Falls, N.
Wales - signed - oil - 15 x 12in.
(Warner, Sheppard & Wade)   **£22**

H. STAUNTON - The Village Path; The
Riverside Path - both signed and dated
1858 - 9½ x 17½in.
(Sotheby's Belgravia)   **£160 Pair**

JOHN SYDNEY STEEL - Still Life Of
A Duck On A Ledge - signed - 21½ x
29½in.
(Sotheby's Belgravia)   **£160**

E. STEELE - Studies Of Fruit And
Flowers, In And Around Vases On Stone
Ledges - signed and dated 1904 - oil on
canvas - 23½ x 17½in.
(Bearnes & Waycotts)   **£240 Pair**

E. STEELE - Roses, Daisies And Other Flowers - oil - on canvas - 15 x 19in.
(Chrystal Bros. & Stott) **£150**

EDWIN STEELE - Still Life Of Roses And Other Flowers - signed - 9½ x 13½in.
(Sotheby's Belgravia) **£65**

STEELE - Still Life Of Fruit On A Table - 20 x 36½in.
(Sotheby's Belgravia) **£14**

GOURLAY STEELL - "Cash", A Study Of A Black Bull In A Landscape - oil - signed and dated 1889 - canvas laid down - 68.5 x 88.5cm.
(Phillips in Scotland) **£270**

STEEN - A Peasant Reading A Letter, A Woman Seated Behind Him - bears signature and dated - 12½ x 8¾in.
(Sotheby's) **£360**

STEEN - A Peasant Smoking, Seated At A Table - canvas - on panel - 6½ x 5in.
(Sotheby's) **£130**

J. STEEN - Peasants Embracing In An Inn - on panel - 8½ x 7in.
(Christie's) **£380**

JAN STEEN - The Backgammon Players - signed - on panel - 16 x 14in.
(Christie's) **£18,000**

JAN STEEN - Peasants Paying Tithes - signed and dated 1679 - 18½ x 15½in.
(Christie's) **£9,500**

H. VAN STEENWYCK, THE YOUNGER - The Interior Of A Palace, Two Men And A Woman Conversing Beneath An Elaborate Gilt Chandelier - on panel - 11 x 8in.
(Sotheby's) **£1,900**

JOHN STEEPLE - The Gypsy Camp - signed - inscribed and dated 1853 on the reverse - circular - diameter 7in.
(Sotheby's Belgravia) **£240**

HENRY REYNOLDS STEER - Cecilia, Touchstone And Rosalind, 'As You Like It', Act II, Scene IV - 20½ x 13½in.
(Sotheby's Belgravia) **£170**

STEER

HENRY REYNOLDS STEER - Portrait Of A North African Tribesman - signed and dated Oct. 1883 - 12¾ x 8¼in.
(Sotheby's Belgravia) **£70**

HARRY REYNOLDS STEER - A Moroccan Smoking A Pipe - watercolour - signed and dated 1881 - 19 x 13¾in.
(Christie's) **£120**

THEOPHILE-ALEXANDRE STEINLEN - Les Chanteurs Du Mois De Marie - pencil and coloured crayons - 20 x 13in.
(Sotheby's) **£120**

J. STELLA - The Madonna And Child With St. Elizabeth And The Infant St. John The Baptist - 18½ x 14½in.
(Christie's) **£650**

JACQUES STELLA - The Rest On The Flight Into Egypt - 49 x 61½in.
(Christie's) **£3,000**

STEPHANOFF - Scene From Woodstock And Gil Blas - both bear another signature - each 11¼ x 9in.
(Sotheby's Belgravia) **£170 Pair**

FRANCIS PHILIP STEPHANOFF - Prince John Welcoming King Richard On His Return - 24 x 36in.
(Christie's) **£420**

ROMAIN STEPPE - Seascape - oil on wood - signed - 12 x 16cm.
(Galerie Moderne) **£62**

ROMAIN STEPPE - Seascape - oil on canvas - signed - 53 x 75cm.
(Galerie Moderne) **£365**

ROBERT MACAULAY STEVENSON - "Rhapsody", An Evening River Landscape - oil - signed - 37.5 x 82.5cm.
(Phillips in Scotland) **£60**

ALLAN STEWART - The Charge Of The Scots Greys At Quenlin - signed and dated 1915 - 48 x 76in.
(Sotheby's) **£620**

L. STEWART - Moated Country House - watercolour - 20 x 30in.
(G. A. Key) **£34**

G. B. STICKS - 'Glentilt', Highland Landscape - signed and dated 1885 - on canvas - 18 x 15in.
(Morphet & Morphet) **£195**

GEORGE BLACKIE STICKS - The Kyles Of Bute, From Glen Calloc At Sunset - oil - signed and dated 1876 - 41 x 59½in.
(Henry Spencer & Sons) **£400**

HARRY STICKS - A Stormy Day - signed - 19½ x 29in.
(Sotheby's Belgravia) **£70**

HARRY STICKS - Rocky Coastal Scene With Stormy Sea - oil - 20 x 30in.
(Thomas Love & Sons Ltd) **£12**

EDWIN ST JOHN - An Italian Lakeside Town - heightened with bodycolour - signed - 17 x 27¼in.
(Sotheby's Belgravia) **£75**

JAN STOBBAERTS - Horses In A Stable - on panel - 13 x 16¼in.
(Sotheby's) **£200**

HENRY JOHN STOCK - The Stars - signed and dated 1887 - 19½ x 13in.
(Sotheby's Belgravia) **£60**

JAN VAN DER STOFFE - An Extensive Cavalry Skirmish In An Open Landscape - signed and dated 1637 - on panel - 46.5 x 96cm.
(Phillips) **£1,400**

C. STOITZNER - Portraits Of Fishermen - 20 x 14.5cm.
(Edmiston's) **£700 Pair**

O. STOITZNER - An Old Pipe Smoker - signed - 8¼ x 6¼in.
(Sotheby's) **£260**

M. STOKES - The Jewel - indistinctly signed with monogram and dated 1884 - on board - 11 x 7¼in.
(Sotheby's Belgravia) **£120**

M. BOELEMA DE STOMME - A Still Life, A Roemer, An Overturned Nautilus Cup, A Beaker, A Pewter Plate Of Oysters And A Peeled Lemon, On A Table Covered By A White Cloth - 21 x 30in.
(Sotheby's) **£1,600**

STONE - On The Coast - on board - 9½ x 17½in.
(Sotheby's Belgravia) **£15**

A. STONE - A Wooded Path - signed - 15½ x 11½in.
(Sotheby's Belgravia) **£120**

HENRY JOHN STOCK - Portrait Of Richard Chamberlain - signed and dated 1899 - 7¾ x 9½in.
(Sotheby's Belgravia) **£60**

HENRY JOHN STOCK - Portrait Of Emily Agnes Chamberlain - signed and dated 1896 - 8 x 6½in.
(Sotheby's Belgravia) **£120**

HENRY JOHN STOCK - Portrait Of Gertrude Chamberlain - signed and dated 1895 - 8¼ x 7in.
(Sotheby's Belgravia) **£95**

W. R. STONE - An Extensive Landscape With A Train in the distance - signed - 12 x 16in.
(Sotheby's Belgravia) **£65**

STONE

W. R. STONE - A Riverside Castle; A Village On A River - 12 x 17¼in.
(Sotheby's Belgravia) **£300 Pair**

W. STONE, JNR - A Roadside Cottage - signed and dated 1884 - 10 x 18in.
(Sotheby's Belgravia) **£110**

DIRCK STOOP - Sportsmen Coursing Hares, A Horseman With A Pack Of Hounds, Followed By Two Huntsmen On Foot - 28½ x 42½in.
(Sotheby's) **£6,500**

STORCK - Shipping In A Calm, An Offshore Scene At Sunset - on panel - 9 x 12in.
(King & Chasemore) **£480**

A. STORCK - A States Yacht, A Boier Yacht And Men-O'-War Offshore In A Stiff Breeze - bears Backhuysen signature - 22 x 27in.
(Christie's) **£38,000**

ABRAHAM STORCK - A View Of the Ij, Amsterdam With The Shreierstoren, Shipping And Figures - signed and dated 1659 - 32½ x 44in.
(Christie's) **£8,000**

ABRAHAM STORCK - A Dutch Harbour Scene with a yacht at a jetty, men-o'-war and other shipping beyond, and boys swimming in the foreground - 25 x 32¼in.
(Christie's) **£15,000**

JACOBUS STORCK - A River Landscape, with sailing barges, a palace below a hill town, and a church to the right - 23 x 32½in.
(Christie's) **£2,400**

JACOBUS STORCK - A Harbour Scene, with numerous buildings, a fortified gateway and a Dutch man-o'-war offshore - signed - 24 x 44in.
(Christie's) **£4,200**

THOMAS STOTHARD - A Chinese Street Seller; And A Rat Catcher - both signed - watercolour - 10 x 7½in. and smaller.
(Christie's) **£100 Two**

H. VAN STRAATEN - Arranging The Flowers, A Mother And Child In A Rustic Interior - 15 x 11in.
(Sotheby's) **£220**

JURRIAEN VAN STREEK - A Still Life With A Roemer And Fruit - 63 x 56cm.
(Sotheby's) **£3,800**

ARTHUR STREETON - Australian Homestead Beneath A Wooded Hillside - signed - 13¾ x 18¼in.
(Phillips) **£3,800**

PHILIP EUSTACE STRETTON - A Terrier In The Gunroom - signed - 11 x 15in.
(Sotheby's Belgravia) **£320**

ABRAHAM VAN STRIJ - Elegant Dutch Interiors, A Mother And Child Seated By A Window; A Gentleman Reading - both signed - on panel - 28½ x 23½in.
(Sotheby's) **£5,200 Pair**

J. VAN STRIJ - Cattle And Sheep In A Wooded Landscape - both indistinctly signed - each 13 x 16in.
(Sotheby's) **£380 Two**

STUART - Portrait Of The Reverend John Atkinson, half length, Seated, His Right Hand Resting On An Open Book - 28¾ x 23¾in.
(Sotheby's) **£30**

ALLAN STUART - The Young Pretender Arriving At Holyrood House - signed and dated 1904 - 39½ x 49½in.
(Christie's) **£550**

R. EASTON STUART - Portrait Of A Lady Wearing A Black Hat, half length - signed and dated 1897 - 29½ x 17½in.
(Sotheby's Belgravia) **£32**

LINT

HENDRIK VAN LINT, called STUDIO -
A wooded river landscape with peasants
cattle and sheep and a village beyond -
17½ x 26½ ins.
(Christie's) £1,300

**HENDRIK FRANS VAN LINT, called
STUDIO** - Italianate Coastal Landscapes
With Shepherds And Cattle - 8¾ x 13¼in.
(Christie's) £,800 Pair

F. W. STURGE - Rocky Coast, Sunset;
Breakers On The Coast - both signed and
dated '96 and '89 - each 36½ x 26½in.
(Sotheby's Belgravia) £20 Two

E. LE SUEUR - Diana And Actaeon -
30 x 24½in.
(Christie's) £600

E. LE SUEUR - Portrait Of A Young
Man, half length, In A Black Habit -
26½ x 22¼in.
(Christie's) £320

SUFFOLK SCHOOL - Cattle Resting
By Stream At Evening - oil - 11 x 17in.
(G. A. Key) £160

W. H. SUGDEN - Furness Abbey -
watercolour - signed - inscribed and
dated 1907 - 9½ x 14in.
(Christie's) £40

ARTHUR SUKER - A Rocky Coast -
signed - 16½ x 28in.
(Sotheby's Belgravia) £28

LEOPOLD SURVAGE - Couples A La
Poire Et Feuille - pencil - signed - signed
with initials and dated '36 - 10¾ x 8¾in.
(Sotheby's) £100

J. SUSTERMAN - Portrait Of A Lady,
half length, As Saint Catherine - 35 x
31½in.
(Christie's) £600

SUSTRIS - The Temptation Of Saint
Jerome - 66 x 47in.
(Christie's) £600

L. SUSTRIS - Portrait Of A Bearded
Gentleman, Seated, three-quarter length,
Wearing A Fur-Trimmed Robe, A View
Of Venice Beyond - inscribed - 48 x
44in.
(Christie's) £800

JOHN SUTTON - Extensive Norfolk
Landscape With Cottages And Mill -
oil - 20 x 30in.
(G. A. Key) £40

JAN SUYVER - Figures And Boats In A
River Landscape - oil - signed - 25.5 x
35.5cm.
(Phillips in Scotland) £145

SWABIAN SCHOOL, circa 1520 - Christ As
Salvator Mundi With The Twelve Apostles,
half length, behind a parapet - on gold ground
panel - 17 x 53in.
(Christie's) £8,500

HERMAN VAN SWANEVELT - A
Wooded Landscape With Washerwomen -
26 x 36¾in.
(Sotheby's) £2,800

SWAINE - Fishing Boats And Men-O'-War Offshore In A Calm - on copper - oval - 5½ x 6½in.
(Christie's) £260

JOHN MacALLAN SWAN - A Female Nude Study - coloured chalks on blue paper - 17½ x 11in.
(Sotheby's Belgravia) £5

JOHN MacALLAN SWANN - Arabs Hunting Lion In Desert - watercolour - 14 x 18in.
(G. A. Key) £50

JOHN WARKUP SWIFT - Shipping Scenes - signed - oil on panel - oval - 5¼ x 7½in.
(Bearnes & Waycotts) **£400 Pair**

SWISS SCHOOL - Landscape - oil on lined canvas - 48 x 59cm.
(Galerie Moderne) **£10**

PHILIPPE SWYNCOP - A Man Seated - oil on canvas - signed and dated 1926 - 1m. x 80cm.
(Galerie Moderne) **£700**

J. SYER - A Barge Off The Coast In Rough Seas - on board - 6¾ x 8½in.
(Sotheby's) **£70**

JOHN SYER - Cattle By A Ruined Castle - signed and dated 1881 - 9½ x 13½in.
(Sotheby's Belgravia) **£80**

JOHN SYER - A View Of Capel Curig, North Wales - signed and dated '67 - 12¼ x 17¾in.
(Christie's) **£500**

W. CHRISTIAN SYMANS - 'Parting Advice' - signed and dated 1873 - oil - 30 x 25in.
(Warner, Sheppard & Wade) **£260**

JOHN SYER - Fishing boat on a beach at low tide - signed and dated '62 - 6¼ x 14¼ins.
(Christie's, S. Kensington) **£160**

WILLIAM CHRISTIAN SYMONS - Rule Britannia - heightened with bodycolour - signed - 21¼ x 30½in.
(Sotheby's Belgravia) **£55**

WILLIAM CHRISTIAN SYMONS - The Dream - signed - 49½ x 40in.
(Sotheby's Belgravia) **£110**

WILLIAM CHRISTIAN SYMONS - Boys Together - signed - signed on the reverse - 19½ x 29½in.
(Sotheby's Belgravia) **£260**

DOROTHEA TANNING - Deux Femmes Enlacees - signed - signed and dated 1953 on the reverse - 23¾ x 11½in.
(Sotheby's) **£1,100**

ADRIEN HENRI TANOUX - La Modele, A Young Girl Wearing A Red Embroidered Bolero And A Brown Shawl - signed and dated 1912 - 28½ x 23½in.
(Sotheby's) **£300**

ANDERSON TARBET - Extensive Landscape With Loch in foreground - oil - 25 x 35in.
(Thomas Love & Sons Ltd) **£50**

EDWARD TAYLER - Portrait Studies of Four Ladies And A Young Girl - four coloured chalks - one heightened with bodycolour - three signed - each 17½ x 14½in.
(Sotheby's Belgravia) **£60 Five**

EDWARD TAYLER - Portraits Of Two Ladies, A Girl And A Boy - two coloured chalks, two heightened with bodycolour - one signed with monogram - 14 x 11in.
(Sotheby's Belgravia) **£45 Four**

TOM TAYLER - Coming From Market - 17¾ x 13½in.
(Sotheby's Belgravia) **£90**

A. TAYLOR - Extensive Highland Landscape With Loch And Cattle in foreground - oil - 24 x 42in.
(Thomas Love & Sons Ltd) **£220**

A. TAYLOR - Highland Landscape With Loch And Cattle in foreground - oil - 20 x 30in.
(Thomas Love & Sons Ltd) **£60**

A. TAYLOR - Highland Cattle - 50 x 75cm.
(Edmiston's) **£23**

EDWARD TAYLOR - Spanish Lady - watercolour - 17 x 14in.
(G. A. Key) **£12**

JOHN FREDERICK TAYLOR - Figures, Dogs And A Pony Outside A Bothy - signed and dated '61 - watercolour - 13 x 20in.
(Woolley & Wallis) **£160**

W. TIMPERLEY - English Landscape With Boy And Cattle, Cottage in background - oil - 23 x 16in.
(G. A. Key) **£36**

T. TEMPLE - 'The Run In' - signed, inscribed and dated 1865 - 44 x 75in.
(Christie's) **£3,000**

TENIERS - A Rocky Coastal Landscape With Peasant Selling Fish By A Ruined Arch - bears signature and dated - 40½ x 53in.
(Christie's) **£5,000**

TENIERS - The Interior Of A Cottage, A Woman Peeling Apples To The Left, Chickens To The Right, A Man Entering Through A Doorway Beyond - on panel - bears signature - 14½ x 21¾in.
(Sothebey's) **£800**

TENIERS - The Interior Of A Kitchen, A Peasant And A Servant Girl in the foreground, An Old Woman Scolding Them To The Right - on panel - bears signature - 15¾ x 19¼in.
(Sotheby's) **£1,505**

D. TENIERS, THE YOUNGER - Peter Denying Christ, With Soldiers Playing Cards - bears signature and dated 1648 - on copper - 14½ x 20½in.
(Christie's) **£4,000**

D. TENIERS, THE YOUNGER - Fortune-Tellers By A Manor House, A River Beyond - on panel - 10 x 13½in.
(Christie's) **£5,500**

D. TENIERS, THE YOUNGER -
The Temptation Of Saint Anthony -
bears signature - on panel - 13½ x
20½in.
(Christie's) **£900**

D. TENIERS - A Dutch Canal Scene
With Figures In The Moonlight in
the foreground - on panel - 8½ x 11½in.
(King & Chasemore) **£720**

DAVID TENIERS, THE YOUNGER -
A Farmyard Scene: 'Le Marchand De
Cochons' - signed - on panel - 20½ x
28¼in.
(Sotheby's) **£6,500**

DAVID TENIERS THE YOUNGER - The
Artist At Work In A Picture Cabinet -
signed - one of the pictures displayed is
dated 1633 - on panel - 21½ x 30½in.
(Christie's) **£40,000**

DAVID TENIERS THE YOUNGER - David
And Bathsheba - 21 x 32in.
(Christie's) **£7,500**

DAVID TENIERS, THE YOUNGER -
A Peasant Feeding Chickens Outside
A Cottage - signed - on panel - 8½ x
6½in.
(Christie's) **£4,500**

D. TENIERS, THE YOUNGER -
Peasants Smoking Outside A Cottage
With A Landscape Beyond - bears
signature - on panel - 10½ x 14½in.
(Christie's) **£10,000**

GERARD TERBORCH - Gesina Terborch
And Her Sister As Shepherdesses - 19¼ x
13in.
(Sotheby's) **£26,000**

HENDRICK TERBRUGGHEN - A Laughing Man With A Dog - signed with monogram and dated 1628.
(Christie's) **£9,000**

B. TERNDONCK - Boats At The Quay - oil on wood - signed - 50 x 40cm.
(Galerie Moderne) **£31**

JOHN TERRIS - A Church By A Riverside - signed - 11½ x 17½in.
(Sotheby's Belgravia) **£42**

JOHN TERRIS - Lunan Bay, East Coast - watercolour - 34 x 50cm.
(Edmiston's) **£44**

JOHN TERRIS - East Coast Fishing Village - watercolour - 51 x 39cm.
(Edmiston's) **£60**

AUGUSTIN SALINAS Y TERUEL - Italian Fiesta - signed and inscribed 'Roma' - on panel - 9½ x 15¾in.
(Sotheby's) **£2,600**

A. TERWESTEN - The Three Graces - 58½ x 42in.
(Christie's) **£1,800**

HENRY HERBERT LA THANGUE - A Study Of A Young Peasant Girl - signed - 27 x 22in.
(Sotheby's) **£500**

J. P. VAN THIELEN - A Swag Of Tulips, Roses And Carnations Suspended From Ribbons Decorating A Cartouche - 41 x 33in.
(Christie's) **£2,000**

JAN PHILIPS VAN THIELEN - Roses, Tulips, Daffodils And Other Flowers In A Bowl On A Ledge - 29 x 20in.
(Christie's) **£7,000**

J. THIRTLE - Extensive Open Landscape With Figures - watercolour - 6 x 9in.
(G. A. Key) **£22**

JOHN THIRTLE - A Farmhouse With A Timber Drag - dated May 6, 1806 - pencil and grey wash - 9¾ x 13½in.
(Christie's) **£400**

GROSVENOR THOMAS - The Old Mill - signed - 23¼ x 15½in.
(Sotheby's) **£140**

JOSEPH THOMAS, Austrian School - Alpine Landscape With Chalet, Horses And Figures - oil on panel - signed - 19 x 14in.
(J. Francis, T. Jones & Sons) **£600**

THOMAS THOMPSON - Sheep In A Landscape - oil on board - signed - 6 x 7in.
(J. Francis, T. Jones & Sons) **£34**

E. M. M. THOMSON - Basket Of Roses - 50 x 60cm.
(Edmiston's) **£11**

J. MURRAY THOMSON - Sunset Over A Highland Landscape - oil - signed - 48.5 x 74cm.
(Phillips in Scotland) **£26**

LESLIE THOMSON - On A Beach,
Evening - signed - 36 x 60in.
(Sotheby's Belgravia) **£300**

W. J. THOMSON - Figures On A Path In
A Wooded Landscape - oil - 35 x 45cm.
(Phillips in Scotland) **£50**

ARCHIBALD THORBURN - Grouse And
Partridge - both gouache - signed and dated
1932 and 1933 - 7¼ x 10in.
(Sotheby's) **£1,250 Pair**

ARCHIBALD THORBURN - Landing A
Salmon - grisaille - signed and dated 1900 -
19½ x 13½in.
(Sotheby's) **£320**

ARCHIBALD THORBURN - Pheasants
Flying From Wood - signed - 12 x 18in.
(G. A. Key) **£82**

ARCHIBALD THORBURN - Study Of
A Buzzard Hawk By It's Nest - signed
with initials - grey monochrome - 3¼ x
5½in.
(Bearnes & Waycotts) **£125**

ARCHIBALD THORBURN - Woodcock
With Their Chicks - grey wash heightened
with white - signed and dated 1897 - 14¼
x 20in.
(Christie's) **£260**

ARCHIBALD THORBURN - Bullfinches -
heightened with bodycolour - signed and
dated 1908 - 10½ x 7in.
(Sotheby's) **£600**

THORN

N. THORN - A Farm In A Wooded Setting, Pond in the foreground - oil on canvas - 11½ x 17¾in.
(Hollingsworths) £18

WILLIAM THORNBERY - Fishing Boats Off The Coast - signed - 11¼ x 8½in.
(Sotheby's Belgravia) £320

ROBERT THORNE-WAITE - The Harvesters - signed - 10½ x 18in.
(Christie's) £750

W. THORNLEY - Beached Fishing Boats - bears signature - 9½ x 15½in.
(Sotheby's Belgravia) £95

WILLIAM THORNLEY - St Michael's Mount - signed - 9½ x 16½in.
(Sotheby's Belgravia) £260

JOSEPH THORS - A Cottage On The Edge Of A Wood - signed - 24 x 36in.
(Sotheby's Belgravia) £1,000

JOSEPH THORS - Rustic Cottages - both signed - each 9¾ x 13½in.
(Sotheby's Belgravia) £850 Pair

JOSEPH THORS - Feeding The Geese - signed - 13½ x 20½in.
(Sotheby's Belgravia) £550

JOSEPH THORS - An Extensive Autumn Landscape, With A Milkmaid Fetching Water From A Stream in the foreground And A Cottage With Farm Buildings Amongst Trees Beyond - signed and dated - 107 x 173cm.
(Phillips) £920

JOSEPH THORS - A Rural Landscape At Sunset, With A Woman And Child Walking Towards Cottages, Amidst Trees in the foreground, A Church Tower in the distance - oil - signed - 12 x 15½in.
(Henry Spencer & Sons) **£320**

JOSEPH THORS - Figures Gathering Brushwood in Oak Wood - signed - 29 x 19½in.
(Phillips) **£400**

JOSEPH THORS - A Peasant On Horseback, In A Wooded Avenue - signed - 29½ x 24½in.
(Christie's) **£550**

J. THORS - Cottages And Figures By A Pond - oil - 6 x 13in.
(G. A. Key) **£33**

ALESSANDRO TIARINI - The Madonna And Child With The Infant Saint John The Baptist - 37½ x 31in.
(Christie's) **£3,200**

BERTHA TICKELL - Illuminated Manuscripts - heightened with bodycolour and gold - signed - 12¾ x 18¾in.
(Sotheby's Belgravia) **£10**

TIEPOLO - A Bacchante And Satyr In A Landscape - on panel - 5 x 9in.
(Christie's) **£260**

TIEPOLO - A Venetian Carnival Scene With Dancers - 65 x 80in.
(Sotheby's) **£2,200**

G. B. TIEPOLO - The Madonna And Child Appearing To Saint Philip Neri - arched top - 22½ x 12in.
(Christie's) **£8,500**

GILLIS VAN TILBORCH - A Man Holding A Stoneware Wine-pot, And A Woman Seated At A Table Behind Which A Young Man Is Slicing Bread, To The Right A Woman Preparing Artichokes; On The Wall Copper And Pewter Vessels And Paintings - 21½ x 29in.
(Sotheby's) **£2,300**

TILLEMANS

P. TILLEMANS - A River Landscape With Numerous Figures On Horseback And Others Unloading A Barge in the foreground, By Classical Ruins - 39 x 57in.
(Sotheby's) **£2,800**

P. TILLEMANS - A View Of The City Of Nottingham - 23 x 47½in.
(Christie's) **£2,800**

E. TILLETT - River Scene With Bridge And Houses - oil - 14 x 17in.
(G. A. Key) **£10**

HENRI TIMMERMANS - The Lecture - on wood - signed - 35 x 57cm.
(Galerie Moderne) **£130**

DOMENICO TINTORETTO - Portrait Of A Gentleman, standing three-quarter length, wearing black costume, a crucifix on a table nearby - dated 1589 - 44¼ x 34¼in.
(Christie's) **£1,800**

J. TINTORETTO - Portrait Of A Gentleman, seated, three-quarter length, wearing a black, fur-lined coat, holding a book - 47 x 53½in.
(Christie's) **£1,600**

J. J. TISSOT - At The Ball - inscribed on panel 8¾ x 4½in.
(Sotheby's) **£450**

TITIAN, After - Portrait of Francesco Filetto transformed into Saint James the Great - on panel - 9 x 6½ ins.
(Christie's) **£2,200**

FOLLOWER OF TITIAN - Landscape With St. Jerome And The Lion - on panel - 23¾ x 37¼in.
(Sotheby's) **£2,500**

TITIAN, After - The Fisherman Showing St Mark's Ring To The Doge - on panel - 8½ x 6¼in.
(Sotheby's) **£90**

TITIAN, After - The Martyrdom Of Saint Pieter Martyr - in a painted arch - 39 x 29in.
(Sotheby's) **£110**

S. DI TITO - Portrait Of A Little Boy, Head And Shoulders, Turned Half Left, In A Black Doublet With Gold Buttons And Gold Braid - 15 x 12in.
(Sotheby's) **£500**

PHILIPP PIETER ROOS, called ROSA DA TIVOLI - Washerwomen And A Peasant Family By A Water Trough in an extensive landscape - 38 x 53in.
(Christie's) **£1,800**

ROSA DA TIVOLI - A Herdsman With Cows, Sheep And Goats, in the foreground Of A Mountainous Landscape - 40 x 50¼in.
(Sotheby's) **£580**

PIETER ROOS, Called ROSA DA TIVOLI - A Herdsman With Cattle On A Path In A Mountainous Landscape - 28½ x 23½in.
(Christie's) **£600**

PHILIPP PIETER ROOS, called ROSA DA TIVOLI - Herdsmen And Animals By A Bridge In An Italianate River Landscape - 38 x 53in.
(Christie's) **£1,900**

LOUIS TOCQUE - Portrait of a Young Lawyer, three-quarter length in a red cloak and white tabs - 35 x 26in.
(Christie's) **£3,500**

LOUIS TOCQUE - Portrait Of A Gentleman, half length, In A Brown Coat, And Gold-Embroidered Waistcoat - 28½ x 22½in.
(Christie's) **£1,400**

LUC TONDERE - Still Life With Apples - oil on canvas - signed - 50 x 60cm.
(Galerie Moderne) **£8**

ROBERT TONGE - Hesketh Bank Near Southport - signed and dated 1851 - 13½ x 25¾in.
(Christie's) **£460**

FRANK WILLIAM WARWICK TOPHAM - A Surrey Garden In Spring - signed - 15 x 19¾in.
(Sotheby's Belgravia) **£85**

FRANCIS WILLIAM TOPHAM - The Spinning Wheel - 11½ x 15½in.
(Woolley & Wallis) **£200**

FRANCISCO TORRESCASSANA - The Opening Of The Suez Canal - signed and dated 1870 - 23 x 62in.
(Christie's) **£8,500**

F. J. TORROME - Bringing Up The Guns - signed and dated 1904 - 15 x 21½in.
(Sotheby's) **£190**

FERNAND TOUSSAINT - Portrait Of A Woman - oil on canvas - signed - 1m. x 80cm.
(Galerie Moderne) **£472**

LODEWIJK JAN PETRUS TOUTENEL, After BAROB HENDRIK LEYS - Burgermeister Six Inspecting Pictures In Rembrandt's Studio - signed - on panel - 28¼ x 22¼in.
(Sotheby's) **£2,600**

CHARLES TOWN - River Scene With Boat Houses - oil - 11 x 14in.
(G. A. Key) **£44**

CHARLES TOWNE - A View Of Annefield With Figures In The Garden And Glasgow Beyond - 21 x 34in.
(Christie's) **£4,000**

CHARLES TOWNE - 'Old Robin', With
A Groom, In An Extensive Wooded
Landscape - signed and inscribed
Liverpool - 25½ x 33½in.
(Christie's) **£2,600**

CHARLES TOWNE - A View Of Caernar-
von Castle With Drover, His Son And His
Dog Resting With Sheep And Castle On
The River Bank - oil on canvas - 27½ x
35in.
(Bonham's) **£1,200**

CHARLES TOWNE - A View Of The
Stable Block And Lodge Gates Of
Annefield And Glasgow Beyond -
21 x 34in.
(Christie's) **£7,000**

FRANCIS TOWNE - North Hill, Near
Porlock, Somerset - inscribed on the
reverse - pen and brown ink, grey and
pale blue wash, watermark Britannia -
6½ x 8½in.
(Christie's) **£650**

FRANCIS TOWNE - Lydford, Devonshire - inscribed on the reverse - pen and
grey ink and watercolour - 10¼ x 7in.
(Christie's) **£1,300**

FRANCES TOWNE - Near Dulwich College;
A Parkland Landscape With Figures And
Mansion - watercolour - 4¼ x 7in.
(Woolley & Wallis) **£220**

MARY TOWNE - The Jay - pencil and
watercolour - signed 'Drawn By Mary
Towne/Woolsthorpe Lincolnshire' and
inscribed - 12¼ x 11¼in.
(Christie's) **£240**

WILLIAM TRAIES - 'On The Teign,
Devon' - signed and dated 1828 - 51 x
67cm.
(Phillips) **£420**

JOHANN GEORG TRAUTMANN – The
Denial Of Saint Peter, With Christ Before
Caiaphas Beyond - on panel - 17 x 21in.
(Christie's) **£1,000**

JOHANN PETER TRAUTMANN - A
Pair Of Village Scenes With Children
Playing, In One With A Goat, In The
Other With A See-Saw - 11¼ x 13¼in.
(Sotheby's) **£1,600 Pair**

WILLIAM TRAUTSCHOLD - Die
Muhlsturzhorner In The Bavarian
Highlands, Early Morning - pastel -
signed and dated 1869 - inscribed
on label attached - 45 x 35½in.
(Christie's) **£120**

C. TRAVERS - On The Beach - both
signed - 14 x 21in.
(Sotheby's Belgravia) **£100 Pair**

F. TREVISANI - Saint Catherine Receiving
The Palm Of Martyrdom - 18 x 14in.
(Christie's) **£500**

FRANCESCO TREVISANI - The Madonna
And Child Appearing To A Bishop Saint -
on copper - 12½ x 9½in.
(Christie's) **£1,600**

TROOST - A Gentleman Conversing With
Two Ladies, In An Interior - 14 x 11in.
(Sotheby's) **£240**

TROUILLEBERT - River Landscapes
With A Punt And Figures Picking
Flowers in the foreground - 19 x 25½in.
(Sotheby's) **£850 Pair**

A. J. TRUEMAN - A Country Lane - signed
and dated 1892 - oil - 23 x 35 ins.
(Neale & Son) **£26**

EDWARD TUCKER - In The Hills,
Evening - signed - 8¾ x 17¼in.
(Sotheby's Belgravia) **£45**

EDWARD TUCKER - An Extensive
Hilly Landscape - signed - 15 x 13½in.
(Sotheby's Belgravia) **£50**

F. TUDGAY - Sailing Ship 'Windsor
Castle' - 1875 - 50 x 76cm.
(Edmiston's) **£680**

FRANCIS TUDGAY - A Three Decker Off
Gibralter - signed and dated 1834 -
35 x 64in.
(Christie's) **£1,800**

ALESSANDRO TURCHI, Studio Of -
Christ's Entry Into Jerusalem - 78 x
92in.
(Sotheby's) **£1,800**

TURNER

TURNER - Richmond Bridge - watercolour - 8¾ x 13½in.
(Christie's) **£25**

TURNER - The Farm On The Hill; The Path To The Sea - both inscribed in pencil with note to engraver - 2¾ x 4in.
(Sotheby's) **£38 Pair**

DANIEL TURNER - A View Of Lambeth From The Thames - signed - on panel - 5 x 6½in.
(Christie's) **£90**

DANIEL TURNER - Lord Nelson's Funeral Barge At The Duke Of York's Steps On The Way To St. Paul's Cathedral - signed and dated 1807 - on panel - 16 x 25¼in.
(Christie's) **£2,200**

F. C. TURNER - Sportsman Standing By A Bay Hunter And Terrier Dog - indistinctly signed and dated 1833 - 17 x 13½in.
(Christie's, S. Kensington) **£560**

GEORGE TURNER - 'Near Barrow-On-Trent' - signed and inscribed on the reverse - oil on canvas - 15½ x 25½in.
(Bearnes & Waycotts) **£460**

GEORGE TURNER - 'A Highland Road Near Crianlarich - millboard on panel - signed and inscribed - 11 x 18¾in.
(Bearnes & Waycotts) **£140**

G. TURNER - A Shepherd With His Flock - on board - 8½ x 12½in.
(Sotheby's Belgravia) **£75**

JOHN TURNER - Imaginary Reconstruction Of A Classical Building - signed and dated 1829 - watercolour - 19¾ x 26in.
(Bearnes & Waycotts) **£20**

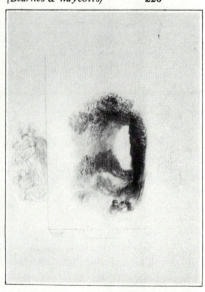

JOSEPH MALLORD WILLIAM TURNER - Fingal's Cave - inscribed 'Lord Of The Isles' 'vol' and 'Fingals Cave' - pencil and watercolour heightened with white, vignette - 11½ x 8½in.
(Christie's) **£3,800**

JOSEPH MALLORD WILLIAM TURNER -
The Bridgewater Sea Piece: Dutch Fishing
Boats In A Gale With Fishermen
Endeavouring To Put Their Fish On Board -
64 x 87½in.
(Christie's) £340,000

JOSEPH MALLORD WILLIAM TURNER
- Llanvihangel, Crucorney, Monmouth-
shire - signed - inscribed on an old label
attached to the backing - watercolour -
6¼ x 8½in.
(Christie's) £950

W. TURNER - Ruined Abbey With
Sailing Boats And Barges On Calm Sea
in foreground - oil - 11½ x 15½in.
(Thomas Love & Sons Ltd) £28

WILLIAM TURNER OF OXFORD -
Carriage Horses And A Groom Outside
A Coach House - indistinctly signed -
on panel - 15½ x 22½in.
(Christie's) £1,400

WILLIAM TURNER OF OXFORD -
A Cock Pheasant - signed with initials
and dated Jany 28th 1856 - watercolour heightened with white on blue
paper - 6 x 13¼in.
(Christie's) £240

W. E. TURNER - 'Gyp', A Study Of Hunter
In A Stable - inscribed on the reverse - oil -
21 x 25in.
(Warner, Sheppard & Wade) £40

WILLIAM EDDOWES TURNER - Pastoral
Scene With Cattle, Sheep And Poultry -
signed and dated 1886 - oil - 23½ x 36in.
(Neale & Son) £19

W. H. TURNER - The Horse Fair; And
The Horse Dealers - both signed and
dated 1859 - 9 x 12in.
(Christie's) £1,500 Pair

WILLIAM L. TURNER - St. John's
Vale, Cumberland, With Helvellyn In
The Background - signed - canvas
laid on board - 9½ x 14¼in.
(Sotheby's Belgravia) £65

TUSCAN SCHOOL, 17th Century -
A Portrait Of A Lady, In Black With A
White Ruff, Seated three-quarter length -
charged with a coat of arms - 40½ x
30in.
(Sotheby's) £350

LEON TUTUNDJEAN - Composition
Abstraite - oil - on canvas - signed -
inscribed Paris - 19¾ x 24in.
(Sotheby's) £540

WALTER TYNDALE - Thomas Hardy's
Cottage - heightened with bodycolour
and inscribed on the reverse - 9 x 6in.
(Sotheby's) £100

WALTER TYNDALE - The Doppelite
Brucke, Rothenburg - heightened with
white - signed and inscribed on the
reverse - 8½ x 14½in.
(Sotheby's) £50

UDELL - A Harbour Scene With Figures in the foreground - inscribed on the mount - indistinctly signed - 4½ x 6½in.
(Sotheby's) £120

FREDERICK UNDERHILL - Going to Church - signed - 27½ x 35½in.
(Sotheby's Belgravia) £220

FREDERICK CHARLES UNDERHILL - Shipping In A Tub - signed - 12 x 16in.
(Sotheby's) £250

FRANZ RICHARD UNTERBERGER - Naples - signed - 49 x 42in.
(Bonham's) £6,200

FRANZ RICHARD UNTERBERGER - The Lower Bazaar, Simla - signed - 35 x 22in.
(Christie's) £1,500

FRANS RICHARD UNTERBERGER - The Boat Houses, Venice: A View Of The Bacino - signed - on panel - 23 x 13in.
(Christie's) £1,900

FRANZ RICHARD UNTERBERGER AND EUGENE VERBOECKHOVEN - An Alpine Landscape, With Figures And Cattle By A Lake - signed F. R. Unterberger - 25 x 36in.
(Christie's) £2,000

MURRAY URQUHART - A Summer's Day By The River - signed and dated 1921 - 15½ x 19¼in.
(Sotheby's Belgravia) £50

A. VAN UTRECHT - A Still Life, With A Dead Hare, A Head Heron, And A Basket Of Vegetables, On A Table - on panel - 29½ x 24½in.
(Christie's) £2,200

SCHOOL OF UTRECHT, 17th Century - Putti Playing By A Fountain, A Town Beyond - on panel - 8½ x 11in.
(Sotheby's) £400

MAURICE UTRILLO - Rue A Sannois - signed - 23¾ x 32in.
(Sotheby's) £38,000

MAURICE UTRILLO - La Rue Norvins au Printemps - gouache - signed - 14¼ x 12½in.
(Sotheby's) £8,000

PIETER UYTEWAEL - A Shepherd With Bag-Pipes, With Sheep And A Dog; and A Shepherdess Holding A Pitcher, With Sheep And A Dog - 41½ x 55in. and 40½ x 51in.
(Christie's)   **£8,500 Pair**

A. VACCARO - Venus And Cupid - 58 x 54in.
(Christie's)   **£1,200**

DE VADDER - A Wooded River Landscape, With Cattle Watering And Figures Resting in the foreground - on panel - 28 x 40in.
(Christie's)   **£850**

LODEWYCK DE VADDER - An Extensive Woody Landscape, With Travellers On A Road - 19 x 25¾in.
(Christie's)   **£7,000**

PIERRE HENRI VALENCIENNES – An Italian Landscape In Central Italy, with trees by a town wall - on panel - 13 x 15¾in.
(Christie's)   **£1,600**

HENRY VALENSI - Vitesse - La Voiture De Sport - oil - on canvas - 20¾ x 32in.
(Sotheby's)   **£800**

VALENTIN - Joseph And His Brothers - 37 x 51in.
(Christie's)   **£600**

VALENCIAN SCHOOL

VALENCIAN SCHOOL, circa 1500 -
The Visitation - on panel - 34 x 25in.
(Christie's) **£2,000**

VALENCIENNES - Figures And Goats
In A Rocky Landscape - on panel -
12 x 15½in.
(Sotheby's) **£150**

J. PIO VALERO - The Young Troubador
- signed - 29¼ x 21in.
(Sotheby's) **£2,200**

M. VALKENBORCH - A Wooded Landscape, With A Village And Workmen
Constructing A House And A Town in
the distance; and A Woody Landscape,
With Sheep In A Village Street - on
panel - 10 x 14½in.
(Christie's) **£1,700 Pair**

FREDERIK VAN VALKENBORCH - An
Extensive Rocky Landscape, with
episodes from the life of Saint John the
Baptist - on copper - 16 x 22in.
(Christie's) **£7,000**

WERNER VAN DEN VALKERT - Allegories Of The Doctor As Seen By
The Patient - on panel - 37½ x 37½in.
(Christie's) **£19,000 Four**

H. VANDECAPEL - Seascape - oil on wood - signed - 21 x 28cm.
(Galerie Moderne) **£38**

Circle of **LIPPO VANNI** - The Madonna And Child, half length - on gold ground panel - 11 x 8in.
(Christie's) **£6,500**

FRANS VANNISTEBROECK - The Fish Pond - oil on canvas - signed - 40 x 50cm.
(Galerie Moderne) **£70**

L. VANNUE TTEN - Paysage Enneige - oil on canvas - signed - 39 x 56cm.
(Galerie Moderne) **£18**

M. VANTYGHEM - Winter Landscape - oil on canvas - signed - 60 x 79cm.
(Galerie Moderne) **£62**

VARLEY - Bamborough Castle, Northumberland - inscribed on the mount - arched top - 9¾ x 13¾in.
(Sotheby's) **£50**

J. VARLEY - Evening On The River Bann, Northern Ireland - sepia wash - inscribed on the reverse - 5¼ x 8¾in.
(Sotheby's) **£45**

J. VARLEY - English River Scene With Wherry - watercolour - 5 x 7in.
(G. A. Key) **£60**

JOHN VARLEY - An Imaginary Landscape With A Castle Overlooking A Lake - signed and dated 1842 - watercolour and gum arabic - 18½ x 35¾in.
(Christie's) **£600**

JOHN VARLEY - Anglers By A River Near A Windmill - watercolour - signed and dated 1837 - 3¾ x 7¼in.
(Christie's) **£130**

JOHN VARLEY - Snowden, North Wales And Riverscape - water colours - signed - 9½ x 6½in.
(Dacre, Son & Hartley) **£625 Pair**

JOHN VARLEY, JNR - Middle Eastern River Scenes - signed and dated 1874 and 1875 - watercolour - 10¼ x 17¼in.
(Bearnes & Waycotts) **£210 Pair**

VAUCLEROY

PIERRE DE VAUCLEROY - The Chestnut Trees - oil on canvas - signed - 60 x 80cm.
(Galerie Moderne) **£53**

VAUTIER - The Reluctant Assistant - 15 x 11½in.
(Sotheby's) **£350**

PIETRO DELLA VECCHIA - Lucius Junius Brutus Holding Lucretia's Dagger - inscribed - 29½ x 27in.
(Christie's) **£500**

J. PALMA, IL VECCHIO - The Madonna And Child - 21 x 14½in.
(Christie's) **£1,500**

O. VAN VEEN - Christ And The Woman Taken In Adultery - on panel - 34½ x 25in.
(Christie's) **£140**

VELAZQUEZ - Portrait Of The Infant Maria-Teresa Of Spain, Standing, three-quarter length, In A Red And Silver Dress; And Portrait Of Don Balthasar Carlos Standing, three-quarter length, In Red Costume And A Silver Lined Cloak - 45½ x 35½in.
(Christie's) **£1,500**

A. VAN DE VELDE - A Peasant, Cattle And Sheep In A Wooded River Landscape - canvas laid down on panel - 14 x 18¾in.
(Christie's) **£700**

ADRIAEN VAN DE VELDE - An Italianate Woody Landscape With A Shepherd, A Shepherdess And Cattle, A Sportsman And Dogs On A Path Beyond - signed and dated 1663 - 18½ x 24in.
(Christie's) **£12,000**

WILLEM VAN DE VELDE THE YOUNGER - Dutch Shipping Offshore In A Rising Gale With A Smallship Close-Hauled in the foreground And A Man-O'-War Preparing To Sail Beyond - signed - 51 x 74½in.
(Christie's) **£65,000**

WILLEM VAN DE VELDE THE YOUNGER - The Surrender Of The 'Royal Prince', June 3rd 1666 - signed with initials - 29¾ x 41¾in.
(Christie's) **£60,000**

W. VAN DE VELDE THE YOUNGER - Men-O'-War And Other Shipping In A Calm - bears initials - 16½ x 25½in.
(Christie's) **£5,000**

J. P. VAN VELREN - Wooded Landscape With Timber Dwelling And Peasant Workers On A Country Road, With Pond in foreground - oil on canvas - signed - 13½ x 16½in.
(Lalonde Martin) **£340**

WILHELM VELTEN - A Woody River Landscape With Cattle Watering - signed and inscribed Munchen - 16½ x 30½in.
(Christie's) **£2,600**

JOHANNES PETRES VAN VELZEN - An Extensive Wooded Landscape With Figures in the foreground And A View Of A Town Beyond - signed - on panel - 33 x 44cm.
(Phillips) **£850**

VENETIAN MASTER, After a - Portrait of a gentleman wearing a black fur-lined robe and holding a letter - on canvas laid down on panel - 6½ x 4¾ ins.
(Christie's) **£1,400**

VENETIAN MASTER, after a - Portrait of a woman wearing a white dress - on panel - 9 x 6½ ins.
(Christie's) **£2,200**

VENETIAN SCHOOL, 18th century - A Capriccio Of Classical Ruins With Numerous Figures - oil - 48 x 39.5cm.
(Phillips in Scotland) **£860**

VENETIAN SCHOOL - A View Of The Giudecca - on panel - 9¾ x 12¾in.
(Sotheby's) **£120**

VENETIAN SCHOOL, 18th Century - Southern Landscapes: In One Figures Dancing By A River; In The Other Peasants Shearing Sheep - each 14½ x 18½in.
(Sotheby's) **£1,700 Pair**

VENETIAN SCHOOL, After GIOVANNI DOMENICO TIEPOLO - The Minuet - 168 x 231cm.
(Phillips) **£1,000**

LORENZO VENEZIANO - A Triptych: In the centre, the Crucifixion - on gold ground - on panels - 32¾ x 23½in.
(Christie's) **£38,000**

MORIZ VENGS - Animal Caricatures - two inscribed - 10 x 7½in.
(Sotheby's) **£55 Four**

CHARLES VENNEMAN - A Mother Nursing Her Baby In The Company Of Three Other Members Of The Family; A Family Saying Grace And With A Child In A Cradle - oils - signed - 18½ x 24½in.
(Graves Son & Pilcher) **£5,500 Pair**

A. P. VAN DE VENNE - Peasants Merrymaking In A Village Street - on panel - 11¼ x 16in.
(King & Chasemore) **£900**

ADRIAEN PIETERSZ. VAN DE VENNE - Peasants dancing to a Bagpiper - traces of signature - inscribed with a proverb - grisaille - on panel - 13¾ x 25¼ ins.
(Christie's) **£1600**

E. VERBOECKHOVEN - Sheep At Pasture - oil on canvas - signed - 59 x 51cm.
(Galerie Moderne) **£665**

EUGENE VERBOECKHOVEN - Sheep And Poultry In A Farmyard - signed and dated 1863 - on panel - 20 x 16½in.
(Christie's) **£1,500**

EUGENE VERBOECKHOVEN - Sheep, Lambs And Poultry In A Barn - signed and dated 1857 - on panel - 30 x 39½in.
(Sotheby's) **£4,600**

EUGENE VERBOECKHOVEN - A Hare And Poultry At A Trough - signed and dated 1855 - on panel - 12¼ x 14¾in.
(Christie's) **£4,500**

EUGENE VERBOECKHOVEN - 'In The Meadows', Sheep, Lamb And Hens Under Tree - oil - dated 1877 - 13½ x 11¾in.
(J. Entwistle & Co.) **£2,100**

LOUIS VERBOECKHOVEN - The Fishing Boats - oil on wood - signed - 24 x 37cm.
(Galerie Moderne) **£86**

LOUIS VERBOECKHOVEN - Sailing Vessels Offshore In A Calm; And Sailing Vessels Offshore In A Choppy Sea - both signed - on panel 8 x 12in.
(Christie's) **£3,400 Pair**

VERBOECKHOVEN - Three Small Schooners Off The Coast In A Breeze - 9 x 10¾in.
(Sotheby's) **£70**

WILLEM HENDRICSZ. VERBOOM - A Wooded River Landscape With A Peasant In A Boat And A Cottage Beyond - signed and indistinctly dated - on panel - 11¾ x 15½in.
(Christie's) **£4,200**

A. G. VERBRUGGE - Figures Promenading In Formal Gardens, both signed - 14¾ x 18½in.
(Christie's) **£3,500 Pair**

VERBRUGGEN - Tulips, Roses, Sunflowers, Carnations And Other Flowers In Urns, With Carpets On Ledges - 43½ x 43½in.
(Christie's) **£2,600**

G. P. VERBRUGGEN - Tulips, Roses and other flowers in a vase on a pedestal 39½ x 28½ ins.
(Christie's) **£1,100**

GASPAR PIETER VERBRUGGEN, THE YOUNGER - Mixed Flowers In A Vase On A Stone Plinth, With A Melon, Grapes And Other Fruits - signed - 33 x 26in.
(Christie's) **£6,000**

GASPAR PIETER VERBRUGGEN - Still Life With Flowers On A Stone Ledge - signed - 32½ x 25¾in.
(Christie's, S. Kensington) **£2,345**

VERCLUSSEN - Cavalry Skirmish - on panel - 16 x 21 ins.
(Christie's, S. Kensington) **£500**

JAN PEETER VERDUSSEN - A Cavalry Engagement - signed and dated 1720 - 47½ x 72½in.
(Christie's) **£2,000**

VERELST - A Still Life Of Flowers, Including Tulips, Poppies And Other Flowers In A Glass Vase On A Ledge - 21 x 18in.
(Sotheby's) **£650**

NICOLAES VAN VERENDAEL - Tulips, Roses, Carnations And Other Flowers, And Butterflies, In A Glass Vase On A Stone Ledge - signed - 21½ x 16½in.
(Christie's) **£22,000**

HENRI VERGE-SARRAT - Le
Ruisseau - pen and indian ink and
watercolour - signed - 9¼ x 13in.
(Sotheby's) **£60**

CHARLES PIERRE VERHULST – The
Toast - signed and dated 1800 - on panel -
24 x 20in.
(Christie's) **£1,600**

J. VERLEYE - Cock And Hens - oil on
wood - signed - 20 x 27cm.
(Galerie Moderne) **£20**

ALBERTUS VERHOESEN - Studies
Of Poultry With A Peacock And Turkey -
signed and dated 1877 - oil on panel -
5½ x 6¾in.
(Bearnes & Waycotts) **£780 Pair**

ALBERTUS VERHOESEN - A Cowherd
And A Bull In A Rural Setting - signed
and dated 1853 - on panel - 13 x 10in.
(King & Chasemore) **£320**

VERMEER, Circle of - The Minuet:
Figures in an interior - 22½ x 16 ins.
(Christie's) **£6,000**

443

VERNEAU

A. VERNEAU - Marshal Foch And
Private Soldier - dated 1915 - 13 x 24cm.
(Edmiston's)   **£38**

ALFRED VERNET - Portrait Of
Napoleon, three-quarter length - oval
miniature on ivory - 3 x 2½in.
(Buckell & Ballard)   **£80**

CLAUDE-JOSEPH VERNET - A View Of
Lake Nemi, in the foreground Three
Country Men And A Woman On A Road
Running Down To The Lake; Sails On The
Sea On The Horizon - signed and dated
J. Vernet f. Roma/1748 - 24 x 29in.
(Sotheby's)   **£19,000**

CLAUDE JOSEPH VERNET - A Rocky
Coastal Landscape In An Early Morning
Mist, with fisherfolk and their boats in the
foreground, a man-o'-war and other shipping
beyond - signed and dated 1759 - 38½ x 53in.
(Christie's)   **£20,000**

CLAUDE JOSEPH VERNET - A Rocky
Coast In A Storm with shipwrecked travellers
on the shore, a British man-o'-war and a
castle on an island beyond - signed and dated
1759 - 38½ x 53in.
(Christie's)   **£20,000**

EMILE VERNON - The Tambourine
Player - signed - oil on canvas - 26 x
20in.
(Bonham's)   **£1,600**

ALEXANDRE RENE VERON - A
Wooded River Landscape In Autumn -
signed - 14½ x 21½in.
(Sotheby's)   **£850**

MICHELE DA VERONA - Perseus And
Andromeda; And Bellerophon And The
Chimaera - on panel - 5½ x 11½in.
(Christie's)   **£12,000 Two**

VERONESE, After - The Presentation In The Temple - 23¼ x 31in.
(Sotheby's) **£130**

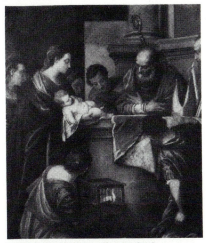

PAOLO CALIARI, called PAOLO VERONESE - The Presentation In The Temple - 60 x 49in.
(Christie's) **£13,000**

LIEVE PIETERSZ. VERSCHUIR - A States Yacht, a large Flute and other shipping, in a calm, off a harbour town - 41 x 60½in.
(Christie's) **£5,500**

WOUTERUS VERSCHUUR - Stabling The Horses - signed - on panel - 13¾ x 19in.
(Sotheby's) **£8,800**

WILLEM VERSCHURING - A Vegetable Seller, A Woman Weighing Chestnuts At A Table On Which Are Parsnips, Artichokes etc. A Boy To The Left And Buildings Beyond - signed and dated - on panel - 9¼ x 8¼in.
(Sotheby's) **£2,400**

L. VERSCHUYS - Sheep And Shepherd In A Landscape - 38 x 58cm.
(Edmiston's) **£300**

ANTONIE VERSTRALEN - A Dutch Winter Landscape with figures skating and playing golf, a village beyond - signed with monogram and dated 1637 - on panel - 13 x 21in.
(Christie's) **£7,500**

SALOMON LEONARDUS VERVEER - A River Landscape With Fisherfolk In Breezy Weather, A Village Beyond - signed and dated - 7½ x 11in.
(Christie's) **£2,000**

J. VERVISCH - Vase Of Roses - on wood - signed and dated 1941 - 80 x 65cm.
(Galerie Moderne) **£150**

VERVOORT

MICHIEL VERVOORT - A Spaniel And
A Hedgehog, Fruit And Flowers in the
foreground; A Fox Standing By A Dead
Chicken And Rabbit - both signed and
dated 1821 - approx. 31½ x 34in.
(Sotheby's) **£1,100 Pair**

LOUIS PIERRE VERWEE - A Study
of Sheep - 20 x 28 ins.
(King & Chasemore) **£230**

FRANCOIS VERWILT - Saint Jerome
In The Wilderness - signed on panel -
8 x 10½in.
(Christie's) **£400**

JULES JACQUES VEYRASSAT - 'The
Barge Team' - signed with initials - on
panel - 13 x 25cm.
(Phillips) **£800**

JULES JACQUES VEYRASSAT - After
The Harvest - signed and dated 1879 -
23½ x 39½in.
(Christie's) **£4,000**

JULES JACQUES VEYRASSAT -
Harvest Time - signed - on panel -
12¼ x 25in.
(Christie's) **£2,000**

JEAN GEORGES VIBERT - Watching The
Sea - signed and dated 1867 - oil on canvas
- 24 x 37in.
(Bonham's) **£950**

GIUSEPPE VICENZINO - A Still Life
With An Urn; And A Still Life Of Flowers
And Fruit - 51¾ x 37¼in.
(Sotheby's) **£8,000 Pair**

A. VICKERS - 1810-1837 - Scottish Loch
Scene With Steamer And Mountainous
background - oil on canvas - signed and
dated 1829 - 23½ x 15½in.
(J. Francis, T. Jones & Sons)   **£100**

A. G. VICKERS - Lake Scene, Figures
in the foreground - 11 x 16¼in.
(Sotheby's)   **£55**

ALFRED GOMERSAL VICKERS - Off
Dover - signed - 29¾ x 47in.
(Sotheby's Belgravia)   **£900**

ALFRED GOMERSAL VICKERS -
Llangollen Bridge - signed and dated
1856 - oil on board - 7 x 10in.
(Christie's)   **£240**

A. H. VICKERS - River Landscape With
Fishermen And Nets in foreground -
signed - 17½ x 31½in.
(Phillips)   **£400**

ALFRED VICKERS, SNR - Shore Scene -
oil on panel - signed and dated 1865 -
8 x 12in.
(King & Chasemore)   **£480**

ALFRED VICKERS, SNR - Near
Bembridge, Isle Of Wight - signed and
dated 1862 - inscribed on the reverse -
16¼ x 23½in.
(Sotheby's Belgravia)   **£300**

JAN VICTORS - Diana And Her
Maidens At The Hunt, In White,
Seated Beneath A Tree With A Bow In
Her Head, A Girl In Green Beside Her,
To The Left A Girl In Pink With A
Hound And In The Centre Another,
In A Brown Tunic, Holding A Hare -
29½ x 36¾in.
(Sotheby's)   **£1,200**

VICTOR ALFRED PAUL VIGNON -
Still Life With Wine And Brie -
signed - the beginnings of an oil
sketch on the reverse - on panel - 7¼
x 9¼in.
(Phillips)   **£540**

CHARLES VIGOR - Interior Scene,
A Young Lady Sits By An Open Window
Reading To Her Grandmother - 70 x 90cm.
(Phillips)   **£690**

LUCAS VILLAMIL - The Cathedral
Wedding - on panel - 12½ x 27½in.
(Sotheby's)   **£2,200**

VINCENT - A Wooded Landscape, With
A Peasant Family Near A Cottage - on
panel - 11½ x 15½in.
(Christie's)   **£320**

G. VINCENT - Moonlight River Scene
With Boy On Bridge - oil - 12 x 16in.
(G. A. Key)   **£70**

VINCENT

G. VINCENT - St Benets Abbey - oil -
16 x 13in.
(G. A. Key) £26

G. VINCENT - A Wooded River Land-
scape With Peasants By A Cottage And
Cattle Watering - on panel - 13 x 18in.
(Christie's) £550

DA VINCI, After - Portrait Of The
Artist - oval - on board - 8½ x 7in.
(Sotheby's) £40

VINCKEBOONS - Saint John The
Baptist Preaching In The Wilderness -
33 x 46in.
(Christie's) £4,500

DAVID VINCKEBOONS - A Village
Festival - on panel - 25½ x 44in.
(Christie's) £14,000

F. VIOTTO - Italian Peasants - both
signed - on panel - each 5½ x 4¼in.
(Sotheby's) £110 Pair

J. VITA - Othello - on panel -
39 x 51cm.
(Edmiston's) £42

F. VITALI - Landscape With Two Ladies
Conversing - signed - 21 x 27in.
(Woolley & Wallis) £170

MAURICE DE VLAMINCK - Les
Trembles - signed - 25½ x 32in.
(Sotheby's) £15,000

MAURICE DE VLAMINCK - Vase De
Magnolias - signed - 23½ x 17¼in.
(Sotheby's) £11,500

DE VLUGHERS - The Return Of The
Hunter - oil on canvas - signed - 78 x
58cm.
(Galerie Moderne) £472

A. DE VOIS - A Young Woman, small
half length, Wearing A Blue Dress,
Before A Ledge - bears signature -
dated 1665 - on panel - 9 x 6½in.
(Christie's) £350

FRIEDRICH VOLK - A Fisherman - oil -
on board - signed - 28 x 18in.
(Stewart & Gore) £88

JOHANN CHRISTIAN VOLLERDT -
A Mountainous, Wooded, River Land-
scape With Figures At A Well Outside
A Village - signed and dated 1760 -
on panel - 22 x 36cm.
(Phillips) £1,900

A. VOMERMORT - The Pond - oil on
canvas - signed - 50 x 70cm.
(Galerie Moderne) £66

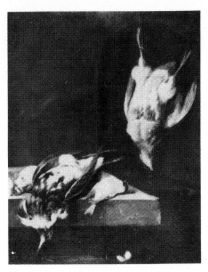

JAN VONCK - A Dead Ruff, A Bullfinch And A Pipit On A Ledge and a partridge hanging in a niche - signed - on panel - 22 x 18in.
(Christie's) £3,000

VAN DER VOORT - A Housemaid Asleep - signed - on panel - 7 x 5½in.
(Sotheby's) £450

S. VRANCX - A Woody River Landscape With A Peasant Selling Cherries in the foreground And A Farm Beyond - on panel - 10¼ x 14¾in.
(Christie's) £1,500

SEBASTIAN VRANCX - A Church Interior With Numerous Figures And Dogs In The Aisle - signed with monogram and dated 1647 - 81 x 119cm.
(Phillips) £3,000

SEBASTIAN VRANCX - Beggars Brawling In A Village In Winter - on panel - 19 x 25½in.
(Christie's) £5,000

SEBASTIAN VRANCX - A Market In A Town Square, with numerous figures - signed with monogram - on panel - 33 x 56¼in.
(Christie's) £17,000

SEBASTIAN VRANCX - A Military Cavalcade In An Extensive Landscape - on panel - 77 x 117cm.
(Phillips) £4,800

SEBASTIAN VRANCX - Autumn: an
avenue in a town, with flowers, fruit,
vegetables and pastry in the foreground -
figures making offerings to a statue beyond -
on panel - 33 x 56¼in.
(Christie's) **£10,000**

EDOUARD VUILLARD - Madame
Hessel Dans Un Interieur - stamped
with signature - 22 x 19in.
(Sotheby's) **£13,000**

EDOUARD VUILLARD - Nu Assis,
Les Jambes Croisees - signed - on
board - 13¼ x 12in.
(Sotheby's) **£6,500**

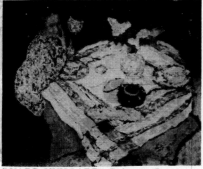

EDOUARD VUILLARD - Dejeuner Du
Matin - signed - on board - 16½ x 20in.
(Christie's, New York) **£48,500**

EDOUARD VUILLARD - Femme A
Villerville - stamped with signature -
pastel - 22 x 16½in.
(Sotheby's) **£18,500**

CORNELIS DE WAEL - A Market Scene With A Woman Suffering Torture - 23 x 43in.
(Christie's) **£1,000**

ARTHUR DE WAERHERT - A Country Road - oil on canvas - signed - 31 x 47cm.
(Galerie Moderne) **£110**

ARTHUR DE WAERHERT - Bergere Et Chevre - oil on canvas - signed - 33 x 43cm.
(Galerie Moderne) **£110**

V. WAGEMAEKERS - Interieur Animee - oil on canvas - signed - 60 x 80 cm.
(Galerie Moderne) **£157**

VICTOR WAGEMAEKERS - The Farmyard - oil on canvas - signed - 50 x 65cm.
(Galerie Moderne) **£24**

THOMAS WAGEMAN - Castle Of Falaise, Normandy - watercolour - 20 x 15cm.
(Edmiston's) **£10**

G. WAGEMANS - The Orchard - on wood - signed - 59 x 49cm.
(Galerie Moderne) **£60**

MAURICE WAGEMANS - Reclining Nude - oil on canvas - signed - 55 x 75cm.
(Galerie Moderne) **£141**

FRITZ WAGNER - 'The Notary' - signed and inscribed - 71 x 81cm.
(Phillips) **£2,600**

LOUIS WAIN - Imaginary Houses And Country Scenes - all heightened with bodycolour - five signed - one with initials - various sizes.
(Sotheby's Belgravia) **£80 Six**

JOHN WAINWRIGHT - Still Life Of Flowers, Including Sweet Peas, Passion Flowers, Rhododendrons, Azaleas, Primulas And Poppies - signed and dated 1865 - circular - diameter 21½in.
(Sotheby's Belgravia) **£1,400**

JOHN WAINWRIGHT - Still Life With Flowers in a Classical Urn, signed and dated 1805 - circular - 21½in. diam.
(Christie's, S. Kensington) **£900**

WILLIAM JOHN WAINWRIGHT - Study Of A Man Wearing A Ruff Collar, head and shoulders - signed - on board - 7 x 4in.
(Sotheby's Belgravia) **£80**

451

E. W. WAITE - A Northern River -
19¼ x 29in.
(Sotheby's Belgravia) **£160**

HAROLD WAITE - Bringing Home The
Sheep - signed - 17½ x 23½in.
(Sotheby's Belgravia) **£70**

ROBERT THORNE WAITE - Gathering
Sheep - signed and dated '91 - 14¼ x
20½in.
(Sotheby's Belgravia) **£200**

ERNEST WALBOURN - Feeding Ducks -
signed - 30 x 20in.
(Sotheby's Belgravia) **£380**

WALBOURN - After The Hunt -
indistinctly signed - 23½ x 19½in.
(Sotheby's Belgravia) **£120**

WILLIAM WALCOT - The Eiffel Tower,
Paris - heightened with bodycolour -
signed and dated 1907 - 16¼ x 17½in.
(Sotheby's Belgravia) **£160**

R. D. WALDIS - Farmyard Scene depicting
Farmyard, Rustics Milking Cows, And
Horses and Duckpond in foreground -
signed and dated 1885 - oil on canvas -
23½ x 17½in.
(Boulton & Cooper) **£140**

VICTORINE DE WALE - A Beach Scene
With People And Boats - oil on wood -
signed and dated 1707 - 28 x 30cm.
(Galerie Moderne) **£173**

FRANCIS SWAINE WALKER - Millfield
Lane, Highgate; Near Armathwaite - one
signed - both inscribed on the reverse -
on panel - each 7¾ x 10in.
(Sotheby's Belgravia) **£80 Pair**

FREDERICK WALKER - 'Caught': A
Woman Holding A Mousetrap - pencil
and watercolour - signed with initials -
5¾ x 3½in.
(Christie's) **£95**

JOHN EATON WALKER - An Edinburgh Shoe Shiner - signed - 7½ x 5½in.
(Sotheby's) £110

MARCELLA WALKER - Sunday Morning - heightened with bodycolour - signed - 7½ x 6½in.
(Sotheby's Belgravia) £80

ELLEN WALLACE - Gleaners Returning - signed - on board - 6¾ x 8¾in.
(Sotheby's Belgravia) £120

J. WALLACE - Shipping Off The Dover Coast - signed - oil on canvas - 19½ x 29½in.
(Bearnes & Waycotts) £280

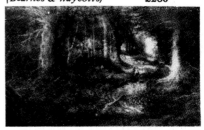

JOHN WALLACE - On The Edge Of A Wood - signed and dated '80 - 29¼ x 40½in.
(Sotheby's Belgravia) £190

WILLIAM WALLS - Goats And Their Kids - signed - 48 x 36in.
(Sotheby's) £180

WILLIAM WALLS - Jaguars At Play - signed - 36 x 48in.
(Sotheby's) £310

M. WALLWYN - Granton Cottage, Goodrich, The Residence Of the Late Joshua Cristall, Esquire - inscribed on the reverse and dated 1835 - 9 x 13½in.
(Sotheby's) £35

THOMAS WALMESLEY, Attributed To - Abbey Crusis Near Llangollen - 11¼ x 16in.
(Sotheby's) £35

WALRAVEN

J. WALRAVEN - The Broken Pitcher - indistinctly signed - on panel - 15¾ x 12in.
(Sotheby's) £1,300

WALSCAPELLE - A Still Life Of Flowers, Including Roses, Tulips, Chrysanthemums And A Peony In A Glass Vase On A Ledge - on panel - 17½ x 12¾in.
(Sotheby's) £480

F. WALTERS - Autumn And Winter - both signed - each 29½ x 19½in.
(Sotheby's Belgravia) £200 Pair

GEORGE STANFIELD WALTERS - Sailing Barges In The Thames Estuary - watercolour heightened with white - signed - 12½ x 19½in.
(Christie's) £95

GEORGE STANFIELD WALTERS - Sailing Barges On A River At Sunset; And Sailing Boats Near A Lightship - watercolour heightened with white - 9½ x 16½in.
(Christie's) £85 Pair

J. WALTERS - On The Thames Near Twyford - signed - inscribed on the reverse - 23½ x 15½in.
(Sotheby's Belgravia) £28

WARD - Defending The Rock - 33 x 28in.
(Sotheby's Belgravia) £70

FRANCIS SWAIN WARD, Attributed To - Portrait Of Lord Macartney's Aide-De-Camp, Standing small full length, In Uniform, With The Fort St. George And The Tower Of St. Mary's Church, Madras, Beyond - inscribed on the reverse - 42½ x 36½in.
(Christie's) £2,000

H. WARD - The Undergrowth - oil on canvas - signed - 51 x 76cm;
(Galerie Moderne) £150

H. WARD - Old Windsor And Castle Through The Mist - signed and dated 1872 - watercolour - 7¼ x 13½in.
(Warner, Sheppard & Wade) £34

JAMES WARD - Children Feeding A Donkey - 19½ x 25½in.
(Christie's) £1,400

JAMES WARD - Children Playing In A Wooded Landscape - signed - 19½ x 25½in.
(Christie's) £2,000

JAMES WARD - A Wooded River
Landscape With Cattle - signed with
monogram and dated 1827 - on panel -
11½ x 16½in.
(Christie's)   **£2,600**

JAMES WARD - The Baptism Of Christ -
signed with monogram and dated 1841 - on
paper laid down on canvas - in a painted
arch - 59 x 26½in.
(Christie's)   **£320**

VERNON WARD - Seagulls - signed
and dated 1927 - on board - 9½ x 13½in.
(Sotheby's Belgravia)   **£50**

A. WARDLE - Hawkcombe, Ex moor -
bears signature - paper laid on board -
11½ x 18in.
(Sotheby's Belgravia)   **£70**

ARTHUR WARDLE - 'Strangers' -
signed - oil on canvas - 23½ x 18½in.
(Bearnes & Waycotts)   **£520**

ARTHUR WARDLE - Cattle Watering -
heightened with bodycolour - signed -
10 x 14½in.
(Sotheby's Belgravia)   **£50**

ARTHUR WARDLE - 'The Culprit',
A Terrier Dog With a Pet Rabbit - signed -
oil - 24 x 21in.
(Warner, Sheppard & Wade)   **£180**

ARTHUR WARDLE - Sportsman And A
Pointer In A Kale Field - signed -
11½ x 18½in.
(Woolley & Wallis)   **£140**

ARTHUR WARDLE - 'Will He Bolt', Fox Terriers in a Woodland Scene - watercolour - signed - 14½ x 20in.
(King & Chasemore) **£270**

HENRY DE WAROQUIER - L'Assiette De Fraises - oil - on canvas - signed and numbered - 10¾ x 13¾in.
(Sotheby's) **£180**

WILLIAM WATSON - Highland Cattle Resting - signed and dated 1911 - 23½ x 35½in.
(Sotheby's Belgravia) **£160**

ELIZABETH MARY WATT - Study Of Roses In A Vase - oil - 24 x 19½in.
(Thomas Love & Sons Ltd) **£20**

EDMUND GEORGE WARREN - In The New Forest - signed - 55½ x 85in.
(Sotheby's Belgravia) **£900**

CHARLES WATELET - Portrait Of A Gentleman - oil on canvas - signed and dated 1948 - 81 x 71cm.
(Galerie Moderne) **£40**

GEORGE WATSON - A Flower Filled Garden - oil - signed and indistinctly dated - 59.5 x 39.5cm.
(Phillips in Scotland) **£29**

R. WATSON - Highland Cattle By A Loch - signed - 23½ x 35¼in.
(Sotheby's Belgravia) **£32**

JEAN-ANTOINE WATTEAU (after RUBENS) - Putti With Lions And A Chariot - 39½ x 62in.
(Christie's) **£5,500**

WATTS - The Lake District, Cottages And Figures in the foreground - on panel - 14 x 20in.
(Sotheby's) **£380**

ROBERT WATSON - Sheep By A Loch - signed and dated 1892 - 23½ x 35½in.
(Sotheby's Belgravia) **£400**

F. W. WATTS - A Riverside Castle - 18½ x 25in.
(Sotheby's Belgravia) **£140**

FREDERICK WILLIAM WATTS - A View Of Chepstow - signed - 19½ x 26¼in.
(Christie's) **£1,000**

FREDERICK WILLIAM WATTS - At
Tadworth - inscribed and dated Sep.
1829 on the reverse - oil on card - 6¾
x 4½in.
(Christie's) **£400**

G. F. WATTS - Portrait Of A Shepherd -
oil - 17 x 14in.
(G. A. Key) **£50**

GEORGE FREDERICK WATTS - Adam
And Eve Before The Temptation - signed
and dated 1896 - 25½ x 14½in.
(Christie's) **£600**

JAMES THOMAS WATTS - The Pet
Rabbit - signed - 13½ x 9¼in.
(Sotheby's Belgravia) **£50**

CHARLES JONES WAY - What O'Clock? -
heightened with bodycolour - signed with
monogram - 9 x 13¾in.
(Sotheby's Belgravia) **£115**

W. H. WEATHERHEAD - A Countrygirl
With A Basket In A Wooded Lane - signed -
oil - 21 x 30in.
(Warner, Sheppard & Wade) **£140**

WILLIAM HARRIS WEATHERHEAD -
The Sailor's Return - signed with
initials and dated 1869 - 24¼ x 29½in.
(Sotheby's Belgravia) **£820**

THOMAS WEAVER - 'Little Jack' - A
Hunter And A Spaniel In A Landscape -
signed, inscribed and dated 1806 - on
canvas - 25 x 30in.
(King & Chasemore) **£520**

G. WEBB - Continental Town Scenes -
both signed - on board - 11½ x 8¾in.
(Sotheby's Belgravia)   **£200 Pair**

JAMES WEBB - View Of A Town On
The Rhine, Barges in the foreground -
signed and dated 1879 - 77 x 127cm.
(Phillips)   **£800**

JAMES WEBB - 'Ehrenbreitstein' -
Figures And Boats In A River Landscape
- signed and dated '81 - on board -
14 x 12in.
(King & Chasemore)   **£520**

JAMES WEBB - 'On The Lazy Scheldt' -
signed and dated '64 - inscribed on a
label on the reverse - 35½ x 59½in.
(Christie's)   **£4,000**

JAMES WEBB - Sunset After Rain -
signed and dated 1878 - inscribed on
the reverse - 23½ x 35½in.
(Sotheby's Belgravia)   **£2,600**

W. E. WEBB - 'Harbour Scene' - signed -
oil on canvas - 40 x 25in.
(Southam & Sons)   **£750**

W. E. WEBB - Fishing Boats, Lake
Maggiore - on board - 7½ x 11½in.
(Sotheby's Belgravia)   **£75**

WILLIAM WEBB - Busy Harbour Scene With Barges And Sailing Boats in foreground - oil - 21½ x 37½in.
(Thomas Love & Sons Ltd) **£470**

WILLIAM WEBB - A Bay Race Horse In An Extensive Landscape - signed, inscribed and dated 1861 - 30½ x 39in.
(Christie's) **£800**

THEODORE WEBER - Fishing vessels off a quay - signed - 12 x 21 ins.
(Christie's, S. Kensington) **£500**

WEBSTER - The Proposal - 21¼ x 17½in.
(Sotheby's) **£38**

GEORGE WEBSTER - Shipping Off Table Bay, Cape Of Good Hope, In A Strong Breeze - signed - 24½ x 31in.
(Christie's) **£2,000**

W. WEEKES - The Eavesdropper - oil - 28 x 23in - oval.
(G. A. Key) **£38**

WILLIAM WEEKES - An Intruder - signed - on board - 8 x 13½in.
(Christie's) **£550**

J. WEENIX - Portrait Of Two Sportsmen, half length, Holding Flintlock Firearms, With A Dead Teal, Stock Dove, Goldfinches And Chaffinches Before Them, In A Landscape - 112 x 164cm.
(Phillips) **£3,600**

J. B. WEENIX - Dead Wildfowl On A River Bank - 27 x 35in.
(Christie's) **£1,100**

JEAN JOSEF WEERTS - Portrait Of A French Officer - signed and dated 1916 - 13¾ x 10½in.
(Sotheby's) **£70**

WEISSENBRUCH - A River Landscape, With Farm Buildings Surrounded By Trees - bears signature - on panel - 11¾ x 15¾in.
(Sotheby's) **£150**

JOSE WEISS - Landscape Study - signed - oil on canvas - 16¼ x 29¼in.
(Bearnes & Waycotts) **£160**

E. WELBOURN - 'Country Scenes With Buildings, Figures And Sheep' - oil - each 29 x 13½in.
(J. Entwistle & Co.) **£370 Pair**

LINA DE WEILER - Le Petit Marchand - indistinctly signed - on panel - 14¼ x 11in.
(Sotheby's) **£500**

G. WELLS - Wooded Lakeside Scene - oil on canvas - signed - 15¾ x 21¾in.
(Hollingsworths) **£30**

JOHN SANDERSON WELLS - More Free Than Welcome - signed - on board - 8¾ x 10½in.
(Christie's) **£190**

JOHN S. SANDERSON WELLS - 'Heavy Load And Behind Time' - signed - on panel - 23 x 41cm.
(Phillips) **£1,300**

JOHN S. SANDERSON WELLS - Stags In The Highlands - both heightened with white - signed - 10½ x 14¼in.
(Sotheby's) **£75 Pair**

JOHN S. SANDERSON WELLS - Cattle Watering - signed - 17½ x 23½in.
(Sotheby's Belgravia) **£90**

J. SANDERSON WELLS - A Hunting Scene - oil on panel - signed - 13½ x 9½in.
(J. Francis, T. Jones & Sons) **£140**

WILLIAM WELLS - House By The River - 31.5 x 24cm.
(Edmiston's) **£150**

VAN DER WERFF - The Expulsion of
Hagar - bears Kauffmann signature - 30½
x 25 ins.
(Christie's, S. Kensington) **£440**

PIETER VAN DER WERFF - A Group
Portrait: A Woman Seated, full length,
With Two Children, A Maid Holding A
Dish Of Fruit - signed and dated 1699 -
69½ x 52½in.
(Christie's) **£1,300**

PIETER VAN DER WERFF - A Family
Portrait: A Lady And A Gentleman
Seated Before A Curtain, full length,
The Lady Holding A Rose, With A
Young Boy Standing At Her Side -
69½ x 52½in.
(Christie's) **£1,300**

WEST - The Rich Man Unwilling To Give
Up His Wordly Goods - 19½ x 15½in.
(Sotheby's) **£40**
WEST - Manlius Imperiosus Torquatus
After The Battle Against The Latins -
43½ x 60in.
(Christie's) **£300**
B. WEST - The Last Supper - 40 x 50in.
(Christie's) **£320**

BENJAMIN WEST - Edward, The Black
Prince Receiving King John Of France After
The Battle Of Poitiers - 16½ x 25½in.
(Christie's) **£1,200**
I. H. WEST - 'Seascape - Lugger Driving
Home In Stormy Seas' - 8 x 12in - 'Out-
ward Bound' - 7¼ x 10in - both signed -
oil on card.
(Lalonde Martin) **£30 pair**

JOHN WESTALL - A Tributary Of The
Avon; Monsal Dale - both signed -
inscribed on the stretcher - each 9¼ x
15½in.
(Sotheby's Belgravia) **£170 Pair**

RICHARD WESTALL - A Wooded Landscape, With Peasants And Cattle By A
Footbridge - signed with initials and dated
1827 - 50½ x 64in.
(Christie's) **£320**

WILLIAM WESTALL - New Bailey Bridge, Manchester - pencil and watercolour - 3½ x 5½in.
(Christie's) **£140**

WESTALL - Two Young Lovers Caught In A Storm - oil - 73 x 60.5cm.
(Phillips in Scotland) **£75**

PHILIP WESTCOTT - Portrait Of Master Henry Collison, full length, With His Dog Rover In A Coastal Landscape - signed and dated London 1859 - inscribed on the reverse - 55½ x 39½in.
(Christie's) **£1,200**

THOMAS WESTER-LLOYD - Pigsticking - watercolour heightened with white - signed - 7½ x 12¼in.
(Christie's) **£45**

JACOB DE WET - Diogenes Searching For An Honest Man - on panel - 27 x 21½in.
(Christie's) **£1,000**

JACOB DE WET - Crossing The Red Sea - indistinctly signed - on panel - 23½ x 32½in.
(Christie's) **£1,700**

J. DE WET - A Cabalistic Scene - on panel - 24½ x 26¼in.
(Sotheby's) **£160**

T. WHAITE - The 'Queen Of Trumps' With Jockey Up - 24½ x 29½in.
(Christie's) **£380**

G. R. WHEATER - River Landscapes - both signed and dated 1900 and 1901 - each 11½ x 17½in.
(Sotheby's Belgravia) **£220 Pair**

WHEATLEY - A Fishing Expedition - oval - on metal - 16½ x 22½in.
(Sotheby's) **£340**

WHEELER - A Saddled Horse - 12 x 14½in.
(Sotheby's Belgravia) **£50**

J. WHEELER, Attributed to - Huntsman On A Horse - oil on board - 8 x 6½in.
(J. Francis, T. Jones & Sons) **£40**

JOHN ARNOLD WHEELER - 'Patchwork', 'Clown', 'Kaleidoscope' And 'Rainbow', The Winning Team Of The Stage Coach Show, Ranelagh, 1899 - signed - inscribed and dated Hanwell 1900 - 28 x 40½in.
(Christie's) **£450**

JOHN ARNOLD WHEELER - Gold Drop - signed with monogram - inscribed - on board - 14½ x 17½in.
(Sotheby's Belgravia) **£150**

JOHN ARNOLD WHEELER - The 'Nimrod', Bath And Devizes Coach, Outside the George Inn At Sandy Lane - signed and dated Hanwell 1892 - 33 x 57in.
(Christie's) **£1,200**

HENE WHEELWRIGHT - Study Of A Kitten And Two Butterflies - signed - watercolour on ivory - 4¾ x 2¾in.
(Bearnes & Waycotts) **£105**

R. WHEELWRIGHT - Two Horses Ploughing - oil on board - signed - 29½ x 21½in.
(J. Francis, T. Jones & Sons) **£60**

WHELDON

F. WHELDON - The S.S. Fairy Under Full Steam And Sail - signed and dated '68 - 19½ x 29in.
(Christie's) **£340**

JOHN WHIPPLE - Scene At Hurley On Thames - inscribed on the stretcher - 15½ x 23¼in.
(Sotheby's Belgravia) **£260**

THOMAS WHITCOMBE - The East Indiaman 'Bombay Castle' Seen From Two Positions Off Dover - signed and dated 1795 - 37 x 57½in.
(Christie's) **£3,200**

THOMAS WHITCOMBE - British East Indiamen Off Penang With Swedish And Dutch Ships Beyond - signed and dated 1821 - 37 x 58in.
(Christie's) **£7,000**

THOMAS WHITCOMBE - Shipping Off The Island Of Sark - signed and dated 1811 - 36 x 54in.
(Christie's) **£4,000**

GEORGE FRANCIS WHITE - The Bazaar Near Calcutta - pencil heightened with white on grey paper - 10¾ x 16¼in.
(Sotheby's) **£50**

THOMAS WHITTLE, SNR - Southdowns, Hastings - signed and dated 1870 - inscribed on the reverse - 19¾ x 29½in.
(Sotheby's Belgravia) **£280**

JOSIAH WOOD WHYMPER - Morning Mists On The Thames - signed - 5¾ x 12½in.
(Sotheby's Belgravia) **£65**

WILHELM WIDER - A Nun's Blessing; The Nun's Recital - both signed - 25¼ x 19½in.
(Sotheby's) **£500 Pair**

F. J. WIDGERY - Views On Dartmoor - signed - pastel - 10 x 14in.
(Neale & Son) **£34 Pair**

WILLIAM WIDGERY - View Of Lyndford Gorge - signed and dated 1875 - oil on canvas - 25½ x 38½in.
(Bearnes & Waycotts) **£210**

WILLIAM WIDGERY - Crossing A Bridge - heightened with white - signed and dated 1869 - 13 x 19½in.
(Sotheby's Belgravia) **£60**

ALFRED VON WIERUSZ-KOWALSKI - Cavalry Encamped By A Cottage - signed - on panel - 15¼ x 21¾in.
(Sotheby's) **£6,800**

CHARLES M. WIGG - Yarmouth Dock Scene With Boats Being Loaded Ahd Unloaded, Figures Fishing etc. - watercolour - 10 x 14in.
(G. A. Key) **£44**

JAN WILDENS - An Extensive View of Antwerp Across the River Scheldt with shipping, and figures in a village street in the foreground - 46 x 92½in.
(Christie's) **£6,500**

M. WILIQUET - Vase Trimmed With Flowers - oil on canvas - signed - 40 x 30cm.
(Galerie Moderne) £17

D. R. WILKEN - Boats Entering Harbour - watercolour - 5 x 7in.
(G. A. Key) £2

WILKIE - A Visit By The Minister - 12½ x 17½in.
(Sotheby's Belgravia) £230

SIR DAVID WILKIE - Study For 'The First Ear Ring' - pencil and watercolour heightened with white on buff paper - 21 x 14in.
(Christie's) £550

SIR DAVID WILKIE - Soothing The Child - 8¼ x 12in.
(Sotheby's) £130

WILKIE, After - The Blind Fiddler - 24 x 33in.
(Sotheby's Belgravia) £70

ARTHUR WILKINSON - Master Carpenters Court, Hampton Court - signed - heightened with bodycolour - 11 x 7¼in.
(Sotheby's) £30

NORMAN WILKINSON - Shelling The Dardanells - watercolour - 9 x 13in.
(G. A. Key) £56

ADAM WILLAERTS - Settlers Landing On A Rocky Coast - signed and dated 1640 - 24½ x 30in.
(Sotheby's) £3,600

ADAM WILLAERTS - A Rocky Coastal Landscape, With Settlers Disembarking - signed and dated 1640 - 24½ x 30in.
(Christie's) £1,600

ADOLPHE WILLETTE - Le Remords De Mahomet - pen and indian ink and blue crayon - signed - titled - inscribed and dated 1912 - 11¼ x 7½in.
(Sotheby's) £30

A. WILLIAMS - A Quiet Day's Fishing; A Rest By A Cottage - one signed and dated 1873 - 17¾ x 26in.
(Sotheby's Belgravia) **£820 Pair**

EDWARD CHARLES WILLIAMS - 'On The Banks Of The Thames': An Extensive View Of The River, With A Drover Taking His Herd To Water And Figures Unloading A Hay Barge Beyond - signed with monogram - dated 1853 and dated Jan. 1853 - inscribed on a label on reverse - 77 x 127cm.
(Phillips) **£2,000**

EDWARD CHARLES WILLIAMS AND WILLIAM SHAYER, SNR - The Midday Halt - signed by both artists and twice dated 1851 - 24¼ x 37in.
(Sotheby's Belgravia) **£4,500**

E. C. WILLIAMS - A River Landscape, With A Man In A Punt - on panel - 11½ x 18½in.
(Christie's) **£200**

G. A. WILLIAMS - Wooded River Scene - oil - 17 x 23in.
(G. A. Key) **£44**

G. A. WILLIAMS - A Wooded Landscape With A Woman Conversing With A Horseman On A Path - 9½ x 11½in.
(Christie's) **£190**

GEORGE AUGUSTUS WILLIAMS - On The Banks Of A River - signed with initials - 9½ x 22¼in.
(Sotheby's Belgravia) **£700**

HUGH WILLIAM 'GRECIAN' WILLIAMS - The Gulf Of Corinth - pencil and watercolour - 23½ x 35¼in.
(Christie's) **£1,100**

HUGH WILLIAM 'GRECIAN' WILLIAMS - Dalhousie - pencil and watercolour - 23½ x 32½in.
(Christie's) **£65**

TERRICK WILLIAMS - View of a fishing port - oil on canvas - signed 16 x 20 ins.
(King & Chasemore) **£500**

WALTER WILLIAMS - Fishermen putting off - signed and inscribed on the reverse - 6 x 8 ins.
(Christie's, S. Kensington) **£160**

WALTER HEATH WILLIAMS - Anglers By A Stony Bridge, Harvest Time - 26 x 40in.
(Sotheby's Belgravia) **£1,000**

WALTER HEATH WILLIAMS - By A Country Pond - 27½ x 35½in.
(Sotheby's Belgravia) **£750**

W. WILLIAMS - A Rocky River Landscape With Mountains Beyond - 25½ x 36in.
(Christie's) **£50**

WILLIAM WILLIAMS OF PLYMOUTH - Border Of Dartmoor Near Okehampton - pencil and watercolour - signed - inscribed on the reverse - 8 x 12½in.
(Christie's) **£28**

SCHOOL OF WILLIAMS, 19th century -
Country Landscape; Cottage With River,
Fisherman, Cattle With Distant Land-
scape And Evening Sun - oil - on canvas -
23½ x 35½in.
(Charles R. Phillips) **£450**

W. J. WILLIAMS - An Extensive Landscape With A Gypsy Encampment -
signed with initials - indistinctly
inscribed - 11¼ x 20¾in.
(Sotheby's Belgravia) **£100**

W. J. WILLIAMS - A Wooded River
Landscape With Fishermen In A Punt
And Cottages Beyond - signed - 17½ x
25½in.
(Christie's) **£300**

WILLIAMSON - Herdsmen With Cattle
And Sheep In An Extensive Landscape -
on panel - 9¾ x 7½in.
(Christie's) **£150**

W. H. WILLIAMSON - Shipping Off
The Coast - both signed with initials -
indistinctly dated - each 7¾ x 14½in.
(Sotheby's Belgravia) **£260 Pair**

W. H. WILLIAMSON - Coastal Scenes
With Fishing Boats Leaving Harbour In
Squally Seas And A Tall Masted Sailing
Ship At Anchor - signed and dated
1880 - on canvas - 10 x 18in.
(Morphet & Morphet) **£430 Pair**

W. H. WILLIAMSON - On A Rocky
Coast - signed with initials and dated
1869 - on board - 6½ x 15½in.
(Sotheby's Belgravia) **£65**

JOHN WILLSTEED-ASH - Barnstable
Bay - watercolour - 10 x 13in.
(G. A. Key) **£14**

J. LASCELLES WILLIAMSON -
Evening In The New Forest - signed -
inscribed on the reverse - 17½ x 23½in.
(Sotheby's Belgravia) **£38**

WILLIS - Cattle And Sheep By A River -
10 x 14in.
(Sotheby's Belgravia) **£80**

CHARLES WILLIS - Model Of A
Warship - signed - 19¼ x 26½in.
(Sotheby's Belgravia) **£350**

CHARLES WILLIS - Weighing The
Fish - signed - 19¼ x 26¼in.
(Sotheby's Belgravia) **£240**

CHARLES WILLIS - His Choice - signed
- 19¼ x 26¼in.
(Sotheby's Belgravia) **£380**

CHARLES WILLIS - The Recitation - signed - 19¼ x 26¼in.
(Sotheby's Belgravia) **£390**

CHARLES WILLIS - The Shortest Route - signed - 19¼ x 26½in.
(Sotheby's Belgravia) **£350**

CHARLES WILLIS - Recounting His Experiences At The Wars - signed - 19¼ x 26¼in.
(Sotheby's Belgravia) **£260**

RICHARD WILLOUGHBY - Whaling In The Arctic - signed and dated 1817 - 27½ x 39½in.
(Christie's) **£2,400**

WILSON - Classical Landscape With A Ruin On Skyline, Figures And A Bridge in foreground - 20½ x 32in.
(Graves Son & Pilcher) **£460**

JOHN WILSON - Fishing Boats In A Choppy Sea - signed - oil on canvas - 15½ x 25½in.
(Bearnes & Waycotts) **£440**

J. J. WILSON - Fishing Vessels Off The Coast - 11½ x 23½in.
(Sotheby's Belgravia) **£130**

JOHN JAMES WILSON - Shipping Off The Coast - signed with initials and dated 1870 - 25¼ x 44¼in.
(Sotheby's Belgravia) **£1,000**

JOHN JAMES WILSON - Shipping Off The Coast - both signed - 12 x 19½in.
(Sotheby's Belgravia) **£600 Pair**

JOHN JAMES WILSON - Near The Needles, Isle Of Wight - signed with initials and dated 1863 - 25¼ x 44¼in.
(Sotheby's Belgravia) **£1,700**

JOHN JAMES WILSON - French Fishing Boats Putting Into Entretat - signed with initials and dated 1860 - 15¼ x 23¼in.
(Sotheby's Belgravia) **£900**

LYMORE WILSON - Coastal Scene With Numerous Figures And Shipping - watercolour - 8 x 18in.
(G. A. Key) **£24**

P. MacGREGOR WILSON - Coast Scene With Fishing Boats, Sunset - 40 x 60cm.
(Edmiston's) **£40**

R. WILSON - Classical Landscape - oil on canvas - 7½ x 10¼in.
(Bearnes & Waycotts) **£80**

R. WILSON - A View Of The River Arno, With A Woman And Baby On Her Lap, And A Boy Fishing - 40 x 49½in.
(Christie's) **£290**

RICHARD WILSON - Two Shepherds In An Italian Landscape By A Clump Of Trees - black chalk - 6 x 5in.
(Christie's) **£200**

RICHARD WILSON - Cock Inn, Cheam Common - 32 x 56in.
(Christie's) **£6,000**

W. WILSON - A View Of A Loch With Fishing Boats - signed - 39.5 x 59.5cm.
((Phillips In Scotland) **£50**

H. B. WIMBUSH - River Landscape - watercolour - 19 x 30in.
(Thomas Love & Sons Ltd) **£20**

EDMUND MORISON WIMPERIS - Pangbourne On Thames - signed with initials - pencil and watercolour - 11 x 18½in.
(Christie's) **£350**

EDMUND MORISON WIMPERIS - Moorland Landscape With Cattle And Cowherd - signed with initials - watercolour - 13½ x 18in.
(Woolley & Wallis) **£165**

EDMUND MORISON WIMPERIS - At The Stile; Willows At Houghton - both signed with initials - 9¼ x 6½in.
(Sotheby's) **£200 Pair**

SIDNEY P. WINDER - On The Banks Of A River - signed and dated 1920 - 19¼ x 25½in.
(Sotheby's Belgravia) **£240**

SIR J. L. WINGATE - A Croft By A Loch - heightened with white - 21 x 29½in.
(Sotheby's Belgravia) **£14**

JAMES DIGMAN WINGFIELD - At Hampton Court - signed and dated 1852 - 12 x 19¼in.
(Sotheby's Belgravia) **£220**

PETER DE WINT - Cattle Watering, Near Bidford On Avon - watercolour - 9 x 12½in.
(Christie's) **£350**

PETER DE WINT - A Rickyard In Lincolnshire - pencil and watercolour - 8½ x 11¾in.
(Christie's) **£650**

PETER DE WINT - Haymaking - pencil and watercolour - 9¼ x 12¾in.
(Christie's) **£1,300**

PETER DE WINT - Corn Stooks In Front Of A Wood And A Farmhouse - watercolour on two adjoined sheets - 9¾ x 21in.
(Christie's) **£3,800**

PETER DE WINT - Palermo From The Gardens Of The Convent Of St. Maria Di Jesu; And View Near Palermo - brown wash - 5 x 7¾in.
(Christie's) **£220 Two**

PETER DE WINT - Lake Near The Faros At Entrance Of Straights Of Messina, Opposite Scilla (sic); And Ruin Called Abazia - brown wash - 3¾ x 8½in.
(Christie's) **£220 Two**

P. De WINT - Wooded River Scene With Cattle Resting - watercolour - 6 x 9in.
(G. A. Key) **£26**

DE WINTER - Vieille Ferme - oil on canvas - signed - 40 x 52cm.
(Galerie Moderne) **£20**

GILLIS DE WINTER - The Interior Of An Inn; And A Violinist Performing Outside An Inn - both signed - on panel - 15½ x 12½in.
(Christie's) **£2,600 Pair**

TATTON WINTER - Study Of A Watermill - watercolour - 6 x 10in.
(G. A. Key) **£5**

PETER WISHART - A Coastal Scene - signed - 14¼ x 21in.
(Sotheby's Belgravia) **£18**

PETER WISHART - The Fringe Of The Wood - oil - signed with initials - on board - 22.5 x 30cm.
(Phillips in Scotland) **£38**

WISSING - Portrait Of Charles II, half length, Wearing Armour And A White Cravat - on panel - 15 x 12in.
(Sotheby's) **£60**

WISSING - Portrait Of A Lady, three-quarter length, Seated, Wearing A Low-Cut White Dress With A Brown Cloak, Feeding A Lamb, An Extensive Landscape Beyond - 48 x 37in.
(Sotheby's) **£140**

WISSING - Portrait Of A Lady, three-quarter length, Wearing A Low-Cut Brown Dress With A King Charles' Spaniel On Her Left - 48 x 37½in.
(Sotheby's) **£170**

JACOB DE WIT - The Immaculate Conception - signed with monogram and indistinctly dated - shaped ceiling painting - 102½ x 104in.
(Christie's) **£1,500**

WILLIAM FREDERICK WITHERINGTON - Landscape Study - signed and dated 1860 - oil on panel - 8¾ x 14¾in.
(Bearnes & Waycotts) **£230**

EMANUEL DE WITTE - The Interior of a Church with a congregation listening to a sermon - signed and dated 1671 - 21½ x 19½ ins.
(Christie's) **£6,000**

FRANZ XAVER WOLFE - A Musical
Interlude - signed and stamped with
artist's seal on the reverse - on panel -
23 x 19½in.
(Christie's)   **£1,500**

GEORGE WOLFE - A Vessel Beached
At Low Tide At Sunset - watercolour
heightened with white - signed - 13½ x
20¾in.
(Christie's)   **£130**

WOLSTENHOLME - The Kill - on panel -
25 x 36½in.
(Christie's)   **£70**

DEAN WOLSTENHOLME - The Kill -
20½ x 28½in.
(Christie's)   **£750**

DEAN WOLSTENHOLME - The Meet;
Full Cry; At Fault; and Treeing The
Fox - bearing signatures - 11½ x 17¼in.
(Christie's, S. Kensington)   **£1,500 Four**

DEAN WOLSTENHOLME - The Essex
Hunt 1831 The Meet at Matching Green -
signed - oil on panel - one of a set of **Four**
(Bonham's)   **£1600**

CATHERINE M. WOOD - Weapons
Of The Gentle Art - 17½ x 29½in.
(Sotheby's Belgravia)   **£400**

CHRISTOPHER WOOD - The Three
Headed Man, Luna Park Ballet, 1930 -
15½ x 9¾ ins.
(Sotheby's)   **£420**

FRANCIS DERWENT WOOD - An
Open Landscape - pen and black ink
and watercolour - signed and dated 1917
- 11 x 14½in.
(Christie's)   **£20**

FRANK WOOD - "Portsmouth Harbour"
and "Sunset On The Solent" - watercolours - 7½ x 15½in.
(Thomas Love & Sons Ltd)   **£35 Pair**

LEWIS JOHN WOOD - A Continental
Market Place - signed - 13½ x 9½in.
(Sotheby's)   **£95**

D. WOODCOCK - Farmyard Scene With
Boy Playing Pipe - signed - watercolour -
18 x 23½in.
(John H. Raby & Sons)   **£115**

WOODMAN - In Windsor Great Park -
19½ x 29¾in.
(Sotheby's Belgravia)   **£45**

ARTHUR WOODS - Study Of An
Orchard With Children And Sheep -
signed and indistinctly dated - oil on
canvas - 23¼ x 29¼in.
(Bearnes & Waycotts)   **£160**

HENRY CHARLES WOOLLETT -
Peasants Smoking In An Interior -
signed and dated 1836 - on board -
12 x 10in.
(Christie's)   **£210**

ALFRED JOSEPH WOOLMER -
The Slave - 11¾ x 9½in.
(Sotheby's Belgravia)   **£320**

WOOLMER

ALFRED JOSEPH WOOLMER -
Dreaming - oval - 10 x 11½in.
(Sotheby's Belgravia) **£260**

ALFRED JOSEPH WOOLMER - Lady
Godiva - signed on the reverse - oval -
31 x 24½in.
(Sotheby's Belgravia) **£750**

ALFRED JOSEPH WOOLMER - The
Swing - on panel - 16½ x 13in.
(Christie's, S. Kensington) **£440**

ALFRED JOSEPH WOOLMER - Wild
Flowers - oval - 16¼ x 12½in.
(Sotheby's Belgravia) **£200**

JOHN WOOTTON - The Godolphin Arabian
- signed and dated 1731 - 39 x 49in.
(Christie's) **£10,000**

J. WOOTTON - An Italianate Wooded
River Landscape With Cattle, Sheep And
Pastoral Figures - 37 x 29½in.
(Christie's) **£1,500**

T. WORSEY - Still Life Berryfruits
With Butterflies - signed - watercolour -
13 x 17½in.
(Charles R. Phillips) **£110**

EDOUARD WOUTERMAERTENS -
The Break Up Of The Herd - on wood -
signed - 56 x 43cm.
(Galerie Moderne) **£700**

FRANCHOYS WOUTERS - The
Finding Of Moses - 67.5 x 92cm.
(Phillips) **£620**

WOUWERMAN - Two horsemen On A
Country Path - oil - bears initials - on
panel - 32 x 44.5cm.
(Phillips in Scotland) **£390**

WOUWERMAN - A Cavalry Skirmish -
21½ x 26in.
(Christie's) **£800**

SCHOOL OF WOUWERMAN -
Groups of Horsemen And Other
Figures - oil on canvas - 10¾ x 9¾in.
(Bearnes & Waycotts)   **£680 Pair**

PHILIPS WOUWERMAN - Bandits
Plundering a Village - signed - on panel -
18½ x 24½in.
(Christie's)   **£9,500**

PHILIPS WOUWERMAN - The Con-
version Of Saint Paul - signed with
monogram - on panel - 10¾ x 14in.
(Christie's)   **£6,000**

PIETER WOUWERMAN - Wooded River
Landscapes, with travellers - one signed with
initials - 50 x 67½in.
(Christie's)   **£5,200 Three**

WRIGHT - Teatime - 22 x 24in.
(Sotheby's Belgravia)   **£130**

WRIGHT - Portrait Of A Gentleman,
half length, Wearing A Red Cloak And
White Ruff - oval - 29½ x 25½in.
(Sotheby's)   **£80**

GEORGE WRIGHT - A Coach And Four
On An Open Road - signed - 19½ x 29½in.
(Christie's)   **£1,500**

GEORGE WRIGHT - After The Hunt -
signed - 9 x 13in.
(Sotheby's Belgravia)   **£700**

GEORGE WRIGHT - Landscape With A
Stagecoach Passing A Training Ground
For Horses - signed - oil on canvas - 23 x
35¼in.
(Bearnes & Waycotts)   **£2,500**

WRIGHT

GILBERT S. WRIGHT - Halt For
Refreshment - signed - 19½ x 29½in.
(Christie's) **£1,050**

GILBERT S. WRIGHT - The Fugitives -
signed - 19½ x 35½in.
(Sotheby's Belgravia) **£1,800**

GEORGE WRIGHT - Royal Mail Coach
Halted By The Hunt - signed - 14 x 20in.
(Christie's, S. Kensington) **£1,300**

GEORGE WRIGHT - The Royal Mail
Crossing A Bridge - signed - 19½ x 29½in.
(Christie's) **£2,200**

GEORGE WRIGHT - Taking A Fence -
signed - 15½ x 23½in.
(Sotheby's Belgravia) **£1,800**

GEORGE WRIGHT - Halt For Refreshment Outside The Clayton Arms - signed -
19½ x 29½in.
(Christie's) **£2,300**

J. WRIGHT OF DERBY - Portrait Of
Erasmus Darwin In A Brown Coat - half
length - 29 x 24¼in.
(Christie's) **£800**

J. M. WRIGHT - Portrait Of A Woman,
Said To Be Mary, Lady Aston, three-
quarter length, Seated At A Writing
Table Wearing A White Dress - 48½ x
38½in.
(Christie's) **£900**

J. M. WRIGHT - Portrait Of Elizabeth
Buddle, three-quarter length, Wearing A
Black Dress And Lace Hood - bears
inscription and dated 1658 - 47 x 39½in.
(Christie's) **£580**

J. MASEY WRIGHT - The Characters From
Chaucer's Canterbury Tales, On Horseback -
10¼ x 37½in.
(Woolley & Wallis) **£100**

RICHARD WRIGHT OF LIVERPOOL -
British Frigates And Fishing Vessels
Off A Rocky Coast With Figures On A
Jetty in the foreground - 30½ x 59½in.
(Christie's) **£1,100**

T. WRIGLY - Snips And Woodcock
Feeding On Marshes - watercolours -
both 6 x 10in
(G. A. Key) **£20 Pair**

JAN WYCK - A Stag Hunt - signed -
43 x 69in.
(Christie's) **£5,000**

J. WYCK - Women Laundering In An Italianate Landscape - on panel - 15½ x 13in.
(Christie's) **£4,200**

T. WYCK - Peasants Merrymaking In An Interior - bears Dujardin signature and dated 1665 on the reverse - on panel - 10 x 7¾in.
(Christie's) **£650**

WILLIAM WYLD - A River Carnival, Holland - indistinctly signed and dated 1875 - 15½ x 25in.
(Christie's) **£750**

WILLIAM WYLD - An Extensive Venetian Scene - oil on canvas - signed - 20 x 32in.
(King & Chasemore) **£500**

WILLIAM LIONEL WYLLIE - The Isolde - signed - on panel - 17¾ x 11¾in.
(Sotheby's Belgravia) **£950**

W. L. WYLLIE - Pool Of London With Tower Bridge - watercolour - 9 x 14in.
(G. A. Key) **£34**

WILLIAM LIONEL WYLLIE - Venice - The Dogana And Santa Maria Della Salute From The Molo With Shipping in foreground and background - oil on board - signed - 10 x 14½in.
(Graves Son & Pilcher) **£300**

J. WYNANTS - An Extensive Landscape With Travellers On A Sandy Lane - bears signature - 9½ x 11¾in.
(Christie's) **£320**

JAN WYNANTS - An Extensive Wooded Landscape, with peasants and sportsmen on a path - signed - 26½ x 33½in.
(Christie's) **£9,500**

JAN WYNANTS and JOHANNES LINGELBACH - A Wooded Landscape with anglers by a stream and travellers on a path - signed by Wynants - on panel - 16 x 20in.
(Christie's) **£11,500**

A. WYNANTZ - A Wooded River Landscape, A Woman On Horseback To The Right, Cottages Beyond - on panel - 9½ x 12½in.
(Sotheby's) **£220**

F. YANI - The Market Place - signed - 15 x 11 in.
(Sotheby's) **£120**

JOSEPH YARNOLD - The Swallow Falls - a pair - both signed and dated - 9/79 and 11/79 - each 36 x 28 in.
(Sotheby's) **£120 Pair**

YANKEL - Portrait Of Jean-Paul Sartre - brush and indian ink and gouache - signed - 27½ x 17¼ in.
(Sotheby's) **£160**

GIDEON YATES - London Bridge, From The South Bank - signed - watercolour - 12¼ x 21½ in.
(Christie's) **£460**

W. YATES - On The Edge Of A Wood; On A Pond - both signed - 11¾ x 9½ in.
(Sotheby's Belgravia) **£300 Pair**

T. YEOMANS - Prize rams by a fence signed and inscribed and dated 1841 - 27 x 35 ins.
(Christie's, S. Kensington) **£660**

T. YEOMANS - Prize ram in a wood landscape - 24 x 29 ins.
(Christie's, S. Kensington) **£460**

FRANCOIS YKENS - Apples And Grapes And Other Fruit In A Bowl, with lemons, plums and dead birds, on a table - signed - on panel - 23½ x 32in.
(Christie's) **£6,500**

J.T. YOUNG - A View of Fort Regent overlooking St. Helier Harbour, Jersey, with cattle in the foreground - 21 x 28½ ins.
(Christie's) **£7000**

J. T. YOUNG - An Extensive Wooded Landscape - rustics in the foreground - signed and dated 1823 - on panel - 8¼ x 11in.
(Sotheby's) **£200**

W. YOUNG - Ely Cathedral From The Canal Basin - signed - 31¾ x 49¾in.
(Christie's) **£520**

W. YOUNG - Highland Landscape And Stream - 34 x 45cm.
(Edmiston's) **£70**

L. YOUNGS - Wayford and Irstead Church - both signed and inscribed - watercolour - 6½ x 9½in.
(Neale & Son) **£19 Pair**

YSENBRANDT - The Agony In The Garden - on panel - 10¼ x 8¼in.
(Sotheby's) **£120**

ADRIAEN YSENBRANDT - The Virgin And Child in a landscape - on panel - 19 x 13½in.
(Christie's) **£19,000**

BERNARDINO ZAGANELLI - The
Virgin And Child Enthroned With Saints
Mountainous Background - on panel -
9¾ x 7¾in.
(Sotheby's) **£23,000**

GIUSEPPE ZAIS - A Landscape with
pastoral figures fishing by a tower; Landscape with a peasant family by a bridge;
Landscape with figures resting by a path;
and Landscape with figures and cattle near
a town - 21 x 27½in
(Christie's) **£10,000 Four**

GIUSEPPE ZAIS - Country People In A
Landscape, Men And Women With A
Cow And A Dog On A Road Between
Trees Leading Into The Background -
21 x 28in.
(Sotheby's) **£4,000**

EDOUARDO ZAMPIGHI - The Morning
News - signed - oil on canvas - 10 x 14in.
(Bonham's) **£1,200**

EDUARDO ZAMPIGHI - 'Loves Me, Loves Me Not' - signed - 60 x 46cm.
(Phillips) **£1,800**

EDUARDO ZAMPIGHI - First Steps - signed - 29¼ x 41in.
(Christie's) **£2,800**

EDUARDO ZAMPIGHI - Her First Born - signed - 21½ x 29½in.
(Christie's) **£3,400**

FARUNISSA ZEID - Eastbourne - pen and indian ink and watercolour - signed - 9½ x 12¾in.
(Sotheby's) **£15**

FARUNISSA ZEID - Spanish Street Scene - oil and gouache on paper - on board - signed - 18¼ x 24in.
(Sotheby's) **£60**

J. ZEITTER - Frozen Well In The Hartz Mountains, peasants surrounding well - 19th century - oil on canvas - signed - 49 x 30in.
(Boulton & Cooper) **£145**

JANUARIUS ZICK - A Herdswoman Playing The Pipe To Two Shepherds - 19 x 15in.
(Christie's) **£3,000**

FELIX ZIEM - A Venetian Capriccio Scene, The Doge's Palace to the left - signed - 18 x 25½in.
(Sotheby's) **£1,200**

FELIX ZIEM - View On The Bosphorus - oil on wood - 24 x 36cm.
(Galerie Moderne) **£440**

A. SOLARIO, LO ZINGARO - Saint Jerome In Penitence, In A Landscape - on panel - 35½ x 29½in.
(Christie's) **£1,000**

UMBERTO ZINNY - Venetian Girl With Roses - signed - watercolour - 11 x 14¾in.
(John H. Raby & Sons) **£32.50**

G. ZOCCHI - 'Mother's Darling', A Roman Interior With A Woman In White Robes And A Child On Her Knee - oil on panel - 9 x 13in.
(Henry Spencer & Sons) **£920**

GUGLIEMO ZOCCHI - The Morning Meal; Her Favourite Author - both signed - 30½ x 17in.
(Sotheby's) **£600 Pair**

A. L ZORN - Skeri-Kulla - etching.
(Edmiston's) **£120**

ANDERS ZORN - Prof. John Berg Etching - signed in pencil - slightly time-stained where not hidden by mount - on Van Gelder paper, with margins.
(Sotheby's) **£120**

ANDERS ZORN - Sappo Etching - signed in pencil - slightly foxed in right margin, with margins.
(Sotheby's) **£250**

ANDERS ZORN - Shallow Etching - signed in pencil - time-stained where not hidden by mount - on Van Gelder paper, with margins - 29.3 x 19.4cm.
(Sotheby's) **£400**

ANDERS ZORN - Ida Etching - printed with tone - signed in pencil - three soft folds - one crossing plate horizontally, with margins - 23.9 x 16cm.
(Sotheby's) **£220**

FRANCESCO ZUCCARELLI - A Wooded River Landscape, with pastoral figures and a town beyond - signed and dated '18 Agosto 1742' - 29 x 45in.
(Christie's) **£30,000**

HEINRICH JOHANN ZUEGEL - A Herdsman Driving Cattle On A Wooded Path - signed and dated '99 - 48 x 36½in.
(Christie's) **£6,500**